THE POWER
WORSHIPPERS

THE POWER WORSHIPPERS

*Inside the Dangerous Rise
of Religious Nationalism*

KATHERINE STEWART

BLOOMSBURY PUBLISHING
NEW YORK · LONDON · OXFORD · NEW DELHI · SYDNEY

BLOOMSBURY PUBLISHING
Bloomsbury Publishing Inc.
1385 Broadway, New York, NY 10018, USA

BLOOMSBURY, BLOOMSBURY PUBLISHING, and the Diana logo are trademarks
of Bloomsbury Publishing Plc

First published in the United States 2019

ISBN: HB: 978-1-63557-343-5; eBook: 978-1-63557-345-9

LIBRARY OF CONGRESS CATALOGING-IN-PUBLICATION DATA IS AVAILABLE

2 4 6 8 10 9 7 5 3

Typeset by Westchester Publishing Services
Printed and bound in the U.S.A. by Berryville Graphics Inc., Berryville, Virginia

To find out more about our authors and books visit www.bloomsbury.com and sign up
for our newsletters.

Bloomsbury books may be purchased for business or promotional use. For information on
bulk purchases please contact Macmillan Corporate and Premium Sales Department at
specialmarkets@macmillan.com.

For my family

CONTENTS

INTRODUCTION

T HIS IS NOT a book I could have imagined writing a dozen years ago. When an older couple from another town attempted to set up and lead a Bible club at my daughter's public elementary school in Southern California in 2009, they might as well have been alien visitors showing up at a beach party. The purpose of the club was to convince children as young as five that they would burn for an eternity if they failed to conform to a strict interpretation of the Christian faith. The club's organizers were offered free and better space in the evangelical church next door to our school, but they refused it; they insisted on holding the club in the public school because they knew the kids would think the message was coming from the school. They referred to our public school as their "mission field" and our children as "the harvest." I thought their plan was outrageously inappropriate in our religiously diverse public school. I also thought it was a freak occurrence. They seemed completely out of place in the sunny land of stand-up paddle boarders and open-air wine tastings. In my eyes they came out of the American past, not the future. I was quite wrong about that.

Sometimes it takes a while to realize what is happening in your own backyard. As I researched the group behind these kindergarten missionaries, I saw that they were part of a national network of clubs. I soon discovered that this network was itself just one of many initiatives to insert reactionary religion into public schools across the country. Then I realized that these initiatives were the fruit of a nationally coordinated effort not merely to convert other people's children in the classroom but to undermine public education altogether. Belatedly, I understood that the conflict they provoked in our local community—I was hardly the only parent who found their presence in the public school alarming—was not an unintended consequence of their activity. It was of a piece with their plan to destroy confidence in our system of education and make way for a system of religious education more to their liking.

In 2012, I published what I had learned about the topic in my book *The Good News Club*. As I was completing that project, I realized I had latched onto only one aspect of a much larger, more important phenomenon in American political culture. The drive to end public education as we know it is just part of a political movement that seeks to transform the defining institutions of democracy in America. This movement pretends to represent the past and stand for old traditions. But in reality it is a creature of present circumstances and is organized around a vision for the future that most Americans would find abhorrent.

For the past ten years I have been attending conferences, gatherings, and strategy meetings of the activists powering this movement. I have sat down for coffee with "ex-gay" pastors determined to mobilize the "pro-family" vote. I have exchanged emails late into the night with men and women who have dedicated their lives to the goal of refounding the United States according to "biblical law." I have walked alongside young women as they marched for "life" and followed them into seminar rooms where they receive training in political messaging and strategy. Along the way, I have made some friends and learned something like a new language. I no longer see members of this movement as alien visitors under the California sun. I know them to be very much a part of modern America. And that alarms me all the more.

Now and then I wish I could go back to those happy afternoons on the California coast, where none of this would have seemed worthy of placing before the public. But I can't so easily forget what I have learned. Anyone who cares about what is happening in American politics today needs to know about this movement and its people. Their issues—the overwhelming preoccupation with sexual order, the determination to unite the nation around a single religious identity, the conviction that they are fighting for salvation against forces of darkness—have come to define the effort that has transformed the political landscape and shaken the foundations upon which lay our democratic norms and institutions. This is the movement responsible for the election of the forty-fifth president of the United States, and it now determines the future of the Republican Party. It is the change that we have been watching—some with joy, others in disbelief, others in denial. And it isn't going away anytime soon.

I don't doubt that many of the people I have met on my journey mean well. I have seen them showing kindness to friends and strangers with equal conviction, and I know that among them are many generous spirits. But I am convinced that they are dead wrong about the effect of their work on the future of the American republic. They may believe sincerely in the righteousness of their cause and want as much as anyone to build a secure and prosperous America. But that just makes their story—the subject of this book—an American tragedy.

For too long now America's Christian nationalist movement has been misunderstood and underestimated. Most Americans continue to see it as a cultural movement centered on a set of social issues such as abortion and same-sex marriage, preoccupied with symbolic conflicts over monuments and prayers. But the religious right has become more focused and powerful even as it is arguably less representative. It is not a social or cultural movement. It is a political movement, and its ultimate goal is power. It does not seek to add another voice to America's pluralistic democracy but to replace our foundational democratic principles and institutions with a state grounded on a particular version of Christianity, answering to what some adherents call a "biblical worldview" that also happens to serve the interests of its plutocratic funders and allied political leaders. The movement is unlikely to realize its most extreme visions, but it has already succeeded in degrading our politics and dividing the nation with religious animus. This is not a "culture war." It is a political war over the future of democracy.

Political movements are by their nature complex creatures, and this one is more complex than most. It is not organized around any single, central institution. It consists rather of a dense ecosystem of nonprofit, for-profit, religious, and nonreligious media and legal advocacy groups, some relatively permanent, others fleeting. Its leadership cadre includes a number of personally interconnected activists and politicians who often jump from one organization to the next. It derives much of its power and direction from an informal club of funders, a number of them belonging to extended hyper-wealthy families. It took me some time to navigate the sea of acronyms, funding schemes, denominations, and policy and kinship networks, and I will lay out much of this ecosystem in this book. Yet the important thing to understand about the collective effort is not its evident variety but the profound source of its unity. This is a movement that has come together around what its leaders see as absolute truth—and what the rest of us may see as partisan agitation. My aim is to describe the common, often startling political vision that has united this movement.

Names matter, so I will take a moment here to lay out some of the terms of my investigation. Christian nationalism is not a religious creed but, in my view, a political ideology. It promotes the myth that the American republic was founded as a Christian nation. It asserts that legitimate government rests not on the consent of the governed but on adherence to the doctrines of a specific religious, ethnic, and cultural heritage. It demands that our laws be based not on the reasoned deliberation of our democratic institutions but on particular, idiosyncratic interpretations of the Bible. Its defining fear is that the nation has strayed from the truths that once made it great. Christian nationalism looks backward on a fictionalized history of America's allegedly Christian founding. It looks forward to a future in which its versions of the Christian religion and its adherents, along with their political allies, enjoy positions of exceptional privilege and power in government and in law.

Christian nationalism is also a device for mobilizing (and often manipulating) large segments of the population and concentrating power in the hands of a new elite. It does not merely reflect the religious identity it pretends to defend but actively works to construct and promote new varieties of religion for the sake of accumulating power. It actively generates or exploits cultural conflict in order to improve its grip on its target population.

Other observers may reasonably use terms like "theocracy," "dominionism," "fundamentalism," or "Christian right." I use those terms where appropriate, but often prefer "Christian nationalism" in referring to the whole, because it both reflects the political character of the movement and because it makes clear its parallels between the American version and comparable political movements around the world and throughout history.

This is not a book about "evangelicals." The movement I am describing includes many people who identify as evangelical, but it excludes many evangelicals, too, and it includes conservative representatives of other varieties of Protestant and non-Protestant religion. This movement is a form of nationalism because it purports to derive its legitimacy from its claim to represent a specific identity unique to and representative of the American nation. And I join with others who study the field in calling it "Christian nationalism" in deference to the movement's own understanding of this national identity, which it sees as inextricably bound up with a particular religion. However, I do not mean to suggest that Christian nationalism is representative of American Christianity as a whole. Indeed, a great many people who identify as Christians oppose the movement, and quite a few even question whether it is authentically Christian in the first place.

I have been following this movement for over a decade as an investigative reporter and journalist. I remain as impressed with the organization and determination of its leaders as I am alarmed by the widespread lack of awareness of its influence among the general public. The aims of the movement's leaders have been clear for some time, often openly stated in the forums that they share. Their recent achievements have exceeded reasonable expectations. Yet much of the public continues to believe that little has changed.

Perhaps the most salient impediment to our understanding of the movement is the notion that Christian nationalism is a "conservative" ideology. The correct word is "radical." A genuinely conservative movement would seek to preserve institutions of value that have been crafted over centuries of American history. It would prize the integrity of electoral politics, the legitimacy of the judiciary, the importance of public education, and the values of tolerance and mutual respect that have sustained our pluralistic society even as others have been torn apart by sectarian conflict. Christian nationalism pretends to work toward the revival of "traditional values" yet its values contradict the long-established principles and norms of our democracy. It has no interest in securing the legitimacy of the Supreme Court; it will happily steal seats and pack the Court as long as it gets the rulings it wants. It cheers along voter suppression and gerrymandering schemes that allow Republicans to maintain disproportionate legislative control. It collaborates with international leaders who seek to undermine the United States' traditional alliances and the postwar world order built up over the past seven decades. And it claims to defend "the family," but treats so many American families with contempt.

The widespread misunderstanding of Christian nationalism stems in large part from the failure to distinguish between the leaders of the movement and its followers. The foot soldiers of the movement—the many millions of churchgoers who dutifully cast their votes for the movement's favored politicians, who populate its marches and flood its coffers with small-dollar donations—are the root source of its political strength. But they are not the source of its ideas.

The rank and file come to the movement with a variety of concerns, including questions about life's deeper meaning, a love and appreciation of God and Scripture, ethnic and family solidarity, the hope of community and friendship, and a desire to mark life's most significant passages or express feelings of joy and sorrow. They also come with a longing for certainty in an uncertain world. Against a backdrop of escalating economic inequality, deindustrialization, rapid technological change, and climate instability, many people, on all points of the economic spectrum, feel that the world has entered a state of disorder. The movement gives them confidence, an identity, and the feeling that their position in the world is safe.

Yet the price of certainty is often the surrendering of one's political will to those who claim to offer refuge from the tempest of modern life. The leaders of the movement have demonstrated real savvy in satisfying some of the emotional concerns of their followers, but they have little intention of giving them a voice in where the movement is going. I can still hear the words of one activist I met along the way. When I asked her if the anti-democratic aspects of the movement ever bothered her, she replied, "The Bible tells us that we don't need to worry about anything."

The Christian nationalist movement is not a grassroots movement. Understanding its appeal to a broad mass of American voters is necessary in explaining its strength but is not sufficient in explaining the movement's direction. It is a means through which a small number of people—quite a few of them residing in the Washington, D.C., area—harness the passions, resentments, and insecurities of a large and diverse population in their own quest for power. The leaders of the movement have quite consciously reframed the Christian religion itself to suit their political objectives and then promoted this new reactionary religion as widely as possible, thus turning citizens into congregants and congregants into voters.

From the perspective of the movement's leadership, vast numbers of America's conservative churches have been converted into the loyal cells of a shadow political party. Here, too, there is a widespread misunderstanding of the way Christian nationalism works. Its greatest asset is its national infrastructure, and that infrastructure consists not only of organizations uniting and coordinating its leadership, and a burgeoning far-right media, but also in large part the nation's conservative houses of worship. The churches may be fragmented in a variety of denominations and theologies, but Christian nationalist leaders have had considerable success in uniting them around their political vision and mobilizing them to get out the vote for their chosen candidates. Movement leaders understand very well that this access to conservative Christians through their churches is a key source of their power, and for this reason they are committed to over-turning regulatory, legal, or constitutional restrictions on the political activity of churches.

A related source of misunderstanding is the comforting yet unfounded presumption that America's two-party system has survived intact the rise of the religious right as a political force. The conventional wisdom holds that the differences between America's two parties, now as before, amount to differences over questions of domestic and foreign policy, and that politics is just the art of give-and-take between the two collections of interests and perspectives they represent. Yet the fundamental difference today is that one party is now beholden to a movement that does not appear to have much respect for representative democracy. Forty years ago, when both sides of certain cultural issues could be found in either party, it made sense to speak of the religious right as a social movement that cut across the partisan divide. Today it makes more sense to regard the Republican party as a host vehicle for a radical movement that denies that the other party has any legitimate claim to political power.

True, there are some Republicans concerned primarily with a conservative economic agenda and willing to practice the traditional politics of compromise and sharing of power. But few Republican politicians can achieve influence without effectively acting as agents for Christian nationalism, and almost no Democratic leaders can realistically cede enough ground to earn the movement's support.

Many critics of the Republican party today trace its present corruption to the influence of big money. This explanation is true enough yet incomplete. In the age of Trump, the party's resolute rejection of the democratic and constitutional norms that it once at least pretended to champion would not have been possible without the prior success of Christian nationalism in training millions of supporters to embrace identity-based, authoritarian rule over pluralistic, democratic processes. The roots of the present crisis in the American political party system lie at the juncture of money and religion.

In recent years the movement has come to depend critically on the wealth of a growing subset of America's plutocratic class. Without the DeVos/Prince clan, the Bradley Foundation, Howard Ahmanson Jr., the foundations of the late Richard Scaife, the John M. Olin Foundation, the Lynn and Foster Friess Family Foundation, the Maclellan Foundation, Dan and Farris Wilks, the Green family, and a number of other major funders I will discuss in this book—to say nothing of the donor-advised funds such as the National Christian Foundation, which channel hundreds of millions of dollars in annual donations anonymously, and the massive flow of right-wing dark money targeting the courts—the movement would not be what it is today. At the same time, the movement has developed a large-scale apparatus for raising funds from millions of small donors. Indeed, the Christian right rose to prominence through aggressive direct-marketing operations, and much of its daily activity can be understood as part of an effort to milk its base of supporters.

Just as important as the pursuit of private money to Christian nationalism is the effort to secure public sources of funding. The movement has learned to siphon public money through subsidies, tax deductions, grants, and other schemes. This flow of funds has in turn shaped the ambitions and tactics of the movement. The calls for "religious freedom" that characterize much of its activism today, though undoubtedly bound up in a sincerely held belief that conservative Christians should be permitted to discriminate against LGBT people and members of religious minority groups, are as loud and passionate as they are because they are grounded in the fear among movement leaders that their discriminatory inclinations might cost them their lucrative tax deductions and subsidies.

Christian nationalists have put particular emphasis on the intersection of money and education. The Christian right has been hostile to public education at least since Jerry Falwell of the Moral Majority called for an end to public schools in 1979. This hostility has its roots in a combination of racial animus and fears of secularism, as I will explain. But Christian nationalists now see in school vouchers—and even charter programs—a potentially vast source of public funding, too. Furthermore, by planting churches in public school buildings for nominal fees rather than purchasing and funding their own buildings or renting private facilities at market rates, they are exploiting the public schools on a widespread scale to subsidize their religion.

In their pursuit of money, just as in their efforts to mobilize voters, Christian nationalists have displayed a high degree of sophistication and technological capability. There is a tendency on the part of those outside it to view the movement as a premodern phenomenon clinging to ancient doctrines that have long been destined for the archives of history. In fact, this is a modern movement in every respect. It is modern in its methods, which include high-tech data-mining operations and slick marketing campaigns. It is also modern in its doctrines, which notwithstanding their purported origins in ancient texts have been carefully shaped to serve the emotional needs of its adherents, the organizational needs of its clerical leaders, and the political needs and ambitions of its funders.

At every step in its rise, popular commentators have declared that the movement is in terminal decline. Secularization and modernization, we have been told, are the immutable laws of history, and demography will put the nail in the coffin. When journalists do draw attention to the authoritarian and theocratic ambitions of the movement, some have been quick to minimize concern and complain of alarmism. It is "a movement that could fit in a phone booth," wrote former George W. Bush speechwriter Michael Gerson in the *Washington Post*. Now that the "phone booth" has been installed in the White House and in the Capitol, the time has come to set aside these premature dismissals.

I wish to underscore, because the question always comes up, that my concern here is not with religious belief systems, either in general or in particular. I do not for a moment imagine that Christian nationalists represent all Christians. I leave it for theologians to decide whether their views are consistent with Christian teachings. I am not interested in judging other people's religious beliefs. But I think we all have a stake in understanding their political actions.

I believe that some of the most powerful resistance to Christian nationalism may ultimately come from those who identify as Christians themselves. As of this writing, many individuals and groups who identify as religious moderates or who call themselves part of a "religious left" are organizing to meet the challenge. They have many good arguments and can draw on a long tradition in the American past to support their cause, and they may have the future on their side. But they are not in the saddle of history today, and they are not the subject of this book.

In *The Power Worshippers* I will introduce you to the movement's power players and the foot soldiers. I will tell their stories, in their words, though my real subject is the political vision that ties them together. I will take you to gatherings in Northern California, where agri-business men team up with pastors who have direct access to the Trump White House; to North Carolina, where Christian nationalist leaders recruit clergy to their partisan activism; to Arizona, where charter school operators with sectarian agendas are indoctrinating schoolchildren on the taxpayer's dime; and to Verona, Italy, where American representatives of what they call a "global conservative movement" gather with international far-right leaders to declare war on global liberalism. We will revisit the strategy meetings of the late 1970s in which it was decreed, several years after *Roe v. Wade*, that abortion would be packaged and sold as the unifying issue of the movement. We'll go back further in time to historical antecedents of Christian nationalism in some

of the most fraught chapters of America's theological past—most importantly, the chapter in which the theological ancestors of today's religious
authoritarians wielded the Bible in support of slavery and segregation. And
we will examine the movement's affinities and connections with religious
nationalist movements in other countries. I will trace the flow of funds from
America's most pious plutocrats to the organizations that are packing the
courts and upending electoral politics. We will sit in on gatherings organized by national activists to motivate pastors to get out the vote for Republican candidates. And we will spend time with some of the movement's
most intriguing personalities as they cast aside their "unbiblical" longings,
make war against their "demonic" enemies, and stride confidently on the
path to power.

CHAPTER I

Church and Party in Unionville

If you don't know your enemy and you don't know yourself, you're going to get conquered every time. If you don't know yourself and you know your enemy, you can win every other time. But if you know yourself and you know your enemy, you can prevail.

—TONY PERKINS, FAMILY RESEARCH COUNCIL PRESIDENT, AT THE UNIONVILLE BAPTIST CHURCH, OCTOBER 2018, PARAPHRASING SUN TZU, *THE ART OF WAR*

WITH THIRTY-THREE DAYS to go before the 2018 midterm elections, I am headed for the fellowship hall of the Unionville Baptist Church, about forty-five minutes outside of Charlotte, North Carolina, in the passenger seat of a Ford Explorer SUV. The car seats and toys strewn in the back belong to my friend Chris Liles, a father of two and head pastor at a Baptist church in a midsized town in South Carolina. With his khaki pants and neat polo shirt and jacket, Chris looks the part of a young, sincere pastor. But the trip seems to be making him a little uneasy.

Chris's church is a member of the Southern Baptist Convention as well as a partner with the Cooperative Baptist Fellowship, which takes a philosophically and theologically moderate stance on issues including women's ordination. Chris is avowedly a Bible believer, yet his reading of Scripture is miles away from the interpretations of the fellow believers with whom we are about to gather. As we set off across the verdant farmland close to the South Carolina border, he reminds me that care for the poor and down-trodden lie at the very heart of the faith, no matter what others seem to say. "It's just hard for me to imagine how you can read the Bible and not see themes of social justice throughout," he says squarely. "Or where you find America's current political landscape in a text that was finished eighteen hundred years ago."

When I asked Chris to add my name as his guest at the event, there was only one available box for pastors to check: "Wife." So he checked it. Chris is about thirty years old—young enough, in theory, to be my son—and his winsome smile and baby cheeks make him look even younger. I'm not going to be his wife. I'm not going incognito, either, but I also don't want to attract attention in any way that might affect the event.

I've chosen a floral print blouse with a complicated arrangement of ribbons off to one side, a coordinating pink cardigan, and pearl earrings. Chris glances at my camouflage with a dubious look. As we pull into the parking lot he hands me the Bible he keeps in his car, a compact New International Version translation. Its black leather binding has been soft-ened to a buttery texture from habitual use.

"Maybe this will help," he says laconically.

Unionville Baptist Church is a solid brick building on a country road surrounded by farmland. We enter the spacious fellowship hall on the ground floor and take our seats at one of the round tables with a clear view of the podium. Purple-and-white floral arrangements adorn the tables, and the walls are lined with colorful booths displaying promotional materials from the various right-wing policy groups in attendance.

From the flyer publicizing the event, which is sponsored by the Watchmen on the Wall, an affiliate of the Washington, D.C.–based Family Research Council (FRC), a passerby might have formed the impression that this would be a nonpartisan occasion involving discussion of policy issues of interest to church members and their leaders. The FRC, one of the most powerful and politically connected lobbying organizations of the Christian right, has organized dozens of similar "Pastors Briefings" through its network of "Watchmen," which claims to have nearly 25,000 members. According to its promotional material, the briefings are "focused on shaping public policy and informed civic activism." The organization's website boasts an endorsement by Vice President Mike Pence: "Keep being a 'Watchman on the Wall.' Keep doing what you're doing. It's making a difference."[1]

With the approach of the 2018 midterms, the rhetoric on the Watchmen's website took a turn to the apocalyptic. "Do you not already hear the warnings of God? Do you not see that the enemy is coming in like a flood? And God is trying to raise up a standard against it. And you and I are that standard," read one quote on the home page from the influential pastor Dr. Henry Blackaby.

If there was any pretense of neutrality at Unionville, in any case, it didn't survive more than a few sentences into the opening remarks by FRC president Tony Perkins. "I believe this last election, 2016, was the result of prayer," said Perkins. "We've seen our nation begin to move back to a nation that respects the sanctity of life." Perkins speaks in the calm, mid-Atlantic voice of a Beltway operator, but his words are all sulphur and rage. The host of a weekly radio show to which he invites prominent guests, he is a practiced and effective speaker and knows the anger buttons of his audience well.

"'Put on the whole armor of God that you may be able to withstand the wiles of the devil, for we do not wrestle against flesh and blood but against principalities, against powers, against the rulers of the darkness of this age, against the spiritual host of wickedness in heavenly places,'" he says, quoting a Bible verse from the book of Ephesians. "If we don't know that to be true after what we've seen in the last three weeks, I don't know what it will take," he adds, referring to the recent fight to place Judge Brett Kavanaugh on the Supreme Court.

A woman seated to my left wearing a conservatively cut red-and-black suit is nodding intently. Perkins is speaking to his people, and the room is punctuated by spontaneous encouragements from members of the crowd: "Preach, brother," and "Amen!"

"Folks, we're headed in a new direction as a nation. And that's what this battle over the court is all about," Perkins continues. "This battle over the court is not about Brett Kavanaugh." He runs through a familiar litany of how "the Court has been used to impose a godless set of values on America," tapping all the well-worn talking points about how the Bible was "taken out of school" and replaced with "calls for abortion on demand." "It was the Court that imposed it on America and made all of us complicit with the taking of innocent human life," he inveighs. "Folks, is this an evil day?"

Then he gets to the point of the gathering. "Christians need to vote," he says. "The members of your congregations need to vote. As pastors, you need to—I'm not going to say 'challenge them'; you need to *tell them* to vote."

Although Perkins never says the word "Republican," there isn't the slightest doubt about which way he expects pastors to tell their congregants to vote. One party is "the party of life," he suggests, and supporting it is a matter of eternal salvation. "We are a divided nation, and someone's values will dominate," he warns, leaving little doubt that in his view "the rulers of the darkness" and "the spiritual host of wickedness" are to be found on the Democratic Party's side of the aisle. "We will be held accountable for what we do with this moment," he tells the assembled pastors. "My question to you this morning is: What will you do? What will you do with this moment that God has entrusted to us?"

In his talk at Unionville, Perkins asks pastors to "pray, to vote, and to stand." "Stand" appears to be a synonym for activity that will lead congregants to vote "biblical" values. An FRC video encourages pastors to form "Culture Impact Teams across the country." These "CITs" are, alongside the Pastors Briefings, central tools in the FRC's campaign to turn out the vote. The idea is for pastors to create within their churches teams of congregants that will "advance Kingdom values in the public arena." Pastors are instructed to figure out which members of their congregation are politically active, well-connected with other members, and motivated to persuade them to vote according to "biblical values," and then draft them as team leaders "to accomplish the Culture Impact Team's mission of defending and advancing faith, family, and freedom." Congregants on the CIT can take lead roles in the areas of communications (including written and social media outreach), research, strategy, and mobilization. Other team members will encourage "grassroots outreach" and "involvement in pregnancy support centers, school board meetings, civil government gatherings," and the like. Team members then set up a "Culture Impact Center" for church members to "give people an opportunity to become informed and, in turn, involved."

A fundamental motivation behind the creation of the elaborate architecture of Culture Impact Teams is to skirt legal prohibitions on the direct endorsement of candidates by church organizations. Current IRS guidelines require that pastors refrain from campaigning for candidates through their office—that is, from the pulpit. But nothing stops congregants from undertaking their own church-based political activism if it's all about "culture." "It wasn't me; it was the CIT" is thus seen as an alibi against any theoretical charge that pastors may be organizing de facto political action committees.

In order to guide the CITs in their actual mission—to turn out the vote for Republican and hyper-conservative candidates—the FRC supplies dense, information-packed manuals. At Unionville, I spot a stack of such manuals, some 180 pages of material in a three-ring binder, bound in a white cover, at the FRC booth, and I take one for myself.

According to the CIT manual, the Bible is very clear about the right answers to the political issues American voters face in the twenty-first century.[2] Scripture, it says, opposes public assistance to the poor as a matter of principle—unless the money passes through church coffers. God has challenged believers "to help the poor and widows and orphans," but He expects governments to step aside. The Bible also votes against environmentalism, which is a "litany of the Green Dragon" and "one of the greatest threats to society and the church today," according to the CIT manual's sole recommended resource on environmental issues, the Cornwall Alliance for the Stewardship of Creation.[3] The Cornwall Alliance has produced a declaration asserting, as a matter of theology, that "there is no convincing scientific evidence that human contribution to greenhouse gases is causing dangerous global warming."[4]

According to the CIT manual, the Bible also opposes gun regulations, favors privatization of schools through vouchers, and tells us that same-sex relationships are an abomination. It emphatically does not want women to have access to comprehensive, twenty-first-century reproductive medical care. The CIT manual directs readers to additional sources. I recognize one of them, Ken Ham, an author and activist known for promoting the claim that the earth is six thousand years old.

Tami Fitzgerald, executive director of the NC Values Coalition, follows Perkins onstage. A seasoned activist with soft blond hair, a smartly cut black skirt suit, and a composed manner, Fitzgerald leads a group with a "dual focus on impacting elections and on advancing Christian values in law and public policy." Yet she offers some carefully worded language that seems intended to make clear to the authorities that she is not a Republican Party operative. After urging pastors to support candidates with the right values, she adds, "Notice I didn't say members of a certain party because party doesn't guarantee they are fearing God and living according to biblical values. We never want to be the pawns of a political party," she points out. "Instead, as Christians, we want to use political parties as a means to an end."

In a curt nod to the letter of the law, she advises the pastors to speak with her privately if they are worried about what they are legally permitted to do. "I'm telling you, you can talk about issues all day long as a pastor, you can tell people who you're going to vote for," she assures them. But, she cautioned, "you must not publish that information in a church newsletter or state it from the pulpit."

From her tone of voice, I can tell that Fitzgerald's talk is haunted by the Johnson Amendment, the federal law that bars houses of worship, charitable nonprofits, and private foundations from endorsing and financially supporting political parties and candidates. Passed in 1954 at the urging of then senator Lyndon B. Johnson, the amendment was intended to prevent public money from passing through churches via tax deductions into the hands of politicians. In theory, according to the Johnson Amendment, religious organizations that engage in activities to directly sway elections could lose their tax-exempt status. It has been a favorite target of Christian nationalists, who regularly decry it as an infringement of their religious freedom.

As Fitzgerald starts to explain the importance of the upcoming elections in North Carolina, however, she becomes more animated. She loosens her grip on the bureaucratic rhetoric and swiftly banishes the specter of the Johnson Amendment. There are three congressional districts in North Carolina in play, all currently held by Republicans, she says. One of them happens to be right here in Unionville. In fact, it is more than likely that's why this meeting is being held here in the first place, and not on the other side of Charlotte. "If we lose those three seats to progressives—I'm using a term to describe people who don't hold our values—then the whole Congress could be lost," warns Fitzgerald.

The Republican Party candidate in one of those districts, Mark Harris, a pastor who served as president of the Baptist State Convention of North Carolina, is right here with us, as it happens, in a blue jacket, red tie, and talk-show hair. Earlier in the election season Harris drew national attention for sermons in which he argued that God's straightforward message for women is that they should "submit" to their husbands.[5] His race is very tight. In the coming months, after Harris supposedly wins by a whisker, his campaign will become embroiled in broadly reported allegations of election fraud. But in this room he is hailed as the kind of godly political leadership America truly needs.

Later in the day Harris comes up on the stage to address the assembled crowd. It is a campaign speech all right, although it sounds a lot like a sermon—which is unsurprising, given that Harris is also a preacher. "The greatest destroyer of love and peace is abortion," he says, paraphrasing a speech by Mother Teresa. "The mother who is thinking of abortion should be helped to understand that she is to give until it hurts. *Her* plans, *her* free time, to respect the life of her child." He declares, "We are reminded time and again that God wants us to deliver his word in a straight and unapologetic way." From the stage, he urges pastors to get their congregations registered to vote. He promises to deliver a "church video" in time for Sunday. In this briefing, there is no easy place to draw the line between preacher and politician, just as there is no space between church and political party.

Mark Harris's views may seem far from the mainstream. An hour away from here, after all, sits the third-largest banking capital of the United

States, surely powered by many women enjoying egalitarian partnerships and voluntary parenthood. Yet Harris's outlook is far from the fringe within Christian nationalist circles, and it reflects something central to the current politics of North Carolina.

Looking only at the top line, this is a purple state. Trump won by three points in 2016, but Obama carried it before that, and Democrats recently managed to capture the governorship. But, thanks to aggressive gerrymandering, or what Faith & Freedom Coalition president Ralph Reed has proudly termed "the Republican reapportionment advantage," ten of thirteen of the state's congressional representatives were Republican as of 2016. And Republicans dominate the state legislature and the courts.

But these weren't just any old Republicans. The hard right controls the party here, and that means they control the state, too. Over the past several years the Republican-controlled state government has enacted laws that restrict access to reproductive care, broaden the ability of taxpayer-subsidized organizations to discriminate on the basis of their religion, and strip public education of critical funding.

The red tide in the state capital really has one godfather, and his name is Art Pope. A wealthy businessman from the retail sector with a libertarian political vision, Pope decided some years ago to seek control of the state government. He invested millions of dollars in political think tanks, funded fellowships, and flooded campaign coffers. Payday has been sweet to Pope and his super-wealthy, hyper-conservative friends. North Carolina has advanced an agenda that includes the privatization of schools and lowering of the state's income and corporate tax rates.

Today, North Carolina is one of the states most affected by the self-inflicted reduction of Medicaid funding. Its public school system has been deflated by the expansion of fiscally unaccountable charter networks, many of which are run by big GOP donors. Koch brothers money speaks loudly in North Carolina, too, now rivaling Pope's for influence, and the state can be ranked alongside Wisconsin and Texas as a model of plutocratic governance. In purely demographic terms, North Carolina is almost exactly balanced between Democratic and Republican voters. In power politics, however, it represents the fusion of money and religion that supplies the foundation of the Christian nationalist movement.

In demographic terms, it is also fair to say that North Carolina is a religious state, but it would not be accurate to suppose that its faith is uniformly conservative. Indeed, North Carolina is the site of a large and fairly active progressive political movement that draws much of its strength from liberal Christianity. Christian Church (Disciples of Christ) Reverend Dr. William J. Barber II, the leader of progressive religious voices, initiated "Moral Mondays" protests to draw attention to issues of economic equality and social justice. He is a member of the Red Letter Christians, a group committed to "combining Jesus and justice." Yet the religion that dominates in North Carolina hardly reflects the diversity of religion among its people.

The faction of Republicans that are in control is so radical that, in 2013, fourteen North Carolina legislators put forward a bill, known as the Rowan County Defense of Religion Act, that declared that states are free to make laws they choose regarding religion. The U.S. Constitution's church-state separation provision, they claimed, only applied to the federal government. Think of it as a new nullification provision, only aimed directly at the First Amendment. The bill would have allowed, say, public schools to insist that principals prove they had been "born again." It could have mandated that candidates for public office prove weekly church attendance and that all public meetings begin with prayers that infidels will come to know the Lord.

In 2013, even in North Carolina, this bill was never going to pass, and it was promptly referred to the Committee for Rules, Calendar, and Operations, which is where wacky bills are sent to die. But passing the bill wasn't the point of the exercise. The sponsors put it forward because they believed—rightly—that this kind of posturing is just the way to gain popularity among the right-wing evangelical base and win power in North Carolina.

It is the same spirit that seems to move Mark Harris to double down on his extreme social conservatism in Unionville. Glancing around at the nodding heads in the crowd, I get a sense of how it works. Beyond the relentless, binary, life-or-death messaging, what Harris and his fellow pastor-politicians offer is a pathway to involvement. There is an undercurrent of rage that flows among the flower-bedecked tables here, and Harris seems to offer his listeners a way to channel it into a kind of political therapy. Here the anxieties over shifting gender roles and the resentments over fading economic privilege are transmuted into personal salvation—and political gold. Setting aside the big money, the key to hard-right Republican power in this state is an army of volunteer activists, people with the time and energy to canvass voters, run for minor political offices, and do whatever it takes to save the country from "the humanists" and "the homosexual agenda" and take it back for God.

When the group breaks for a lunch of barbecue, baked beans, and coleslaw, Chris and I wander outside to check out a red-and-blue "Values Bus"—the FRC claims to operate two of them—that is parked in front of the church. Sizable and eye-catching, it has been repurposed as a mobile get-out-the-vote unit.

The side of the bus bears the enlarged signatures of identical twin brothers Jason and David Benham, two of the featured speakers at today's event. They are accompanied by their father, Philip "Flip" Benham, a longtime antiabortion activist and associate of Tony Perkins, who takes in their presentation with pride. Popular draws on the right-wing speaking circuit for their farm-boy-wholesome looks and lightly competitive banter, Jason and David are former minor-league baseball players turned real estate entrepreneurs. In 2014 they attracted national attention when the media outlet Right Wing Watch reported that David spoke with conservative radio host Janet Mefferd and warned against "homosexuality and its agenda that is attacking the nation."[6] He also claimed that "demonic ideologies" are taking hold in colleges and public schools. In the flare-ups that followed, the Benhams' anticipated reality television series on HGTV was scrapped. Not to be outdone, their father, Flip Benham, went on television to back Judge Roy Moore in his Senate race in Alabama in order to beat back allegations of child molestation leveled against the judge.

Along with its crew of firebrand speakers, the Values Buses cross the country delivering hundreds of thousands of "voter guides." The voter guides are one of the essential tools of the movement. They are everywhere in the Unionville church. A voter guide created by the North Carolina Family Policy Council has been placed at every seat, and piles of them are dispersed throughout the fellowship hall, including a table in the middle of the room that holds thousands of them in neat stacks, ready to be loaded into the trunks of pastors' cars.

"Take as many voter guides as you can, as you believe you can use effectively, giving one to every member of your church and then beyond," says John Rustin, president of the North Carolina Family Policy Council. "We survey all the candidates, over four hundred candidates, running for U.S. House, the North Carolina Senate, the North Carolina House, the North Carolina Supreme Court, and the North Carolina Court of appeals." Rustin directs the audience to the organization's voter guide website. "Type in your name and address and it will generate a personalized guide specifically for you . . . Those are provided free of charge!"

Voter guides escape IRS limitations on campaigning for candidates on the theory that they offer voters a nonpartisan assessment of where the candidates stand on key issues. However, every voter guide I come across here has a pretty unambiguous message. The candidates from one party are in favor of "life." Candidates from the other party apparently favor death. One party's candidates support "religious freedom." The other party's candidates presumably endorse religious tyranny.

A glance at the Values Buses' schedules indicates that the FRC's presence in this swing district in North Carolina is far from accidental. The itineraries match the Republican Party's geographical needs with some precision. Later in the month, Values Buses will hit congressional swing districts in Dallas, Houston, and Oceanside, California. Along the way, the buses will make stops in states with hot Senate races: Florida, Tennessee, Montana, and Missouri.

After lunch, we head back into the building, and I notice a display case offering a dozen-odd different pocket-sized tracts for free: *The Truth About Hell*; *The Truth About Abortion*; *The Truth About Mormonism*; *The Da Vinci Con*. I pick up a pamphlet with the curious title *New International perVersion*. It turns out to be a screed against the New International Version (NIV) of the Bible, a 1978 effort to make the Bible more comprehensible. There are reportedly tens of millions of copies of the NIV in circulation, including the one covered in supple black leather that Chris handed to me earlier today and I'm carrying with me now. According to the pamphlet, "The NIV perverts Jesus Christ into Lucifer."

Chris notices the pamphlet and leans toward me. "Some people revere the King James version like they were the precise words of, say, Paul, written in English rather than Greek," he says, "as opposed to a translation that has been updated as we make advances in the field of translation and scholarship. I think it's about familiarity and fear. People memorized those specific words when they were children, and now, if those words change, the fear is everything else might be up for grabs."

The greatest terrors of translation, in Chris's view, have to do with sex. New words could mean a new gender order. "In Romans there's a woman named Junia, whom Paul said was outstanding among the apostles," he explains. "Many early writers believed that she was indeed a woman. At some point, though, there was this thought that 'apostle' wasn't a role women should have, and you see a masculine form of the name, 'Junias,' start to appear. Some translations highlight this tension in the footnotes, but others don't mention it. She just became a man."

We settle into our seats for the after-lunch program featuring Lieutenant General (ret.) William Boykin. Boykin is a living legend at events like these, an old warrior with an affable manner best known as the commander of the raid depicted in *Black Hawk Down*. Boykin seems willing to say out loud things that usually don't come out until the bottle is nearly empty. But to view Boykin's influence as marginal would be to underestimate the role he has played in nurturing Christian nationalist networks in the military and among "disaster relief" NGOs working abroad.

Boykin starts off with a lengthy reminiscence about "the longest day of my life," the eighteen-hour firefight that ended with "fifteen of my men brought back dead." Referring to President Bill Clinton, who authorized the raid, Boykin says, "We were sent in there to do this job by a man who was a philanderer. As far as I'm concerned, and I will tell you right now, he was a lowlife. Because he didn't understand the concept of integrity. He didn't understand that a vow is a vow. Like when you stand before God and you say, 'I'll honor and respect this woman I'm about to marry till death do I part.' That's why elections matter."

"Go on, brother," says the square-jawed young pastor seated just behind me. The roomful of Trump loyalists nod their heads with righteous certitude. Chris scribbles a note and passes it to me: "Do they have no sense of irony?"

Boykin pivots from adultery to communism, which he seems to think remains the greatest threat to our nation today. One of his friends in the audience, on cue, holds up a book with a red cover titled *The Naked Communist*. "If you want to understand what's going on in America right now," Boykin says, "you need to read that book right there."

The Naked Communist, by W. Cleon Skousen, was first published in 1958. Skousen was one of the founders of the National Center for Constitutional Studies, a conservative Mormon group that holds seminars across the country and promotes "a bizarre version of American history," according to the Southern Poverty Law Center.[7] Skousen was much-admired by the catastrophist Glenn Beck, who aggressively promoted Skousen's ideas on his TV show and wrote a foreword to one of his books. Skousen's teachings are also disseminated through a network of Arizona-based, taxpayer-funded charter schools, Heritage Academy, whose curriculum is suffused with ideological "principles," such as the notion that "free market and minimal government best supports prosperity." Textbooks in Heritage Academy's mandatory American government class have included the claim that the U.S. Constitution is based on "biblical principles" and asserted that "God" destroyed a French fleet that threatened the American colonies.[8] The Heritage Academy network, along with state officials, has been sued over alleged misuse of public money.[9] And yet the network remains a favorite within Arizona's "school choice" movement. In early 2019 the deputy secretary of the U.S. Department of Education participated in a "School Choice Week" celebration at a Heritage Academy campus.

In spite of his affinity for fringe figures like Skousen, Boykin's career has taken him close to the heart of American military power. He served at the Central Intelligence Agency as deputy director of special activities and was made deputy director for operations, readiness, and mobilization on the army staff. In 2003 he was appointed deputy undersecretary for intelligence and war fighting. In that capacity he worked with contractors with strong links to dominionist groups, who believe that Christians should seek to occupy all positions of power in government and society.[10]

One group that Boykin was closely involved with, Humanitarian International Services Group (HISG), led by a man named Kay Hiramine, received government contracts for work in disaster relief, emergency management, and intelligence gathering. Boykin "used his position not only to pay Hiramine and his missionaries to spy, but also to create work for his fundamentalist friends," according to the journalist Sarah Jones writing for the Wall of Separation Blog, a publication of Americans United for Separation of Church and State.[11]

An aid worker and missionary, Hiramine had "used shipments of clothing to disguise smuggled Bibles," Jones writes. But even before that, Hiramine worked for the late C. Peter Wagner, serving for a time as the executive director of the Wagner Institute for Practical Ministry. Wagner, a former professor of "church growth" at Fuller Theological Seminary who authored more than seventy books and founded various ministries, is widely referred to as the godfather of dominionist ideology.

In his 2008 book *Dominion! How Kingdom Action Can Change the World*, Wagner explains that God has commanded true Christians to gain control of the "seven molders" or "mountains" of culture and influence, or seven areas of civilization, including government, business, education, the media, the arts and entertainment, family, and religion. "Apostles," he says, have a "responsibility for taking dominion" over "whatever molder of culture or subdivision God has placed them in," which he casts as "taking dominion back from Satan."[12] Although Wagner is not a household name outside of Christian nationalist circles, his work is broadly influential within it.

Boykin's focus on "Kingdom action" has never wavered. He is presently the FRC's executive vice president and is a frequent guest on Tony Perkins's radio show, *Washington Watch*. The organization he founded, Kingdom Warriors, promises to "help believers in Christ to understand the concept of spiritual warfare." Boykin told an interviewer, "We're in a spiritual battle every single day and we wish to help equip them to fight this spiritual war that we're in."[13] He is on the council of POTUS Shield, a prayer initiative of "Warriors, Worshippers and Watchmen" supporting the Trump presidency.[14] "Points of discussion" on the POTUS Shield website include, "The

Church & Kingdom Trump & Resistance Changing the Laws—The the [*sic*] Supreme & Federal Court System Abortion Turning back Globalization Israel & Jerusalem Space Force and dominance."

At the podium in Unionville, Boykin speaks at length about the communist threat. By the time he sits down, it feels like we've been on a trip down memory lane in a neighborhood shaped by red scares and Dr. Strangelove. Other, more youthful, speakers brought to us by the Values Bus, however, take to the stage with forward-looking ideas.

Perhaps the most dynamic presenter at the Unionville event is a pastor and political activist named J. C. Church. Mr. Church, who now serves as the FRC's national director of ministry engagement and who also happens to be a council member of POTUS Shield, is here to tell us about the time he turned Ohio red. In vivid terms he recounts how twelve years ago he packed his family into a motor home, drove 14,000 miles up and down Ohio, and visited 2,500 churches in eighty-six of the state's eighty-eight counties.

That initiative, called Awake 88, is still in place today. The website for Awake 88 promises "timelines, tools, suggested messaging videos," and other support for pastors. "We need your help to mobilize the voters in your church!" the website exclaims. One tool advertised by Awake 88 is the Church Voter Lookup, which essentially marries a church database with a voter database. "You'll then receive a report that tells you what percentage of your congregation is registered to vote and what percentage actually voted in the last election!"[15]

The payoff for all those years of work, J. C. Church exults, came in 2016. "If you watched, the map was turning red, eighty-one of eighty-eight counties in Ohio went red. You know why? We had to beat the money, the media, our party, the left, our governor, et cetera. And you know why? Because pastors partnered together, were preaching and praying, and they mobilized and used their influence to get people to turn out and vote."

Mr. Church makes clear that turning Ohio red has nothing to do with keeping it white. In fact, much of the Awake 88 effort is targeted specifically at Latino pastors. This lines up with a message I've been hearing at activist gatherings. At the September 2018 Values Voters Summit, super-lobbyist Ralph Reed made the point bluntly. Mocking the mainstream pundits, he said, "They're always talking about racial issues, it's all about race and ethnicity. Not true! If you back evangelicals out of the white vote, Donald Trump loses with whites." Reed is absolutely right about the top-line numbers, but he appears to brush off the ways in which conservative white evangelical religion and racism often reinforce each other. This reality stands in uncomfortable contradiction with the leaders' goals of expanding Christian nationalism to religious people of color. Reed, like others in the movement, is hopeful that large numbers of Latino and Black Americans will soon be on the "right" side of history.

Black pastors, too, are part of the target group. While most of the attendees in Unionville are white, perhaps a half dozen Black pastors and associates are in the room. "There is a sleeping giant out here, it is the Black community and the Black church," says Bishop Larry Jackson, another presenter at the conference. A bald man with an attentive expression, he speaks in somewhat plaintive tones about the power of effecting change through racial unity. "I'm thinking about the need in the Black community and the need that they're waiting to be delivered from what they're under," he tells the crowd. "And I want you to understand that your voice to them will mean more than you can ever imagine. Many times more than my voice to them even as a Black man . . .

"It's not revival until the entire church is working as one together," he adds.

For Mr. Church, in any case, the agenda extends well beyond the colors of Ohio. Reaching the climax of his stemwinder, he thunders that "the number one thing" anybody can give another person is "the supreme Christ." But "the second greatest thing we can give this generation," he swiftly adds, "is the Supreme Court."

And then he opens a window on the vision that drives him and his fellow passengers on the Values Bus relentlessly forward. "What's hanging in the balance in the next thirty-three days will determine the next thirty-three years of this nation," he announces. "If we can secure the judiciary, from the Supreme Court on down, we can build a firewall for our children and grandchildren that they just might scale the seven mountains of influence."

The "seven mountains," of course, are the seven areas of human civilization that C. Peter Wagner wrote about and that, according to dominionist theology, "true" Christians must seek to control. I glance over at General Boykin's table, and it occurs to me that if the dominionist agenda calls for military action, he is a designated hitter. Once atop those seven mountains, the plan is to convert the world to Christianity and prepare for the second coming of Jesus. Which could involve an apocalyptic end for the earth, rapture for the faithful, and eternal torment for everyone else. That, it would seem, is the intended final destination of the Values Bus.

As the program winds down, Chris and I head out into the sunlight. Even though it is early October, the temperature outside is nearly 90 degrees. I take off my cardigan and enjoy the warmth of the sun on my shoulders. We get into the car and Chris steers it back toward Charlotte.

For the first few minutes Chris is silent. We pass barns and trees and cows and pretty houses with vegetable gardens and orchards, old and modestly constructed wooden churches, the lush landscape of the South. Chris cracks the silence. "It's ten degrees hotter than normal, and these people don't believe in climate science," he grumbles. Then his words start tumbling out like a waterfall.

"Do we not owe people more than simply reducing 'pro-life' to one issue?" he says. "I mean, no one wants babies to die. No one is 'pro-abortion.' That is a false dichotomy. Do we not owe more to people than to force them into one box or another? As much as abortion is a pro-life issue, so is affordable health care, access to contraceptives, and real, comprehensive sex education. Minimum wage. Fighting poverty. These should all be part of the 'pro-life' conversation."

Chris falls into silence for a few minutes, then speaks again.

"And shouldn't we show compassion to people regardless of how they identify? They, too, are made in God's image. We find in Scripture the imperative to love our neighbors and care for the least of these. That is by far one of the clearest messages we receive."

I feel bad for Chris; he seems dismayed by the event precisely because the Bible is his greatest source of comfort and moral direction. He tells me he is hesitant to encourage civic duty from the pulpit, because he doesn't see it as his role. "I don't see myself pastorally as having an obligation to the U.S.A. I see my obligation as being to the kingdom of God," he says. "Our church hosts the Rotary Club each week, and I'm a member. I will stand during the Pledge of Allegiance, but I won't recite it. Because that space for me is sacred, and in that sacred space, I'm not willing to pledge allegiance to anything but God.

"I will occasionally mention political topics from the pulpit but not partisan ones," he continues. "The Bible is inherently political in that it routinely speaks against people who abuse their power in order to oppress other people."

Stopping at a red light, Chris picks up his Bible and turns to the Old Testament book of Amos.

"Here, for instance, in chapter five, the prophet says, 'You, Israel, you were supposed to take care of the poor and you're not doing it,'" Chris says. "'You're using power and wealth to tilt the system in your favor.' For society to be just, it was necessary for everyone to be seen as equal." He falls silent for a few moments, "Sometimes," he adds, "it's almost like people are reading a different Bible. That's the trick with Scripture. You can make the Bible say just about anything you want it to."

Chris directs me to Psalm 121, which he likes to read aloud to bedridden or hospital-bound congregants, or those facing the end of life. "The LORD watches over you—the LORD is your shade at your right hand; the sun will not harm you by day, nor the moon by night. The LORD will keep you from all harm—he will watch over your life . . ."

The psalm is soothing, comforting, uplifting. It reminds me of the complexity of the Bible and also its flashes of lucidity, which makes it so open to interpretation and exploitation.

Coming in off the highway, I remind myself that North Carolina is a much bigger place than the fellowship hall at the Unionville Baptist Church. Many people who identify as Christians here—in fact, perhaps most—live a world apart from the dark, paranoid visions of the day's Pastors Briefing. I think of the Reverend William Barber again, and the voices of progress that have gathered around his "Moral Mondays." And I think of

Episcopal bishop Michael Curry, previously the bishop of the Diocese of North Carolina and perhaps best known for delivering the sermon at the 2018 wedding of Prince Harry and Meghan Markle. Curry, too, is an outspoken opponent of Christian nationalism and a committed supporter of marriage equality, interfaith dialogue, and other progressive causes.

The same voices of progress can be heard across the nation. In July 2019, hundreds of clergy representing a variety of mainline and progressive Christian denominations endorsed a new initiative, Christians Against Christian Nationalism.[16] In October 2018 the National Council of Churches, an organization representing dozens of Protestant denominations and millions of U.S. congregants, issued a rare statement opposing the appointment of Brett Kavanaugh to the Supreme Court. Many other Christians have aligned themselves against President Trump and his policies. The progressive Jesus-follower activists behind the Vote Common Good tour have made their own, shorter peregrinations through Ohio. Since 2016, hundreds of progressive pastors have gathered in Washington, D.C., to rally in support of the Affordable Care Act and to oppose several of Trump's cabinet and Supreme Court picks. And the Evangelical Environmental Network, a faith-based environmentalist movement, advocates for sensible climate policies by urging fellow evangelicals to "walk together as disciples of Christ faithfully following God's call to be good stewards of creation."[17]

But, for now, progressive religious voices have figured out only how to grab a headline here or there for the benefit of sympathetic audiences. They do not know how to seize the reins of political power. The leaders of the Unionville Pastors Briefing do.

While Chris was finished with the Pastors Briefing, it was not finished with him. After settling back in at home, Chris dodged the inevitable follow-up calls from representatives of FRC for several days. But he continued to receive emails from the organization through the midterm elections, after which he finally unsubscribed.

"Dear Chris," one email read, "We have a number of FREE Tools for you to use on the next two Sundays to encourage your people to get out and vote their Biblical values on November 6."

Penned by Dr. Kenyn M. Cureton, vice president for Christian Resources, the email promised an "Announcement Slide"; a "full-text Sermon Starter" on the theme of "For the Sake of America"; a printable, downloadable "Values Voter Bulletin Insert"; and videos from Tony Perkins to air at church. Such sophisticated tools promote a clear message for how congregants ought to vote and make it easy for the pastor to deliver the "correct" talking points.

"Point your people to 501c3 IRS compliant Voter Guides available at iVoterGuide.com where they can simply put in their zip code and get federal and state race guides," the email urged. "A basic patriotic action step is to vote biblical values."[18]

As one of his first acts in office, President Trump vowed to "totally destroy" the Johnson Amendment.[19] At the Values Voter Summit in 2018, Vice President Mike Pence boasted that the Johnson Amendment "will no longer be enforced under this administration." But he vowed to repeal it anyway.

As the gatherings like this one at Unionville make clear, the point of talking about the repeal of the Johnson Amendment is not, in fact, to repeal it. It has already been vetoed on the ground. Churches and preachers are some of the most valuable political operatives in America today, and they work mostly (though not exclusively) on the side of the Republican party. Since churches are subsidized with public money through tax deductions and other tax advantages, one could say that the United States now has a publicly subsidized political party that promotes an agenda of religious nationalism.

The point of talking up the nonexistent horror of the Johnson Amendment, in fact, is to feed the sense of persecution that is so central to Christian nationalism today. This is why Trump's and Pence's promises to neutralize the Johnson Amendment and to "stand up" for "religious freedom" play well to conservative Christian audiences. The narrative that government is stomping all over the rights of Christians and their churches may have little basis in fact, but it is one of the most powerful messages the movement has to drive voters to the polls.

Meanwhile, Watchmen on the Wall continues to gain favor with the Trump-Pence administration and allied politicians. Along with the ringing endorsement of the organization from Vice President Mike Pence, it is clear that the pretense of neutrality has vanished. One political party endorses ultraconservative varieties of religion and it is exploiting them to lock in power. This is how the Christian nationalist movement works.

All of this has been building up so slowly, and become so familiar, that Americans have come to take for granted that it is part of the natural order of things. We have become so used to the identification of "values voters" with the Republican Party that we no longer remember a time when neither party had a monopoly on God. We have heard the single-issue, pro-life or -death refrain so many times that we no longer remember a time when America's houses of worship, including conservative ones, tended to approach a vast range of issues that affect our society with the humility and appreciation of their complexity that is their due. We have been exposed to so much extreme rhetoric—and so many apocalyptic visions for world domination—that we no longer remember the time when such ideas and those who espoused them were nowhere near the center of political power.

Yet there was such a time, and it wasn't so long ago. How we got from there to here is the subject of the remaining chapters of this book.

CHAPTER 2

Ministering to Power

T HE GAME OF power really has two sides. You reach outside to voters
and tell them what they need to hear so they will vote in your favor.
But you also step inside and gather with the powerful individuals who actually call the shots. In recent years the Christian nationalist movement has
had extraordinary success in playing the inside game.

Even while some missionaries organize bus tours to mobilize pastors and
voters in swing districts across the nation, others are walking the hallways
of power, cultivating leaders and brokering deals between big money and
big government. In the Trump administration, activists who in an earlier
time would have been identified as extremists lead prayer and "Bible study"
sessions with officials at the highest levels of the executive and legislative
branches, in federal and state governments. At the same time they work
with some of America's wealthiest individuals and families, many of whom
fund the careers of the same politicians, to bring forth policies that are
favorable to plutocratic fortunes and advance their political vision.

Outside observers tend to think that the political religion of the movement emanates from the large population of conservative Christian voters
to whom it appeals. According to the conventional wisdom, the movement
is simply an effort to preserve so-called traditional values and, perhaps more
critically, to restore a sense of pride and privilege to a part of the American
population that feels that its status is slipping. But a closer look at the

substance of that political religion, in the context of the movement's involvement with political elites, tells a very different story. Most of the political vision of Christian nationalism is decided in the inside game. After all, the Bible can be used to promote any number of political positions. Many would argue that it generally favors helping the poor, for example. But the Bible of Christian nationalism answers to the requirements of the individuals who fund the movement and grant it power at the highest levels of government.

In the past two years, perhaps no Christian nationalist leader has had better luck playing the inside game than Ralph Drollinger. A onetime athlete and sports evangelist from California, Drollinger now leads weekly "Bible study" in the White House for cabinet secretaries and other officials—Mike Pence has reportedly attended—and his operation is rapidly expanding, both domestically through state capitols and among political leaders overseas. In hopes of learning more about the keys to his success, I find myself on the road to Tulare, a city in California's inland empire, where Trump's secretary of agriculture, Sonny Perdue, headlines a $10,000-a-table celebration of Capitol Ministries, the group that Drollinger founded.[1]

Tulare is surrounded by some of the most productive farmland in the United States. Kale, cherries, peaches, brussels sprouts, almonds—nearly half of America's fruit, vegetables, and nuts are grown in California, along with 20 percent of the nation's dairy. Multigenerational mom-and-pop farms are sandwiched between agribusiness conglomerates. The landscape is dotted with taco stands, gun shops, and community health centers.

Signs about water policy punctuate the highway like mile markers of a changing political topography. "No Water = No Jobs," says one. "Is growing food a waste of water?" asks another. "No to Bullet Train; Yes to Water Dams!" says a third, referring to the plan, favored by coastal elites, for a high-speed rail connecting north and south. In national political discussions, California counts as a blue state. But this is California, too: culturally conservative, steeped in resentment directed at the people flying overhead or populating the coastline, and largely Republican. This part of California, as it happens, is also heavily dependent on government subsidies, government-sanctioned water distribution rights, and undocumented labor.

Tulare is host to the World Ag Expo, an annual agricultural outdoor exposition bringing together hundreds of businesses supporting the food-growing sector, from harvest machine manufacturers to agricultural colleges to producers of cattle feed supplements. In the large tents focusing on various aspects of the agricultural business—viticulture, dairy, education—guests chat with vendors at the booths, learning about new services and talking shop. Outside, families in jeans and cowboy boots walk through the dusty grid inspecting the farming equipment on display and snacking on tri-tip sandwiches and baked beans.

The World Ag Expo in Tulare isn't as unlikely a locale for the celebration of a politically focused ministry as one might think. From its earliest years, Drollinger's ministry has benefited from the generous donations of agribusiness kings. But Capitol Ministries has come a long way since then. For Drollinger, the gritty fairgrounds in the red lands of California is a fitting backdrop for a triumphant homecoming.

Over in a white VIP tent on a corner of the fairground, hundreds of guests gather to honor the success of Capitol Ministries. The crowd consists of affluent agribusiness owners and executives, local lawmakers, bankers, law enforcement people, and a few stragglers. The gender balance tips male; the invitation specified "cowboy formal," and most guests are wearing cowboy hats or boots paired with sport jackets. A number of attendees have guns visibly holstered on their belts. I spot one man with four.

The crowd mingles over sodas—Drollinger disapproves of alcohol—and a bountiful assortment of vegetables and cheeses, chatting about growing seasons, agricultural technologies, and the great opportunity that comes with having elected Donald Trump. Many are excited about the recent confirmation of Supreme Court justice Neil Gorsuch. "This generation *will* end abortion," a woman is saying with a knowing look. Her companion smiles. "God is good."

The guests make their way to the dining area. I purchased an individual ticket for $175 and am seated at a table toward the back, which I figure is for stragglers. Nearby, a man in a plaid shirt and navy jacket is engrossed in conversation with a woman wearing a silver-and-turquoise Navajo-style bracelet. He's letting her know that "political correctness" is what's destroying America. She nods back at him.

Across the room, I think I spot Steve Taylor in jeans and a sport jacket, although I can't be sure. Taylor is a member of the board of Capitol Ministries since 2013. He is also on the board of directors of the Family Policy Alliance, the public policy arm of Focus on the Family, a well-funded Christian organization promoting socially conservative, often political viewpoints and policies. Focus on the Family was for a time merged with the Family Research Council; today, the organizations frequently work side by side on issues of mutual interest.

Taylor's involvement in both Capitol Ministries and the Family Policy Alliance is unsurprising, as the two entities pursue largely similar agendas in many areas. In a "ministries update" on the Capitol Ministries website, Steve Taylor said, "I have worked with candidates who have become U.S. Senators and House of Representatives members and God really impressed upon me the importance of speaking spiritual truths into their lives. It became apparent that is what Ralph [Drollinger] is doing every day."[2]

Steve Taylor is the brother of Bruce Taylor, who headed up the large produce grower Taylor Farms; they are scions of a multigenerational agribusiness conglomerate. Steve is also the former CEO of Fresh Express, which developed packaged salads in the 1980s and was acquired in 2005 by Chiquita Brands International for $855 million. Taylor and his partners from Fresh Express, including Mark Drever, started Organicgirl in 2007; the company is known to upscale shoppers for its lettuce and greens sold in sleek plastic clamshells at high-end grocery stores.[3]

When a Whole Foods shopper reaches for a package of Organicgirl premium salad mix, she might be under the illusion that its contents were brought to market by a yoga mama with rainbow flags on her hydroponic greenhouse. But to anyone sitting at the table here in Tulare, these kings of the organics business are very much on board with the hard-right religion and even harder-right politics of Capitol Ministries. As the evening gets underway, Jeff Taylor, another member of the clan, who comes in late and is seated at our straggler's table, leads a chorus of

"Hallelujahs" from our corner of the tent. From time to time he claps for emphasis and fires off: "Praise the Lord!"

Ralph Drollinger grew up in Southern California, the son of a successful and wealthy real estate magnate known for developing an area of Los Angeles near the LAX airport. Seven feet two inches tall, Drollinger began his career as a sportsman. He excelled at college basketball at UCLA, then played with an evangelistic team, Athletes in Action, before a brief stint with the Dallas Mavericks. He and his wife, Karen Rudolph Drollinger, an athlete and author, had three children. Then, as Drollinger told a writer with the German newspaper *Welt Am Sonntag*, Karen left him in order to take up a relationship with a woman.[4]

It had to have hurt. Drollinger, who has characterized same-sex relationships as "detestable acts," "profane actions of immorality," and an "abomination," is a committed and unapologetic advocate of gender hierarchy in the home and at church. "The respect of the submissive wife to her husband then, becomes a tremendous physical picture of the interrelationships existing amongst the members of the Trinity, i.e. the Son's respect for the Father's authority. This human modeling is essential to the woof and warp of successful cultures," he writes. But "the forces and events of evil continually labor to expunge God's model of marriage from the face of the earth."[5]

Although Drollinger endorses these ideas, he didn't invent them. He appears to have absorbed them while pursuing his master of divinity degree at The Master's Seminary in Los Angeles, which adheres to a strict Calvinist and patriarchal brand of theology. The school has been led since 1986 by John MacArthur, a hyper-conservative pastor who assumed the pastorate of Grace Community Church in Sun Valley, California. In a 2009 survey by LifeWay Research, the survey arm of an organization that "equips church leaders with insights and advice that will lead to greater levels of church health and effectiveness," MacArthur won a spot on a list of most influential living Christian pastors.[6]

MacArthur's sermons and writings leave an indisputable record of his commitment to the doctrine that female subordination and "wifely submission" are ordained by God and cemented in Scripture. According to a

February 19, 2012, sermon titled, "The Willful Submission of a Christian Wife," MacArthur instructs women to "rank yourself under" husbands. Castigating women who are employed, he says, "Your task is at home. A woman's task, a woman's work, a woman's employment, a woman's calling is to be at home." The problem, he explains, is that "working outside removes her from under her husband and puts her under other men to whom she is forced to submit."[7]

To those who worked with him, MacArthur's condemnation of gender equality was palpable.[8] Dr. Dennis M. Swanson, presently the dean of Library Services at the University of North Carolina at Pembroke and who worked in various capacities at The Master's Seminary for twenty-four years, asserts that few women on campus held positions of consequence, and female academic visitors were distinctly unwelcome. When the acclaimed German Protestant theologian Eta Linnemann paid a rare visit to the area, Swanson said, she was compelled to meet with students off campus. Even at the library, he says, which he ran for some time, the acquisition of books by female writers was frowned upon.

"If MacArthur found out your wife worked, he'd fire you," says Swanson. "Or, if he liked you, he'd give you a raise so she could quit her job."

Drollinger, Swanson believes, took his cues from MacArthur. "Drollinger's theology is hard-line within evangelical Christianity," he says. "But if you read his work side by side with what's in MacArthur's books, you'll see that's where Drollinger got it from. I don't think it's any great secret."

Drollinger graduated from The Master's Seminary with his career on an upward trajectory. He became friendly with James Dobson, founder of Focus on the Family, and created and participated in a variety of athletics ministries in hopes of evangelizing sportsmen. Soon he was proselytizing with so much force, and with such extreme views, that the world of pro sports was spinning with controversy. Few Christian sports ministers can "match the sledgehammer outspokenness with which onetime AIA basketball team member Ralph Drollinger connects sports and evangelical religion to the political sphere," observed Tom Krattenmaker in his 2009 book *Onward Christian Athletes: Turning Ballparks into Pulpits and Players into Preachers.*[9]

In 1997, Drollinger decided to raise his sights from the playing fields to the state legislature. With his new wife, Danielle Madison, who formerly worked at Focus on the Family and ran a right-wing political action committee, he moved to Sacramento and began spreading the Word among state legislators. He founded Capitol Ministries with the tagline "Making Disciples of Christ in the Capitol."

"Scripture is replete with illustrations, examples and commands to underscore the importance of winning governmental authorities for Christ," explains Drollinger. "A movement for Christ amongst governing authorities holds promise to change the direction of a whole country."[10] In quick order, Capitol Ministries secured a conference room in the governor's suite at the Capitol to lead weekly Bible study classes for lawmakers, and sought to establish similar ministries in other states. The group was familiar enough to be known by its own abbreviation: "CapMin."

Drollinger's talent for eliciting controversy was soon on display again. In 2004, Drollinger angered many in Sacramento when he denounced female lawmakers with children at home as sinners. "It is one thing for a mother to work out of her home while her children are in school," he wrote. "It is quite another matter to have children in the home and live away in Sacramento for four days a week. Whereas the former could be in keeping with the spirit of Proverbs 31, the latter is sinful." The controversy cost CapMin its conference room in the governor's suite.[11]

Questions about Drollinger's involvement in the political arena continued when he published a blog post on his website, titled "A Chaplain's Worst Nightmare," in February 2008. Drollinger claimed that God was disgusted with many lawmakers in the state. "In the past several weeks, I have visited with a Jewish legislator, a Catholic legislator and a liberal Protestant legislator—all of whom reject the Jesus of Scripture," he wrote.[12]

More conflict followed. In 2009, the California state director of Drollinger's organization, Frank Erb, resigned from Capitol Ministries and began working with a competing ministry, Capitol Commission, which describes itself as "Reaching Capitol Communities for Christ." The two organizations became embroiled in a trademark dispute. Around the same time, five Capitol Ministries board members resigned. Representatives of

MacArthur's Grace Community Church in Sun Valley, which Drollinger had previously attended, announced that "it is the estimation of these men that Ralph Drollinger is not biblically qualified for spiritual leadership."[13]

Drollinger sensed early that Donald Trump would be the savior of Capitol Ministries. A passionate supporter of Trump's presidential candidacy from the start, Drollinger claims he and Trump became "pen pals" during Trump's 2016 campaign. Although Drollinger undoubtedly has many reasons to support Trump, a key to his thinking about the 2016 election may be best encapsulated in his views on child-rearing.

Drollinger is an enthusiastic advocate of corporal punishment. In a Capitol Ministries Bible study guide titled "God's Word on Spanking," one of his study guides aimed at political leaders, Drollinger quotes Proverbs 23:13–14: "Do not hold back discipline from the child, although you strike him with the rod, he will not die. You shall strike him with the rod and rescue his soul." In his exegesis Drollinger elaborates: "When rebellion is present, to speak without spanking is woefully inadequate."[14] Drollinger's views on presidential authority would appear to be taken from a page of the same book. "The institution of the state" is "an avenger of wrath," he explains in another sermon, and its "God-given responsibility" is "to moralize a fallen world through the use of force."[15] President Trump, he believes, excels in these biblical criteria for leadership.

Trump, of course, is the man who by all accounts has the least claim of any public figure in recent memory to those virtues that are commonly identified as "Christian." But that is, perhaps, precisely why leaders like Drollinger embrace him. While many Americans still believe that the Christian right is primarily concerned with "values," leaders of the movement know it's really about power. Trump's supposedly anti-Christian attributes are in fact part of the attraction. Today's Christian nationalists talk a good game about respecting the Constitution and America's founders, but at bottom they prefer autocrats to democrats. Trump believes in the rule of force, not the rule of law. He is not there to uphold values but to impose the will of the tribe. He is a leader perfectly suited to the cause.

"Good laws are informed by Biblical morality, over and above personal liberty," as Drollinger writes. "Opposite the theory of Theocracy when it comes to lawmaking (wherein every precept and tenet of the religion is incorporated into the laws of the State) is Libertarianism," which he disparagingly characterizes as tending "toward amorality."[16]

At the end of the day, it's all about consolidating the power of the in-group. "Christian believers," he writes, "will someday (soon I hope) become the consummate, perfect governing authorities!"[17]

By the spring of 2018, Drollinger's weekly White House Bible study gatherings, some reportedly taking place in the West Wing, included as many as eleven of fifteen cabinet secretaries. Alex Azar and Tom Price from the Department of Health and Human Services; Mike Pompeo, now the secretary of state; NASA administrator Jim Bridenstine; former attorney general Jeff Sessions; former secretary of labor Alexander Acosta; Education Secretary Betsy DeVos; Housing and Urban Development Secretary Ben Carson; former EPA administrator Scott Pruitt; Energy Secretary Rick Perry; and other senior officials, including Vice President Mike Pence, counted as participating members.

With additional study groups targeting the Senate and House of Representatives, Drollinger is coming face-to-face with some of the most powerful lawmakers in the country. At a 2018 event at the Museum of the Bible as part of Ralph Reed's Road to Majority conference, an annual gathering of activists and policymakers organized by his Faith & Freedom Coalition, Representative Barry Loudermilk of Georgia exulted, "How many of you know that we have a church service every Wednesday night right here in the Capitol building?" Conference-goers, who filled the auditorium, nodded their heads and beamed back at him. "We have dozens of Bible studies that happen throughout the week," Loudermilk continued. "We have ministers that do nothing but walk the halls of the office buildings and drop in and pray with members."[18]

The dividends in policy have already begun to show. In 2018, Capitol Ministries Bible study group member Jeff Sessions issued guidelines for the Justice Department giving religious individuals and groups "protections to express their beliefs" when they come into conflict with government regulations. The initiative was similar in approach to the formation in 2018 of a Conscience and Religious Freedom Division of the Department of Health and Human Services Office of Civil Rights, which was formerly led by CapMin member Tom Price, and whose purpose is in large part to ensure that health care providers can deny services to individuals whose sexual orientation, "lifestyle," or other characteristics offend their religious sensibilities.

Drollinger's teachings appear to be touching other areas of policy. Using language straight from the Cornwall Alliance, the anti-environmentalist organization referenced in the Family Research Council's Culture Impact Team manuals, Drollinger called environmentalism a "false religion" and asserted that certain initiatives to protect animal species and preserve natural resources "miss the clear proclamation of God in Genesis."[19] This position must have been encouraging to EPA head Scott Pruitt, who told the Christian Broadcasting Network that it was "wonderful" to be able to attend and participate in CapMin's cabinet Bible study.[20] In May 2018, reflecting on his first year in office, Pruitt celebrated the rollback of twenty-two environmental regulations under his watch.

Secretary of State Mike Pompeo, who has also attended CapMin Bible study, also seems to be allowing his personal religious beliefs to influence American policy. In January 2019, speaking at the American University in Cairo, Egypt, a country riven with sectarian struggle, Pompeo highlighted his own sectarian leanings, saying he had come to the region "as an evangelical Christian" and adding, "I keep a Bible open on my desk to remind me of God's word, and the truth."[21] That March, in an unprecedented move, Pompeo held a State Department telephone conference restricted to reporters from "faith-based media only." No transcript was provided, and the list of invitees was not disclosed.

Drollinger is not the only evangelical pastor to target the upper reaches of government. The Family, a secretive organization that cultivates political leaders in the U.S. and around the world, has long organized prayer gatherings among the powerful. In addition, perhaps mindful of Drollinger's successes, the politically connected pastor Jim Garlow, whom I will discuss in a subsequent chapter, founded along with his wife, Rosemary Schindler Garlow, a ministry called Well Versed that claims to hold weekly Bible study in the United Nations, Congress, and the State Department, as well as among "prime ministers, kings and other influential leaders across the globe." The ministry hosts and sponsors "gatherings where governmental leaders can meet with people of faith as we teach them to be 'well versed' in biblical principles in order for them to be equipped to speak to the world's complex cultural issues" and "lead biblically in decisions they are faced with."[22] Garlow makes regular appearances at the World Congress of Families, an annual event that brings together representatives of the "Global Conservative Movement," including Catholic, evangelical, and Russian Orthodox leaders and an international cohort of far-right politicians and activists. In 2019, the WCF was held in Verona, Italy, which has become a flashpoint of far-right activity.

"I want to stop and thank the Catholics and the Orthodox who have led the charge in ways that many times the evangelicals should have," Garlow said, referring to the growing global movement to defend the "natural family" against the supposedly corrosive forces of feminism, liberalism, and LGBT equality. "We often are oblivious to the fact that the Scripture speaks to the civil government's principles."

In Drollinger's mind, burrowing into the upper reaches of the federal government is just the first part of God's plan. Drollinger seeks to institute similar Bible study groups in all fifty state capitols. And he claims to have already established or contributed to satellite ministries in over forty centers of state politics. "A movement for Christ amongst our nation's political leaders will only occur to the degree we establish strong, fruitful ministries in the federal and state Capitols of our nation and in addition, in the thousands of local city and county government offices throughout our land," Drollinger writes. "It can be achieved only by healthy Bible-believing churches taking up the cause of founding and building (for starters) weekly Bible studies in these public buildings."[23]

And the United States is just the beginning. Drollinger aims "to create 200 ministries in 200 foreign federal capitals." In the fall of 2018, Drollinger held a training conference for some eighty international associates at the newly created Museum of the Bible in Washington, D.C., on the topic of "creating and sustaining discipleship ministries to political leaders."[24] By 2019, CapMin claimed to have "birthed ongoing outposts for Christ" in dozens of countries throughout the world, adding Latvia, Ghana, Tanzania, Malawi, and Brazil to the list.

Drollinger has long had his eye on eastern Europe and Russia and it appears they have their eyes on him. In 2015, his group was invited to "plant a discipleship Bible study ministry" in Belarus for the benefit of that nation's political leaders. His wife, Danielle, attended as a representative of the Museum of the Bible, with a promise that the museum's Bible curriculum would soon be translated into Russian. In 2017, following Drollinger's visit to eastern Europe, CapMin's director of the "Eurasia Affinity Sphere," Oleg Rachkovski, urged members to "please pray that God will bless our efforts to establish new ministries this month in the countries of Romania, Moldova, and Ukraine." Rachkovski translated Drollinger's 2012 book, *Rebuilding America: The Biblical Blueprint*, into Russian; it was retitled *Building a Nation*.[25]

In May 2019, Capitol Ministries reported that a Ukrainian politician who had "linked arms" with the organization over a decade ago had established Bible studies to the Ukrainian parliament and members of the Ukrainian president's administration, and was planning a similar group for the Cabinet of Ministers. Similar initiatives, according to CapMin, "are continuing to multiply as word of them spreads and catches fire." Speaking of a member of the Romanian parliament to the journalist Mattathias Schwartz, Drollinger said, "One of the reasons he's so close to me is, I give him access to the cabinet in America."

Political leaders in numerous Caribbean and South Pacific nations have joined the network, too, establishing affiliated ministries in their own corridors of power. Capitol Ministries has placed ten "global directors" around the world and hired a director of international ministries to help manage and direct its explosive growth.

"A German conservative theologian came to America last week, met with me, brought an entourage, and long story short he says the way to start ministries in foreign federal capitals throughout Western and Eastern Europe is to first start at the EU," Drollinger tells the assembled gathering in Tulare. "There are 600 parliamentarians in Brussels that come from 26 Eastern and Western European countries. And if we can . . . have a discipleship Bible study with full-time ministry there, chances are we can disseminate that ministry throughout European capitals."

Under the VIP tent at the Ag Expo, Drollinger continues to bring people the happy tidings of his progress toward world conquest. "It's amazing how fast we are expanding overseas," he says. Exulting over new outposts in Fiji, Papua New Guinea, and the Congo, he says, "Because England colonized sixty-eight countries of the world, a lot of Caribbean nations, a lot of South Pacific nations, these nations have a link to Protestantism that makes for fertile soil to plant the Capitol Ministries vision." He informs the crowd about alliances forged with believers in Muslim-majority countries, "going into enemy territory, spiritually speaking."

"I just got an email from our discipleship leader in Beijing and he just sent me a nice picture of him and the prime minister of Papua New Guinea; he wants to start a discipleship in the capitol there," he chortles. "And I'm not even sure where that is!"

The opening act in Tulare is Lincoln Brewster, a onetime member of the band of former Journey vocalist Steve Perry; Journey keyboardist Jonathan Cain is presently married to Trump faith outreach adviser Paula White. Punk-rock skinny, with a hipster haircut, Brewster has, like Cain, remade himself as a contemporary Christian musical artist. He plays a few bars of the Journey hit "Lights" before launching into Chris Tomlin's ubiquitous Christian music hit "Our God."

"I have so much gratitude about the people who are leading our country," Brewster ad-libs. "To know that if you look at a dollar bill and it says, 'In God We Trust,' that we are so firmly getting back to that!"

The first speaker to take the podium in Tulare is Congressman Jeff Denham, Republican of California's 10th Congressional District. Denham celebrates the large number of cabinet members attending Drollinger's study groups and claims that 10 percent of the members of the U.S. Senate attend the groups, too. "This is a special type of ministry that I don't think we've seen before," he says. Praising the organization and its expansion "across the world," he says, "You can worship with other members, build relationships, and really interpret these decisions that you are making for your state from a Biblical perspective."

Michele Bachmann takes the stage in a long coat and a pinch-me-to-make-sure-this-isn't-a-dream expression of wonder on her face. As a Republican primary candidate in the 2012 presidential election, she was derided by progressives as a stilted speaker and criticized both for her own anti-gay activism and for that of her husband, Marcus Bachmann, who offers "gay conversion therapy" through his counseling service. But to sympathetic audiences she is relaxed and uplifting, at times exuding a campy charm. "We're from Minnesota; we put on our coats in October and don't take them off until June!" she quips, and the room laughs along with her. Bachmann seems overjoyed with the Trump presidency and the opportunity it presents to Christian nationalists. "It is a new day in Washington, D.C.," she enthuses. "Think of this: you have a man in the Oval Office who is not ashamed of prayer. Who is not ashamed of the gospel. And in the vice president's office. And in the cabinet. And in the Senate. And in the House of Representatives. In governors' offices. In our state capitols. Is this amazing what is going on in our day?"

To enthusiastic applause, she adds, "And the trajectory of growth is like nothing we have ever seen before!"

Praising the Capitol Ministries program as "the highest quality material I have ever seen," Bachmann explains, "Every week it plumbs deep into different biblical issues, which incidentally tend to intersect with the decisions we are making every day in Washington, D.C." The Drollingers, she says, "are trying to cover the government offices at the beginning levels, which would be your city, your school board, your county offices, all the municipal elections, they want to see Bible studies there. Because they know the people who start at that level tend to want to move up and serve in their state senate and serve in your state house." From there, she says, "people tend to go on to serving in Congress and in the Senate."

Bachmann wants to assure the crowd that Drollinger's ministry is not just ceremonial, nor intended merely for the private spiritual edification of its participants. "I can tell you from personal experience that members of the House, members of the Senate, members of the cabinet, are transformed by this word," she says, and those "transformed lives" are leading to "a transformed nation."

Ralph Drollinger takes the stage in an exuberant mood, thanking state and regional directors and attributing his success to support from California's Central Valley. "Capitol Ministries really grew up on carrots and milk," he says, a reference to Central Valley businessmen such as Rob Hilarides, a prosperous dairyman who sits on the board of Capitol Ministries, and conglomerates like the Bolthouse Foundation, which gets its money from Bolthouse Farms, one of the largest carrot producers in the region. For at least seven years, starting in 2001, the Bolthouse Foundation made donations to CapMin of up to $200,000 each year.

Onstage, Drollinger swiftly communicates how close to power he has become. "I always send [the president] notes and copies of my weekly study," says Drollinger. "The president always sends me handwritten thank-you notes and expresses his gratitude for my support." Clearly he sees his focus on Trump as biblically righteous. "The strategicness [sic] of fulfilling the Great Commission relative to political leaders is easy to see throughout the pages of the New Testament," he says. "One-third of the New Testament is written to try to convert one political leader for Christ."

Drollinger is keen to assure the crowd that their donations will be put to good use. "Most of the money goes to expansion overseas," he says. "Because the fields are wide-open, it's amazing how fast we are expanding overseas. Our biggest limiting factor is our ability to resource. So that's what this partnership with you can be all about."

What is the difference between Bible study and policy advocacy? In the curriculum that Drollinger offers to powerful officials through Capitol Ministries, it isn't clear that there is much difference at all. He lays it all out in *Rebuilding America: The Biblical Blueprint*, and he fills in many of the details in publicly available manuals for his weekly Bible study sessions. Copies of his book are available here in Tulare, and Drollinger helpfully touches upon some of the main themes at his dinner speech.

The expansiveness of Drollinger's positions on domestic, economic, and foreign policy hits home the fact that Christian nationalism is a political movement, not merely a stance in the "culture war." Like his fellow radicals at the forefront, Drollinger strives for an ever-widening domain of control.

According to Peter Montgomery, a senior fellow at People for the American Way who has been studying and writing about the religious right and right-wing movements for two decades, Drollinger instructs public officials "that the Bible mandates adherence to right-wing policy positions on a wide range of issues, including environmental regulation, the death penalty, abortion, LGBTQ equality and more." The Bible, for example, has a very clear message on United States fiscal policy. Just a few weeks prior to the Tulare event, Drollinger published a Bible study titled "Solomon's Advice on How to Eliminate a $20.5 Trillion Debt."[26] The study guide makes clear that God believes in deregulation. "Leaders must incentivize individuals and industries (which includes unencumbering them from the unnecessary burdens of government regulations)," Drollinger writes.

Drollinger has words of wisdom for laborers, too. In a Bible study titled "Toward a Better Biblical Understanding of Lawmaking," he cites 1 Peter 2:18-21, "Servants, be submissive to your masters with all respect, not only to those who are good and gentle, but also to those who are unreasonable." Here Drollinger explains, "The economy of Rome at the time of Peter's writing was one of slave and master. The principle however, of submitting to one's boss carries over to today."[27]

This is all music to the ears of agribusiness leaders. Major issues confront managers of agricultural concerns these days, among them government policy with respect to labor, foreign trade, water access, subsidies and other regulation. It is not surprising that industry leaders may look to a certain kind of religion for answers—not in the sense of praying for rain (although speaker Sonny Perdue, the secretary of agriculture, has done that, too) but in the sense of working with religious nationalists to elevate the policies and politicians that work to their benefit.

Of course, those policies, which favor low regulation and minimal workers' rights, may exacerbate existing wealth inequalities in the Central Valley. But this is a feature of the system, not a bug. That's the way inequality works. On the one hand, it creates concentrations of wealth whose beneficiaries are determined to manipulate the political process to hold on to and enhance their privileges. On the other hand, it generates a sense of instability and anxiety among broad sectors of the wider public, which is then ripe for conversion to a religion that promises authority and order.

Drollinger is just one particularly successful example of the kind of religious entrepreneur that such times invariably call forth.

In keeping with this line of logic, Drollinger's Bible has strong views on compensation for lawmakers. "If Congress passed a balanced budget and policies that lead to a 7% increase in GDP, then every legislator should receive a 7% bonus the following fiscal year," he says.[28] Thus, for godly civil servants, getting right with the Lord involves the accumulation of personal riches under the right circumstances.

Drollinger's Bible is also firmly on the side of the wealthy. "God is pro private property ownership," he writes, asserting that a flat tax is "God-ordained." When one individual earns more than another, he says, "it is not just or fair for the Government to tax that person at a higher percentage." Illustrating the point, he writes, "If a couple earns a joint income of under $16,700 they pay the lowest rate of 10% of their income, whereas on the other end of the progression, if one makes over $372,000 one pays the highest rate of 35%. This is not how God taxed Israel. All paid 10% no matter what they earned."[29] And he declares his "growing personal conviction" that "if there is not a change to a flat tax soon, citizens who are now both on government subsistence programs and paying no income tax should have the privilege of voting curtailed until their case proves otherwise."[30] So much for democracy.

While politicians and business leaders are free to increase their own pay packets, according to Drollinger's Bible, they may turn a cold shoulder to the less fortunate. Mr. Drollinger believes that social welfare programs "have no basis in Scripture." "The responsibility to meet the needs of the poor lies first with the husband in a marriage, secondly with the family (if the husband is absent) and thirdly with the church," Drollinger stipulates. "Again, nowhere does God command the institutions of government or commerce to fully support those with genuine needs."

I glance at my tablemate Jeff Taylor and wonder what members of his clan, including Steve, think of the proceedings. It's not a stretch to imagine that they bring an economic agenda to involvement with the ministry, consciously or not. Taylor Farms has come under scrutiny for its labor practices. According to a report by the California-based investigative journalism outfit Capital & Main, first published in 2014 and updated in 2017, "Taylor represents the platinum standard for corporate industries that seek to maximize profits by treating their workforce as someone else's problem—whether they be the temp labor contractors or the taxpayers who must pick up the tab when it comes to providing workers' medical care, food stamps and other social services." Possibly Mr. Taylor finds something spiritually uplifting in the theology of low taxation and minimal regulation. But he can be quite confident that it is economically uplifting for him and his family firm.

Drollinger insists that "Lawmakers must be men and women who are willing to be informed by Scripture."[31] To be clear, Drollinger does not mean to include those whose understanding of Scripture happens to deviate from his. "The Social Gospel movement, which infiltrated and captured many mainline Protestant denominational seminaries and subsequently their pulpits," he says, is an expression of "aberrant theologies."[32]

Drollinger also anchors an ardent passion for male supremacy in his reading of the Bible. Women, he has maintained, should not be allowed to teach—or be placed in positions of leadership over—men in church. "If you look in the Bible all the leaders are male. It may not be what I would choose," he says with an air of feigned helplessness, "but that's what God wants."[33]

Women, or at least the right kind of women, may be allowed in the halls of power, according to Drollinger, but they must be handled with extreme caution. "If I need to follow up with, say, Betsy DeVos, it's better that my wife Danielle is with me or that she follows up with Betsy DeVos," he told *Welt Am Sonntag*. "I would not write Betsy DeVos emails about her issues and whatever. It's just safer in terms of the integrity of the ministry and the optics of the ministry that Danielle handles the female workload rather than me. Like I'll never go into an office, shut the door with a female member and talk about her marital issues, you know. That's just asking for trouble."

Drollinger's Bible is also unflinchingly pro-natalist. Government policy should "incentivize population growth," he argues, quoting Psalm 127:5, "Blessed is the man whose quiver is full of them." The same passage is a favorite among conservative Christians who eschew birth control in their pursuit of very large families.

Those lawmakers seeking guidance on immigration policy can turn to a study guide titled "What the Bible Says about Our Illegal Immigration

Problem." Citing the story of the Tower of Babel, Drollinger maintains that the Bible requires "the nations" to be kept separate through "borders and boundaries," and that "God's Word says He frowns on *illegal* immigrants."[34] It's a curious message to bring to a room full of agribusiness people, many of whom rely critically on cheap, often undocumented labor from "other nations."

Drollinger's Bible is a source of political theory as well as political advocacy, although it does not turn out to be a democratic political theory. One of Drollinger's frequently used words, and perhaps a central concept of his political theory, is "kingship." He even turns it into a verb phrase, as in "kinging," or getting ready "to king." "Why is reaching 'kings and those who are in authority' so important?" he asks in his book. "Political leaders and political Capitols represent the hubs of power, influence, communications, and transportation, with influence reaching into the countryside. Winning leaders for Christ and planting churches in these focal points makes sense for the practical reason of greater efficiency, effectiveness, and impact on the nation as a whole."

Drollinger's antidemocratic political theory, and in particular his obsession with kings, is revealing of the relationship between the Christian nationalist movement and President Trump. "It is God that raises up a king," Trump evangelical advisor Paula White declared in a TV interview about her longstanding relationship with the president. After Trump won, Franklin Graham, son of the late Billy Graham and one of Trump's most trusted evangelical advisors, declared, "God's hand intervened." In 2019 he announced a "special day of prayer for the President, Donald J. Trump"; the initiative was cosigned by more than 250 pastors and faith leaders. Other evangelical leaders, including David Barton, have called Trump "God's candidate" or "God's guy." Even former White House press secretary Sarah Huckabee Sanders said God "wanted Trump to become president." Noting Trump's propensity for vulgarity and name-calling, Christian TV personality Mary Colbert declared defiantly, "My Jesus was a name-caller. So get over the name-calling!" Addressing her viewers, she said, "You have to line up with what God wants."

Whether by design or—more likely—the unfortunate accident of character, Trump seems pleased to play the role that his followers have assigned him. He is obliging them by behaving like a monarch—or, some might say, a mad king. Meetings with cabinet members have consisted of members praising him one by one and even thanking God for his leadership. Meetings with business leaders have had a similar tone. Trump continues to praise himself and then turns around and models the same sucking-up behavior in his relations with despots like the leader of North Korea, Kim Jong-un, Philippines president Rodrigo Duterte, Turkish president Recep Tayyip Erdoğan, and Russian president Vladimir Putin. Trump demands military parades, threatens to punish his critics, refuses to cooperate with government investigations, and claims he is above the law.

The Trump family, too, appears to have gotten in on the act of modeling monarchical behavior. Like royal families of yore, they make little distinction between the public purse and their private interest. The Trump sons travel the world conducting Trump Organization business on the taxpayer's dime, while son-in-law Jared Kushner has bought and sold as much as $147 million of real estate and other assets since joining the White House. Meanwhile, foreign political leaders and representatives pay for expensive rooms and hold lavish events at the Trump International Hotel. In a democracy answering to the rule of law, such corrupt and nepotistic practices would register as major scandals. In a monarchy, or pseudo-monarchy, however, they are merely business as usual.

For Drollinger and his fellow travelers, in any case, Trump's king-like behavior seems far from troublesome. On the contrary, it may satisfy their craving for a certain type of political leadership. When God sends a ruler to save the nation, He doesn't mess around; He sends a kingly king. And kings don't have to follow the rules.

Dinner is a plate of chicken and steak, washed down with soda, iced tea, or chocolate milk. At the table in front of us, I spot five men with holstered guns. At least some of them appear to be sheriffs. Other guests are perusing Drollinger's books and study guides that are handed out at the back of the tent.

Sipping chocolate milk, I watch attendees work the room. Between the "Hallelujahs" and "Praise the Lords," wealthy growers and other agriculture-minded entrepreneurs trade business cards and discuss partnership opportunities. Funders of the event even included some banks. It isn't obvious that they all believe in Drollinger's version of the Bible, but it seems safe to assume that—like the leaders of South Pacific nations appealing to the club associated with the U.S. president's golden touch—they are betting that an affiliation with Capitol Ministries will help their bottom lines.

Like Steve Taylor, whose family's business practices have come under scrutiny for its temporary labor contracts, many of the agribusiness kings here have treated their workers as other peoples' problems, leaning on taxpayers to pick up the tab for laborers' medical care, food stamps, or other social services even as they cozy up to a religious leader who argues that the government has no business providing such services. But we're not here in Tulare to think about the needs of the working poor. If your aim is to rise in the ranks of—or obtain favors from—a future theocratic administration, it behooves you now to get in with the in-club. It's that power of the network, more than any lessons in Scripture, that Capitol Ministries delivers.

I decide it's time to head for the exit. Strolling out of the dusty fair-ground, past the vast exhibition halls full of tractors and fertilizer displays, it strikes me that the theology of the evening is all but inseparable from a certain form of life. It is the string that ties together a bundle of costumes, assumptions, business dealings, and political favors. It is the latest form of a certain political and social vision that entitles a select few to work the earth with other people's hands.

Many Americans still mistakenly believe that leaders of the religious right confine their attention to a few hot-button concerns and that if we could just find "common ground" on, say, abortion, the hostilities would cease. The religion I found in Tulare, however, is mostly about money and power. The speakers on Drollinger's stage declare their intention to domi-nate every aspect of life in America, from government to education to the economy, in accordance with their religious "principles." The real issue at the Capitol Ministries fund-raiser is that the proponents of this antidemo-cratic vision no longer seem to feel the need to disguise their ambitions. They, too, are getting ready to king.

CHAPTER 3

Inventing Abortion

THE MOST POPULAR origin story of Christian nationalism today, shared by many critics and supporters alike, explains that the movement was born one day in 1973, when the Supreme Court unilaterally shredded Christian morality and made abortion "on demand" a constitutional right. At that instant, the story goes, the flock of believers arose in protest and threw their support to the party of "Life" now known as the Republican Party. The implication is that the movement, in its current form, finds its principal motivation in the desire to protect fetuses against the women who would refuse to carry them to term.

This story is worse than myth. It is false as history and incorrect as analysis. Christian nationalism drew its inspiration from a set of concerns that long predated the Supreme Court decision in *Roe v. Wade* and had little to do with abortion. The movement settled on abortion as its litmus test sometime after that decision for reasons that had more to do with politics than embryos. It then set about changing the religion of many people in the country in order to serve its new political ambitions. From the beginning, the "abortion issue" has never been just about abortion. It has also been about dividing and uniting to mobilize votes for the sake of amassing political power.

* * *

On a crisp morning in January 2018, tens of thousands of marchers throng the National Mall in the annual March for Life. The crowd tilts female and young, and the overwhelming majority is white. A good number are clustered in church or campus youth groups and facing down the cold with parkas and Uggs or duck boots to protect their feet from the chill.

I spot a young woman I'll call Megan in a placard-wielding group near the corner of Constitution and Fifteenth Street. Wearing a gray knitted pom-pom hat over light brown curls, she is marching with other members of a pro-life group at her college, where she majors in English. I first met her several years ago at a gathering of young antiabortion activists, where she was taking copious notes on a laptop plastered with stickers: "Cru," "A Child Not a Choice." Finding her here, though unanticipated, is not terribly surprising. With her cheery disposition and uncomplicated certainty of her views, Megan seems to embody the ideal that Phyllis Schlafly, a godmother of the antiabortion movement and founder of the conservative interest group the Eagle Forum, famously advertised in the title of one of her books: *The Power of the Positive Woman.*

That ideal lives on in the movement leaders today, including Penny Young Nance, president and CEO of Concerned Women for America, who made waves in recent years with her opposition to the Disney movie *Frozen* (it's anti-male)[1] and, more recently, the "weaponization" of the #MeToo movement.[2] Glamorous and effusive, she is true to the title of her recent book, *Feisty and Feminine: A Rallying Cry for Conservative Women.* "We expect to devote considerable resources to this effort, and we expect to win," said Nance, commenting on the appointment of prolife Supreme Court justices. "Our happy warrior/activist ladies relish the fight and shine in these historic moments."[3]

Like other young activists at the march today, Megan is being groomed for glory in the conservative movement. As a convivial high school student, she was inspired by a friend to join a local chapter of Students for Life of America. Over a summer Megan attended the Young America's Foundation's National Conservative Student Conference in Washington, D.C., where, along with some 1,000 other students, she learned from speakers like Dinesh D'Souza and Ben Shapiro about the importance of traditional values, free markets, and the left's assault on free speech.

Megan, like other "student leaders" at the event, also received media coaching, including tips on crafting op-eds and appearing on camera. She hopes her networking will soon pay off in the form of a post-graduation internship at a right-wing policy organization. The Heritage Foundation, for instance, offers subsidized housing and free lunch—a sweet gig for an English major. "When I was younger, I never imagined I could be on TV," Megan says with confidence. "Now I know I can."

As I'm chatting with Megan, Jeanne Mancini, president of March for Life, takes the stage and the crowd erupts in a roar of joy. "Jeanne! Jeanne!" Megan's voice joins the collective thunder. Mancini previously worked for the Family Research Council, and before that on behalf of the Catholic Church.

Speaker after speaker follow onstage to condemn abortion and offer messages of praise for "the most pro-life president in history!" With the exception of Congresswoman Jaime Herrera Beutler, whose mother is white and father is Mexican American, every speaker at the 2018 March for Life rally program appears to be white.[4]

Donald Trump at last appears on a giant television screen live via satellite from the White House Rose Garden. The crowd greets the supersize image with enthusiasm, and it is clear that many believe that God, acting through the pro-life movement, put Trump in the White House. The president declares that the marchers are "a truly remarkable group" and then runs through a list of his own amazing achievements in office. "On the National Day of Prayer, I signed an executive order to protect religious liberty," he says. He is referring to a declaration that, as Rob Boston, senior advisor for Americans United for the Separation of Church and State aptly put it, amounts to "one more attempt . . . to redefine religious freedom to mean the freedom to discriminate against those who do not share our religious belief." The crowd bursts into applause, and Trump nods his head, smiling. "Very proud of that."

I watch Megan watching Trump. It's as if I can see the lines of power traced in her eyes. But when I ask her what she makes of the fact that Protestants by and large did not oppose abortion rights fifty years ago, and neither did many Republicans, she gives me a blank look. "Christianity is pro-life," she says with certainty. "Republicans are the party of life."

The annual scene on the mall, though familiar enough by now to count as reaffirmation rather than protest, serves mainly to drive home the brute fact that, for Republican politicians, abortion demagoguery is the path to power in America. Donald Trump clearly grasped that fact. Most of the people here, like most of the people catching snippets of the event on the evening news, take for granted that it is the way things have always been.

Except that it isn't.

In the late 1970s a curious combination of religious and political activists assembled to ponder the strategy of a new political movement, sometimes by letter or phone, and sometimes in conference rooms or at a hotel in Lynchburg, Virginia. Some of the more vocal members of the group included Southern Baptist pastor Jerry Falwell; conservative activists Ed McAteer and Paul Weyrich; Nixon appointee Howard Phillips; attorney Alan P. Dye; and Robert J. Billings, an educator and organizer who would later serve as Ronald Reagan's liaison to the Christian right.

This was an angry group of men. "We are radicals who want to change the existing power structure. We are not conservatives in the sense that conservative means accepting the status quo," Paul Weyrich said. "We want change—we *are* the forces of change."[5] They were angry at liberals, who threatened to undermine national security with their unforgivable softness on communism; they were angry at the establishment conservatives, the Rockefeller Republicans, for siding with the liberals and taking down their hero, Barry Goldwater; they were angry about the rising tide of feminism, which they saw as a menace to the social order; and about the civil rights movement and the danger it posed to segregation, especially in education. One thing that they were *not* particularly angry about, at least at the start of their discussions, was the matter of abortion rights.

Weyrich was "the man perhaps with the broadest vision," according to his fellow conservative activist Richard Viguerie. "I can think of no one who better symbolizes or is more important to the conservative movement."[6] In matters of religion, Weyrich was personally conservative: he abandoned the Roman Catholic Church, which he believed had become too liberal, for the Melkite Greek Catholic Church after the Second Vatican Council. But his politics weren't necessarily centered on religion. He formed his political creed as a twenty-something in the Barry Goldwater uprising of 1964, and it consisted of visceral anticommunism, economic libertarianism, and a distrust of the civil rights movement. Jimmy Carter's famous religiosity did nothing to redeem him in Weyrich's eyes. Indeed, in 1978 and 1979, Weyrich's immediate priority was to make sure that Carter would be a one-term president.[7]

Weyrich began to identify himself in the late 1970s with a movement whose name Richard Viguerie put on the title of his 1980 manifesto: *The New Right: We're Ready to Lead.*[8] Weyrich came to be known as the "evil genius" of the movement[9]—or sometimes "the Lenin of social conservatism"[10]—and Viguerie, who is considered the pioneer of political direct mail, came to be known as its "funding father."[11]

From the beginning, the New Right sought radical change. They would establish themselves "first as the opposition, then the alternative, finally the government," according to Conservative Caucus chair Howard Phillips.[12] "We will not try to reform the existing institutions. We only intend to weaken them and eventually destroy them," said Weyrich protégé Eric Heubeck, writing for the Free Congress Foundation. "We will maintain a constant barrage of criticism against the Left. We will attack the very legitimacy of the Left. We will not give them a moment's rest . . . We will use guerrilla tactics to undermine the legitimacy of the dominant regime."[13]

Weyrich went on to call for a constitutional convention in hopes of producing a form of government more congenial to conservatism. "I don't want everybody to vote," he said at a gathering in the fall of 1980. "As a matter of fact, our leverage in the elections quite candidly goes up as the voting populace goes down."[14] Richard Viguerie emphatically endorsed Weyrich's radicalism, which in turn led both men to adopt a kind of experimental pragmatism in pursuing their ends. "One of the major differences in this group of new conservatives was that we weren't afraid to try even when there was only a 20 per cent chance of success," Viguerie wrote. "We knew that if you expected to hit a lot of home runs, you had to expect to strike out a lot."[15]

At the core of the concerns of the New Right was the perception that American capitalism was under dire threat from mortal enemies—some of them internal, some external, most of them communist. "Liberal national defense policies have resulted in the United States, long the world's strongest military power, falling behind Soviet Russia in every major area of conventional and strategic weaponry," wrote Viguerie.[16]

Activist Phyllis Schlafly shared Viguerie's obsession with the communist menace. In the 1950s she wrote, "The plain facts are that Communism is advancing over the surface of the globe with such rapidity that if it continues at the same rate for the next thirteen years that it has been advancing during the past thirteen years, America will be Communist by 1970."[17] But Schlafly also gave voice to another motivating concern of the emerging right-wing consensus: the specter of feminism. Schlafly rose to prominence in her campaign against the Equal Rights Amendment. The feminist movement, she asserted, "is the most destructive element in our society."[18]

For Weyrich and his fellow political operatives, the rise of the civil rights movement presented a historic opportunity to advance their own agenda. From Reconstruction through the 1960s, southern whites had been a critical part of the Democratic Party coalition. Their support had been essential in realizing the New Deal, although it burdened the progressive legislation of the period with racist policies. When Democrats took the lead in civil rights, however, the southern white population was suddenly in play. Nixon famously committed the Republican Party to the "Southern Strategy"— that is, appealing to the southern, white, formerly Democratic popular vote through populism, racism, and nativism. This in turn created a tension with the Republican Party's other base, the so-called Rockefeller Republicans, who consisted, on balance, of economic conservatives with largely moderate social views.

As the Lynchburg crowd commenced their conversations, Weyrich had already formulated a general idea for an electoral strategy that would take the New Right from opposition to power. He had studied the successes of the left in the 1960s and 1970s, and now he thought he knew what the left had that the right lacked: the right needed to get religion. The left had successfully appealed to religious feelings and organizations in forming the coalition that advanced civil rights, promoted Great Society programs, and opposed the Vietnam War. Just as reformers around the turn of the century had deployed the Social Gospel on behalf of progressive causes, Martin

Luther King Jr. has used his pulpit to mobilize change. If the right could access the religious vote, Weyrich reasoned, power would be in its grasp. Together with Phillips, he devoted "countless hours cultivating electronic ministers like Jerry Falwell, Jim [James] Robison, and Pat Robertson, urging them to get involved in conservative politics," according to Viguerie.[19]

Weyrich eventually founded or played a critical role in a number of prominent groups on the right. They included the Heritage Foundation, the American Legislative Exchange Council, and the Free Congress Foundation. Arguably the most consequential of the groups Weyrich played a role in founding was the Council for National Policy, a networking organization for social conservative activists that the *New York Times* once referred to as a "little-known group of a few hundred of the most powerful conservatives in the country."

Weyrich did not act alone. Other cofounders and early members of the CNP included Tim LaHaye (then head of Moral Majority), billionaire Nelson Bunker Hunt, Pat Robertson, and Jerry Falwell. A leaked 2014 membership directory of the CNP, posted on the website of the Southern Poverty Law Center, shines a spotlight on this powerful subsection of the reactionary right.[20] The directory includes Steve Bannon, Kellyanne Conway, and the National Rifle Association's Wayne LaPierre; Christian right leaders such as Tony Perkins, Ralph Reed, and James Dobson; and antiabortion advocates Phyllis Schlafly, Penny Nance, and Kristan Hawkins. The group also brought into the fold leaders of right-wing economic policy groups and media conglomerates; masterminds of the right-wing legal movement including Alan Sears, Jay Sekulow, and Leonard Leo; and various members of the DeVos and Prince families, including Betsy DeVos's brother Erik Prince and her husband, Richard, who served as president twice. "The Council for National Policy went on to assemble an impressive network of media and organizations that worked to advance their cause, with a special focus on mobilizing the fundamentalist vote in key districts," says Anne Nelson, author of *Shadow Network: Media, Money, and the Secret Hub of the Radical Right*.[21]

Weyrich came to Lynchburg armed with a clear knowledge of where to find the hot-button issues of religious conservatives. First and foremost, it lay at the intersection of federal power, race, and religion. As Weyrich knew,

Jerry Falwell and many of his fellow southern, white, conservative pastors were closely involved with segregated schools and universities, and they had come together as a political force out of fear that their institutions would soon be deprived of their lucrative tax advantages. To be sure, Falwell, the founder of the Thomas Road Baptist Church and Lynchburg Baptist College—later Liberty University—suffered from no lack of hot buttons. On his nationally syndicated radio and television show, he regularly fulminated against emblems of moral decay: divorce, pornography, sex education, "secular humanism," and public education.[22] But the thing that got him up in the morning, as Weyrich knew, was the threat that the Supreme Court might end tax exemptions for segregated Christian schools.[23]

In the first decades of his career, Falwell practiced segregation even in religion.[24] In the early 1960s, when Black high school students attempted to pray at the Thomas Road Church, they were ejected by the police.[25] When Falwell went on to set up a Christian academy, he made sure it stayed just as white as his church. He attracted national attention with a 1965 sermon impugning "the sincerity and nonviolent intentions of some civil rights leaders such as Dr. Martin Luther King" and—with immense irony, in retrospect—arguing that ministers had no business getting involved in politics. He suggested that the faithful should concentrate their reform ambitions on alcoholism rather than civil rights, since "there are almost as many alcoholics as there are Negroes."[26]

Bob Jones Sr., founder of the college that later became Bob Jones University, was an especially ardent segregationist, and he centered his defense of segregation clearly in his religion. In an April 17, 1960, radio address, "Is Segregation Scriptural?" he declared "God is the author of segregation" and called the practice "God's established order." He referred to desegregationists as "Satanic propagandists" and "religious infidels" who are "leading colored Christians astray" with their "Communistic agitation to overthrow the established order of God."[27]

Evidently imagining that there might be some Black listeners with whom he had any credibility, Jones added, "After the Civil War the colored people wanted to build their schools and churches, and white friends made financial contribution to the building of these schools and churches. Back in those days it was not easy when the white people were paying most of the taxes—don't you colored friends forget that when you are inclined to turn away from your white friends."[28]

Bob Jones University excluded Black students, but this was not uncommon among southern educational institutions at the time. In response to the desegregation orders that flowed from the Supreme Court's *Brown v. Board of Education* decision of 1954, a number of white families in southern states wished to avoid sending their children to integrated schools. Public officials began promoting "schools of choice," a euphemism for private schools that were, in effect, white-only. Such "choice" schools were also known as "segregation academies." In many cases they were, like Falwell's, affiliated with churches and other religious entities.[29]

Christian academies soon came to depend heavily on public support. In Falwell's Virginia, for example, state-sponsored tuition grants allowed students to take public money to the school of their choice. As religious entities, moreover, the schools and the organizations running them benefited from significant tax exemptions. But in the late 1970s, following a string of court cases, the IRS began to threaten the tax-exempt status of religious groups running race-segregated schools. For conservative religious leaders, the previous decades had seemed like a long string of defeats. And now they had a chief bogeyman in the IRS, which was coming after their schools and their pocketbooks.

It would be hard to overestimate the degree of outrage that the threat of losing their tax-advantaged status on account of their segregationism provoked.[30] As far as leaders like Bob Jones Sr. were concerned, they had a God-given right not just to separate the races but also to receive federal money for the purpose. Emerging leaders of the New Right were prepared to defend them. They began to meet regularly, to discuss politics, and to look for ways to make their voices heard in Washington. Weyrich stoked the flames with sympathetic words about the unjust efforts "to deny them tax-exempt status on the basis of so-called de-facto segregation." In the grievances of the segregationists, he saw the opportunity to found a movement.[31]

The correspondence between the religious conservatives and the New Right conservatives now crackled with energy. At their meetings in Lynchburg, common ground began to emerge. As Harry R. Jackson Jr. and Tony Perkins relate the story in their 2008 book, *Personal Faith, Public Policy*, "At one point during the wide-ranging discussion, Weyrich is reported to have said that there was a moral majority who wanted to maintain the traditional Christian values that were under assault in America. Falwell asked Weyrich to repeat the statement and then spun around and declared to one of his assistants, 'That's the name for this organization—the *Moral Majority.*'" That day, say Jackson and Perkins, "marked the beginning of a new force in American political landscape . . . At the rebirth of the Conservative civic involvement in 1979, the new leaders were determined not to repeat the "sins" of the fathers. They would not shy away from controversy, nor would they yield to criticism; they would work with others to restore the moral foundations of the nation."[32]

But they had a problem. As Weyrich understood, building a new movement around the burning issue of defending the tax advantages of racist schools wasn't going to be a viable strategy on the national stage. "Stop the tax on segregation" just wasn't going to inspire the kind of broad-based conservative counterrevolution that Weyrich envisioned. They needed an issue with a more acceptable appeal.

What message would bring the movement together? The men of Lynchburg considered a variety of unifying issues and themes. School prayer worked for some, but it tended to alienate the Catholics, who remembered all too well that, for many years, public schools had allowed only for Protestant prayers and Bible readings while excluding Catholic readings and practices. Bashing communists was fine, but even the Rockefeller Republicans could do that. Taking on "women's liberation" was attractive, but the Equal Rights Amendment was already going down in flames. At last they landed upon the one surprising word that would supply the key to the political puzzle of the age: "abortion."

As the historian and author Randall Balmer writes, "It wasn't until 1979—a full six years after *Roe*—that evangelical leaders, at the behest of conservative activist Paul Weyrich, seized on abortion not for moral reasons, but as a rallying-cry to deny President Jimmy Carter a second term. Why? Because the anti-abortion crusade was more palatable than the religious right's real motive: protecting segregated schools."[33]

More than a decade later, Weyrich recalled the moment well. At a conference in Washington, D.C., sponsored by a religious right organization called the Ethics and Public Policy Center (to which Balmer had been invited to attend), Weyrich reminded his fellow culture warriors of the facts: "Let us remember, he said animatedly, that the Religious Right did not come together in response to the *Roe* decision. No, Weyrich insisted, what got us going was the attempt on the part of the Internal Revenue Service (IRS) to rescind the tax-exempt status of Bob Jones University because of its racially discriminatory policies."[34]

As Balmer tells it in his book *Thy Kingdom Come: How the Religious Right Distorts the Faith and Threatens America*, Weyrich then reiterated the point. During a break in the proceedings, Balmer says, he cornered Weyrich to make sure he had heard him correctly. "He was adamant that, yes, the 1975 action by the IRS against Bob Jones University was responsible for the genesis of the Religious Right in the 1970s." It was only after leaders of the New Right held a conference call to discuss strategy, Balmer says, that abortion was "cobbled into the political agenda of the Religious Right."[35]

In those earlier days of the emerging New Right, Balmer reports, activist Robert Billings, in correspondence with Falwell, marveled with delight that abortion would "pull together many of our 'fringe' Christian friends."[36] Falwell, Weyrich, and their fellow operatives at last recognized that support for reproductive rights from feminists and liberals "had imbued the abortion issue with associations that could be tapped to mobilize a wide array of cultural conservatives," according to Linda Greenhouse and Reva B. Siegel.[37] Five years after the *Roe v. Wade* decision, Jerry Falwell began denouncing abortion, along with same-sex intimacy and pornography, in his sermons.[38] In a 1980 book chapter titled, "The Right to Life," he declared that abortion is "murder according to the Word of God."[39]

The matter advanced when the influential evangelical theologian Francis Schaeffer was converted to the cause by his son. In 1979, Schaeffer, in collaboration with the pediatric surgeon C. Everett Koop, produced a book and film series decrying abortion titled *Whatever Happened to the Human Race?* and screened it at churches around the country. A subsequent movie, *The Silent Scream*, was produced in 1984 in partnership with the National Right to Life Committee. Premiering on Reverend Jerry Falwell's television program, it aired on several major television networks and was widely used as a lobbying tool. "It's been said that if every member of the Congress could see this film of an early abortion," President Reagan declared, "that Congress would move quickly to end the tragedy of abortion. And I pray that they will."[40]

Abortion henceforth would be the key to unlocking power for the conservative movement. But before it could be used to control the future, it was necessary first to change the past. The flock would have to learn to forget that for decades abortion was just one among many moral concerns, and it played little role in dividing the faithful from the damned.

The Catholic Church first prohibited abortion at any stage of pregnancy by canon law in 1869.[41] But when abortion was criminalized across most of the United States in the late nineteenth century, the sentiments of the Catholic Church had little to do with it. Two groups in particular spearheaded the antiabortion cause. The first was Protestant nativists who feared an onslaught of immigrant and Catholic babies and saw a ban on abortion as a way of producing the more "desirable" kind of babies. Leaders of the eugenics movement, too, were initially hostile to both abortion and birth control, fearing they would suppress the birth rates of wealthy, "better" women. According to historian Leslie J. Reagan, professor of history at the University of Illinois, "White male patriotism demanded that maternity be enforced among white Protestant women."[42]

Standing shoulder to shoulder, if at times awkwardly, with these Protestant nativists was a faction of the medical establishment led by the Boston physician Horatio Robinson Storer, who sought to reverse widespread acceptance of early abortion. Storer also railed against the education of girls, asserting that "To stimulate a girl's brain to the utmost, during the access of puberty, is a positive loss to the State."[43] In a widely distributed tract, he lamented that "abortions are infinitely more frequent among Protestant women than among Catholic," and wondered whether America's western and southern territories would be "filled with our own children or by those of aliens? This is a question that our women must answer; upon their loins depends the future destiny of the nation."[44]

By the middle of the twentieth century, abortion was both mostly illegal and yet widely practiced in the United States. Somewhere between 200,000 and 1.2 million procedures took place every year (estimates vary), with a large number occurring in unsafe circumstances. One indication of the prevalence of the procedure was the death toll. According to the Guttmacher Institute, in 1930 there were an estimated 2,700 deaths attributed to illegal abortions—though some researchers suggest the true number was higher. With the invention of antibiotics, the procedure became safer, but in 1965 deaths from illegal abortion still accounted for 17 percent of all deaths attributed to childbirth and pregnancy.

In the 1950s and 1960s, two opposing forces emerged around the issue. While many first-wave feminists declared their opposition to abortion, casting it as a consequence of male promiscuity and the degradation of women, feminists in the second wave saw the criminalization of abortion as an intrusion on women's right to bodily autonomy and private decision-making regarding health and family. Many religious leaders agreed with them, and came together to form the Clergy Consultation Service on Abortion, which assisted women in obtaining abortions from licensed medical professionals. The effort to reform laws criminalizing abortion was also driven by public health–minded doctors, who pointed out that the risk of injury and death from illegal abortion "disproportionately harmed poor women and women of color, who could not afford to pay the 'right' doctor or travel to a jurisdiction where abortion was legal," according to Reva B. Siegel.[45]

These doctors, feminist activists, and pro-choice religious leaders, together with allies in the Protestant political establishment, took the fight to state legislatures. In response, a number of Catholics mobilized to oppose the expansion of abortion rights. Thus, the abortion battles of the middle decades of the twentieth century did not divide the religious against the secular, nor did they divide one party from the other. On the contrary, as Daniel K. Williams, professor of history at the University of West Georgia, points out: "The early political battles over abortion in state legislatures pitted Catholic antiabortion lobbyists against Protestant proponents of abortion law liberalization, with most Republican legislators siding with the Protestants."[46] As Williams goes on to note, "many Republicans supported the liberalization of state abortion laws, believing that abortion law reform accorded well with the party's tradition of support for birth control, middle-class morality, and Protestant values."[47] Billy Graham echoed widely shared Protestant sentiments when he said in 1968, "In general, I would disagree with [the Catholic stance]," adding, "I believe in planned parenthood."[48] Indeed, the most liberal abortion law in the country was signed in 1967 by California's Republican governor, Ronald Reagan.

It is important to note that, among the populace at least, the issue did not reliably divide Catholics and Protestants. "It is incorrect to assume that the Catholic Church has always organized against abortions or that all Catholics subscribe to the views of their church leaders," writes Leslie J. Reagan. "Indeed, many Catholics shared what I have described as a popular ethic supporting abortion ... More tolerant attitudes toward abortion, rooted in material experiences, persisted in the face of a public discourse that denounced it."[49]

Contrary to myth, when the Supreme Court handed down its decision on *Roe v. Wade*, many secular and religious conservatives responded with delight. Here is what W. Barry Garrett, Washington bureau chief of the *Baptist Press*, a wire service run by the Southern Baptist Convention, wrote upon the announcement: "Religious liberty, human equality, and justice are advanced by the Supreme Court abortion decision."[50] Garrett's position wasn't exceptional. The 1971 convention of the Southern Baptists endorsed a resolution calling for the legalization of abortion to preserve the "emotional, mental, and physical health of the mother" as well as in cases of rape, incest, and "deformity." The convention approved the same resolution after *Roe*, in 1974, calling it a "middle ground between the extreme of abortion on demand and the opposite extreme of all abortion as murder," and again in 1976.

Even Phyllis Schlafly, a key player in the antiabortion movement, did not center her political activism on the abortion issue in the initial stages of her career. In Schlafly's mind, "the day we invented the pro-family movement" was not the day after *Roe v. Wade* but April 26, 1976—the day she brought more than one thousand people to Springfield, Illinois, for a demonstration against the Equal Rights Amendment.[51] As for abortion, it mattered, too, as one part of the alleged attack on family values and the dignity of women's traditional role within it. "Since women must bear the physical consequences of the sex act, men must be required to bear the other consequences and pay in other ways," Schlafly said. Laws and customs, she added, "decree that a man must carry his share by physical protection and financial support of his children and of the woman who bears his children, and also by a code of behavior which benefits and protects both the woman and the children."[52]

Many leading members of the Republican establishment were nevertheless thrilled with the outcome of *Roe v. Wade*. The first lady, Betty Ford, hailed it as a "great, great decision."[53] Conservative senator Barry Goldwater—Paul Weyrich's beau ideal of the modern statesman—also initially hailed its passage. "I think abortion should be legalized because whether it is legal or not, women are going to have it done," he wrote in a draft of a letter to a constituent in 1973.[54] Goldwater's wife, Peggy, was a founding member of Planned Parenthood in Arizona. When the Republican National Convention gathered in Kansas City in 1976—"nailing an anti-abortion plank onto the Republican platform," in the words of one stunned observer[55]—fewer than 40 percent of the delegates opposed abortion rights.[56] Public opinion polls at the time showed that a greater percentage of Republican voters were pro-choice than their Democratic counterparts.

Up through 1979, members of both major parties, in a variety of ideological flavors, inhabited all sides of the abortion issue. Democratic opponents of abortion included Sargent Shriver, who campaigned against Maryland's liberal abortion laws in 1992. Hubert Humphrey was also personally opposed to abortion, although he did not favor a constitutional amendment to overturn *Roe v. Wade*. Ted Kennedy, Jesse Jackson, and Al Gore adopted antiabortion positions early in their careers and later evolved toward choice. In 1982, while serving on the Senate Judiciary Committee, Joe Biden voted for a constitutional amendment to overturn *Roe v. Wade*, although his views also dramatically shifted over time. On the other side of the aisle, Republicans such as Barbara Bush, Arlen Specter, William Weld, and Pete Wilson were unabashedly pro-choice and sought to strip antiabortion planks from the party platform.

The closing of the Republican mind took more than a decade. A pro-choice movement persisted in the Republican Party all the way up through the early 1990s.[57] Yet it grew increasingly isolated and forlorn. At the

Republican National Convention in 1996, the influence of Christian conservatives had become so strong that pro-choice Republicans Weld and Wilson were "bumped from prime speaking roles."[58] Until at long last it was over, and the Republican Party became the party of Life.

In order to achieve political unity around abortion, the leaders of the emerging Christian nationalist movement understood, it was also necessary to change the deep frame of American religion. So that is what they set about to do. The modern pro-life religion that dominates America's conservative churches and undergirds a variety of their denominations is a political creation.

One thing that the politico-theological leaders of the movement appeared to understand was that the greatest danger to the antiabortion party might come from liberal Christian thinkers. The Bible and 2,000 years of Christian apologetics, after all, has provided ample material to those who argue that abortion rights are compatible with Christian belief and practice. It was therefore necessary to purge theology of any position inconsistent with the idea that all the moral and religious attributes of human life are invested in the zygote at the moment of fertilization. This in turn meant making "life begins at conception" something close to a foundational doctrine—which in turn helped to bring about a convergence of the many variations on conservative forms of the Christian faith. The new dividing lines in American religious life were no longer between Protestant and Catholic, or between this sect and that, but between conservatism and liberalism—or, as the conservatives saw it, between the faithful and the godless, who came to be defined by their evident contempt for "life."

Francis Schaeffer was an important theological catalyst, popularizing the pro-life cause in a multitude of books and films. Other voices included the evangelical theologian Carl F. H. Henry, who wrote antiabortion opinion pieces for Christian media, and Harold O. J. Brown, a divinity school professor who founded a Protestant pro-life organization in 1975. Evidence of their swift success came in the response to D. Gareth Jones's 1984 book *Brave New People: Ethical Issues at the Commencement of Life.*

In his book, which was published by the respected Christian publisher InterVarsity Press, Jones lays out a case that would have seemed unremarkable in an earlier time. The embryo, he argues, has moral value but is not the equivalent of a human child. He also takes the trouble to review the long and complex history of Christian approaches to reproductive health issues. Had the book been published twenty years previously, it would likely have received mild commentary on what would have counted as a mainstream position. But in 1984, with conservative hopes for power resting increasingly on unifying the religious right around abortion, Jones's work met with brutal denunciations. It was a "monstrous book," the leaders of the religious right raged, and Jones was on a "bandwagon bound for hell." For the first time in its history, InterVarsity Press felt compelled to withdraw a book from publication.

As the pro-life view came to dominate conservative Christian theology, an alliance between conservative Catholics and conservative evangelicals that could scarcely have been imagined in the America of earlier times began to take hold. Here, too, Schlafly took the lead. "Schlafly's political genius owed to her prescient certitude that religious conservatives— Catholics, evangelicals, Mormons, and even Orthodox Jews—could abandon their longstanding separatist ways and unite on behalf of shared political goals," writes Neil J. Young, author of *We Gather Together: The Religious Right and the Problem of Interfaith Politics.* "In the 1980s, Jerry Falwell would take (and receive) credit for being the mastermind of this ecumenical conservative movement," says Young, but "Schlafly had imagined that unthinkable prospect as early as the 1950s, long before Falwell, and begun translating it into reality with her STOP ERA organization in the 1970s."[59]

Furthering the alliance was a cohort of conservative Catholic intellectuals who would later be termed "theoconservatives." Led by Richard John Neuhaus and Michael Novak, among others, several of the movement's key figures had started off in life as 1960s radicals. Disillusioned with what they perceived as the moral nihilism of the age, they pivoted sharply to the right and coalesced as a scholarly movement and political force in the Reagan years. Conversion may have made them more zealous than native believers, and perhaps the most zealous of the bunch was Neuhaus, who had crossed over all the way from progressive Lutheranism to conservative Catholicism. They were as committed as any of their evangelical brethren to rebuilding America on the basis of religious principles, and they proved instrumental in uniting conservative Catholics, evangelical Protestants, and, at least for a time, neoconservative Jews around a political vision.

The process of détente advanced considerably with a 1994 declaration of Catholic-evangelical solidarity, Evangelicals and Catholics Together: Toward a Common Mission.[60] The collaboration strengthened further with the Manhattan Declaration: A Call of Christian Conscience, the 2009 culmination of a multi-decade process. Manhattan Declaration signers, who included nearly 150 leading evangelical and conservative Catholic thinkers, pastors, and prelates, all agreed on three main points: "life," traditional marriage, and "religious liberty." The Manhattan Declaration ushered in a robust era of "co-belligerency"—that is, a dedication to strategic cooperation.

The new alliance might have been less successful had it not also been paired, over time, with an organizational effort dedicated to capturing America's churches for "life." In the early 1980s, Novak and Neuhaus joined the board of the recently formed Institute on Religion and Democracy, which was created to oppose the social justice positions and liberal theologies of mainline Protestant churches. The IRD claimed to promote church "renewal" by amplifying conservative theological positions, but its real goal, as critics put it, might better be described as "steeplejacking."

In their 2007 book, *Steeplejacking: How the Christian Right Is Hijacking Mainstream Religion*, Sheldon Culver and John Dorhauer assert the IRD used "covert methods" to wage a shadow war on mainline churches such as the United Methodist Church, Presbyterian Church (USA), and the United Church of Christ. "In alliance with fundamentalist and evangelical Christians, the IRD uses trained activists, skillfully developed propaganda and clandestine tactics to infiltrate and hijack—or 'steeplejack'—mainline churches in order to force out 'liberal leadership' and replace it with those who share their conservative world view," according to Culver and Dorhauer. Through the use of same-sex marriage as a wedge issue, congregations are persuaded to separate from their denomination, the authors say, and when possible to seize control of the church-owned real estate and take it out of the denomination, too.[61] The IRD's initial sources of funds included Scaife family foundations, the Lynde and Harry Bradley Foundation, the John M. Olin Foundation, and others.

Unfortunately, as the authors report, the response to such attacks has been anemic. "There is an awareness that something nefarious is going on," they write, "but the cost of confronting the bullies is more than the leadership is willing to pay."[62]

In her foreword to their book, the author and journalist Michelle Goldberg, whose 2006 book *Kingdom Coming: The Rise of Christian Nationalism* foretold the political crisis of the present moment, echoed the alarm. "It's hard to tell this story without sounding like a conspiracy theorist—it is, after all, a tale of power-seeking reactionaries enacting a plan to infiltrate and undermine established institutions," she pointed out. "Yet Culver and Dorhauer have carefully marshaled evidence linking fights in individual congregations to larger organizations like the Institute on Religion and Democracy." Just as planned, Goldberg notes, "right-wing groups have formed parallel organizations inside mainline congregations all over the country, often attempting coups against more liberal church leadership." The outcome of these struggles, she says, "will determine whether America's historic Protestant churches remain firm voices for social justice or become mere adjuncts of the political right."[63]

Not all efforts to drag American religion to the right came from the IRD, of course. The Southern Baptist Convention, for example, fell to what was in effect a coup.

"The leadership of the Southern Baptist Convention has been taken over by ultraconservatives," writes Leon Howell in *United Methodism @ Risk: A Wake-Up Call*.[64] "Although not a liberal church to begin with . . . [i]t was taken over from the top in the 1980s. Purges, schisms, and acknowledged right-wing loyalties have followed."[65]

In conversation with me, the historian Diana Butler Bass, whose books include *Standing Against the Whirlwind: Evangelical Episcopalians in Ninetheenth-Century America*, describes concurrent efforts to bring the Episcopalian church, too, under more conservative leadership. "On the national level, there were people who were troubled by what they saw as a turnaway from orthodoxy," she says. "They abandoned the traditional policy structure of elected representatives and adopted a strategy of succession in order to have as many dioceses as possible secede and form the 'true'

Episcopal church, and thus leave the old Episcopal church, with gay people and women leaders, in the dust." These conflicts, Bass notes, "function as predictors, or canaries in the coal mine, about larger political movements."

While that action was taking place on the ground, new activist groups were reordering the relationship between American religion and politics. One was Pat Robertson's Christian Coalition. By now Robertson had founded the Christian Broadcasting Network and CBN University (whose name was later changed to Regent University). In 1989, Robertson and his allies, including Ralph Reed, whom he tapped as executive director, created a nationwide grassroots political organization. A key tool was the mailing list—mined, in part, from Robertson's failed 1988 presidential campaign.[66] It soon became clear that the Christian Coalition was a vehicle intended for the control of the Republican Party. By working from the grassroots up and training pro-family candidates for public office, the group set out to reshape Republican politics. Communicating the message to voters in innovative ways, such as papering church parking lots with voter guides and penning lurid fund-raising appeals warning of "a feminist agenda . . . that encourages women to leave their husbands, kill their children, practice witchcraft, destroy capitalism and become lesbians," they had an outsized influence in primaries and elections.

Dogged by organizational challenges, including a long battle over its tax status, by the late 1990s the Christian Coalition's star began to fade. Some religiously moderate and secular observers declared the death of the religious right, a narrative that fit comfortably within their views about progress. But they confused their own visions of history with observations of reality. As the Christian Coalition (following the Moral Majority) waned in importance, other organizations stepped up, often with the same key people in the lead.

Ralph Reed launched the Faith & Freedom Coalition, an advocacy group organized under the auspices of the section of the tax code that supposedly limits activity expressly to promote candidates. That restriction has not prevented Ralph Reed from turning his organization into an extension of the Republican party's political machine. At the 2019 Road to Majority Conference, Reed's annual gathering of activists and policymakers in Washington, D.C., Reed had nothing but praise for the president. "There has never been anyone who has defended us and fought for us who we have loved more than Donald J. Trump," he said. "He is everything he promised us he would be and more."[67] Reed declared the organization would invest $50 million dollars in get-out-the-vote efforts in 2020, with a special focus on swing states and Latino voters of faith. The effort, he said, would include five hundred paid staff and five thousand volunteers.

Other organizations that rose to the vanguard of the Christian nationalist movement include Concerned Women for America, Focus on the Family, the Family Research Council, the Alliance Defense Fund (now Alliance Defending Freedom), the American Family Association, and dozens of others, many with state and local affiliates, all promoting their understanding of the correct stance on religion and policy matters. Meanwhile, smaller coalitions of movement elite, including the Council for National Policy and the Fellowship Foundation, also known as "The Family," work to align money, resources, technology (including media and campaign operations), political leadership, and other sources of power.

By the election of 2016, the creation of a new American religion of "life" and its merger with a single political party was plain for all to see. Every presidential candidate for the Republican nomination took a stand against abortion and disagreed only on whether rape, incest, and life-of-the-mother exceptions should be allowed. And every Christian nationalist activist hammered home the message. "There is literally no more important issue than the life of a child prior to its birth," said Buddy Pilgrim, an activist and businessman who has been closely involved in political campaigns and legislation-focused initiatives. "That is supreme, and we cannot stand before a righteous and holy God and say, 'I voted for a pro-abortion candidate because I liked their economic policies better.'"[68] Christian nationalists and their allies continue to stand behind the most corrupt, divisive, and chaotic president in history because they believe that he can supply, via the courts, the abortion ban that they see as a necessary prelude to making America a righteous nation again.

It is another crisp, winter morning, one year later, and I am back at the March for Life in Washington, D.C. The official theme of the march this year is "science." "Pro-Life is Pro-Science," the banners read. The unofficial theme might well have been "Girl Power." I spot an abundance of placards reading "I am a Pro-Life Feminist," "A Woman's Rights Begin in the Womb," and "Pro-Life, Pro-Woman." And yet the whole affair feels even more like a Trump rally than last year's event.

This year, of the twenty-two members of Congress whose names Jeanne Mancini reads out onstage, twenty-one are Republican and none are women. But, perhaps mindful of the blowback from last year's nearly all-white speaker's panel, the organizers have been careful to offer more racial diversity in the lineup, bringing in antiabortion activist Alveda King and Louisiana state representative Katrina Jackson. Like last year, the crowd at the mall is largely white, with a light sprinkling of red MAGA hats. Vice President Mike Pence is there with his wife, Karen, to declare, once again, that Trump is "the most pro-life president in history."

I approach one of the young women present, a representative of an affiliate of Concerned Women of America called Young Women for America, and ask her what she makes of the link between abortion and women's rights. She offers a swift, practiced response: "Half of the babies that are killed are female babies, and those women, those very young girls, they don't have a choice." I chat with the Northern California regional coordinator of Students for Life, and she gives me pretty much the same answer: "Abortion is discrimination based on their age," she says. "And that's a message that plays pretty well with young people, because our generation is all about equal human rights and equality for all," she nods.

I approach another two dozen or so women and I hear versions of the same response. The talking points match those found in widely disseminated "apologetics" intended to help pro-life activists refute progressive arguments for abortion rights. The Students for Life of America National

Conference, which takes place the day after the march, offers a breakout session on "Pro-Life Apologetics for College Students," which promises "tips based on actual experience on college campuses." There is also an "Advanced Apologetics" course that provides answers to "the most difficult pro-life questions that would've previously left you stumped."

I get mixed results when I test the apologetics on the connection between abortion access and economic insecurity. While virtually every antiabortion activist speaks of connecting pregnant women with "resources," and some mention government assistance, none have a ready response when I press them on whether they would favor investments in the kind of education, safety net, and social service programs that their party, the Republican Party, has aggressively undermined. One woman tasked with developing a pro-life apologetics at her church cheerfully volunteers that she organized a dona-tion drive, collecting a roomful of castoff toys and maternity clothes. Another activist says, with a sanguine, straightforward air, "Poverty has always been with us."

There are a handful of delegations from Jewish and liberal Christian groups, a lonely band of atheists, and a dash of pro-life Democrats. But there is no mistaking that this is a Christian nationalist event. The spirit of the day belongs to groups like the Crusade for Life, a Fountain Valley, California–based organization whose pamphlets express a fervent hope that a constitutional amendment banning abortion will help return the nation to the time of the founders, when, it supposes, there was no separation between church and state. Or groups like 40 Days for Life, a Bryan, Texas–based international prolife advocacy organization with hundreds of groups and initiatives around the world. They have a close relationship with a program in Colombia, for instance, where abortion is largely banned. The program, called Choose Life Colombia, trains teenagers to seek repeal of the country's "relaxed" restrictions on abortion, which presently permit the procedure in cases of rape, incest, extreme fetal abnormality, and to save the life of the mother. Apparently even these exceptions are objectionable.[69]

The marchers' commitment to "science"—the official theme of this year's March for Life—is similar to their commitment to female empowerment. They have learned the language, but they have mostly changed its meaning. The marchers I meet have adopted a scientistic rhetoric but evince little interest in the social science of reproductive rights, which shows that an especially effective way to reduce abortions is to promote access to long-acting contraception. The most vocal members of the movement remain committed to antiscientific positions in biology and climate science.

They also show a stunning disregard for the science of reproduction, particularly as it relates to complications in pregnancy or fetal development. It is not uncommon to hear birth control characterized as abortion, or pronouncements that abortion is "almost never" necessary to save the life of the mother. And they characterize late-term abortions as whimsical decisions when the research shows that such abortions are almost always done in the event of complications that threaten the life and health of either or both mother and fetus. What they mean by "science," it becomes very clear, is simply the images delivered by scientific instruments—high-resolution images of fetuses in the womb—which they see as powerful tools in advancing the belief that "life begins at conception."

In much of the reporting on the 2019 March for Life, attention focused on the Catholic boys' school from Covington, Kentucky, whose MAGA-hatted students fell into a viral encounter with a Native American drummer from Michigan. But the telling detail of that story is not what happened on the mall but the form of the Pledge of Allegiance that the Covington boys are compelled to recite at their school. Every day they amend the pledge, "with liberty and justice for all, born and unborn."[70] The implication is clear: real Americans belong to one party alone, the party that opposes abortion.

As in last year's event, Donald Trump once again appears, Oz-like, on the giant video screen. He reads from a prepared text in a somewhat robotic tone. He drones through all the expected language about his sincere commitment to "life." The crowd cheers; the deal is done. He sounds genuinely bored. I wonder if it's because it has become so easy.

CHAPTER 4

The Mind of a Warrior

AT A MINI-MALL Starbucks in southern San Diego, I'm staring into my coffee and wondering whether coming here was such a good idea. I have written about the most emotionally fraught chapters of Jim Domen's life in a column for the *New York Times*. I did it not to invade his privacy but because by his own account those intimate details are part of what define him as the public figure that he is. Still, as I take in the glow of the late-afternoon California sun reflecting off the Home Depot across the parking lot, I'm on edge. Did I get him right? Will he be angry? Two months ago, he retweeted @realDonaldTrump's claim that the "FAKE NEWS media"—including the "failing @nytimes"—is "the enemy of the American People!"

A black sedan pulls up and Jim Domen pops out of the back seat sporting a broad smile. He is exquisitely attired in an upscale plaid shirt with a coordinating plaid tie and well-cut navy vest. Every article of clothing trumpets red, white, and blue. Even his socks are Stars-and-Stripes. Trim and athletic, with his short blond hair curled at the top, he radiates a kind of kinetic energy.

"Wow, you look fantastic!" I say. Then I catch myself. I wonder if I'm building some assumption about his sexuality into the way that I am speaking to him. Domen has built a whole new identity and career out of the idea that he is "ex-gay." I worry that he'll take offense. But he immediately puts me at ease.

"Thank you for that incredible article!" he exclaims. "I am so blessed by your piece." He asks for a hug, which I happily supply, and invites me to dinner, adding that his wife is eager to meet me. In an instant I feel the warmth and charisma that has made Domen a leader in conservative Christian circles in this part of the state.

"Sometimes the Latino pastors call me *Jefe*," he laughs, then shakes his head modestly. "But I say, 'No, please don't call me that. Because only Jesus is Lord.'"

Domen's story is an irresistible one for anyone interested in understanding the Christian nationalist movement. His issues are the issues of the movement. But the part of the story that many outside observers don't get—and the main reason I'm back in Southern California—has to do with those Latino pastors.

The Christian nationalist movement is frequently characterized as a white movement. And for some of the white people in the rank and file of the movement, it is indeed implicitly a white movement. For them, it surely is part of a vision that involves recovering a nation that was once, supposedly, both Christian and white.

But the leaders of the movement can read the demographic future just as well as you or I can. Many of them understand very well that the electoral future of Christian nationalism is not ethnically homogenous. They can also see, as some members of majority-white American congregations cannot, that some of the fastest-growing varieties of evangelicalism in America are in the charismatic and Pentecostal vein, and these are explicitly multiracial movements. A number of the more farsighted leaders are therefore making a conscious effort to include and empower conservative Christians of color. At the very least, they are doing what they can to collect their votes.

Jim Domen is one such leader. A California pastor and the founder of a group called Church United, he has built his voter-outreach machine around the idea of racial inclusiveness. Like Watchmen On the Wall, Church United holds gatherings in which the organization is introduced to pastors across the state, and the aim is to get them to engage with political leaders and persuade their congregations to vote their "biblical" values. A substantial number of Church United gatherings are conducted in the Spanish language, and the organization has spawned at least one affiliate, Alianza de Pastores Unidos de San Diego, whose members minister to largely Spanish-speaking audiences.

It wasn't always this way, of course, and it isn't going to change overnight. Many of the southern white evangelical groups that remain entrenched in the national leadership of the religious right hail from a tradition that long maintained the separation of the races is central to the Bible's plan. In the 1959 case *Loving v. Virginia*, for example, Judge Leon M. Bazile spoke for many of his fellow Bible believers when he argued that God "did not intend for the races to mix."[1] Yet while the movement's demands for purity are as intense as ever, they understand that the sorting of the pure and impure now answers to different rules. This gives activists like Domen an opening—not only for redemption, but for a path to political power. "God wired me for government and church," he tells me. As Domen fills me in on the details of his life story, he invites me to a pastors' event that evening, and I promise to meet him there.

Perched on a knoll in a southern section of San Diego, the Ocean View Church is a sturdy, attractive complex decorated in soothing shades of green and blue. From the back of the property, behind the youth chapel, you can catch a distant glimpse of the Pacific. When I arrive at 6:00 P.M., families are gathered around the alfresco buffet, filling paper plates and bowls with fruit salad, ceviche, and ham and roast beef sandwiches. There are a few Anglos in the crowd, but most of the attendees are Latino, and they chat quietly in small groups as they enjoy the evening breezes. The women are dressed in modest yet stylish fashions. The men, most of them pastors, are wearing guayaberas or sport jackets. The conversations around me are all in Spanish.

The event is cohosted by Church United and its affiliated organization, Alianza de Pastores Unidos de San Diego. I chat with Hugo Campos Sr., Spanish pastor of the Ocean View Church and president of the Alianza de Pastores Unidos, who appears to be in his mid-forties and sports a robust mustache.

"We need to get involved in politics to the extent that it impacts the family," Campos says to me in a temperate voice. "Hispanic people are very family-oriented, and we are uncomfortable speaking about sex very openly. For us, this is an issue for parents. The things they are putting in public schools are messages that we don't feel comfortable exposing our children to.

"You have to pay attention," he adds, gesturing around the outdoor patio and the families enjoying the early evening air. "Because your kids are the most valuable thing you have."

From conversations with Campos and others at the event, it is clear that the Latino pastors present have a stake in other issues, too. Community health and safety, access to quality education, economic opportunity, and immigration policy come up, at times in somewhat guarded tones. Latino voters have traditionally gravitated toward the Democratic Party, but today the pastors know that they will hear a different message.

A pastor who is among the small number of Anglos at the gathering explains that breaking the news to congregants can be a delicate business. "They came up in tears and said, 'I was born in this political party and I've always voted in this political party. But now I understand I have to vote on issues.' Or: 'My husband has always told me who to vote for. But, before God, I can't vote for a candidate who believes in abortion.' I've had people coming up crying, and they've said, 'The company or the union told me how to vote. And I can't vote for that person.'"

As I head inside for the main event, an usher wearing a crisp black pant-suit greets me. "*¿Es pastora?*"—Are you a pastor?—she asks. "No," I respond in Spanish, "I am a guest of Jim Domen." Her face lights up and she guides me to what I gather is a place of honor in the auditorium. I settle into my seat, eager to witness the work that has made Domen a fast-rising star of the movement.

By the time he was in middle school, Jim Domen knew he was different. He found boys sexually attractive, and that confused him. His thoughts, he knew, would shock and offend those he loved the most.

Domen's father, a stern figure who worked as a sheriff for Los Angeles County, came from a Catholic family. His mother's background was Epis-copalian. Around the time Jim turned seven, both parents were "born again."

The family was financially stable and religiously devout. They lived in Yorba Linda, the birthplace of Richard Nixon, and attended the Rose Drive Friends Church, an evangelical ministry affiliated with the Evangelical Friends Church Southwest. Though nominally descended from Quaker heritage, the group in fact practices a conservative, nondenominational form of evangelicalism. The pastors at Rose Drive Friends Church left no doubt that same-sex relationships are an abomination.

"I tried to read the Bible and I prayed to change the sinful desires," Domen told a radio interviewer in 2013, but "they weren't changing." He also tried dating girls, but that didn't seem to work, either.

At night he liked to watch Michael J. Fox in the popular eighties TV series *Family Ties*. Alex Keaton, the character played by Fox, was his hero, fresh-faced and precocious. "He was this conservative kid surrounded by liberal family members," says Domen. "I wanted to be like him."

In a moment of crisis, Domen entrusted his secret to a youth pastor at church. The pastor told him to confess his sin to his parents. Domen did as he was asked. If he had been hoping for acceptance, he was sorely disappointed.

"They were shocked and devastated," he said.

Domen resolved to change his sexual orientation. He sought out treatment from a Christian counselor to help with the transition. It didn't work.

The attractions persisted through his teen years and into young adulthood. At twenty-four, Domen announced to his parents that he had fallen in love.

"Is it with a woman or a man?" His mother asked. It was a man.

"She just started bawling," he later recalled. "My sister started just screaming over the phone and said, 'Don't call here ever again.' My brother started praying for me."

Fearing he would be forsaken by his family and faith, Domen abandoned both. He moved to the desert luxury town of Palm Springs and embraced the "homosexual lifestyle," he says. His boyfriend was a successful paper sculptor fourteen years his senior, and the couple established an art gallery. "He made the art and I would sell it," Domen recalls. "The most expensive piece sold for $30,000."

Among the attractions of Palm Springs is its lively gay scene, and Domen was living at the heart of it all. His partner was involved in the city council, and the pair frequented White Parties, where guests circulated in all-white clothing and costumes. Many of their friends were prominent Hollywood industry insiders who came down from Los Angeles on weekends.

But sometimes Domen felt it couldn't last. "When I was in the lifestyle, I knew what I was doing was wrong," he says.

The denouement was abrupt. "I came home one day with my eyelashes and eyebrows dyed black. And [my partner] screamed at me, 'I don't want to be with a woman!'" Domen recalls. His partner demanded that he leave the house. "He switched all the bank accounts and filed a restraining order. I went from being well off to having nothing."

A taste of bitterness lingers in Domen's version of the story. "I started to see a lot of alcoholic behaviors in [him]," he says. "I had been planning to leave anyway."

Homeless and penniless, Domen fell into a depression. In his lowest moment, he turned to prayer: "God I'm yours again."

The next morning he found a $5 bill on the sidewalk. When Moses had been lost in the desert, Domen reminded himself, God had shown him a path. Now God was showing that He would provide for him, too. Domen used the money for breakfast at Denny's. Then he resolved to return home to Yorba Linda, a broken man, ready to wield his own pain as a weapon in the fight for redemption.

He arrived at the Rose Drive Friends Church with quite a lot to prove. "When he showed up in those days, 2002 and 2003, he seemed intent on projecting an ultra-masculine persona," says Bradley Onishi, who was a member of Rose Drive Friends Church for ten years and served as a youth pastor at the church for seven. "At the summer camp where we took our high school and junior high school students, occasionally a bear would come into the camp. Jim made it his life's mission to hunt the bear down and kill it." Domen took up endurance sports with intentional vigor, running, biking, and swimming his way into triathlon competitions.

Everyone knew the story. "He was the prodigal son coming home from the wilderness of the gay lifestyle," says Onishi.

Domen evinced only pity for the earlier version of himself, the young man careening through the gay party scene in all-white outfits. When driving past Palm Springs on a church road trip, Onishi recalls, Domen asked everyone in the vehicle to pray. "We were praying for the den of sin that is Palm Springs; it was like praying for the Castro," says Onishi. "My take is that it was clear that that was on his mind all the time. Taking part in triathlons, riding his bike—he seemed to me like someone who was always moving and never wanted to stop, because it wasn't clear what would happen if he did."

Upon his return, Domen also revealed a sharply partisan aspect to his personality. He fell into clashes with the leadership and culture of Rose Drive Friends Church and developed a reputation as an outspoken, political person. "Rose Drive was full of mainly white folks and older leadership, and Jim wanted to shake things up," says Onishi.

At the same time, with reparative therapy, Domen claims, his sexuality began to shift toward heterosexuality. "I had a blast dating all kinds of women, white, black, short, skinny, godly and ungodly," he told a radio interviewer in 2013. But, he added, "I really kept my sexual purity and wanted to honor my body and save myself for marriage."

As religion became ever more central to his identity, Domen decided it was time to enroll in a seminary. He chose Azusa Pacific University, a private evangelical Christian university in Azusa, California, to obtain an advanced degree in theology. It was at Azusa that he met Amanda Stanfield, his future wife.

With his theological credentials and pastoral experience in hand and a family life on the way, Domen took to organizing political rallies, which soon led to a position at the California Family Council, a state affiliate of Focus on the Family.

With an annual budget of approximately $90 million, the national right-wing powerhouse Focus on the Family produces a variety of media programming that promotes traditional "family values." The organization has funded campaigns against state legislators who support LGBT rights and anti-bullying programs in public schools. Focus on the Family aggressively supported Proposition 8, the 2008 statewide ballot measure that sought to eliminate the rights of same-sex couples to marry. Domen was all in. A photo from election night shows him celebrating the passage of Proposition 8 with fellow activists, arms raised high in victory.

In more than one sense, the man in the photo was starting to resemble a grown-up Michael J. Fox from *Family Ties*. Domen, just like his hero on the show, was a precocious young man defending conservative values against the misguided relativism of the liberal community that had once welcomed him in Palm Springs. He loved them—truly he did!—but he knew they were wrong.

Domen believes same-sex attractions to be a consequence of poor or unresolved parent-child bonding. "I wasn't athletic like my brother," he explains, referring to his previously strained relationship with his own father. Now the prodigal son had transformed himself into an athlete, too. From 2011 to 2014, Domen served as leader of Multisport Ministries, "running, biking, and swimming to win as God's men, competing in the character of Christ," according to the website. In describing his own journey, Domen says, "The need for connection with other men was real, but sexual activity is wrong." Today, he says, he enjoys "hanging around healthy heterosexual men really teaching on me what it is to be a true man, the true masculinity." Posing for the cameras with the famously pious athlete Tim Tebow, Domen wears a slightly startled expression, his arm lightly draped around Tebow's waist.

Today, Domen makes regular appearances at government buildings and other public spaces in Sacramento and Santa Ana, often bringing with him squadrons of fellow ex-gay allies, or "formers," as they sometimes identify themselves. In 2018 he staged an event at Los Angeles's Pershing Square with eighteen speakers including two survivors of the Pulse nightclub massacre in Orlando, Florida, all sharing their "stories of transformation from homosexual, lesbian, bisexual, and transgender lifestyles."

A popular guest speaker at churches in California and beyond, Domen continues to disparage same-sex relationships and their acceptance in the wider culture. "Now you've got [the popular television show] *Modern Family* and you've got two homosexual men and they have two children," he said from a Texas pulpit in 2018. "This is horrible. It's horrific. It is abnormal."

As of this writing, his Twitter bio reads: "Pastor, Ironman, Husband, Daddy, Triathlete and Deplorable. I want the world to know I live for the glory of Jesus Christ."

Although the trajectory that led Jim Domen to the forefront of evangelical political activism has its share of idiosyncratic twists, the place in which he has landed must seem familiar to anyone who travels in conservative evangelical circles. Hypermasculinity, if not always drawing from the same sources, is a leitmotif of conservative Christianity in America. Reverend Jerry Falwell disdained androgynous, gentle representations of Jesus, insisting that his savior was hypermasculine. "Christ wasn't effeminate," Falwell asserted. "The man who lived on this earth was a man with muscles ... Christ was a he-man!"[2] The Family Research Council's Jerry Boykin said Jesus "was a man's man, but we feminized him in the church,"[3] adding, "I believe that sword he'll be carrying when he comes back is an AR-15."[4] Mark Driscoll, a celebrity preacher who cofounded the Acts 29 parachurch network, got the point across in flowery language: We "live in a completely pussified nation," he said.[5] If Christian men "do not man up soon," he warned, "the Episcopalians may vote a fluffy baby bunny rabbit as their next bishop to lead God's men."[6]

The testosterone rhetoric reflected a renewed forcefulness in cultural and political engagement as well as anxieties about gender, sexuality, and family structure that preoccupy religious nationalists around the world.

In America, at least in part, it was a response to a gender gap in church attendance that has tended to skew female. At the Yorba Linda Friends Church (which is close to but not affiliated with Domen's Rose Drive Friends Church), director of the men's ministry Steve Craig said in 2006, "We're beginning to take out the flowery songs and replace them with the warrior-type lyrics and more masculine things that men identify with."[7] Today, many conservative evangelical networks promote the idea of "male headship" at church and in the home as part of "God's created design"—even as more women than men fill their pews.

Jim Domen's remarkable ability to step outside of himself, to shed an earlier personality like an old skin then hold it up to his own contempt—this, too, has ample precedent in a tradition that loves nothing more than tales of souls redeemed for their opposites. His irrepressible drive to share his beliefs, to convert others so that he may believe in himself, is equally characteristic of a religion that is, after all, built to proselytize. But in recent years, at least, the most familiar aspect of the life that Domen has carved out of a conflicted childhood in Orange County is the strangest one: namely, the way in which his religious, sexual, and personal concerns are inseparable from his politics.

Notwithstanding the successful campaign for Proposition 8, it wasn't until 2014 that Domen founded Church United and really hit his stride in the political arena. It is in this capacity that Domen has become someone to know for those who want to understand American political life today. If the Republican Party enjoys electoral success in the future, it will be thanks to the efforts of Domen and others like him.

"Goliath must fall in California," Domen has written on his blog, explaining the mission of Church United.[8] "California's progressive Legislature is defiling the armies of God." Shortly after founding the group, he added: "The state's liberal leadership has persistently—and consistently—stripped away those values we hold closely to our core: life, traditional marriage, and religious freedoms. Let's face it: at the core of our struggle is a mighty spiritual battle between light and darkness." Borrowing from the same playbook that so many other Christian nationalist leaders have turned to, Domen rhetorically asked, "Who better to lead us in these battles than our spiritual shepherds?"

Church United started with six affiliated pastors in 2014. In 2015 it counted twenty-seven affiliated pastors. By 2018 the number had grown to approximately five hundred pastor members, all organized into "pastor clusters," each with a leader who answers to a central committee.

The clusters are established up and down California's coastal and inland areas. "These slow, intentional, servant-heart, relationship-building efforts have resulted in successful statewide senior pastor and regional pastor relationships," Domen wrote on his blog, "reaching Redding, San Francisco, San Jose, Sacramento, the Central Valley, Los Angeles" and other locales.[9] Dozens of sub-networks create a dense infrastructure crisscrossing the state.

Church United members meet with elected officials to discuss issues of local and statewide concern and attend gatherings at the state and national capitols. They also offer support to the growing numbers of Christian nationalists holding public office. "Briefings" draw representatives of church and state together, so that "members of Congress, the California Legislature, and county and city elected officials speak to the pastors about their faith and how they implement a biblical worldview in policy."[10]

The rapid success of the Church United model has inspired Domen to embrace a breathtakingly ambitious goal: "Imagine if we grew and replicated these efforts in each of the 50 states!" he wrote. For the time being, to be sure, Domen remains focused on California.

California may look to the world like a blue state. But one in five adults are evangelical Christian, and the state has more megachurches than any other. Although Orange County angled blue in the 2018 midterm elections, the margins were wafer-thin. As far as today's Christian right is concerned, California remains a battlefield.

David Lane is one of many evangelical leaders who see the state as political territory ripe for conquest. In the 1990s, Lane first coordinated gatherings of evangelical pastors in California and Texas with the aim of organizing them to get out the vote on behalf of conservative religious causes. The effort was expanded in the 2000s with funding from the American Family Association. Lane founded the American Renewal Project, "people of faith positively affecting public policy," and has led an estimated 15,000 pastors in "Pastors and Pews" dialogues with politicians such as Mike Huckabee, Bobby Jindal, and Ted Cruz, along with figures like the Christian nationalist historian David Barton. In 2010, he coordinated pastor gatherings in politically contested states, including New Hampshire, Ohio, and Iowa. In advance of a July 2016 Pastors and Pews gathering in Orlando, Florida, Lane spelled it out in an interview with the Christian Broadcasting Network. "Our goal is to restore America to a Biblically based culture," he said. "Somebody's values are going to reign supreme."

"What we're doing with the pastor meetings is spiritual, but the end result is political," Lane said in 2011."[11]

Pastor Jim Garlow has also recognized political opportunity in the Golden State. The former leader of a San Diego-area megachurch who coauthored a book with David Barton in 2018, Garlow played a key role in organizing pastoral support for Proposition 8, California's constitutional amendment to ban same-sex marriage. Proposition 8 passed but was subsequently voided by the Supreme Court.

Franklin Graham foresaw electoral fortunes in California, too. One of Trump's earliest and most enthusiastic evangelical defenders, Graham led a three-bus caravan up the center of California in advance of the 2018 election with the goal of turning out the evangelical vote for Republican candidates. "Progressive?" he said, railing against the state's supposedly secular values. "That's just another word for godless."[12] For the tour, which he called Decision America, Graham and his team produced ten campaign-style rallies, complete with worship music and slick videos. Most of the rallies took place in swing districts.

It is Domen, however, who has opened up the most fruitful strategy for the Christian right in California. His Church United initiative rests on two simple insights. The first, which he shares in common with other activist groups, is that pastors drive votes. Church United's raison d'être is to politicize pastors—in the "right" direction. The second insight, which distinguishes Domen from the field to some degree, is that the future of Christian nationalism is not all white. To be sure, other leaders accept this demographic reality, but Domen acts on that strategic insight in a systematic way.

Racial unity in Christ is one of Church United's core themes. When Domen assembled several dozen pastors and "former homosexuals" on the steps of the Ronald Reagan federal building in Santa Ana to oppose California's Assembly Bill 2943, which would have enhanced California's existing prohibition on "sexual orientation change efforts," he made a point of highlighting that diversity. "There are pastors of every color or creed on the steps with us today," he said. "Members of the press, I ask that you use this word for us, as 'formers.'"

To be clear, real power in the Christian nationalist movement is still largely white and male. Yet Domen is a new and different sort of creature in the same movement. As Bradley Onishi observes, "Domen didn't grow up with that southern, segregated racial framework. So he is way more effective than he might be if he were from Texas or Virginia or Georgia. He doesn't come from a context where strict racial binaries are built into the church every Sunday.

He is comfortable with Latino people because they are an unmovable part of his community. It is not surprising to me that he has found a way to expand.

"That's not to say that there wasn't a subtle racism at play," Onishi adds. "I'm a biracial American, and I'd say, casually, that attending Rose Drive made me more white than Japanese American because all of my mentors and my culture became white. It was an implicit agenda, more than an explicitly segregationist agenda. But it wasn't like going to Jerry Falwell's church, or a place where there was a segregation academy."

Like the most famous son of Yorba Linda, Domen seems to have politics in his bones, even as he remains an outsider of sorts. He is fully committed to the politics of division and conquest. But with the benefit of perspective that distance supplies, he understands that the sorting of the pure and impure now answers to different rules. "For the evangelical church right now, membership is no longer based on color," Onishi notes. "It is also not really based in religion anymore, either. Your litmus test for religious belonging comes via your political beliefs."

Inside the Ocean View Church in San Diego, a series of Latino and Anglo speakers take their turns at the podium. Craig Huey, a laconic white-haired businessman, starts off with a presentation of voter guide material.

Speaking through an interpreter, he tells the crowd, "You need to be able to explain to your fellowship these issues. When we talk about abortion, for example, what is more important, talking about the minimum wage, or about 'life'?"

It's all spelled out, in Spanish, in the voter guide pamphlets distributed among the audience. Huey also invites the crowd to consult his own group's website, which rates candidates on "biblical issues." "All people have to do is log in to see how to vote their values," he says. "Other issues are important, but biblically based principles are clear."

Huey impresses on the group the importance of voting these biblical principles. "Muslims vote 84 percent. Only about 40 percent of Christians in California voted. As a result, we see our Christian rights going away," he says. As the audience groans, he runs through a litany of frothy complaints: "Recently they tried to stop homeschooling. They tried to ban the Bible. They just almost passed a bill in California that would have put out of business Christian colleges, like Azusa, Biola, because the people in Sacramento, like many of those in Congress and the Senate and in Washington, D.C., have an ideology that discriminates against Christians and want to take away our rights." To judge from the sighs in the crowd, it appears that these preposterous allegations are accepted here as mostly true.

"I spoke at a Hispanic church. About seven hundred people were in tears because they never heard this before," he adds. "They were in tears because they never knew how to vote their values. They realized that they were voting against their values! They were voting against what was really in their self-interest. And they were not honoring God with their vote."

Huey assures the audience that they need not feel powerless.

"If in your area we had twenty-five churches where we went down the ballot in the church, a good candidate who believes in a biblical worldview would win an election," he says. "Take a stand that you're going to help transform the politics of your community in the state of California!"

Huey also volunteers his services to the group. "My wife, Shelly, and myself or one of our associates would be glad to come to your church and have an election forum," he says. "And you don't have to worry about it. We can do it for you. And if you want to do it, we have a PowerPoint that you can use to go straight down the ballot."

Another Anglo speaker, Jack Hibbs, pastor of Calvary Chapel Chino Hills, takes the stage and continues with a message, also delivered through an interpreter, that reduces both the Bible and politics to a few key issues with yes-or-no answers.

"Regardless of the party, I vote my biblical worldview," says Hibbs. "Why? Because I can stand before God at the end of my life, having lived it without trying to please any man."

Hibbs has made a point of flouting IRS rules on political activism from the pulpit. The IRS requires that certain charities, nonprofits, and other tax-exempt organizations, including houses of worship, refrain from partisan political activism if they wish to maintain their privileged tax status. So, in 2012, Hibbs forwarded to the IRS a video of himself engaging in a sermon that unmistakably favored the Republican platform. "That's the whole point, to cross the line, to draw fire," Hibbs said at the time. "We want to draw the IRS out."[13]

The IRS declined to take the bait. But Hibbs still seems determined to establish a precedent that would allow his church and like-minded religious organizations to operate as taxpayer-funded extensions of the political party of their choice.

His speech to the crowd at the Church United and Alianza de Pastores Unidos event is only fifteen minutes long, yet it packs a day's worth of whoppers.

"Years ago, our church was made aware of the fact that churches in California would have to be funding and paying for abortions," Hibbs claims. "So I refused," he says, "and so we lost our insurance coverage because God is for 'life.'"

This is a blatant distortion. California churches do not pay for abortions any more than they pay for Viagra or for abdominal aortic aneurysm screenings. Instead, through the Affordable Care Act, they participate in health insurance exchanges that allow employers statewide to negotiate insurance coverage for their employees—some of whom happen to be women making use of reproductive care services. Characterizing this as churches paying for abortions is like saying that motorists are compelled to transport tractor-trailers from state to state because they share the same roads. But this sham narrative has become a popular talking point for the California Family Council and is perhaps too valuable in activating the base to set aside just because it's not true.

Hibbs only works harder to heighten the tension in his narrative of martyrdom in the face of his church's alleged complicity in California's baby genocide. "We are currently in a lawsuit with the governor's office to fight for the voice of the unborn child," he says, his voice ringing with sanctimony, and the audience claps.

He pivots to the hot-button issue of the moment: California's Healthy Youth Act, which took effect in 2016 and requires school districts throughout the state to provide students with comprehensive sexuality and health education, including information about HIV prevention. "It is the most radical sex education the state has ever seen," he claims. "If it's not yet in your child's school, it's coming. Listen, parents, pastors, leaders, there's no opt out extended to the family. Your child *must* go through this curriculum."

This, too, is a bending of the truth. There is no single course on offer. Rather, there are multiple courses and curriculum materials in use in various districts. Parents are legally allowed to opt out of lessons about comprehensive sexual health and HIV prevention in their entirety—and many of them do. What they may not opt out of is assemblies on bullying and harassment or social studies classes that discuss the contributions of LGBT people in history.

Domen has a handout, depicting alleged sex education curricula in public schools, to be distributed among the crowd. The one-page sheet is a lurid mash-up of graphics and text. Some of the materials strike me as inappropriate for the age groups that the flyer suggests they are reaching; others seem factually incorrect or even bizarre, and I can see why they might be concerning to parents. On the back of the sheet is a list of seventy-seven California politicians who have supported California's Healthy Youth Act; all but one are Democrats.

When I later check with Laura Dudnick, a representative from the San Francisco Unified School District, she tells me that none of the graphics or materials on the handout are used in any district public school in the manner implied by organizers of this event. A few components of the graphics, which Domen's handout suggests are utilized in elementary schools, are in fact used at the high school level, for example, and are not taught with the other components of the graphics with which they are grouped. Other materials in Domen's handout, says Dudnick, are not taught anywhere in the San Francisco Unified School District.

Hibbs circles back to the bottom line: Vote red. "Christian leaders, who is going to do it? Who will stand for the family? Who will stand for marriage? Who will stand for our culture? So I want to encourage you: Get involved. Have your people—you know, it's legal, register to vote at your church. It's legal . . .

"And just so you know," he adds, in what amounts to a final twisting of the truth, "I'm not a Republican or a Democrat. I'm a Christian—which makes me a monarchist if you think about it!" The crowd whoops and claps their approval.

The organizers of the event are also keen to target their audience with a message about capitalist economics. Here, they turn to a video featuring Gloria Álvarez, a telegenic libertarian activist from Guatemala. The video is from Prager University, which is not a university and does not hold classes—not surprising, perhaps, given that its largest funders include the biblical-literalist fracking billionaires Dan and Farris Wilks.

"Have you ever asked yourself why the U.S. is a country with much more freedom, much less corruption, and is much more prosperous than any of our countries in Latin America?" Álvarez asks in an urgent, rapid-fire tone. "The answer lies mainly in the American belief of having a limited government. Why? Because the more limited a government, the less corrupt it is. And the more limited the government, the more you will have individual freedom and personal responsibility. And given those things, along with hard work and talent, you can accomplish your life's goals."

Álvarez, whose grandparents fled Cuba, identifies as an atheist. But the bond between Christian nationalism and economic libertarianism has become powerful enough for both sides to overlook theological quibbles. In San Diego, activists understand perfectly well that breaking the link between Latinos and the Democratic Party requires undermining the economic message that voters are hearing from unions and other progressive sources.

"Is it because you think that when Democrats offer you free stuff, it means they really care about you?" Álvarez says. "Do you think that when the Republicans talk about enforcing immigration laws it means they are going to send you back? Let's be honest: you didn't come here for free stuff; you came for the economic opportunity that allows you work and earn money." The audience murmurs its assent.

Following the video, a man in jeans and a nicely fitting blue jacket takes the stage. Pastor Netz Gómez comes from the Houses of Light, a "nondenominational" church in Northridge, California, but his role here is apparently to spread a certain amount of darkness around those toward whom the gathered faithful should direct their hate.

"Look, brothers, we're seeing an invasion of humanism," he says in impassioned Spanish. "Our schools, our laws, our senate is full of humanism, brothers, and I feel an outrage." Then he shifts his aim from the dreaded humanists to the even more despised members of the LGBT community. "Homosexual groups, I have nothing against them," he claims, before launching into a diatribe about the things he does, in fact, hold against them. "They are a minimum percentage, not even 3 percent. However, they're influencing the entire population." And "that is why we have to rise up in a holy indignation."

There is a sad irony in inviting people of color who were themselves once—and indeed remain—objects of contempt for other groups of religious nationalists to turn around and discover their own objects of contempt. But for Gómez it is clearly just a matter of redrawing the lines between insider and outsider, and he is careful to reassure his audience that they are on the inside.

"Hispanic brothers, you came to the United States of North America as an instrument of God," he says. "Some of you came here for work, others came here wet, others came here dry!" Everyone in the room laughs knowingly. "I don't know how you guys came here," he continues, "but what I know, brothers, is you are here as an instrument of God. And for those who are here as preachers, we have a tremendous responsibility."

Then Gómez, too, pivots to the bottom line. "I loved what my brother is giving us. Check it out," he enthuses. "He's giving us a voter guide. It is important you see it. He's giving us, on the first page, two governor candidates who were selected in the primary elections. Gavin Newsom, who is a democratic person, is a person who has promoted the homosexual marriage, is one of the spokespersons, one of the people who go to the front of the homosexual groups."

Gómez clearly has no problem spelling out the "correct" conclusions to draw from the "nonpartisan" voter guides.

"Please notice here, for example," he continues, pointing to another part of the voter guide, "where it talks about the lieutenant governor, there are two candidates and they are Democrats. There was no choice for a person with a little more of values." Opening the cover, he says, "These two people who are listed here, one of the lieutenant governor candidates has 99 percent of a secular vision. Nothing of God. And the other candidate is a man who has 97 percent. It means that no one is good. Are you understanding me? There is no one to vote for."

But just to reassure his audience that political talk at church is all well and good, he adds, "A lot of people are going to tell me, 'No, brother, don't meddle in political matters, because they're going to shut down the church.' It's a devil's lie, brothers. This thing is legal. Here it is written," he says, gesturing toward a packet of papers, "so you don't have the slightest doubt."

The material to which he appears to be referring includes content from the Family Research Council associated with its Culture Impact Teams—and it is, if anything, still more partisan. The FRC's manuals twist and spin a few Bible passages to prove that God opposes gun regulations, the Affordable Care Act, tax increases, public assistance (unless it passes through church coffers), climate science, and pretty much every other position associated with the Republican Party's opponents.

Domen himself appears highly pleased with the Ocean View Church event, and it is abundantly clear that its partisan political nature comes directly from him. In the run-up to the gathering, his Twitter posts alternated between praise for Jesus and calls to "arrest Hillary Clinton" (June 18, 2018) and "DRAIN THE SWAMP!" (June 5, 2018). He has also retweeted a number of Trump's statements attacking the Mueller investigation and the media, including one from February 2017: "The FAKE NEWS media (failing @nytimes, @NBCNews, @ABC, @CBS, @CNN) is not my enemy, it is the enemy of the American People!"

Donald Trump, Domen says, has "done more for the Church than many Christian presidents have . . . I believe it's also divine that we are powering up Church United at the same time that America is under new leadership." Domen celebrated Donald Trump's victory in the 2016 election by attending the inauguration in Washington, D.C. In a photograph taken from the event, he appears relaxed and content.

Painting the blue state of California red may seem like a stretch target. But Domen is a picture of optimism. "Even though we have a supermajority liberal worldview in Sacramento," he writes, "I'm hopeful that with Church United we can better partner together to address the spiritual problems affecting our communities so California can be golden once again."

* * *

Church United is Domen's work, and it is also very much the creation of a national movement. Christian nationalist organizations, many of them based in Washington, D.C., have provided him with critical resources, including funding, connections, partnerships, travel opportunities, and ideas.

It is easy to see why so many pastors are happy to sign on. Aside from the opportunity for cross-denominational fellowship, activism, and political engagement, there's the free or subsidized travel. Church United sponsors annual trips to the state capitol in Sacramento, dubbed, "Awakening Tours," where pastors learn about the legislative process, meet public officials, pray loudly under the rotunda, and "strategically target committee members" in order to defeat what Domen has called "the enormous evil facing California from the legislature." Meetings with congressmen are often arranged with assistance from the Christian legal firm Advocates for Faith & Freedom, which also acts as a sponsor of the tours. "Most of the politicians were extremely encouraged by their visit from the pastors," according to a report from one such gathering. "God definitely had His hand in the connection made between the pastors and their elected officials!"[14]

In addition to the Sacramento pilgrimages, Church United invites pastors to "Awakening" conferences in Washington, D.C. Activities have included a luncheon at the Heritage Foundation rooftop patio, which boasts inspiring views of the Washington Monument; a private screening of the antiabortion movie *Gosnell: The Trial of America's Biggest Serial Killer*, special tours of the Museum of the Bible; and meetings with right-wing lawmakers. Visiting pastors rub shoulders with movement VIPs like Christiana Holcomb of Alliance Defending Freedom, Ralph Drollinger of Capitol Ministries, and Star Parker of the Center for Urban Renewal and Education (CURE).

By all accounts, the D.C. visits are a success. As the Family Research Council summarized it, "Each of these pastors commits to pray for the nation, preach Christian citizenship messages, and partner with at least three other pastors. In May, FRC hosted our 13th annual national 'Watchmen on the Wall' conference in Washington D.C. Nearly 700 attendees from 41 states" attended.[15] In this way, Church United acts as a supportive initiative that funnels its members into the Family Research Council's vast pastoral network.

Aware of the need to expand the base beyond the once-familiar racial boundaries, the FRC adds, "We translated the event and key resources into Spanish," and has held dozens of events specifically for Black and Latino communities.

Domen's group relies critically on these tours, both to attract pastors and to provide a focus for their political activism. "The loudest message the pastors heard collectively from Congress was that they cannot change the country through public policy—the country will change through the people of God—especially when pastors engage," Domen wrote after one Awakening tour. "They all understand the Kingdom impact pastors have. It is the people of God who will change California and its cities, one city at a time."[16]

Church United's busy schedule of activities costs money. It is unclear from the organization's reporting where it comes from. The mailing address takes us to the Newport Beach, California, post office box of a real estate investment company run by Larry Smith, a businessman with close ties to other activist organizations. Smith currently sits on the board of Ralph Drollinger's Capitol Ministries. He has also served on the board of the Family Action PAC, which seeks "to recruit and elect qualified leaders who will advance a culture in which human life and family are valued, personal responsibility is encouraged, and liberty thrives." He donated at least $50,000 in support of California's anti–gay marriage amendment, Proposition 8, which Domen campaigned in favor of before it passed in 2008. Domen told me that the FRC also donated approximately $50,000 to Church United efforts in 2018. "I have to raise the rest," he said. "Mainly through the generosity of individual donors."

Domen's efforts appear to be bearing fruit. Fresh from an "Awakening" tour of the Sacramento capitol, Bishop Ed Smith of Zoe Christian Fellowship in Whittier, California, enthused, "I got challenged to tell people in our church to run for public office, to get involved in the legislative process, and to let their voice be heard through voting and in other ways. I want to encourage you as pastors in your church to be a voice and get people involved in the political process."

Shortly after attending a pastor gathering, Smith delivered a sermon about Senate Bill 1146, the Equity in Higher Education Act, which prohibited gender discrimination at institutions receiving state financial aid. As Smith characterized it, SB 1146 would have allowed the government "to take religious freedom away" from faith-based institutions. "If they limit the Christian colleges and universities, then they'll limit the high schools, the Christian high schools and then churches," he warned. "The devil don't know how to stop until we stop him!"[17] Under pressure from religious groups, the antidiscrimination language was removed.

For Pastor Elias Loera of Fresno's Family Christian Assembly, Church United has proved transformative, completely altering his previous understanding of the proper relationship between religion and politics.

"We've believed a lie for so long that the church and the state should be separated," he said in a Church United promotional video.[18] "But in my Awakening tour experience, there was a congressman that gave us a tour of the Capitol after hours, and he spoke up, when that was written by Thomas Jefferson, he was doing it to keep the politics out of church, not to keep the church out of politics. And that was, like, for me an awakening."

As a Church United cluster leader, Loera says, he strongly encourages his members to involve themselves and their congregations in policy issues. "Getting back we had a different perspective. 'Hey, guys, we're *supposed* to be involved in this process,'" he says.

In early 2018, under Loera's coordination, the Fresno-Clovis cluster organized multiple events, including a twenty-one-day schedule of fasting. Twenty-two regional churches of various denominations participated: Baptist, Presbyterian, and charismatic, as well as members of "nondenominational" parachurch networks like Cornerstone and Vineyard. A Facebook notice for the annual Fresno-Clovis pastor's breakfast announced the invited speaker: Tony Evans, the Dallas-based evangelical powerhouse who has established approximately eighty "church-school partnerships" throughout the Dallas area. Evans has flatly stated that the idea of church-state separation is unbiblical: "God never intended there to be such a separation in His world."

Another Church United–affiliated pastor, Bob Branch, who leads the Springs Community Church in Temecula, drew similar conclusions. "I realized that I was conceding the public square to the enemy and to the tide of the culture, and that's unacceptable," he said in a Church United video.[19] "Really in the final analysis, I thought wow, under my watch, I'm conceding the public square to the evil one. And I'm truly sorry and this is not okay. I can't sit on the sidelines anymore."

After attending an Awakening tour in Washington, D.C., Branch implemented a Culture Impact Team at his church to mobilize his congregation. In a sermon titled Finding Your Voice, he said, "You need to actually go and start taking your stand and be part of some pro-life efforts that are going on." He continued, "Every single person in this room has a sphere. And if we actually became God's change agents within those spheres, then we're talking about 150 people impacting perhaps 10,000 people. And that infection spreads."[20]

Mr. Branch makes no effort to disguise his ambition to spread the "infection" in hopes of mobilizing right-wing voters. Rob McCoy, pastor of Godspeak Calvary Chapel in Thousand Oaks, is equally forthright. "If we want to make a difference in this state we have to step into the culture mountain of influence of politics. The only commodity or currency in politics is winning elections," says McCoy. "We have got to get folks in the congregations to step into this political mountain of influence."[21]

For those pastors who happen to disapprove of Republican leadership or who might be leery of church-state entanglements, McCoy has a ready answer, which he articulated in a video on the Church United website: "I speak to these pastors" across the country, he said. "This is the one thing they say: 'Politics is dirty.' My response to them is, 'So is the church. So what's your point?'"[22]

Just five years after its founding, Domen's organization is praised by some of the movement's most prominent leaders. David Barton has appeared at California gatherings and endorsed the group enthusiastically: "One of the things the Bible makes very clear is that pastors should be the leaders in all aspects of community. And that's one of the things Church United helps accomplish is get pastors to lead, not just in the pulpit but out of the pulpit as well."[23]

At the 2018 Road to Majority conference, an annual gathering of religious right activists organized by Ralph Reed's Faith & Freedom Coalition that took place at the Omni Shoreham Hotel in Washington, D.C., Republican representative (now senator) from Tennessee Marsha Blackburn stood on the stage of a large auditorium, backed by an enormous red, white, and blue video screen. "You have all heard the Democrats say they're going to have a big blue wave," she said to the conservatively attired audience members filling the room. "We have to make certain that blue wave goes crashing into the great red wall." With a nod to the West she added, "It looks like they had a little red wall building going on in California this week."

Later at the conference, during a panel on legislative initiatives, Dave Louden, the national field director for the Faith & Freedom Coalition, remarked, "It's incredible the organizing that's happening in California!"

Apart from the obvious electoral advantages that Church United delivers in California, there is something else about Domen that seems to appeal to Christian nationalist leaders across the country. Domen's efforts to build cross-racial unity—even as his group stridently promotes political division—makes him particularly valuable to a movement that must now inoculate itself against charges of racism in the past and in the present.

Another part of the attraction, strangely enough, is Domen's own personal story. The way that Domen wrestles with his sexual demons—not in private but out in the open, in front of makeshift podiums in town squares—makes him the prized embodiment of what the members of his movement might call the "good homosexual." By standing up as living "proof" that those who choose to do so will be redeemed, paradoxically he underwrites the license to revile those who do not. The troubled young man from Yorba Linda has indeed managed to transform his "brokenness" into the source of his own success and that of the movement he so ably represents.

CHAPTER 5

Up from Slavery: The Ideological Origins of Christian Nationalism

O N A HOT afternoon in August 1980, Ronald Reagan strode to the podium at the Reunion Arena in Dallas, Texas, and addressed a crowd of 15,000 pastors and religious activists. President Jimmy Carter had declined the invitation to attend the Religious Roundtable's National Affairs Briefing, so candidate Ronald Reagan had seized the opportunity.

"I know that you can't endorse me," he declared, but "I want you to know that I endorse you and what you are doing."[1] The pastors went wild. Reagan went on to air his personal doubts about the theory of evolution. Then he offered a homespun hypothetical: if he were to be trapped on an island with only one book, he said, he would take the Bible. "All the complex questions facing us at home and abroad," he said, "have their answer in that single book." The performance, according to many political historians, clinched his victory in the election, as conservative Christians abandoned the famously evangelical Carter and put their faith in their newfound Republican savior. "We gave him a ten-minute standing ovation," Paul Weyrich later recalled. "I've never seen anything like it. The whole movement was snowballing by then."[2]

Among those present in the Dallas sports stadium that day was Gary North, an influential thinker in the world of Christian Reconstructionism, a theocratic movement seeking to infuse our society at all levels with a biblical worldview. At Reunion Arena in 1980, however, North was concerned that one name was missing from the roster of speakers.

"We agreed that it was unfortunate that Rousas Rushdoony was not speaking," he observed. "If it weren't for his books, none of us would be here," he said at the time to fellow activist Robert Billings, the former executive director of Jerry Falwell's Moral Majority who was now on staff with the Reagan campaign. "Nobody in the audience understands that," Billings said. "True, but *we* do," North reportedly replied.[3]

Later, North would write, "Rushdoony's writings are the source of many of the core ideas of the New Christian Right, a voting bloc whose unforeseen arrival in American politics in 1980 caught the media by surprise . . . They never did figure out where these ideas were coming from."[4]

A few months after the Dallas event, with Reagan installed in office, Rousas John (R. J.) Rushdoony had the opportunity to make good on the omission. Along with Howard Phillips, Weyrich, and other leaders of the conservative Christian counterrevolution, he showed up at the White House to press the administration to end the outrage of depriving racially segregated religious schools of their tax exemptions.[5]

The band of advisors that gathered in the White House freely acknowledged Rushdoony's foundational role in the new Christian right. Howard Phillips, a right-wing activist with a perch in the Nixon administration, called Rushdoony the "most influential man of the 21st century,"[6] telling author and religious studies professor Julie Ingersoll in 2007 that "the whole Christian conservative political movement had its genesis in Rush."[7] But Rushdoony's close associates were far from alone in their assessment of his contributions. Rushdoony's works were required reading for some classes at Pat Robertson's Regent University and Jerry Falwell's Liberty University, and a standard component of the reading lists among many theologically conservative Protestants.[8] (Several of Falwell's associates later pushed back with an essay critiquing Christian Reconstructionism for advocating positions that some other conservative evangelicals found "scary.")[9] Howard Ahmanson Jr., the reclusive heir to a banking fortune, considered Rushdoony a personal mentor and donated over $700,000 to his organizations.[10] The Christian homeschooling movement, which has played a role in indoctrinating fresh generations in a "biblical" worldview, is explicitly indebted to Rushdoony's work. The Quiverfull movement, which encourages ultraconservative Christian couples to produce as many children as possible, was in large part inspired by Rushdoony.[11] The broadly influential theologian Francis Schaeffer offered Rushdoony "kind words about their mutual work" in a "warm, highly personal 1978 letter," as Ingersoll reports."[12] In a 1990 essay, theoconservative Richard John Neuhaus pointed out that Rushdoony's "theonomy," or idea of a social and political order rooted in "biblical law," has "insinuated itself in circles where people would be not at all comfortable to think of themselves as theonomists" and advised readers that "the distance from Norman Vincent Peale to Rousas John Rushdoony is not so great as may first appear."[13] Christian Reconstructionists were at the table in the early days of the Council for National Policy, which to this day functions as a nexus of power for the right-wing and reactionary Republican machine, and their ideas have left a powerful imprint on "The Family," the secretive yet influential organization of "believers" in politics.[14]

The views of the theologian who lies at the center of so much influence are not hard to state simply and clearly: Rushdoony advocated a return to "biblical" law in America. The Bible, says Rushdoony, commands Christians to exercise absolute dominion over the earth and all of its inhabitants. Women are destined by God to be subordinate to men; men are destined to be ruled by a spiritual aristocracy of right-thinking, orthodox Christian clerics; and the federal government is an agent of evil. Public education, in Rushdoony's reading of the Bible, is a threat to civilization, for it "basically trains women to be men," and represents "primitivism," "chaos," and "a vast 'integration into the void.'"[15] In over thirty books and publications, including *The Messianic Character of American Education* and *The Institutes of Biblical Law*—often hailed as his magnum opus and recommended as one of the Choice Evangelical Books of 1973 by evangelical flagship journal *Christianity Today*—Rushdoony lays it all out in a program that he calls Christian Reconstruction.

There is also little mystery about the historical sources from which Rushdoony drew his own inspiration, as he is careful to lay them out, too. Setting aside the Bible itself, there were the Dutch Reformed Presbyterians whom he studied. A key figure in Rushdoony's personal development was Cornelius Van Til, who maintained that rationality is possible only on the presupposition that the Bible is true—which is to say, in plainer language, that the "Christian worldview" is the only legitimate basis for rational thought. Van Til and Rushdoony both also drew on Abraham Kuyper, also a Dutch Reformed theologian known for his claim that Christianity has sole legitimate authority over all aspects of human life. "There is not a square inch in the whole domain of our human existence over which Christ, who is Sovereign over all, does not cry, Mine!" said Kuyper.[16] But two other intellectual traditions appear to have played critical roles in the development of Rushdoony's thought and expose the real implications of his commitment to radically conservative theology. One is the work of America's redoubtable band of proslavery theologians. Another comes from the theologians who labored on pro-capitalist, libertarian responses to the specter of the New Deal.[17]

To be clear, the Christian nationalist movement is large and diverse in its specific theologies. Many of its representatives know very little about R. J. Rushdoony, and others take pains to distance themselves from him.[18] Some of his extreme positions, such as the idea that homosexuals, blasphemers, adulterers, incorrigible teenagers, and practitioners of "witchcraft" are all worthy of the death penalty, have been loudly repudiated by many conservative religious leaders. Yet it is difficult to understand the ideological origins and structure of Christian nationalism in America today without taking into account Rushdoony's ideas. Just as in that pivotal 1980 conference that put Ronald Reagan on the road to the White House, Rushdoony remains an unacknowledged leader of the movement, a sage whose ideas continue to speak long after he has been silenced.

Few thinkers invent new ways of being out of whole cloth, and Rushdoony was not among them. He himself understood this well and celebrated the fact. His purpose was to rescue a lost cause, not to fabricate it. Although he leaned on many role models from the past, one of the most revealing of his acknowledged antecedents is arguably Robert Lewis Dabney, a Presbyterian minister and theologian born in Virginia in 1820.

To those who knew him as a young man, Robert Lewis Dabney "was even then the most Godly man they had ever met." In old age his students revered him as "St. John."[19] By most accounts, he was generous, passionate, considerate, and a thunderous presence in any church or lecture hall.[20] He dedicated his life to serving the Presbyterian church and to fighting for the rights of true believers.

The beleaguered people to whose cause Dabney rallied were, more precisely, his "oppressed" white brethren of Virginia and neighboring states to the south. Their oppression consisted in, among other things, having to pay taxes to support a "pretended education to the brats of black paupers."[21] These unjustly persecuted white people, as Dabney saw it, were also forced to contend with "the atheistic and infidel theories of physical science."[22] He had two sciences in mind—geology and evolutionary biology—"the one attacking the recent origin of man, the flood, etc., the other presuming to construct a creation without a creator."[23] The malevolent tormentors of the wholesome white taxpayers of America were the secular, liberal elites who dominated national political life. Though hardly a man of the people by temperament—he referred to democracy as "mobocracy"—Dabney was keenly sensitive to the realities of electoral politics.[24] "If . . . the voters among these [faithful Christians] would go together to the polls, they would turn the scales of every election," he declared.[25]

In the first half of his career, before the Civil War, he sermonized loudly about the "righteousness" of slavery and argued that opposing slavery was "tantamount to rejecting Christianity."[26] In this respect he was an unexceptional figure in his time. Upon the outbreak of the war, Dabney joined his fellow Southern Presbyterians in resolving in conference: "We hesitate not to affirm that it is the peculiar mission of the Southern Church to conserve the institution of slavery, and to make it a blessing both to master and slave."[27]

Certainly, many American ecclesial voices rejected slavery. John Wesley, the founder of the Methodist movement, abhorred slavery. The first Methodists in America passed resolutions condemning it, although as both the church and slavery expanded in the first half of the nineteenth century, much of the Methodists' opposition to the practice was sidelined and in the deep South turned into direct support for the institution. Other clerical

voices opposing slavery included ministers such as Reverend Calvin Fair-
bank, who is believed to have aided the escape of dozens of slaves; the
Presbyterian minister Charles Grandison Finney and his disciple Theodore
Dwight Weld; and John Leland, a Baptist minister. In Boston's West
Church, Charles Lowell, a staunch abolitionist, ended the practice of segregated seating, and prior to the Emancipation Proclamation the church
became a safe house on the Underground Railroad. Prominent abolitionist
clerics in England included William Wilberforce and Thomas Clarkson,
who hosted Frederick Douglass on his first UK visit.

But a preponderance of representatives of major American denominations of the time had made their peace with slavery, and either conscien-
tiously refrained from making any judgment that would upset the established
order, or supported it outright. A leading Baptist of Georgia declared, "Both
Christianity and slavery are from heaven; both are blessings to humanity;
both are to be perpetuated to the end of time."[28] The Georgia Annual
Conference of the Methodist Episcopal Church unanimously resolved "that
slavery, as it exists in the United States, is not a moral evil."[29] The Episcopalians of South Carolina found slavery to be "marked by every evidence of
divine approval."[30] The Reverend J. C. Postell of South Carolina stated that
slavery "is supported by the Bible ... [T]he fact that slavery is of divine
appointment would be proof enough with the Christian that it cannot be a
moral evil," adding that it "is a judicial visitation."[31] The Charleston Union
Presbytery resolved that "the holding of slaves, so far from being a sin in the
sight of God, is nowhere condemned in his holy word."[32]

Contrary to popular myth, many representatives of the churches of the
North went along with Dabney's program. Reverend Wilbur Fisk, the
Methodist president of Wesleyan University in Connecticut, agreed that
"the general rule of Christianity *not only permits*, but, in supposable circumstances *enjoins the continuance of the master's authority*. The New Testament
enjoins obedience upon the slave as an obligation *due* to a present *rightful*
authority."[33] Moses Stuart, the top Bible scholar at Andover in Massachusetts, applauded the sentiment: "The precepts of the New Testament ...
beyond all question, recognize the existence of slavery."[34] The president of
Dartmouth College, Nathan Lord, added that any criticism of slavery is
"dishonorable to God, and subversive of his government."[35] John Henry

Hopkins, the Episcopal bishop of Vermont, who published a tract and a lengthy book defending slavery, penned a letter to the abolitionist bishop of Pennsylvania "to prove, *from the Bible*, that in the relation of master and slave there was necessarily no sin whatever."[36] The founder of Yale's Divinity School and the leading Presbyterian theologian at Princeton concurred.[37]

The identification of religious authority with the perpetuation of the institution of slavery reflected something far more important than mere adaptation to the largest concentration of economic power in the nation—although it was that, too. At a deeper level, it was part of a counterrevolutionary response to the perceived liberal and irreligious excesses associated with the American Revolution. The period around the American Revolution was, by most accounts, a low point for fundamentalism and a high one for freedom of thought and what was considered heresy. In a letter to Dr. Benjamin Waterhouse dated June 26, 1822, Thomas Jefferson famously predicted that all Americans would shortly convert to Unitarianism, and Thomas Paine went even further, suggesting that they would abandon all traditional religions in favor of a pure deism, or religion of nature and reason.[38] Yet those prognostications missed the mark by approximately 180 degrees. In the decades following the Revolution, an evangelical surge rolled across the landscape, sweeping aside the Unitarians and other liberal religionists and installing hardline Presbyterian, Methodist, and Baptist sects that, while often popular in their rhetoric and methods, promoted literalism and absolute submission to authority in their doctrines.

In that wave of fundamentalism, two forces played decisive roles. One was the emergence in the early years of the republic of a hard-core theological establishment, centered chiefly in the Northeast, radically opposed to both religious liberalism and political liberalism. Led by men such as Reverend Timothy Dwight, the Yale leader who came to be known as "Federalist Pope of Connecticut," these theologians condemned the French Revolution along with the godless nature of American democracy. The other force was the institution of slavery itself, which benefited from and in turn promoted the values of biblical literalism and absolute submission to authority. Borrowing the language that the Federalist theologians developed in their assaults on liberal religionists and supporters of popular democracy, the new generation of leaders promoted a theological vision that emphasized the divine origins of the existing order, which invariably involved domination and subordination, always of men over women, and frequently of white people over Black people, too.

True, a number of the activists who took up abolitionism, including Reformed Baptist minister Charles W. Denison and Universalist (later Unitarian) minister Adin Ballou, did so in the name of religion and from pulpits. But, as Frederick Douglass acidly observed at the time, these religious abolitionists tended to be a distinctly disempowered minority in their own denominations. Looking back, Douglass noted, "A few heterodox, and still fewer orthodox ministers, filling humble pulpits and living upon small salaries, have espoused the cause of the slave; but the ministers of high standing—the $5,000 divines—were almost to a man on the side of Slavery."[39] At their churches, he added, "so far from being rebuked as an offender, the slaveholder was received and welcomed as a saint." Furthermore, by the end of the antebellum period, according to Douglass, some number of its leading abolitionists (such as the Presbyterian minister Robert Finley) were also committed to colonization schemes, which sought to "solve" the problem of slavery by "repatriating" freed Black people to the west coast of Africa.[40]

Meanwhile, many of the most famous of the abolitionists—Douglass himself, along with William Lloyd Garrison, Theodore Parker, and Gerrit Smith—had moved in the direction of religious heterodoxy, for which they were routinely denounced as heretics; leading orthodox ministers in the North and South repeatedly condemned abolitionism as a breeding ground for "infidelity" and—just as bad—feminism. Douglass famously supported women's suffrage. Gerrit Smith's letter in support for women's rights was read aloud at the opening of the Rochester Women's Rights Convention of 1848. Theodore Parker delivered an 1853 sermon castigating the isolation of women in domestic roles. Charles Grandison Finney's encouragement of female speakers at prayer meetings drew the condemnation of conservatives, who described his gatherings as "promiscuous assemblies." And Adin Ballou founded a religion-based commune committed to women's rights and spiritualism—which only added to his infamy.

"Southern clergymen," according to the author and historian Mitchell Snay, "emphatically countered that slavery was sanctioned in the Bible."[41]

James Henley Thornwell of South Carolina, Dabney's brother-in-arms in the Southern Presbyterian Church, summed up the wisdom of the age well: "The parties in this conflict are not merely abolitionists and slaveholders—they are atheists, socialists, communists, red republicans, jacobins, on the one side, and the friends of order and regulated freedom on the other."[42]

Perhaps the most important aspect of the proslavery theology that Dabney so ably embodied—or at any rate the one that far outlasted its explicit support for the enslavement of human beings—was its fusion of religion with a racialized form of nationalism. Indeed, Christian nationalism came of age in the American slave republic. In the eyes of proslavery theologians, the United States was the "Redeemer Nation"—a "nation which God's own hand hath planted, and on which He has, therefore, peculiar and special claims," as one Alabama cleric put it.[43] When the United States was divided by Civil War, God's hand unmistakably settled on the Confederate States of America, which was understood to be waging a holy war on behalf of Christian civilization against the impious Union.

In the aftermath of the war, even as the formal institution of slavery ceased to exist, the legend of the redeemer nation persisted. And Robert Lewis Dabney was right there to keep the dream alive. In hopes of sabotaging efforts at reconstructing the South as part of a universal, multiracial republic, he trained his polemical guns on "the Yankee theory of popular state education." He asserted that public education was "pagan" and "connected by regular, logical sequence with legalized prostitution and the dissolution of the conjugal tie."[44] Predicting that the growing women's rights movement would "destroy Christianity and civilization," he thundered, "women are here consigned to a social subordination, and expressly excluded from ruling offices, on grounds of their sex, and a divine ordination based by God upon a transaction that happened nearly six thousand years ago!"[45] The woman was "'first in her transgression,'" he helpfully explained, for which God rightly laid upon her "subordination to her husband and the sorrows peculiar to motherhood."[46] And he just couldn't give up on slavery. As late as 1888 Dabney published an article in the *Presbyterian Quarterly* titled "Anti-Biblical Theories of Rights," in which he explained that "the relation of master and bondman was sanctified by the administration of a divine sacrament."[47] God himself "predicted the rise of the institution of domestic bondage as the penalty and remedy for the bad morals of those subjected to it," he said, and "God protects property in slaves, exactly as any other kind of property, in the sacred Decalogue itself." To argue otherwise, he said, is a "hurricane of anti-Christian attack."[48]

It seems unlikely that the typical American today would regard Robert Lewis Dabney as an inspirational leader. But R. J. Rushdoony was far from a typical American. Indeed, Rushdoony drew on his reading of Dabney (as well as Dabney's admirer A. A. Hodge) and his fellow proslavery theologians as he shaped the ideas that supplied an ideological cornerstone of Christian nationalism today.

Perhaps the most important thing to know about Rushdoony is that he was born in 1916 to Armenian immigrants who had narrowly escaped the genocide, in which as many as 1.5 million Armenians were murdered by Turks of the Ottoman Empire. Rushdoony's father, who founded the Armenian Martyrs Presbyterian Church in Kingsburg, California, ministered to a community of fellow Armenian refugees, who agonized and grieved as letters from relatives back home came to a standstill. As R. J. Rushdoony's son Mark Rushdoony commented, "My father grew up with a very keen awareness that the Armenian people had been massacred, their culture extinguished, and their history rewritten because they were Christians in a non-Christian culture."[49]

As Mark Rushdoony tells the story, his father overheard a conversation among a group of older Armenian men in the late 1950s. "They were lamenting the course they saw America was on and issued a condemnation, which given their experiences was stronger than any vulgarity. They said America was becoming like Turkey," Mark said. Amid the ever-present awareness of genocide, Rushdoony developed the conviction that only absolute submission to the word of God could save the human world from chaos.

"In Armenia, there was no neutral ground between Islam and Christianity," Rushdoony wrote in 1997. "And I came to realize there is no neutral ground anywhere."[50]

Rushdoony left his family home in Kingsburg, California, and made his way to college at the University of California, Berkeley. He did not fit in. Advised to further his education by reading the classics, Rushdoony recoiled in horror as he perused Homer, Shakespeare, and the rest of the canon. He later called this "the ugliest experience of my life." The books he read were "humanistic garbage," devoid of wisdom. The ancient classics were, as he later said, "classics of depravity. Classics of degenerate cultures. What they offer at their best is evil."[51]

Rushdoony emerged from Berkeley with all the distinctive features of his intellectual persona in place: a resolutely binary form of thought that classified all things into one of two absolutes; a craving for order; and a loathing for the secular world and secular education in particular—all of which explains much of his attraction to the works of Robert Lewis Dabney. While the rest of the world may have seen in the proslavery ideologue a racist, a sexist, and a partisan of enslavement, Rushdoony "applauded Dabney's defense of slavery."[52] Indeed, he and many of his fellow Reconstructionists regarded Dabney as prophetic. Rushdoony reprinted and disseminated some of Dabney's works through Chalcedon Foundation newsletters and lectures, as well as through his publishing company, Ross House Books.[53] He found himself agreeing with Dabney that the Union victory was "a defeat for Christian orthodoxy."[54] In Rushdoony's mind, Dabney's great adversaries, the abolitionists, were the archetypes of the anti-Christian rebels—the liberals, the communists, the secularists, the advocates of women's rights—who continued to wreak havoc on the modern world. As his fellow Reconstructionist C. Gregg Singer put it, proslavery theologians including Dabney, Thornwell, and their contemporaries "properly read abolitionism as a revolt against the biblical conception of society and a revolt against divine sovereignty in human affairs."[55] Rushdoony himself concluded, "Abolitionist leaders showed more hate than love on the whole."[56]

Rushdoony's vision of a civic order rooted in hierarchy and deriving its legitimacy from its claim to represent an authentically Christian nation forms a central part of an extraordinary revisionist account of American history—an account that would soon insert itself into the heart of the modern Christian nationalist movement. In Rushdoony's telling, it was not the intention of America's founders to establish a nonsectarian representative democracy. He characterized the American political system as "a development of Christian feudalism."[57] The First Amendment, he argues, aimed to establish freedom "not *from* religion but *for* religion"[58]—a phrase widely parroted by Christian nationalists today. "The Constitution was designed to *perpetuate* a Christian order," he said.[59] For Rushdoony, the passage of the Fourteenth Amendment, which included a guarantee that all citizens receive equal protection under the law, "began the court's recession from its conception of America as a Christian country."[60] Now the job was to redeem America from its commitment to godless humanism.

Rushdoony's admiration for southern Christian orthodoxy was such that he adopted a forgiving attitude toward certain forms of slavery. In books such as *Politics of Guilt and Pity* and *The Institutes of Biblical Law*, which is essentially an 890-page disquisition on "the heresy of democracy" and the first of a three-volume series under the same title, he makes the case that "the move from Africa to America was a vast increase of freedom for the Negro, materially and spiritually as well as personally."[61]

"Some people are by nature slaves and will always be so," Rushdoony muses, and the law requires that a slave "recognize his position and accept it with grace."[62]

Rushdoony seemed to believe that involuntary slavery is justified in certain instances. "A man who abuses his freedom to steal can be sold into slavery," he continues, then adds, "State supported and controlled education is theft." And he calls "the claim of ownership to the lives of citizens" by a "humanist state" slavery, too. "In a century's time, the Negro exchanged slavery to an individual for slavery to the State," he writes. "In both conditions there are advantages, but both constitute slavery."[63]

Rushdoony did not agitate for the literal enslavement of Black Americans in his time. But as with his fellow travelers in the dominionist movement, his fascination with proslavery theology was no passing fancy. The idea that the United States is a Redeemer Nation, chosen by God; that it is tasked with becoming an orthodox Christian republic in which women are subordinate to men, education is in the hands of conservative Christians, and no one pays taxes to support Black people; that at some point in the past the nation deviated horribly from its mission and fell under the control of atheist, communist, and/or liberal elites—the stuff of proslavery theology was the life of Rushdoony's political thought. And it remained a cornerstone of Christian nationalism even while Rushdoony's successors disavowed or simply forgot about the origins of their interpretation of the creed, and long after they had erased their earlier hostility to abolitionism from history and convinced themselves that they were the heroes in the story of emancipation.

Some of Rushdoony's successors, as a matter of fact, did not feel the need to disguise their debt to him and his ruminations on "biblical" slavery. One is Douglas ("Doug") Wilson, the Moscow, Idaho, preacher, slavery apologist, and a founder of New Saint Andrews College. "On its Web site, the college treats Rushdoony and Dabney as foundational thinkers on the order of Plato and Aristotle," according to the Southern Poverty Law Center.[64] Doug Phillips, Howard Phillips's son and former president of the now-defunct Vision Forum Ministries, openly embraced Dabney's work and called him a "prophet," too.[65]

Perhaps the most telling example comes from David Barton, whose efforts to reframe our constitutional republic as a Christian nationalist enterprise are at the center of so many of the movement's cultural and legislative initiatives today. Though perhaps not in a formal sense a Reconstructionist, Barton echoes or dances around many of Rushdoony's defining ideas, even on the question of slavery. When it came time to edify his followers on the topic of slavery in the Bible, Barton could have chosen to cite any number of secondary sources. He chose to cite Rushdoony extensively.

In a paper titled "The Bible, Slavery, and America's Founders," posted on the WallBuilders website, Barton argues that "in light of the Scriptures, we cannot say that slavery, in a broad and general sense, is sin. But this brief look at the Biblical slave laws does reveal how fallen man's example of slavery has violated God's laws."[66]

In order to make the case, he relies heavily on Rushdoony's *Institutes of Biblical Law*. He quotes Rushdoony to point out that "Deuteronomy 23:15.16 makes very clear. Biblical law permits voluntary slavery because it recognizes that some people are not able to maintain a position of independence." He draws on Rushdoony to make the further claim that slavery is something of a lifestyle choice: "To attach themselves voluntarily to a capable man and to serve him, protected by the law, is thus a legitimate way of life, although a lesser one." Barton also borrows from Rushdoony in enumerating the freedoms that biblical slaves relinquished in making their lifestyle decisions: "'If his master gives him a wife, and she bears him sons or daughters, the wife and her children shall belong to her master, and he shall go out alone.' (Ex. 21:3–4)."

Perhaps recognizing that all this sounds rather unpleasant for the enslaved person, Barton once again turns to his preferred guide to explain why it all makes sense: "Rushdoony comments: 'The bondservant, however, could not have the best of both worlds, the world of freedom and the world of servitude . . . If he married while a bondservant, or a slave, he knew that in doing so he was abandoning either freedom or his family. He either remained permanently a slave with his family and had his ear pierced as a sign of subordination (like a woman), or he left his family. If he walked out and left his family, he could, if he earned enough, redeem his family from bondage. The law here is humane and also unsentimental.'"

Where Barton strikes out on his own, it is to take a swipe at modern, liberal government as a form of slavery, a gesture that Rushdoony surely would have endorsed. "Since sinful man tends to live in bondage, different forms of slavery have replaced the more obvious system of past centuries," Barton explains. "The state has assumed the role of master for many, providing aid and assistance, and with it more and more control, to those unable to protect themselves."

Among apologists for Christian nationalism today, the favored myth is that the movement represents an extension of the abolitionism of the nineteenth century and perhaps of the civil rights movement of the twentieth century, too. Many antiabortion activists self-consciously identify themselves as the new abolitionists. Mainstream conservatives who lament that the evangelicals who form Trump's most fervent supporters have "lost their way" suggest that they have betrayed their roots in the movements that fought for the abolition of slavery and the end of discrimination. But the truth is that today's Christian nationalism did not emerge out of the religious movement that opposed such rigid hierarchies. It came from the one that promoted them—with the Bible in one hand and a whip in the other.

*　*　*

In Rushdoony's debt to proslavery theology, it is also possible to glimpse the outlines of another cornerstone of the Christian nationalist project he helped create. The defeat of the orthodox side in the Civil War, Rushdoony realized, "paved the way for the rise of an unorthodox Social Gospel."[67] The "Social Gospel," as Rushdoony understood it, is the mistaken belief that Christianity would have us use the power of government to reform society along lines that conform with Jesus's teachings about loving thy neighbor. This unwanted fruit of defeat in the Civil War, Rushdoony came to think, blossomed into the next great enemy of Christian civilization. The enemy was, in a word, the New Deal. And so it was to the defeat of this poisonous heresy that Rushdoony now turned his attention.

It wasn't easy being a conservative in the 1930s and 1940s. The Great Depression and the New Deal, following so closely upon seeming triumphs of the 1920s, seemed like a direct refutation of the conservative vision. Everywhere government seemed to have the upper hand, and socialism or worse loomed on the horizon. Those who remained faithful to the cause of freedom and private property now faced the onus of explaining why history had strayed so far from the correct course. A small but determined number accepted a still greater challenge: How could they, now a scorned minority, regain control and steer the ship of history back to conservative principles?

Fortunately, the times brought forth some extraordinary role models to serve as guides. One such figure was James W. Fifield Jr., an energetic Congregational minister who thought he had the answer to the problem of the age. To combat the horrors of the New Deal, Fifield proposed to energize the nation's Protestant pastors. In 1935 he cofounded and led the Mobilization for Spiritual Ideals, also known as Spiritual Mobilization. His ambition was to broadcast from pulpits and radio stations a simple message: business has a friend in Jesus, and government is the enemy of God and man. He had a theology to back it up, but it was uncomplicated. The welfare state violated several of the Ten Commandments, but especially the Eighth. When New Dealers used the power of government to restrain business and take from the rich to give to the poor, he argued, this was a clear violation of God's word: Thou shalt not steal.

Fifield's main ideological target was the "Social Gospel," which he took to be a mainspring of the New Deal's evils. As the preceding Gilded Age had come to its bumpy end, a number of religious activists had allied themselves with progressive activists to support various social and economic reforms. The movement arguably reached its apogee in William Jennings Bryan's failed presidential campaign of 1896, but it remained a threat in the more liberal churches of the land. In Fifield's mind, the Social Gospel was just another word for communism, and it had to be stopped.

Fifield understood that in a world that had just witnessed catastrophic economic collapse where government had indeed proved vital in rescuing workers, his views would not command immediate support. How would he make this unpopular doctrine appealing?

The secret sauce was money. With a talent for whispering into the ears of plutocrats, Fifield secured major funding for his activities from the moguls of the Sun Oil Company, Chrysler, and General Motors, among others. These corporate sponsors expected, and received, a popular theology that lionized business and demonized labor unions and in general anything that required government to work on behalf of the people. Fifield's methods had ample precedent in American history: it was Rockefeller money that sent baseball player turned evangelist Billy Sunday into the coal mines of the West Virginia hills to preach the sinfulness of striking in 1920.[68]

While Fifield and his clerical allies were working the spiritual angle against the modern welfare state, a new group of libertarian economic thinkers emerged that shared their fear and loathing of government, if not necessarily their religion. Members of the Austrian school of economics, led by Ludwig von Mises, Friedrich Hayek, and their American popularizer Henry Hazlitt, warned that the modern welfare state would soon overwhelm the free market and put humanity on the road to serfdom.[69] They denounced labor unions, public education, redistributive programs, and other governmental interventions in the free market, which they believed would produce peace, prosperity, and the solution to all major social problems if left free to its own devices.

Rushdoony found it all very thrilling. He admired the publications that came out of Fifield's groups and their allies. All they needed, he thought, was a little more theological sophistication and economic firepower. He was also strongly attracted to the libertarians, but in his view they could use a firmer grounding in theology. Extending on Fifield's religion of the Eighth Commandment, Rushdoony began churning out doctrinal works arguing that "*capitalism is supremely a product of Christianity.*" On the other hand, "socialism is organized larceny; like inflation, it takes from the haves to give to the have-nots."[70]

The field of education was the setting for perhaps the most fruitful marriage of libertarian economics and Rushdoony's style of religious ultra-orthodoxy. Both lines of thought dreaded the specter of government involvement in the education of children, if for subtly different reasons. But Rushdoony understood much more clearly than the libertarians the link between this anti-public education agenda and the old, proslavery theology. In 1963 he laid it all out in his 410-page anti-public education screed, *The Messianic Character of American Education.*

Justice in education, for Rushdoony as for Dabney, was not merely a matter of exempting (white) taxpayers from the burden of supporting secular indoctrination. It was also about laying the foundations for the reconstruction of a theonomic society: one whose laws are based on what Christian nationalists today might call a "biblical worldview." Presbyterian theologian A. A. Hodge, who was an avid admirer of Dabney and who Rushdoony admired in turn, delivered a lecture, which was published in 1887 after his death, painting "government schools" as "the most appalling enginery for the propagation of anti-Christian and atheistic unbelief, and of antisocial nihilistic ethics, individual, social and political, which this sin-rent world has ever seen."[71] Citing Hodge and his predecessors directly,[72] Rushdoony amplified the message, arguing that the "government school" has "leveled its guns at God and family."[73] "Liberal education is inevitably pluralistic," he lamented. "It would follow that Southerners are clearly wrong in resisting integration of white and Negro pupils."[74] The implication here was that they were, in fact, right to have resisted integration. In Rush-doony's view, there was nothing wrong in principle with segregation.

Although the immensely influential pastor and radio evangelist D. James Kennedy distanced himself from some aspects of Rushdoony's Reconstruc-tionism, Kennedy's Coral Ridge Ministries broadcast network hosted Rushdoony as a guest in the early 1980s, and Kennedy's tirades against public education are nearly identical in language and content to Rush-doony's.[75] In a sermon titled "A Godly Education," later turned into a widely distributed pamphlet, Kennedy thundered, "The infusion of an atheistic, amoral, evolutionary, socialistic, one-world, anti-American system of educa-tion in our public schools, has indeed become such that if it had been done by an enemy, it would be considered an act of war."[76] Disparaging public education pioneer Horace Mann as "a Unitarian," Kennedy declared, "The modern, public education system was begun in an effort to deliver children from the Christian religion."[77] After Rushdoony's death, Gary North, who had developed a close relationship with the politician Ron Paul, dutifully produced the Ron Paul Curriculum, a homeschooling program with an emphasis on "the Biblical principle of self-government and personal respon-sibility which is also the foundation of the free market economy."[78]

"Let us be blunt about it: we must use the doctrine of religious liberty," North once wrote, "to gain independence for Christian schools until we train up a generation of people who know that there is no religious neutrality, no neutral law, no neutral education, and no neutral civil govern-ment. Then they will get busy in constructing a Bible-based social, political, and religious order which finally denies the religious liberty of the enemies of God."[79]

Libertarians like economist Milton Friedman sometimes expressed dismay when their school privatization schemes were used as a cover to fund segregated religious academies. Friedman took pains to insist that he abhorred racism and opposed race-based segregation laws.[80] But he also opposed federal laws that prohibited discrimination, believing that unfet-tered free markets would magically solve the problem. In conversation with me, Gary North, clearly determined to allow no one to stand to his right, referred to Milton Friedman as "that Communist."

Rushdoony emphatically agreed with the immortal principle articulated by Dabney himself: "Americans, taken as we find them, who do not get their moral restraints from the Bible, have none. Training which does not base duty on Christianity is, for us, practically immoral."[81] The same message spills out of the works of Christian nationalist leaders today.

Borrowing from other anti-New Deal writers such as Albert Jay Nock and mixing in language from the Bible, Rushdoony articulated the doctrine of "the remnant." When history takes a wrong turn, he says, God leaves behind a "remnant" of true believers, tasked with guarding the light in dark times and then retaking civilization—or, as he called it, "the task of reconstruction"[82]—thus bringing about the term Christian Reconstruction. The job of the Reconstructionists, according to Rushdoony, is to remain faithful no matter what. "History has never been dominated by majorities, but only by dedicated minorities who stand unconditionally on their faith," he says.

Libertarian economics came to dominate Christian nationalism. Gary North published a book, *Christian Economics in One Lesson*, that was selfconsciously modeled on Henry Hazlitt's libertarian bestseller, *Economics in One Lesson*. Jerry Falwell, among others, took to tossing around quotes from Milton Friedman and attacking labor unions, redistributive policies like food stamps and Medicaid, and government regulation.[83] The fact that members of his congregation often depended on these same government programs did not seem to trouble him at all.

Ultimately Rushdoony's contribution had less to do with the originality of his ideas—they were in large measure borrowed—than with the clarity and forcefulness with which they were expressed and elaborated upon. To his followers, his moral certainty was inspiring. To the future leaders of the movement, it could prove embarrassing. To much of the rest of the world, it was the kind of clarity that chills the blood. To those who knew him personally, it all came down to a certain paradox. The father of six children, five biological and one adopted, Rushdoony appears to have enjoyed warm relations with his kids (of whom he gained custody after divorcing their mother, Arda) and was welcomed in many groups as a thoughtful, charismatic leader. Yet, in his writings, he reimagined a world in which a particular understanding of the Christian religion dominates every aspect of life, and those who deviate from certain "biblical" orthodoxies could be condemned to death. Many of Rushdoony's ideas justify the politics of today—perhaps in ways that even he didn't intend.

The fusion of hyper-capitalist ideology with hyper-Calvinist theology, purveyed by the likes of Fifield and chiseled in the granite of Rushdoony's ponderous works, secured the financial future of Christian nationalism.

America's plutocrats understood that they had a friend on the Christian right. Just as the moguls of the 1930s and '40s flocked to Fifield, a number of their heirs and successors attached themselves to evangelical leaders who hewed to this brand of thinking. Although few plutocratic families linked themselves in such obvious ways with Rushdoony himself (Howard Ahmanson Jr.'s onetime admiration for Rushdoony was not shared by other members of his clan), others put their money behind figures like D. James Kennedy, who carried, in more palatable packaging, many of the same messages as Rushdoony: that any attempts by government to interfere with the accumulation of great riches was equivalent to theft, and what the people really needed was not equitable tax policy or accessible health care or quality public education but religion.

Sometime in the late 1970s, observers of the American religious land-scape came to a sudden, shocking realization: fundamentalism was back. The revival came as a surprise, because the keepers of popular opinion had formed the firm impression that old-fashioned literalism was a dying taste, doomed to fall behind in the march of science and progress. The defeat of the anti-evolution ideologues in the Scopes "Monkey Trial" of 1925, it was thought, marked the final step in fundamentalism's humiliating exit from the modern world. The secularizing forces that elevated liberal theologians such as Reinhold Niebuhr and Paul Tillich in the 1950s seemed to culmi-nate with *Time* magazine's 1966 scandalous cover story, "Is God Dead?"

Yet, by the 1970s, even as nonbelief continued to capture the headlines and the total number of religious believers drifted slightly downward, the proportion between liberal religionists and their conservative brethren began to shift. With the election of Jimmy Carter in 1976, it suddenly became clear that millions of Americans—as many as 50 million, some claimed—identified as "born-again" Christians, and millions more aligned themselves with an increasingly austere form of Catholicism. What's more, ultraconservative Americans were starting to organize at the polls and vote their religion.

Although the return of old-line religion struck many observers as a novelty, in retrospect it is clear that the new orthodoxy followed the pattern set by the counterrevolutionary revival of the preceding century. The tech-nology in the early days was the revival tent and the empty cornfield; in mid-century it was the radio and television set; and now we may add the cell phone, computer screen, and the megachurch or local outpost of a large parachurch network. But the reactionary character of the message, considered apart from specific policy agendas, was remarkable in its similarities. Then as now, the movement drew its energy from the needs and anxieties of a mass of struggling Americans—even as it allied itself with concentrations of economic power in its time. Just as in the days of proslavery theology, the contradictions were almost too obvious to be seen. Poor whites were, apart from enslaved people themselves, the system's greatest losers, and yet, with the guidance of men like Dabney, they joined with its loudest supporters. The enemy, all agreed, was some form of godlessness, and redemption always came by "reclaiming" the nation.

Just as the activity on the ground fell into a familiar pattern, so, too, did the ideas that accompanied the movement. A surprising number of leaders found themselves making sense of the new world with ideas that had ample theological precedent in Rushdoony and his mentors and predecessors.

They rediscovered a supposedly Christian founding of the American republic and detected a plot to subvert the nation's destiny through secularization. And once again they invented a plan for redemption that involved taking the country "back" to a time that never existed. As the movement grew, new writers and theologians emerged and struck off on their own—only to end up on the ground Rushdoony and his forebears had tilled.

In recent years, it seems, more of Rushdoony's admirers have felt emboldened to step out of the closet. In a 2018 blog post, Watchmen on the Wall, the Family Research Council's alliance of an estimated 25,000 pastors, characterized Rushdoony as a "powerful advocate for the Christian and home-school movements across America" who "challenged Christian leaders of his day to stand on biblical truth in the public square" before quoting extensively from his *Institutes of Biblical Law*.[84] Other leaders have self-consciously distanced themselves from Rushdoony. They reject guilt by association with his philosophies and have done their best to pooh-pooh "alarmism" over his ideas. And yet, Julie Ingersoll aptly observes, "little slivers of Rushdoony's work seem to be everywhere."[85] In the drive for home-schooling and the privatization of public education; in the providential history of Christian nation mythologizers; in their insistence that public officials be guided by a "biblical worldview"; in the unabashed commitment to the subordination of women, part of the order and structure of the universe as God intended; in the fusion of the Bible with libertarian economics— even in their arguments for gun rights and against universal health care— today's Christian nationalists follow the logic, if not necessarily the theology, laid down by Rushdoony.

Although his heirs pursued their own theologies, and in cases explicitly disagreed with him on certain doctrinal matters, an astonishing number settled on one version or another of dominionism, or the fundamental idea that right-thinking Christians should assume power in all spheres of life. C. Peter Wagner, father figure to the New Apostolic Reformation,[86] whose leaders consider themselves to be apostles and prophets, promoted a particularly influential variety of dominionism widely referred to as the "7 Mountain Mandate." Once in the shadows of the religious right, the movement appears to be approaching the mainstream. Seven Mountains dominionist promoter Lance Wallnau was given a featured speaking slot at the 2018 Values Voter Summit, and other prominent speakers at the summit peppered their presentations with references to the "mountains of culture." In his book *Dominion! How Kingdom Action Can Change the World*, Wagner traces the ideas and their genealogy with admirable clarity: "The practical theology that best builds a foundation under social transformation is dominion theology, sometimes called 'Kingdom now.' Its history can be traced back through R.J. Rushdoony and Abraham Kuyper to John Calvin."[87]

Gary North put his finger on the deeper forces at work when he observed that "the ideas of the Reconstructionists have penetrated into Protestant circles that for the most part are unaware of the original sources of the theological ideas that are beginning to transform them."[88] Then again, perhaps some of those circles are aware of the sources of their ideas after all. "Though we hide their books under the bed, we read them just the same," as one person put it to Michael J. McVicar, author of *Christian Reconstruction: R. J. Rushdoony and American Religious Conservatism*.

The evolution of the conservative movement over the past forty years has exposed the inner truth about its origins. "Evangelicals have traded Ronald Reagan's gospel-inspired depiction of America as a 'shining city on a hill' for

Trump's dark vision of 'American carnage,'" writes the journalist Sarah Posner, a reporting fellow with Type Investigations, in a 2017 article for the *New Republic*. "And in doing so, they have returned the religious right to its own origins—as a movement founded to maintain the South's segregationist 'way of life.'"[89]

In the final analysis, Rushdoony and his Reconstructionists were effects of history, too, not its causes. The new nationalists rediscovered—or simply reinvented—their ideas because they answered to a logic that has much deeper roots in American history. Slavery may have ended with the Thirteenth Amendment, but the system of economic exploitation through racial division lived on, and the proslavery theology that sustained it in an earlier time did not simply vanish. The hierarchies that arose in the Gilded Age hit some roadblocks in the progressive era, but that hardly stopped plutocrats from enlisting new champions of theological legitimation. Christian nationalism exploits and intensifies inequality, and dominionism is its logical end point and the actual engine of the so-called culture wars. Its ideas persist not on account of any clandestine texts or secret cabals but because the forces that produced them remain very much at work in shaping the movement today.

The many paradoxes and contradictions of Christian nationalism make sense when they are taken out of the artificial "culture war" framing and placed within the history of the antidemocratic reaction in the United States. To any outside observer, it must seem odd that Christian nationalists loudly reject "government" as a matter of principle even as they seek government power to impose their religious vision on the rest of society. America's slaveholders, too, revealed a similar inconsistency when they championed "states' rights" and at the same time demanded the assistance of the federal government in catching runaway slaves and defending the slave system. Plenty of other political movements, including progressive movements, might say that they like government when it does what they like, and they dislike it when it doesn't. Among Rushdoony's successors, it would become clear that what they actually oppose is simply secular, democratic government, whereas what they invariably support is religious or theocratic government. At bottom, they agree with Rushdoony that there is no neutrality: the state either answers to God or it answers to something worse.

Perhaps the most obvious paradox of Christian nationalism is that it preaches love but everywhere practices intolerance, even hate. Like Rushdoony the man, members of the movement are often kind in person. They love and care for their children, volunteer in their communities, and establish long friendships—and then they seek to punish those who are different. It is not enough for them to assert that they alone are religiously righteous; they want everyone else to conform to their ideas of righteousness. They save some of their most poisonous words for those who dare to identify as Christians of a different sort. In their eyes, the archest of enemies are the misguided souls who would champion "social justice"—or what Rushdoony would have identified as the most recent incarnation of the Social Gospel. As one Texas pastor said, "If Southern Baptists don't rise up and take a stand now, then in a few years they will be seeing books in their Lifeway bookstores promoting liberation theology, black theology, and feminism."[90]

Jerry Falwell more than anyone embodied this unsettling mix of love and hate. A jovial presence with an easy manner, Falwell was often celebrated as a "loving man" and "a big heart." Yet he regularly spewed toxins, as when he blamed "the abortionists, and the feminists, and the gays and the lesbians" for the September 11 attacks. When the journalist Frances FitzGerald profiled Jerry Falwell for the *New Yorker* in 1981, she spoke with Reverend Carl McIntire, a pastor in Falwell's style. "Separation involves hard, gruelling controversy. It involves attacks, personal attacks, even violent attacks . . . Satan preaches brotherly love in order to hold men in apostasy," McIntire told FitzGerald. Therefore, he said, aggression "is an expression of Christian love."[91]

CHAPTER 6

The Uses and Abuses of History

S OMETIMES A MUSEUM is just a museum. And sometimes it is "an 'Ark of the Covenant' for our nation, bearing witness to His goodness." That's what the organizers of Revolution 2017 had to say about the Museum of the Bible in advance of their conference there in December 2017.

At the event, Cindy Jacobs, a featured speaker who identifies herself as an "apostle," went on to describe the Museum of the Bible as "God's base camp." Right there, in the auditorium of the museum, she offered a prophecy: "The army of the heavens marches into Washington, D.C., and marches out of Washington, D.C." Soon enough, she declared, "they go into North Korea."

In order to understand how this museum on the corner of Fourth and D Streets SW, three blocks from the national Capitol, became an Ark, you have to know something about the people behind the museum. I laid plans to visit shortly after the museum opened in November 2017. After catching Jacobs's incendiary prophecies on YouTube, I also added Revolution 2018 to my schedule.

Sometime in 2006, the Green family sat down to have a conversation about the true meaning of the Fourth of July. "We saw a film at church right around that time that really opened our eyes to what was going on in our nation," Barbara Green later recalled, according to the account provided by her son Steve Green in his 2011 book, *Faith in America*.[1] David Green, Steve's father, remembered the film well. "It was centered on all these people of faith who were signers of our U.S. Constitution," he said. "It really got my attention, and I decided we needed to make a statement about the godly heritage of our wonderful country."[2]

The Green family, as it happens, were in a position to make quite a statement. David Green is the founder and CEO of Hobby Lobby Stores, an Oklahoma-based private retail corporation with eight hundred locations and about $4.5 billion in revenue, and Steve Green is its president. The company is best known to the general public as the plaintiffs in a landmark 2014 case, *Burwell v. Hobby Lobby Stores, Inc.*, in which the conservative majority of the Supreme Court decided 5–4 that business corporations may be said to possess religious belief systems and enjoy the right of freedom of conscience. Even if that means refusing to comply with federal law regarding the provision of comprehensive health insurance to female employees.

When the Green family sat down for their chat about the Fourth of July, Hobby Lobby was already known for public expressions of religion, running newspaper ads around Christmas and Easter to signal its adherence to conservative Christian beliefs. David Green instructed his son Steve to get ahold of the producer of the marvelous film they'd seen in church and see if he might help them think up an ad for Independence Day that would "express how we feel about our country."

The film was the work of David Barton, a former math teacher and administrator at a Christian high school who had reinvented himself as a "historian" of "America's Christian Founding." He soon showed up at company headquarters in Oklahoma City bearing a trove of material: "letters, quotes, all sorts of testimonies from all kinds of famous Americans." At his dad's urging, Steve Green had put together an ad stocked with "quotes about our Christian nation from the people in leadership— presidents, judges, congressmen, and the like," all organized under a citation from the Psalms at their most theocratic: "Blessed is the nation whose God is the LORD (Psalm 33:12A)."[3]

Like the bulk of David Barton's own works, the Hobby Lobby ad was a mash-up of quotes wrenched out of context and dragooned into service of the Christian Nation myth. Rob Boston, senior advisor at Americans United for Separation of Church and State and author of *Taking Liberties: Why Religious Freedom Doesn't Give You the Right to Tell Other People What to Do*, posted a lengthy rebuttal on the online publication of Americans United remarking that it would "take a small book to dissect" and catalogue all the distortions and calling it "an insult to the intelligence of its readers."[4] Andrew L. Seidel, a constitutional and civil rights attorney with the Freedom from Religion Foundation and author of *The Founding Myth: Why Christian Nationalism Is Un-American*, built an interactive website to nail down as many misrepresentations as feasible.

The error in the detail was there to provide cover for the great lie at the center of Christian nationalism. What David Barton and the leaders of the Hobby Lobby corporation don't want you to know is that America's founders explicitly and proudly created the world's first secular republic. It seemed the point of the Hobby Lobby ad was not to celebrate America's history but to counterfeit it.

As far as the Green family was concerned, however, the ad was a tremendous success, and they have continued to run versions of it every year. Indeed, it was a step in the direction of a still bolder plan to which Steve Green next turned his attention.

Around the time of the Fourth of July ad, Steve Green and his representatives were scouring the Middle East in search of "biblical" artifacts. It later became evident that they were scouring a little too hard. In 2010, Hobby Lobby agreed to purchase more than 5,500 artifacts for $1.6 million and arranged to have them shipped in packages bearing labels that described contents as "ceramic tiles." In 2017 the corporation paid a fine of $3 million to settle charges over what the government says were intentionally mislabeled and smuggled goods.

In the same period that he was acquiring pricy "ceramic tiles," Green formed a 501(c)(3) nonprofit corporation to create the Museum of the Bible. The mission of the museum, he told the IRS, would be "to bring to life the living Word of God, to tell its compelling story of preservation, and to inspire confidence in the absolute authority and reliability of the Bible." Green would eventually raise and spend $500 million on the project.[5]

In anticipation of this new and colossal undertaking, Green decided to consult with the experts. First, he traveled out to Manitou Springs, Colorado, to visit John Stonestreet, a minister associated with the institute founded by Chuck Colson (the ex-convict of Watergate fame who later founded Prison Fellowship) and promoter of the "biblical worldview" through literature, curricula, and youth-focused conferences and seminars. Green also flew out to Cincinnati to consult with Ken Ham at his office in the Creation Museum in nearby Petersburg, Kentucky. Ham, the founder of Answers in Genesis, has devoted his career to debunking the science of biology and promoting the view that the earth and all living things were created just as the Bible says. The third and perhaps most important source of guidance to whom Green turned was David Barton.

"Tucked away in a tiny Texas town about forty-five minutes west of Fort Worth is the person who arguably has one of the deepest modern understandings of what was going on in the minds of the Founding Fathers when they formed our nation over two centuries ago," writes Green, who visited with Barton at the latter's headquarters in Aledo, Texas. Green goes on to recount some of the many pearls of historical insight that he has gleaned from direct conversation with Barton. "A republic is a representative form of government," Barton told his admirer. "Our forefathers got the idea straight from the Bible."[6]

Flying back home from a visit with the experts, mulling his plans for the Museum of the Bible, Green "realized how privileged I was to spend the time I did with John Stonestreet, David Barton, and Ken Ham—all experts in their chosen fields of study." His conversations had "provided some important information regarding how and why the biblical worldview really is absolute and absolutely from God."[7] Now he was ready to put that information to work in a giant converted warehouse located three blocks south of the Capitol in Washington, D.C.

One summer day in 1987, as David Barton tells the story, God told him to do two things. First, he was to look up the day that the Supreme Court ruled against school-sponsored prayer. Second, he was to gather the data on the past couple decades' SAT scores. At the time, Barton was a

thirty-three-year-old math teacher and school principal at the Aledo Christian School, which grew out of a church started by his parents in Aledo, and
his bachelor's degree in Christian education came from Oral Roberts
University.[8]

SAT scores, Barton discovered, had been on a steady climb until 1963,
when suddenly they dropped as if "they were tumbling down a steep moun-
tainside." Around the same time, he noticed, the rates of divorce, teen pregnancy, and violent crime began to rise. How to explain this mysterious
collapse in the statistics of American educational and social well-being?
Then he looked at the Supreme Court records, and that's when it hit him:
in 1962, in the case of *Engel v. Vitale*, the Supreme Court yanked God out
of America's classrooms. A year later it nailed the schoolhouse doors shut
with the case of *School District of Abington Township, Pennsylvania v.
Schempp*, in which the Court declared that school-sponsored Bible reading
in public schools was unconstitutional. There, Barton claimed, was the
explanation for the crisis in America!

Of course, Barton could just as well have blamed the decline of public
education on the Beach Boys, who also happened to make it big in 1962. In
order to pin the blame for declining SAT scores on the Supreme Court's
school prayer decisions, Barton also has to overlook the massive changes in
American education at the time. Many of them involved the expansion of
the school systems to include previously excluded and disadvantaged groups
of people, which predictably resulted in a significant increase in the number
of test-takers and a decrease in average scores. But clearly Barton does not
seem to know or care about the troves of sociological research on the subject.
He also exhibits little interest in the actual history of religion in public
schools, which would show that the majority of the nation's school districts
had minimized or ceased the practice of school-sponsored, sectarian prayer
long before the Supreme Court allegedly "kicked God out of the
classroom."

But the biggest lie in Barton's first stab at history is what he takes to be
its biggest truth. Once upon a time, in his telling, America was united
around a common religion that served as the foundation of the republic—
until secularists commandeered the Supreme Court and ruined everything.
The reality is that America was a pluralistic land from the beginning and

the United States was founded as a secular republic. Thomas Jefferson said it best when he pointed to the First Amendment and said with awe that it erected "a wall of separation between Church & State."[9] It is why he declared, in the Virginia Statute for Religious Freedom, "that to compel a man to furnish contributions of money for the propagation of opinions which he disbelieves *and abhors*, is sinful and tyrannical."[10] This is why the Treaty of Tripoli of 1798, endorsed by John Adams and other members of America's founding generation, declared explicitly (and uncontroversially) that "the government of the United States is not in any sense founded on the Christian Religion."[11]

The next big lie in Barton's history is about American education. In his telling, American schools were all about God until the Supreme Court decided to throw American heritage to the secular winds. In reality, Massachusetts passed the first law prohibiting the use or purchase of schoolbooks "which are calculated to favor any particular religious sect or tenet" in 1827, and in 1837, Horace Mann, often hailed as "the father of American public education," declared that public schools should be nonsectarian—meaning that schools should restrict religious teachings to commonly shared Protestant values, which he, a Unitarian, regarded as universal and believed could be taught without offending any sectarian sensibilities.[12]

In the middle decades of the nineteenth century an influx of immigrants from Catholic countries sparked bitter and bloody conflicts over religion and public schools in Boston, Maine, Ohio, and elsewhere. At the time, public school textbooks were filled with anti-Catholic tropes, and Protestant nativists sought to exclude Catholic teachings and texts from the schools. Catholic parents and religious leaders, naturally reluctant to have their children inculcated in undermining stereotypes, asked, in vain, for a share of tax money for their own school systems. In the early 1840s, the growing Catholic immigrant community began to pressure school officials to allow their children to read from their Bible, the Douay-Rheims translation, at school.

The conflict took a violent turn in Philadelphia in 1844, when Protestants and Catholics hit the streets for two separate weeks of rioting; when it was over, at least twenty-five residents of the City of Brotherly Love were dead. This episode and others persuaded much of the American public of the inequity and unsustainability of public school–sponsored religion in a diverse society. "Leave the matter of religion to the family circle, the church, and the private school, supported entirely by private contributions," said President Ulysses S. Grant in 1875. "Keep the church and state forever separate."[13]

Indeed, the pair of Supreme Court decisions in 1962 and 1963 that Barton blames for America's downfall were easily decided. They received the support of six out of seven (*Engel v. Vitale*) and eight out of nine (*Abington v. Schempp*) justices, because for a period of four decades or so that began with a pair of landmark decisions in 1947 and 1948, the judiciary had arrived at a straightforward and consistent philosophy intended to answer to the principle of church-state separation, and the decisions answered to those precedents.

These Supreme Court rulings were far from outlier decisions. In fact, they had ample precedent in the states. To give just two examples, the Supreme Court in Wisconsin struck down government-sponsored prayer in schools in 1892 and the Nebraska Supreme Court did the same in 1902.

None of this seemed to matter to Barton. As patient as he was ambitious, Barton soon moved on from the SAT-prayer nexus to other mythical episodes in American history. "To retake lost ground quickly is not the strategy prescribed by the Lord Himself," he wrote. "Commit yourself to this engagement for the long haul—for the duration; arm yourself with the mentality of a marathon runner, not a sprinter. Very simply, be willing to stay and compete until you win."[14] He established WallBuilders, which bills itself as a service for protecting America's Christian heritage and sells books, videos, and merchandise to an eager segment of the public. He has since risen to become the most celebrated and broadly influential Christian nationalist historian in America, leading pastors and politicians on tours of Washington, D.C., to indoctrinate them with the correct talking points on "America's Godly heritage." At speaking engagements, his longtime ally Newt Gingrich advises audiences to read Barton's work, saying, "It's amazing how much he knows and how consistently he applies that knowledge."[15] Mike Huckabee once said, "I almost wish that there would be . . . a simultaneous telecast, and all Americans would be forced—forced at gunpoint, no less—to listen to every David Barton message."[16] Sam

Brownback, currently the U.S. ambassador at large for international religious freedom, said Barton is providing "the philosophical underpinnings for a lot of the Republican effort in the country today—bringing God back into the public square."[17] Although he does not mention him by name, Vice President Mike Pence duplicates some of Barton's talking points. Barton advises right-wing policymakers and lawmakers in charge of approving public school curricula, and frequently teams up with Family Research Council president Tony Perkins for radio appearances and other events.

Yet, even as Barton rose to prominence, the characteristic features of his approach to the rewriting of history never changed. Bartonian historiography invariably begins with the myth of the golden age—the idea, in essence, that America was once a single nation with a single God. It goes on to describe a fall and a cause for grievance as the righteous lose their hold, thanks to the actions of secular liberals. The story of the past thus leads inexorably to a political prescription for the future, which for the most part involves retaking the court system and the rest of government and turning it over to Bible believers.

The historical errors and obfuscations tumbled out of Barton's works fast and furious. Intent on demonstrating that the American republic was founded on "Judeo-Christian principles," Barton reproduced an alleged quote from James Madison to the effect that the Ten Commandments are the foundation of American civilization. Chuck Norris, Rush Limbaugh, *Duck Dynasty* star Phil Robertson, and countless other luminaries of the right recycled the quote in so many iterations that it has become a fixture of Christian nationalist ideology. Yet there is no evidence that Madison ever said such a thing.

In a 1990 video titled *America's Godly Heritage*, Barton acknowledges that Jefferson assures the Danbury Baptists in his famous letter of January 1, 1802, that language in the First Amendment erects "a wall of separation between Church & State," in Jefferson's own words.[18] Then Barton goes on to argue that Jefferson meant only to prohibit "the establishing of a single denomination."[19] The First Amendment "never intended to separate Christian principles from government," he says. The wall, Barton writes, "was originally introduced as, and understood to be, a one-directional wall protecting the church from the government."[20]

But Jefferson did not say anything about a one-directional wall. Rob Boston, who has been tracking David Barton since the 1990s, has said, "If Barton would take the time to actually read Jefferson's letter he would see that he is simply wrong. Jefferson's letter says nothing about the wall being 'one directional,' and certainly does not assert that it was meant to keep 'Christian principles' in government. Such sentiments . . . conflict sharply with our third president's well known advocacy of church-state separation and religious freedom."[21]

By the early 2000s, Barton's historical inaccuracies were beginning to attract notice, and a number of exposés catalogued the errors and distortions. Author Chris Rodda filled three volumes with Barton's crimes against history under the title *Liars for Jesus: The Religious Right's Alternate View of American History*. Yet the adverse coverage did little to stop the Barton juggernaut. If anything, it affirmed his authenticity in the eyes of his followers. In 2012 he released his biggest book yet, *The Jefferson Lies: Exposing the Myths You've Always Believed About Thomas Jefferson*, in which he turns the tables on his critics by supposedly exposing the lies promulgated by those mainstream historians who have characterized Jefferson as a representative of the Enlightenment.

Barton's demagoguery met with immediate scrutiny. According to National Public Radio, "We looked up every citation Barton said was from the Bible but not one of them checked out."[22] The History News Network soon named *The Jefferson Lies* "the least credible history book in print."[23] Ironically, among Barton's most forceful critics were academic historians at evangelical institutions. "David Barton is offering an alternative vision of American history which places God, the providence of God, Christianity, at the center," said John Fea, then chairman of the history department at Messiah College.[24] Two Christian professors at conservative religious colleges, Warren Throckmorton and Michael Coulter, rebutted Barton's claims, eventually publishing a take-down: *Getting Jefferson Right: Fact Checking Claims About Our Third President*. The controversy deepened as ten conservative Christian professors reviewed the book and identified numerous errors and distortions.[25] In August 2012, Barton's Christian publishing house, Thomas Nelson, halted production of the tome, announcing that they had lost confidence in it.

"There were historical details—matters of fact, not matters of opinion, that were not supported at all," said Thomas Nelson senior vice president and publisher Brian Hampton.[26]

At the root of all the controversies over Barton's work, one inevitably finds the same fundamental falsification of American history. Christian nationalism, by its nature, must deny the extraordinary achievement of America's founders in creating the world's first secular republic and replace it with the kind of shabby religious-nationalist mythology that characterizes reactionary movements around the world. Likewise, Bartonian historiography seems to involve a brazen disdain for scholarly norms and the actual facts. But it makes a certain kind of sense: you have to tell lots of little lies to promote one big lie.

But none of that has mattered. Barton's pseudo-history is too valuable to the Christian nationalist machine to let facts and scholarship get in the way, and his standing with his own audience has continued to soar. For at the heart of Barton's project is an assault on the very idea of history as a meaningful subject of scholarly investigation and a source of objective truths. Embedded in Barton's enterprise—and visible in the very title of his magnum opus, *The Jefferson Lies*—is the message that history is just a political battlefield where the votaries of "the Left" spin their secularizing falsehoods from the comfort of "the Academy," and the only alternative is to spin better stories from those who believe rightly. As with the many utterances of Donald Trump—"God's candidate," according to Barton—the fact that liberal critics find no end of lies and contradictions in his work only serves to confirm in the minds of his followers his authentic commitment to a deeper truth.

On a cool December morning in 2017, the line coils around the corner from the front entrance of the Museum of the Bible. A chatty family from Maryland compares schedules for field hockey practice and dental appointments. A man in a black sweatshirt with a torso-size cross emblazoned on the front studies a brochure. A mom who looks like she has just stepped out of a long car ride herds her children away from the curb and hands out snack bars.

The museum is housed in a repurposed, eight-story, 430,000-square-foot 1922 warehouse building just two blocks from the National Mall. Passing through the huge bronze entrance gates inscribed with text from the Gutenberg Bible, the visitor enters a cathedral-like hall, lined with monumental stone columns from Jerusalem, with colorful LED displays gracing the 140-feet-long and 40-feet-high ceiling.

The museum's installations include an immersive sound-and-light show designed to convey "the stories of the Bible" through animated films, kinetic sculptures, and fiber-optical representations of the parting of sea. Another exhibit, "Washington Revelations," literally moves and shakes visitors as it takes them on a virtual helicopter ride through the nation's capital in search of biblical inscriptions. A restaurant on the sixth floor draws on ingredients and flavors of the Mediterranean and Middle East.

The sound-and-light show may strike some visitors as garish, but it isn't inaccurate—inasmuch as a well-executed cartoon may be said to represent the contents of the Bible. Which is, of course, one of the puzzles that any visitor to this museum must consider. There is no hint in the animated sequences and fiber-optic oceans that the texts from which the stories are drawn contain inconsistencies and contradictions, that a certain violence must be done to them even to turn them into picture narratives, or that they have been interpreted in radically divergent ways by scholars and religious traditions. It appears that the guiding assumptions in this museum are that the Bible has only one meaning, that this meaning is directly accessible by dint of individual effort, and that this particular meaning is the foundation of the Christian religion (at the very least). These are very Protestant assumptions. But no matter: the museum has attempted to simulate nonsectarianism by mixing in displays of Jewish and Catholic aspects of the history of the Bible. (Islam, on the other hand, shows up sporadically; the various Orthodox Christian traditions are neglected; and you can pretty much forget about the Mormons.)

An exhibit on the translation of the Bible into many languages features videos of groups of colorfully dressed brown people dancing in jubilation. They are presumably there to provide a chorus of affirmation for the museum's theology in living color.

The artifacts from the Green family's vast collection—scrolls, stone slabs, religious objects, and so on—fill large sections of the museum, mixed in with nuggets of Scripture printed on purple banners unfurled from the ceiling. Amid the various displays, the visitor comes upon a documentary film presentation, *Drive Thru History*, that offers a breathless tour through archaeological work on holy sites. The narrator, Dave Stotts, is a well-known personality in Christian nationalist media circles—he also stars in a video series, *The Birth of Freedom*, that teaches "the biblical roots of liberty" while providing believers with "a resource for countering anti-Christian revisions of history"—and he exudes enthusiasm as he careens around Israel in a series of flashy sports cars. What he does not exude is any sense that the archaeological evidence might contradict the textual claims of the Bible. In this museum the only purpose of archaeology is to confirm what the Bible has already told us. This museum, like the documentary film, doesn't proselytize—at least, not overtly. It simply celebrates. Here the Bible is the Forrest Gump of history. Whenever something big is happening, the Bible is there, and it's always doing good.

The messaging is hardly surprising, when one considers the sources. A glance at the *Drive Thru History* film credits shows it to be the work of ColdWater Media, which has also created content for conservative activist and policy groups such as Students for Life of America, the Colson Center for Christian Worldview, and Focus on the Family. ColdWater Media is also the force behind several American history–themed series of DVDs, including *Drive Thru History—"America: Columbus to the Constitution."* The DVDs offer "stories of history, character, faith, and the hand of God in America's discovery."[27] Dave Stotts stars in that series, too. It appears to cover much of the same ground as a 2006 DVD series also titled, *Drive Thru History America: Foundations of Character*, also featuring Dave Stotts, produced in collaboration with Focus on the Family and "based on the work of Christian historian David Barton."[28]

Where the museum takes on the task of protecting the myth of America's Christian foundations, the pattern of assertion by omission yields to something closer to outright distortion. In "Washington Revelations," the aerial hunt for Biblical inscriptions in the nation's capital, we are taken to the Jefferson Memorial, where the narrator reads from one of the panels: "Indeed I tremble for my country when I reflect that God is just." This, we are assured, was inspired by Psalm 145 ("the Lord is righteous . . ."). The camera does not take us to the panel on the other side of the Jefferson Memorial, which honors the Virginia Statute for Religious Freedom, in support of which Jefferson declared that the mind advances by "reason alone," without appeal to revelation.

Before you know it, we're hovering inside the Lincoln Monument, where the narrator repeats the famous hope of the Gettysburg Address, that "government of, by, and for the people shall not perish from the earth." We are informed that this phrase comes from a line in Scripture where John tells us that believers in Jesus "shall not perish." Yet there is no direct evidence that the line as delivered in Gettysburg actually comes from Scripture. The ride designers are presumably unaware that Lincoln might just as easily have picked up the words from his favorite philosopher, Theodore Parker. Widely denounced in his own time as an abolitionist and an "infidel," Parker asked, in a speech Lincoln read, whether America and its "government of all, by all, and for all" might one day "perish."

As the visitor reels out of the virtual roller-coaster ride of Washington Revelations, he or she may stumble across a large reproduction of Arnold Friberg's iconic painting of George Washington kneeling in prayer in the woods of Valley Forge. The caption on the right tells us that the artist took pains to render the general's uniform true to life. On the left, a little plaque reminds us that the artist made sure the painting was realistic, describing the scene as "an imagined moment of prayer." Nowhere does the museum take the trouble to inform viewers of the actual provenance of this imaginary scene. It was in fact a fiction, concocted by a reverend forty years after the alleged incident, who claimed to have heard about Washington's moment of prayer from a man named Isaac, who is also referred to as "John," and who, it later turned out, was nowhere near Valley Forge in 1777. The story fell apart in 1918 when the National Park Service thought to erect a monument on the alleged spot of the genuflection and conducted an investigation. But in this museum, none of that matters.

It all starts to make more sense, as you leave the museum, when you come across the donor wall. The museum's sponsors, apart from the Green family and Hobby Lobby, are a roll call of powerhouse funders of the Christian nationalist movement. Amway cofounder Richard DeVos's family foundation as well as his son Richard Jr., and daughter-in-law, Education Secretary Betsy, all make it on to the wall for gifts in excess of $250,000. At the time of my visit, the roster of the museum's board extended the list of power players from the Christian right. Board member Bob Hoskins, who has dealings with the Green family at least as far back as 2008, leads a very large and extremely well-funded international ministry, OneHope, dedicated to evangelizing children. The first president of the board, Cary Summers, was also founder of The Nehemiah Group, which works to promote "Biblical" principles of leadership to for-profit and faith-based organizations. Joining them on the board were evangelical mega-pastor Rick Warren and Gregory Baylor, a senior counselor at the Alliance Defending Freedom, which represented the Green family in the *Hobby Lobby* case. Green has declared that all board members are asked to sign a statement of faith.

To judge from what David Barton practices rather than what he preaches, history is a means to an end. It is there to be used, not studied or probed. The domination of the American political system by Bible-believing Christians is always the ultimate goal. And so it came to pass that, even as his Wall-Builders group manufactured mythologies about the American past, he began to lay the groundwork for his political activism. A key early step was the creation of The Black Robe Regiment, an association of conservative clergy members and "concerned patriots" whose mission is to "restore the American Church in her capacity as the Body of Christ, ambassadors of Christ, moral teacher of America and the World, and overseer of all principalities and governing officials (Rom 13), as was rightfully established long ago."[29]

Barton presciently anticipated that the Republican Party would become the principal instrument of the Christian nationalist movement, and he quickly resolved to fashion himself into the vital link between Republican politicians and the nation's conservative pastors. As WallBuilders grew into a propaganda machine, he began to accumulate positions and influence of an overtly partisan political nature. From 1997 to 2006 he was vice-chair of the Republican Party of Texas and also acted as a political consultant to the Republican National Committee on evangelical outreach. He served as a co-director, along with Newt Gingrich, of Renewing American Leadership, whose leadership also included Jim Garlow and whose mission was "defending and promoting the three pillars of American civilization: freedom, faith and free markets."[30] Barton and Gingrich frequently appeared together to deliver keynote addresses at pastors' policy briefings in battleground states.

Another one of Barton's go-to organizations is the American Renewal Project, which is closely aligned with the hyper-conservative policy group the American Family Association and whose briefings bring conservative clergy together with right-wing politicians to foster collaboration on policy initiatives. Every year Barton assembles sympathetic lawmakers for a ProFamily Legislative Network Conference, "an opportunity for conservative pro-family State legislators from across the United States to come together for an insightful briefing session with leading experts in a variety of fields that touch many of the most crucial areas of public service."[31]

Barton's ideas found a warm welcome among Republicans interested in courting the evangelical vote. In 2004 he was hired by the GOP as a consultant, playing a key role in the Republican National Committee's outreach to members of the clergy. He traveled across the country for a year showing pastors a slideshow promoting his views. His efforts, he told the online magazine Beliefnet, were "below the radar . . . We worked our tails off to stay out of the news." The effort proved critical in clinching George W. Bush's narrow win over John Kerry.[32]

Barton also hosted pastor gatherings and tours to indoctrinate clergy with the idea that the U.S. was founded as an explicitly Christian nation and that Christians today should "take it back"—mainly by voting for conservative Republicans. The aim of the gatherings was to encourage participants to mobilize their congregations and organize voter registration drives. Kyle Mantyla, a senior fellow with People for the American Way, reported that Sam Brownback appeared on Barton's radio program and referred to Barton as "one of my big heroes."[33] In 2013, while Brownback was governor of Kansas, Barton headlined the prayer breakfast in that state.

Barton soon waded into education policy. He has served as an "expert reviewer" to the Texas State Board of Education in establishing the state's textbook curriculum standards. In fact, he had such sway with the far-right faction that dominated the Texas State Board of Education that he was permitted to submit his notes and comments separately from a panel of professionally vetted and approved curriculum specialists, and his recommendations were parroted by the far-right faction's members. (Because Texas is the nation's largest purchaser of textbooks, publishers have historically written to the Texas standards.) Barton also serves on the advisory board of the National Council on Bible Curriculum in Public Schools, a program that produces sectarian "Bible study" classes as for-credit courses in public high schools.

Equally concerning, perhaps, is Barton's influence on education in the military. Researcher and author Chris Rodda spotted a David Barton essay about the "myth" of church-state separation in a JROTC American history textbook as far back in 2007. "We're constantly seeing Barton's brand of revisionist history promoted in places like military base newspapers. Barton's books are even in the libraries at West Point and Air Force Academy," she told an interviewer in 2016. "He also speaks at military bases and recently claimed that he was asked to train military leaders, one of his few claims that is unfortunately probably true."

Barton devotes a significant part of his activism to a variety of entrepreneurial projects intended to produce future generations of movement leaders. At the end of his *WallBuilders Live!* radio shows, Barton narrates an advertisement for "the Patriot Academy," a program for the sixteen- to twenty-five-year-old set whose graduates "serve in the halls of Congress, in the film industry and the pulpit and every area of the culture." "Join us in training champions to change the world," Barton exclaims. The program now also includes a "citizen track for adults." The academy presently operates in state capitols around the United States, including Texas, Florida, Idaho, Delaware, and Arizona, producing four weeklong Patriot Academies just about every month.

In recent years Barton has become closely involved in the money side of Christian nationalist politics. In the 2016 race he partnered with Ted Cruz, overseeing a Keep the Promise PAC, one of several similarly named multimillion-dollar super PACs supporting Cruz's presidential bid. "Having David Barton running the super PAC gives it a lot of validity for evangelicals and pastors," said Mike Gonzalez, Cruz's South Carolina evangelical chair.[34] The PAC was one of four affiliated super PACS in the network, including Keep the Promise I, a PAC managed by Kellyanne Conway, which received $11 million from Robert Mercer, and Keep the Promise III, which received $15 million from the families of Texas fracking billionaires Dan and Farris Wilks.

Barton's reputation as a strategist has continued to blossom. In 1992 he presciently pointed the movement in the direction of the courts, writing that "the judiciary is now the primary battlefield."[35] In recent years, even while keeping up the fight for control of the courts, Barton has worked to direct the Republican Party to capture control of state legislatures and governorships. Barton is a central figure in the conceptualization of the "religious freedom movement" as one of four board members for Project Blitz, a broad and ambitious legislative initiative that I will discuss in the next chapter. He was instrumental in focusing the movement's sights on the Johnson Amendment, which was intended to prohibit churches and charities from directly or indirectly participating or intervening in "any political campaign on behalf of (or opposition to) any candidate for elective public office." An aim of the movement, it would seem, is to turn houses of worship into the cash machines of the political system by allowing special interests to pour millions of tax-free dollars into churches, which could then turn around and spend like super PACs to elect or defeat candidates.

In his political commentary, Barton plays just as loose with the facts as he does in his works of history. Speaking on his *WallBuilders Live!* radio program on April 17, 2017, Barton falsely suggested that the Johnson Amendment "violates the First Amendment rights" of churches. He eagerly relayed the views of a fellow pastor who said, "Guys, I'm tellin ya, Christian is the new black. Christian is what you get discriminated against now like blacks were in the '60s."[36]

Show cohost Rick Green, a former Texas State representative, made a similar point in answering a listener's query about the law: "The Johnson

Amendment is what Lyndon Johnson slid in there in 1954 in the appropriations bill to try to muzzle churches and prevent pastors from being able to speak out on the biblical perspectives of different issues in the culture, if they could be labeled as 'political,'" he said. "The government is literally inside our churches trying to muzzle our pastors and prevent them from having free speech or freedom of religion."

"Pastors don't have the same right of free speech that everybody else has," Barton complained.

In fact, pastors are free to say what they like; the Johnson Amendment simply says that they can't also collect their tax subsidies if they electioneer from the pulpit.

With the Trump presidency, Barton believes, America is finally moving in the right direction. President Donald Trump, he has said, is running America on a "CEO model."[37] Christians who fail to support the Trump presidency are taking "a very selfish view of what we do with voting."

"It's not your vote, it's God's vote," says Barton.[38]

Even as he has cultivated links with the big names in Republican politics, Barton has stayed close to some of the most extreme representatives of the Christian nationalist movement. He paired up with evangelists Lance Wallnau, who wrote a book comparing Trump to King Cyrus, and Andrew Wommack, who has said opposition to Trump is "demonic deception" and "one of the signs of the End Times,"[39] in the Truth & Liberty Coalition, an activist and media organization whose mission is "the reformation of Nations by igniting the latent potential in the Body of Christ." The website champions "the 7 Mountain Mandate, a powerful, transformative campaign intended to bring about social transformation," a reference to the idea, popularized by C. Peter Wagner, that Christians who hold similarly radical beliefs are to dominate seven key areas of culture. Under "resources," the website for Truth & Liberty Coalition links to a number of right-wing get-out-the-vote sites, including the iVoterGuide. It also links directly to the Trump campaign via "Trump's Accomplishments (WhiteHouse.gov)," a site promoting Trump's policies and celebrating his successes. Its "coalition partners," who are also referred to as "influencers," include many familiar names, such as Mike Huckabee, Jay Sekulow, Tony

Perkins, Jerry Boykin, Steve Green, and Kristan Hawkins, who launched Students for Life of America. "I believe the 45th president is meant to be an Isaiah 45 Cyrus," Wallnau writes. "With him in office, we will have authority in the Spirit to build the house of the Lord and restore the crumbling walls that separate us from cultural collapse."[40]

Throughout his own rise, Barton has remained close to the family that brought us the Museum of the Bible. Since that early meeting in Aledo, Texas, Barton has lavished praise on the Greens, inviting Steve and his brother Mart on *WallBuilders Live!* on multiple occasions. Characterizing the Bible as "the document that is the true founding document of America," Barton and his cohosts hail the Green family as "champions for getting the Bible in the hands of people all over the world."[41]

Mart Green is founder and CEO of the Oklahoma City–based Mardel Christian & Education, with over thirty stores in six states. He also founded Every Tribe Every Nation, which brings together Bible translation agencies and digital technologies to promote access to the Bible with the aim of "eradicating Bible poverty," as they call it, by evangelizing "unreached people groups."

Barton and Steve Green have also appeared together on various right-wing platforms, including Glenn Beck's BlazeTV in September 2013, to discuss Green's then-ongoing lawsuit *Burwell v. Hobby Lobby Stores, Inc.* Barton opened the conversation with a sympathetic gesture of shared grievance. "You guys are in the middle of a lawsuit that is on its way to the Supreme Court for appeal that may dramatically restructure Obamacare by the fact that they have said you guys are not allowed to have a conscience, a religious conscience," Barton told Green.[42]

In a segment that aired May 1, 2017, Steve Green appeared on *Wall-Builders Live!* to discuss "the need to revive the Bible in America so that we can have that biblical worldview." Barton's cohost, Rick Green, emphatically endorsed Steve Green's work at the Museum of the Bible. "For us to have a biblical perspective, or the nation to have a biblical perspective, we've got to get back to what a biblical worldview actually is," he said. Rick Green went on to praise Steve Green's "incredible effort to restore this book back to its proper place in our culture." Steve Green asserted, "We had a love for God's word. I believe [the Bible] is foundational to our nation, to our lives, and to our business." Rick Green concluded, "The significance and importance of what you guys are doing with the book, the museum, all of it, is huge."[43]

In its official pronouncements, the Museum of the Bible has learned to present itself as just a museum. Its first president, Cary Summers, described the museum as "a non-sectarian institution. It is not political and it will not proselytize." Its aim, he said, is simply to "reacquaint the world with the book that helped make it, and let the visitor come to their own conclusions." Steve Green has also dismissed concerns the museum has a religious agenda. "The theological weeds or the political weeds—we don't have time," he has said.[44]

In 2012 the museum removed from its corporate mission statement the language about inspiring "confidence in the absolute authority and reliability of the Bible" and announced that the museum's purpose was simply "to invite people to engage with the Bible."[45] Yet Green himself has maintained that there was no real change. "The intent had always been to be a nonsectarian museum," he told the reporter Michelle Boorstein at the *Washington Post*.[46] Perhaps Green hews to the belief that being "nonsectarian" and inspiring "confidence in the absolute authority" of the Bible mean exactly the same thing.

The pretense that the museum was just a museum, however, cut no ice with its most fervent champions. Values Voter summits, Road to Majority conferences, Watchmen on the Wall gatherings, and other assemblies of religious right activists invariably include events at the museum, such as film screenings, behind-the-scenes tours, and lectures. In late March 2019 the Museum of the Bible cohosted the International Culture Shapers Summit featuring prominent Seven Mountains dominionists such as Lance Wallnau, Os Hillman, and James and Anna Kramer. Other speakers included Roma Downey, whose husband, Mark Burnett, created President Trump's former television show *The Apprentice* and guided it with Trump at the helm through fourteen seasons; Family Research Council leaders Tony Perkins and Ken Blackwell; and over a dozen other representatives of media-, government-, education-, and business-focused associations.

In May 2019 the Museum of the Bible hosted a special reception and tour for the Watchmen on the Wall's annual national gathering in Washington, D.C. According to an event schedule, speakers at the three-day event included dozens of Christian nationalist activists, including many who appeared at the regional event in Unionville, North Carolina: Tony Perkins, Lieutenant General (ret.) William Boykin, and J. C. Church. Predictably, they were joined by David Barton. The event schedule also promised a handful of Republican politicians, including Representative Vicky Hartzler and Senator Josh Hawley (both R-Mo.) and training sessions before lobbying on Capitol Hill. According to reporting from the National Religious Broadcasters, Mike Pence made a surprise appearance and vowed to "fight until we fully repeal the Johnson Amendment." He added, "I know it is the President's conviction and my conviction that the pulpits you stand at are of much greater consequence than any podium behind which he and I stand."[47]

By now the Museum of the Bible had become a well-trod pilgrimage destination, not just for leaders of the movement, but also for its foot soldiers. In August 2018 the Museum of the Bible hosted a special tour for Generations, the ministry affiliated with homeschool advocate (and Rushdoony acolyte) Kevin Swanson, as part of its four-day Bible Family Conference. Generations advocates "biblical" government, strictly enforced gender roles and the submission of women, and condemns same-sex relationships. There is little in the museum to challenge Generations members' philosophy, or "worldview," as they call it, and that's exactly as organizers of the Bible Family Conference want it. In an article posted to the Generations website, the question "Should I let my kids read books by non-Christians?" is met with the response by one of Swanson's associates that the "bigger question I have is, 'How do I make sure that my grandkids don't turn into Mark Twain?' Because this is one of the defining characteristics of most of the men in these books, they are apostates."[48]

The Museum of the Bible also hosted Revive Us 2, a "national family meeting" organized by evangelical celebrity Kirk Cameron. The event broadcasted live to movie theaters and churches around the country, delivering the message that national unity can only be achieved through allegiance to conservative Christian religion—and by voting "biblical values."[49]

Another group that appears thrilled with the museum is the Center for National Renewal, an initiative of Churches in Covenant, a large international coalition of churches. During their December 2017 conference, the D.C. Renewal Experience, CNR arranged for a special access tour of the museum. In a promotional video for the group, Pastor Stephen Hayes, son of CNR founder Dr. Mike Hayes, said, "God has called us to take possession and dominion of this land and of our government."[50]

In 2019 the Museum of the Bible sponsored the three-day Worldview Conference of Kingdom Education Ministries, "Capturing the Next Generation for Christ Through Kingdom Education." It has also sponsored Passages, a group that provides Christian college students with trips to Israel to promote the political and theological views of Christian Zionism, and which Southern Methodist University professor of religious studies Mark A. Chancey calls "a sort of 'Birthright [Israel] for Evangelicals.'"

And of course the Museum of the Bible is a little piece of heaven for leaders such as Ralph Drollinger, who held a fall training conference for international leaders of his ministry at the Museum of the Bible shortly after its opening in November 2017. "Many of these men were named Global Directors earlier this year, and have made tremendous progress in establishing their own ministries as well as in their charge of finding godly, skilled, and experienced men to take the Gospel to the leaders of nations in their area of the world," Drollinger said.[51] None of these visitors seem to have any doubt that the Museum of the Bible is something like "God's base camp" in the nation's capital, as "apostle" Cindy Jacobs put it during Revolution 2017.

On the eve of my departure for Revolution 2018, I am frankly disappointed to learn that the venue has unexpectedly been switched. But I feel a certain shiver of excitement when I learn of the new venue for the event. With help from the Museum of the Bible, Revolution 2018 has secured space at the Trump International Hotel on Pennsylvania Avenue, just a few blocks from the White House. This, I think, should be interesting.

Lamplighter Ministries, the group behind Revolution 2018, is associated with the New Apostolic Reformation, a fast-growing movement in the charismatic tradition that counts Seven Mountains dominionist C. Peter Wagner as a forefather. Its leaders call themselves apostles, maintaining that they can receive direct communications from God and have influence in the supernatural realm. On a chilly December evening I arrive at the Trump International Hotel, where the rank and file of Lamplighter Ministries move around in curious juxtaposition with the pale interiors, gold trim, and sparkling crystal chandeliers.

A gentle man of about thirty wearing a Mickey Mouse T-shirt tells me he made the long drive with his father to D.C. from Albany, New York. The pair could not afford the hotel's $56 parking fee, so they parked on a faraway street. They could not afford D.C. hotel rates, either, so they decided to lodge outside the city limits. "But it's so good to be here," he says with delight. For a middle-aged attendee who says she's on disability thanks to a workplace-related injury, the trip is a splurge. "I've never been anywhere like this before," she tells me, looking around the white-and-gold ballroom.

I fall into conversation with Johneen and Tom, a friendly, gregarious couple in their seventies who flew in this morning from the Houston area. Johneen, who wears a scarf and sweater in softly coordinating shades of gray, tells me stories about her four children and fifteen grandchildren— "thirteen of them homeschooled!"

She confides, "We had a prophetic moment on the way here. Our plane was delayed because they had to secure a fire extinguisher that had come loose. And here we are heading into 'The Fire!'" she exclaims, her delicate features crinkling with pleasure and wonder.

Johneen's husband, Tom, who is wearing a fine cashmere sweater, works "in oil," she says. Johneen "started getting involved in intercession" when the pair were living in a historic house in London and "we had some issues with demons."

At the front table, organizers are handing out a stapled program and wristbands. The headline on the handout reads: "Compilation—Verdicts from Heaven's Court." Some of the papers, which are printed on both sides, purport to be a "Life Decree: Amendments to Decree of Divorce from Baal," concerning the case of "THE PEOPLE OF GOD, Plaintiff, versus

THE PRINCIPALITY OF BAAL (Incl. Baal, Queen of Heaven, Leviathan, Defendant)."

Under the header "Re-Constitution of the United States (The Turnaround Verdict)," the handout tells us: "It has been decided that the land and government (of the United States) were consecrated to Jesus Christ from inception, and remain in this standing today" and that "the Court now rules according to Psalm 15:3 that the scepter of the wicked must no longer remain on the land allotted to the righteous. The scepter, or enforcement of unjust governance, must now be rescinded. Further, the Court grants the wealth of heaven and Earth to establish this Covenant sworn to your forefathers by the King. The issuance of the King's land grants and inheritances is now authorized for distribution and stewardship to this end."

A giant screen behind the podium features a large graphic of what appears to be a red substance—blood? food coloring?—swirling in water. "I can feel it coming in the air tonight, oh Lord," several hundred worshippers sing the refrain of a Phil Collins's song. On stage, a nine-piece band from Georgia plays the familiar tune slowly. Soon they pick up the pace, transitioning into contemporary worship songs like "Holy Visitation" by Rita Springer, whose voice has the ragged edges that suggest familiarity with the harder side of life. In front of the room, a dancing woman whirls two flags through the air, American and Israeli.

Up at the podium, the speakers take over, wielding a gavel for dramatic effect. Jon Hamill, who founded Lamplighter Ministries with his wife, Jolene, announces, "In Jesus's name, we declare the Deep State will not prevail," before banging the gavel on a podium. A similar prayer ritual, directed at "the false media network," is led by Jolene, who implores members of the audience to "repent of drinking the cup of media, because it is a false cup."

"We have reached a moment now to set a new course for the nation," says "apostle" Chuck Pierce. According to his biography, "Chuck is known for his accurate, prophetic gifting which helps direct nations, cities, churches and individuals in understanding the times and seasons we live in."

"The windows of access over Washington, D.C., are open!" he raises his voice. "Open!"

"*Freedom!*" everyone cries.

Another featured speaker, Rick Ridings, takes the stage to offer the details of one of his apparent conversations with God. "I said, 'How will the nations learn to change?'" Ridings asks. "The Lord said, 'It must play,'" he pauses for emphasis, "'the *Trump card.*'"

As the audience reacts with a cheer, he continues, "It was amazing to see the realignment of Israel, Jerusalem, for America."

This subsection of the Christian nationalist universe may appear to be well outside the mainstream of the movement, and many of its beliefs and practices—including an acceptance of female pastors—are no doubt heretical to hard-line evangelicals in the style of Ralph Drollinger. But the presence of a featured guest—Pastor Andrew Brunson, who appears onstage with his wife, Norine, to deliver a lengthy and impassioned speech of gratitude—shows that this cohort has more avenues of access to power than one might think. Brunson, who lived in Turkey for twenty years and pastored at a small evangelical Presbyterian congregation in Izmir, was arrested and imprisoned for two years on allegations of "support of a terrorist organization" and "political and military espionage." Brunson received legal representation from the American Center for Law and Justice, which is led by Trump counsel Jay Sekulow, and his cause was trumpeted by nearly every major Christian nationalist organization in America, from the Family Research Council to the Alliance Defending Freedom. After Brunson's release was secured and he returned to the United States, he was photographed praying in the Oval Office with President Trump.

Prior to Pastor Brunson's speech, Hamill claims to have prayed, along with other faith leaders, for Brunson's release in Sam Brownback's office at the State Department. Brownback "brought us up privately to his office so we could just hear his heart," Hamill says. "And he pulled out a picture of Pastor Andrew with a personal note that he had written and asked for the Gideon group, our community-within-a-community, and the Lamplighter families to pray for Pastor Andrew."

Brunson is followed on stage by Pam Pryor, who led a "faith and Christian outreach" effort during Trump's presidential campaign. Pryor, an ex-aide to Sarah Palin whose name appears on the leaked 2014 membership list for the Council for National Policy, has landed a job as senior advisor in the office of the undersecretary for civilian security, democracy, and human rights at the State Department and is on hand to help celebrate Brunson's release.[52] "I just want to say if I'm ever in prison, I want Norine!" she says from the podium, and the crowd laughs along with her.

Praising Jon and Jolene Hamill as "royalty among intercessors," Pryor tells us she, too, sets aside time for "intercessory prayer" every Tuesday at 10:00 A.M. "I will say there's still a lot to pray for in the State Department, still a lot to pray for in this administration," she says. "There are a lot of enemies still within the camp. And that's bad, man, they are, yeah, they are still in the camp, so pray . . . but I have such confidence."

As it happens, a Chanukah gathering for members of the Orthodox Jewish community is taking place in the Trump International Hotel on the very same night. For the Lamplighters, this can be no mere coincidence. "Tonight, Jewish leaders are hosted at the Trump hotel for a Chanukah celebration," Ridings says. "We bless President Trump even as he sits with elders of the Jewish community. A righteous revolution has been released to bring America back, to turn America to God. Trump has brought us into alignment with Jerusalem."

Throughout the event, there is only praise for the Museum of the Bible and the sudden relocation of the conference to the Trump International Hotel. I ask Johneen how she feels about the change, and she is effusive. "They're really treating us like royalty," she says, pointing out that the Museum of the Bible is paying for buffet meals in an attempt to compensate for the venue change. "That wasn't included before," she says appreciatively.

When another guest marvels, "Isn't this hotel incredible?" Johneen responds, "Isn't it incredible what God has done?"

Johneen exudes an admirable sense of optimism and wonder, and in some ways I find myself envying her ability to read in creaky floorboards and unsecured fire extinguishers a message sent from on high. No self-doubt stands in the way of her drive to place her own story at the center of the universe. No shimmering displays of political or financial corruption, no glaring examples of political manipulation, will cloud her happy vision.

As the first night of Revolution 2018 winds down, I head to the hotel bar. The men outnumber the women, and they do have a certain swagger. A tall bearded man, about forty, strolls through the lounge in leather chaps and a T-shirt reading, "Bikers for Trump." His lady friend, in Minnie Mouse polka dots and six-inch platforms, giggles on his arm. A number of men in very expensive suits chat in the middle area of the lounge in languages I can't identify. A group of Orthodox Jews are installed in an area near the front of the room. I recognize Rabbi Levi Shemtov, executive vice president of American Friends of Lubavitch in Washington; Shemtov is Jared and Ivanka's rabbi.[53] Four or five young men in slim-fitting suits and fashy hair-cuts, several wearing "Trump 2020" buttons, saunter up to the bar. One has what appears to be a tattoo of an Iron Cross discernible just above his collared shirt.

Over a glass of Trump champagne and some perfectly pickled radishes, I watch the chyrons flow across the overhead television tuned to Fox News. "ANTI-CHRISTMAS CRAZINESS . . . WHERE IS THE TOLERANCE ON THE LEFT? . . . LIBERALS: THE NEW CENSORS . . . DEMOCRATS: THE PARTY OF KILLJOYS . . . CLIMATE CHANGE ALARMISM IS GOING TOO FAR . . ."

CHAPTER 7

The Blitz: Turning the States into Laboratories of Theocracy

IN THE WORLD of investigative journalism, most of the revelations come in pieces—a stray bit of testimony here, a video recording over there—that accumulate in slow motion. But once in a long while it all happens on one day with a discovery that suddenly makes sense of the past and casts the future in a new light. That more or less was the case when Frederick Clarkson, acting on a tip, went fishing in a conservative website and reeled in a 116-page manual for a campaign called *Project Blitz*.[1]

"It was like an archeological find or a scientific discovery," said Clarkson, a senior research analyst at the Massachusetts think tank Political Research Associates, who reported on his findings for the online magazine Religion Dispatches. "You see it for what it is, and suddenly the world has changed."

The discovery of *Project Blitz* was a game changer for understanding the movement's legislative strategy. It is the playbook for a nationwide assault on state legislatures in all fifty states. It does indeed describe a "blitz," for the basic strategy is to flood the zone with coordinated, simultaneous bills in the hopes that they will, eventually, become law.[2] The stated aim of the project is to advance "religious freedom"—in a late 2019 conference call, organizers discussed rebranding the initiative Freedom for All—but this turns out to be the biggest of the many deceptions that characterize the enterprise. Along with the parallel, equally massive, coordinated assault by antiabortion activists on state legislatures, *Project Blitz* aims to inundate as many states as possible with its bills in order to jam the wheels of the state legislative process. On a 2017 conference call for like-minded state legislators, Project Blitz director Lea Carawan thanked the "coalition of government leaders, faith-based organizations, policy and legal groups, media outlets, and businesses who are united to blitz the nation with effective and enduring religious freedom legislation, and also reclaim the narrative in the public square."

Although the initiative was started in 2015, it is evolving rapidly, capitalizing on its previous successes and incorporating lessons learned from its losses. In 2016 the *Project Blitz* playbook was 40 pages long; in 2017 it had grown to 116 pages. By 2018–2019 it had swelled to 148 pages.

Perhaps the most illuminating aspect of the *Project Blitz* manual, however, has to do less with the specifics on the Christian nationalist strategy for state legislation than with what it reveals about the organization and effectiveness of the movement itself. There is no single institution behind Project Blitz, just as there is no single Christian nationalist headquarters, no permanent staff, no charismatic kingpin. There are simply a number of familiar faces, a variety of old and new hats, and a swarm of acronyms. And yet none of these absences seems to diminish the movement's ability to act effectively and decisively. The unity of Christian nationalism, as ever, is to be found in its distinctive political vision.

At the time of Clarkson's discovery, the steering committee of Project Blitz consisted of four individuals, each of whom opens a revealing window on the workings of Christian nationalist leadership. Lea Carawan, the director of the group, is representative of the governmental wing of the movement. Carawan, who obtained her master's degree in Christian theology at Regent University, is cofounder (along with Virginia congressman J. Randy Forbes) and executive director of the Congressional Prayer Caucus Foundation, whose goal is to "protect religious freedom, preserve America's Judeo-Christian heritage and promote prayer," as well as "address and challenge current anti-faith trends" affecting the legal and legislative landscape. "What separation of church and state was designed to do, that Thomas Jefferson himself said, was to ensure that [government] did not interfere with our ability to live out our faith in the public square," Carawan told a TV interviewer in 2018.[3]

"Our country was founded by Christians on Judeo-Christian principles, and they intended for this to be a Christian nation," said the interviewer.

"That's right," Carawan replied. "It simply means that our laws and policies will reflect Judeo-Christian or biblical values and concepts."

Joining Carawan on the steering committee of Project Blitz is Buddy Pilgrim, a businessman and founder of Integrity Leadership, a ministry focused on "equipping Christians with Biblical principles for the workplace." According to Integrity Leadership's website, "We will always exercise and teach dominion in business and politics."[4] Pilgrim is an avid proponent of the merger between the Christian far right and the economic far right. When Pilgrim writes, "Dominion in earthly realms of authority (business & politics) is a Biblical mandate," one can hear the echoes of Rushdoony and his progenitors. "Business is God's system of wealth creation," according to Pilgrim. In an interview, he added, "If you turn it over to people who don't know God you'll only get ungodly results." The "only way to make freedom work," he says, is to have "Godly men and women assuming positions of power and authority in business (and politics)."[5]

For several years Pilgrim has been active in reaching evangelical clergy with the message of the importance of voting. "The evangelical Christian vote is the single most important bloc in any given election and it was in particular in 2016," he told a radio interviewer in 2018. "So we've got this huge voting bloc out there, and we're already organized. Most Christians already meet every week in a church." Hitting the point home, he added, "There was no Republican candidate who can win in 2016 without the evangelical vote, and there was no Republican candidate who could lose if they had the evangelical vote . . . [I]t was essential to that election."

In addition to his convictions and activism, what Pilgrim may also bring to the table is access to money and connections. Lindy M. "Buddy" Pilgrim is the former president of Pilgrim's Pride Corporation and a nephew of Lonnie "Bo" Pilgrim, who founded the chicken processing company in 1946 as a feed store in Pittsburg, Texas. Some sixty years later Pilgrim's Pride was in the Fortune 500. At its peak, the company had operations in seventeen states and Mexico and more than 35,000 employees. Buddy Pilgrim later branched out to other endeavors. He worked as CEO of Simmons Foods and founded start-ups in residential housing, food distribution, and agribusiness. He also established businesses in Moscow and St. Petersburg, Russia.

A Trump supporter from the start—voting against Hillary Clinton was "a simple choice of life over death"—Pilgrim served on President Trump's "Evangelical Leadership Council," as a 2018 radio interviewer called it. Pilgrim glowingly recalled a dinner he attended at the White House for evangelical leaders, including James Dobson, Tony Perkins, Kenneth Copeland, and Franklin Graham. "And here's what was so special about it," he said. "This was the first ever dinner like this, and the dinner was literally named, 'A Celebration of Evangelical Leadership.' Not 'a celebration of faith leadership in general,' with a mix of Buddhists and Hindus and Christians and all these other groups."[6]

Project Blitz lists two other sponsoring organizations: WallBuilders ProFamily Legislative Network and the National Legal Foundation. David Barton, of course, is the founder and president of the first and sits on the board of the second. Not surprisingly, Barton is also on the steering committee of Project Blitz. In fact, to outward appearances, he is an ideas man and a prime mover behind the venture. In several conference calls aimed at coordinating Project Blitz with sympathetic legislators, it was Barton, along with Carawan, who took the lead in laying out the strategy and fielding questions. Barton also shares another connection with Buddy Pilgrim: both men worked on Ted Cruz's unsuccessful bid for the presidency in 2016, with Pilgrim as national director of the Faith and Religious Liberties Coalition directing faith outreach efforts on Cruz's behalf.

Rounding out the fantastic four on the Project Blitz steering committee is Bill Dallas, a convicted embezzler who served time in the San Quentin State Prison in San Quentin, California, before founding a data firm that aims to turn out the conservative Christian vote. Dallas has also become a behind-the-scenes power player; he took a lead role in organizing the June 21, 2016 closed-door gathering between then presidential hopeful Donald Trump and more than 1,000 evangelical leaders from around the country. That gathering, which took place at a hotel in Midtown Manhattan, marked a turning point in Trump's political fortunes. We'll meet Bill Dallas in the next chapter.

*   *   *

In early 2018 the bills started to come in. The people who follow these types of legislation across the states—the lawyers at Americans United for Separation of Church and State and the Freedom from Religion Foundation, for example—sensed that something strange was afoot. In all of 2017 there had been three bills proposing the use of "In God We Trust" in various official forums. Now there were more than that number rolling in every week.

By April 2018 state legislatures had been served with more than seventy bills based on Project Blitz models. Some of them involved the motto "In God We Trust" and other expressions of Christianity in public settings. Project Blitz had kicked into action. While many bills were defeated, bills in at least five states were signed into law. "It's kind of like whack-a-mole for the other side; it'll drive 'em crazy that they'll have to divide their resources out in opposing this," David Barton explained on a conference call about Project Blitz with state legislators from around the country.[7]

Politicians tended to frame the bills in the language of heritage and civil rights rather than religion. That was by design. In one of Project Blitz's conference calls for sympathetic state legislators, David Barton promised to share "very extensive national surveys on where people are with religious liberties. And the kind of words we can use that people respond to much better than other words. And so those are the talking points that we are happy to share with you guys." Later in the call, Carawan added, "Maclellan [possibly a reference to the deep-pocketed Chattanooga, Tennessee–based Maclellan Foundation] funded reports of two years of hearts and minds strategies . . . best practice messaging on religious freedom."

Minnesota was one of the states where the messaging worked and Blitz scored. In May 2018 an "In God We Trust" bill, whose chief sponsor was state senator Dan Hall, passed the Minnesota senate. The bill, describing the words "In God We Trust" as a "national motto," would allow "volunteer groups" to install their "In God We Trust" signs in public buildings, including public schools, throughout the state. Far-right policy groups such as the American Family Association, whose founder Donald Wildmon notoriously accused the Harry Potter franchise of promoting witchcraft, stepped up with their own "In God We Trust" posters designed with the public schools in mind.

The bill immediately provoked controversy; indeed, it seemed crafted for precisely that purpose. "I don't want far-right hate groups like the American Family Association plastering my kids' school with their 'In God We Trust' signs," said Nancy Jackson, a St. Paul mother who organized a letter-writing campaign to state representatives. The debate over the bill lit up the floor of the legislature. Supporters noted that "In God We Trust" was adopted as the national motto in 1956; opponents pointed out that it was a McCarthy-era phenomenon that had displaced *E Pluribus Unum*, or "Out of Many, One," which had been the United States' unofficial motto since the eighteenth century. "I'm wondering if Senator Hall would feel the same if students walked in and instead of the word 'God,' the word 'Allah,' which is the word for God in the Muslim religion, welcomed students to their schools," asked Democratic state senator Scott Dibble. Senator John Marty weighed in, too, characterizing the bill as "offensive."[8]

The last comment in particular was like gold for the right-wing mediasphere. The implication that God is "offensive," or that Islam might claim equal rights before the law with Christianity, was more than worth its weight in conservative rage. Soon the clip showed up on Fox News, CNS News, Breitbart, and other right-wing platforms. The segment was tweeted out by the Family Research Council. "Our nation's motto, 'In God We Trust,' igniting a debate on the Minnesota state senate floor, over a bill that simply allows schools to—get this—*voluntarily* display posters with the saying on it," the Fox anchor announced. "But some lawmakers, Democrats, argue the motto doesn't belong in schools and is offensive."

Fox then invited Dan Hall to defend the bill. "There's no cost to it; the cost would come from the community," Hall told the TV host. "My whole premise was: How about bringing respect back into the schools? We've lost a whole lot of respect for those things in life that we should be respecting."

"Why is God, the mention of God in our schools controversial on the left today?" asked the Fox newscaster incredulously.

"There seems to be an anti-faith movement in the country, to suppress anything that is religious in any way and wipe it out of government," said Hall. "I'm here to tell you we need to bring respect back to our country."[9]

If it felt as though the event had been staged to evoke the grievances of a population steeped in its own feelings of persecution, that's because it was.

On Fox News, Dan Hall told the host with a wide-eyed expression, "I just figured the opposition would be really short, there wouldn't be a whole lot." That sounded like a whopper. The documentation of Project Blitz makes clear that a principal purpose of the "In God We Trust" legislation is to force the opposition to take unpopular stands on seemingly symbolic issues. In fact, the authors specifically seemed to envision using the bills to catch opposition lawmakers on video saying things that can later be used against them.

Dan Hall should have known that, of course: he is cochair of the state legislative prayer caucus, a state wing of the Congressional Prayer Caucus, the organizational sponsor of Project Blitz.[10]

The documentation of the Blitz is particularly valuable in that it shows that Christian nationalists have self-consciously embraced a strategy of advancing their goals through deception and indirection. For many years critics have warned that concessions to the Christian right on "symbolic" issues—erecting religious monuments and emblazoning religious mottos on state property, for example—would set the nation on a course leading to the establishment of religion. We now know that the critics were right—because pushing the states down a slippery slope to a more "bibically based" society is precisely what the authors of Project Blitz propose to accomplish. In multiple states, including Mississippi, Louisiana, Alabama, South Dakota, Tennessee, Kentucky, and Florida, prominently placed "In God We Trust" signs in every public school building are now mandatory.[11]

As Dan Hall also would likely have known, the "In God We Trust" brouhaha was only phase one of Project Blitz. The architects of the Blitz have helpfully grouped their model legislation into three categories or phases.[12] The first consists of symbolic or ceremonial gestures that will receive "some opposition but not hard to beat," according to David Barton. Some, like the Minnesota bill, focus on placing mottos in schools. Others aim to place "In God We Trust" placards and stickers in statehouses, federal buildings, libraries, post offices—even police cars. Still other bills include "Civic Literacy" initiatives that involve the display of other kinds of historical and religious documents favored by movement leaders.

But the point of phase I is just to clear the path for phase II, which consists of bills that propose to inject Christian nationalist ideas more directly into schools and other government entities. Some phase II bills are intended to promote the teaching and celebration of Christianity in public schools, including support for sectarian "Bible literacy" curricula, particularly those that include hefty servings of Christian nationalist history and the declaration of a "Christian Heritage Week."[13] They are a means of spreading the message, among children especially, that conservative Christians are the real Americans and everybody else is here by invitation only. According to Barton, these laws "will also be pretty easy to pass," but the opposition is "going to be a lot more virulent and mean in their attacks." The point of phase II, of course, is to make room for phase III, which legalizes discrimination against those whose actions (or very being) offends the sensibilities of conservative Christians.

While Project Blitz seems to promote the religious right's proverbial Santa's list of culture war issues, one key topic is missing, and that is abortion. The documentation for Project Blitz does not include proposed legislation relating to women's reproductive rights—apart from a model bill advancing the rights of providers to deny services to women on grounds of religious conscience—but this is not the result of any oversight. Project Blitz does not address the topic because it does not need to; the abortion issue is already being handled, with stunning effectiveness, by other entities.

Under the leadership of organizations including Americans United for Life, the Susan B. Anthony List, and National Right to Life, different groups with varying strategies united by common political goals, antiabortion activists have in the past few years pushed more than four hundred bills to restrict reproductive freedom through state legislatures.

This was the blitz before the Blitz, in a manner of speaking. Both the antiabortion and the "religious freedom" prongs of this assault on state capitols consciously intend to emulate the strategy of "bill mills" like the American Legislative Exchange Council, the corporate-funded outfit that has pushed many hundreds of hard-right economic bills through state legislatures.

Women in America have a constitutionally guaranteed right to have an abortion through the right to make decisions about family as well as the principle of bodily integrity. So much was established by *Roe v. Wade*. Yet that has not stopped antiabortion activists from using the coercive power of government to deprive as many women as possible of that right. The first and most obvious strategy is to use the government's power of the purse to go after women who might otherwise rely on public assistance to cover the cost of the procedure. Leading the way in this new strategy was the Hyde Amendment, a legislative provision barring the use of certain federal funds to pay for most abortions. Passed in 1976, the Hyde Amendment was a rider to annual appropriations bills. Because the Hyde Amendment primarily affects Medicaid, it has substantially impacted poor women and families. Subsequent initiatives have targeted this vulnerable population disproportionately.

The Republican Party now has at its disposal a variety of tools to be used in the assault on women's ability to access abortion as well as certain forms of contraception. Six-week abortion restrictions—before many women realize they are pregnant—are just the latest effort in a multipronged strategy. Forced ultrasounds, for instance, compel women to undergo needless expensive and invasive medical procedures. Sham "crisis pregnancy centers," which exist to dissuade women from obtaining abortions, are now receiving unprecedented amounts of state funding; in 2018 more than a dozen states earmarked an estimated $40.5 million in taxpayer funds for these centers.[14] Various methods of birth control, such as emergency contraception and IUDs, have been wrongly labeled "abortion," a designation that defies science and reason and paves the way for onerous regulation or limited access.[15] "Waiting periods" of up to seventy-two hours substantially burden patients, who may be compelled to take time off from work, arrange child care, and pay for hotel accommodations in faraway cities. Laws known as "targeted regulation of abortion providers" (or TRAP laws) encumber the medical practices of abortion providers in the name of "safety," with stunning consequences: From 2011 to 2016, more than 160 abortion clinics in the country closed or stopped performing abortions, and only 21 new ones opened to replace them.[16]

The religious right is quick to extol the principle of free speech when it comes to, say, public school officials preaching to children in their care or shouting at women through bullhorns outside of reproductive health clinics. And yet they are eager to regulate and restrict the speech of medical professionals delivering reproductive health services. In some states doctors are now required to lie to their patients by giving them false or incomplete information about their legal options in pregnancy, or are compelled to make inaccurate statements about a disproven link between abortion and cancer or mental health. And a rule governing Title X, the federal program that finances reproductive health services for low-income women, censors the speech of healthcare workers by prohibiting them from referring patients to abortion clinics.

According to Elizabeth Nash, senior state issues manager at the Guttmacher Institute, a leading reproductive research and policy organization, 231 abortion restrictions were enacted between 2011 and 2014—almost 20 percent more restrictions than the number enacted in the entire preceding decade. Nearly two hundred antiabortion bills were introduced in 2015. In 2016, eighteen states enacted fifty new abortion restrictions. In 2018, fifty states adopted twenty-seven new restrictions.

Considered individually, the hundreds of bills making their way through dozens of state legislatures appear to have a scattershot quality. In reality they are components of a coordinated, overarching strategy that, like Project Blitz, aims to overwhelm state legislatures. The end goal is to create a new reality on the ground in which women have no real ability to exercise a right that they are supposedly guaranteed.

While the right continues to grandstand on the abortion issue, the abortion rate in the United States is in decline for reasons that have much to do with innovations in long-acting birth control. Access is key, however. Multiple studies show that increased contraceptive access, including better insurance coverage policies, over-the-counter availability, and comprehensive sex education, dramatically reduces rates of both unintended pregnancy and abortion. If antiabortion activists were truly interested in lowering abortion rates, they would champion such measures. Instead, they support measures that interfere with access.

That's because the real aim is to cast birth control—and the activity that creates a need for it, particularly among women—as unhealthy and immoral. The 2019 Students for Life conference held a workshop titled "Green Sex." "Many women are already throwing away their birth control pills to join this green sex movement," according to the workshop description. "Join us to find out why!"[17] At the 2018 Values Voter Summit in Washington, D.C., speaking on a panel titled "Restoring a Generation's Identity," Chelsea Patterson Sobolik, a policy director for the Ethics & Religious Liberty Commission of the Southern Baptist Convention, laid the blame for "gender confusion" squarely at the feet of family planning. "I want to dial back about one hundred years ago, to when birth control and the pill were introduced," she said. "What that did is that's the very beginning of breaking down marriage and divorcing intimacy and sex from consequences."

Like the sponsors of Americans United for Life legislative initiatives, the leaders behind Project Blitz are playing a long and ambitious game. They have invested their deepest hopes in the third and most contentious category of model legislation. Recognizing that the initiatives will be unpopular, Project Blitz advises its troops against framing them in religious terms, recommending instead that they "begin a public discourse on these important topics grounded in the language that the opponents themselves use."

For the Blitzers, the dream bill is something that participants in a conference call referred to in awed tones as the "Mississippi Missile." The "missile" is the state's HB 1523, a 2016 law that allows individuals, nonprofits, private businesses, and government agencies to discriminate against targeted groups with impunity (and above all without losing their tax-advantaged status), provided that they do so in accordance with "sincerely held religious beliefs."

Introduced into the Mississippi legislature and signed into law by Governor Phil Bryant in 2016, HB 1523 was one of the most sweeping of the nation's "religious liberty" bills making the rounds in red-state capitals that year. In the press they were and are often referred to as "anti-LGBT bills," because they would give legal cover to those who want to discriminate against LGBT people. Ben Needham, Director of Strategic Initiatives in the Policy and Political Affairs Department at the Human Rights Campaign, has said the legislation is "probably the worst religious freedom bill to date."[18]

The public perception of these bills, often abetted by Christian nationalists themselves, is that they concern only the religious feelings of homophobic cake bakers and florists. But there is an even more radical agenda behind the bills, and depriving LGBT Americans of their right to obtain goods and services on an equal basis is only a part of it. Consider the law's provisions regarding foster care services. The government, we are told, will no longer be allowed to take action against any foster parent that "guides, instructs, or raises a child ... in a manner consistent with a sincerely held religious belief."

It is worth remembering in this context that the culture of the religious right often favors corporal punishment as a form of discipline in child-rearing. Focus on the Family, the Christian right advocacy group, offers handy tips on "Five Biblical Principles for Spanking." Indeed, in his many books on child-rearing, Focus on the Family founder James Dobson emphasizes the message that children must be brought under a strict form of parental authority and taught to fear God. Children, Dobson insists, "are naturally inclined toward rebellion, selfishness, dishonesty, aggression, exploitation, and greed."[19] Even infants may be "defiant upon exit from the womb." But "a well-deserved spanking," he advises his followers, turns "a sullen little troublemaker into a sweet and loving angel."[20] If a toddler disobeys, he once told a live audience, the parent should grab hold of the child's trapezius muscle. "You squeeze that little muscle," he said, and "he goes down to the ground." The audience laughed.[21]

Of course, it's all part of the child's training in submission to an authoritarian form of religion. As Dobson explains, "We should teach our children to submit to our loving leadership as preparation for their later life of obedience to God."[22]

Or, as Ralph Drollinger puts it, "The rod, according to the Bible, is the specific means of dealing with, and is the remedy for, foolishness in the heart of a child. Yes, effective verbal communication is necessary too, but when rebellion is present to speak without spanking is woefully inadequate." Drollinger chides parents who have qualms about striking their children. It "matters little what we might think about spanking. The issue is this: will we obey God on this matter? Will we follow His methods for childrearing or not?" Drollinger goes on to advise, "Think of spanking in this way: as hard as it is for you to spank your child, his or her obedience to God in the future is directly related to yours in the present."[23]

In one of the model bills that picks up where the Mississippi Missile leaves off, the Blitzers intend to get state legislatures to resolve that "this state supports and encourages marriage between one man and one woman and the desirability that intimate sexual relations only take place between such couples." What is perhaps more striking than the direct attempt to legislate against intimacy between consenting adults is the cruelty with which the argument is advanced. In that piece of proposed lawmaking, states are asked to affirm that people who have sexual intimacy outside of a monogamous, heterosexual marriage have a "higher instance of serious disease." It would be touching to think that the leaders of America's latest religious revival have at last turned their attention to health care, but no: their concern here is that all of this sex is costing taxpayers lots of money—"estimated to be in the billions of dollars."

The emotional impact of bills like these really has two sides: It singles out a target population as worthy of state-sanctioned contempt, and it identifies another group as worthy of state-sanctioned respect. That privileged group consists of those who adhere not to any religion but to a specific variety of religion, just as the despised group consists of those that offend the privileged group. In HB 1523, as in the Blitzers' model bills, the variety of religion is indicated with some precision as that which involves a belief in the primacy of heterosexual relationships and the fixity of gender. Those whose religion might sanction a different or more complicated set of beliefs will find no representation in these bills.

Apart from consolidating the privileges of conservative Christians to impose their beliefs on others, the point of bills like HB 1523 has a lot to do with money. A helpful clue can be found in a letter that the American Family Association sent out in support of the Mississippi bill before it was passed. The bill, said the AFA, is crucial because it protects the AFA and groups like it from the "governmental threat of losing their tax exempt status."[24]

There is a revealing irony in that statement. Tax exemption is a kind of gift from the government: a privilege. It is an indirect way of funneling money from taxpayers to groups that engage in certain kinds of activities (like charity work or nonprofit education) and not other kinds of activities (like business and political activism). In articulating their concern for potential threats to their governmental subsidy, the AFA implicitly recognizes that if our society decides that it no longer wishes to subsidize groups that preach homophobia and promote discrimination, the justification for continued subsidies and privileges from the government will evaporate.

The people who drafted the bill on behalf of the Mississippi legislators get it. This is why the very first "discriminatory action" by the government that the law prohibits is "to alter in any way the tax treatment" of any person or organization that abides by the newly sanctioned religious beliefs.

In 2016 a federal district court struck down HB 1523 for the obvious reason that it favored one set of religious beliefs over others. In 2018, however, an appeals court set aside that decision on the grounds that the plaintiffs did not have standing to bring the case, so the law remains in force until some individuals suitably harmed by its manifestly discriminatory intent, and in possession of the bottomless resources that will be required for the inevitable battle with deep-pocketed Christian right legal groups like Alliance Defending Freedom, decide to come forward to oppose it.

The Blitzers understand at some level that their agenda will not command majorities of public opinion. Indeed, the premise of their work is that they can't win in a fair and open debate. Increasingly, Christian nationalists have become comfortable embracing this kind of minority-led politics. As J. Randy Forbes, founder of the Congressional Prayer Caucus, put it, "Our studies and what we have seen is 10 percent of the people in any country in the world can change that country if they have the right strategies, if they persevere, and if they will just find a way to put their differences aside and come together. And that's what we're seeing happening across this country."[25] Referencing David Barton's assertions about the American Revolution, Forbes claimed that "only 10 percent of the population ever did anything in the fight, just 10 percent, and that really hasn't changed much today. Ten percent of the people in this country can change this country. We just have to find that 10 percent, get them together, get the right strategies, the right commitment, and watch how the Lord how he can change this country."

While Forbes directly referenced Barton's work, his statement also likely alluded to the work of evangelical pollster George Barna. Barna, hailed in *Christianity Today* as "evangelicals' most-quoted statistician," is a prolific author and activist who founded the Barna Group, an evangelical market research firm based in Ventura, California, that focuses on cultural and religious trends. Barna identified a cohort of "SAGE Cons," or "spiritually active, governance-engaged conservatives," and introduced the term into movement leadership parlance in his 2017 book *The Day Christians Changed America: How Christian Conservatives Put Trump in the White House and Redirected America's Future.* "The driving force behind their faith is that nine out of ten of them (90%) have developed a biblical worldview," Barna writes. "That compares to just 1% of the rest of the U.S. adult population."[26] According to Barna, SAGE Cons number just 10 percent of the population but vote in highly disproportionate numbers and, more to the point, are motivated to persuade others to vote for their preferred candidates. It was the work of these SAGE Cons, Barna said, that put Trump over the top in the 2016 election.[27]

On October 29, 2018, Forbes appeared on a broadcast from the Truth & Liberty Coalition and "7M Ventures," the initiative cofounded by Barton, Lance Wallnau, Pastor Andrew Wommack, and other dominionist leaders. ("7M" would appear to be a reference to the Seven Mountains.) Forbes boasted that in addition to "100 members of Congress, both in the House and in the Senate" and "almost 1000 state officials" in "33 states," their work has roped in government officials at the local level across the country, from "mayors to police chiefs to fire chiefs across the board."

"So now we have an entire division that is fighting nothing but getting 'In God We Trust' across the country," he exulted. "We've got groups meeting to see what kind of strategies we can use in Hollywood. We have other groups that are looking at the laws we can get passed. Groups looking at how we protect and strengthen our judges."[28]

As far as the organizers of Project Blitz are concerned, things are going according to plan. In a 2017 conference call, Lea Carawan's mood was notably upbeat: "We have this window of opportunity now; I think we're all feeling it," she said. Speaking of "a powerful momentum," she declared, "there is more receptiveness at the administration than in over thirty years, and by working together in a unified strategy we're going to be advancing religious protection in Congress, and in many states in the nation in 2017, but we believe this is just the beginning."

Carawan also appeared on the October 29, 2018, Truth & Liberty Coalition broadcast along with Forbes. Wearing a vivid blue dress and coordinating jacket, she spoke with fellow panelists Karen Conrad and Pastors Andrew Wommack and Richard Harris.

"Faith Impact Network is something we're very excited to tell you about. It's also a component of what we're doing with the Congressional Prayer Caucus Foundation," Carawan said. "In a nutshell we've built the largest network of elected leaders, federal, state elected leaders who are united to make an impact for faith." Carawan explained that "it started with the congressional members . . . We realized we need to go to where the battle is being waged, which is at the state and community levels, and so we built a network across states, now we have thirty-three states that are a part of this and many more will be joining."[29]

In a conference call for state legislators, there was a telling moment that got to the heart of the thinking behind Project Blitz. Former member of Michigan's House of Representatives Ken Kurtz said, "You know one of my favorite songs is 'Onward Christian Soldiers.' The one verse there that I really like, 'Like a mighty army.' And that's what I began to believe the Congressional Prayer Caucus Foundation was, that army put together."

At this point, it would have been apparent to any listener that the agenda of Project Blitz had nothing to do with religious freedom in the proper sense of the term. The point of Kurtz's Christian army was quite palpably to fight on behalf of conservative Christians who wish to discriminate against those who do not share their beliefs. By "religious freedom," participants simply meant privilege for those with the right religion.

CHAPTER 8

Converting the Flock to Data

B Y HIS OWN account, Bill Dallas grew up in an unhappy household.[1] His mother had been sexually abused by her father. She had her first pregnancy at the age of seventeen. Dallas's dad was an alcoholic and a depressive. He died at fifty-one. Bill was an intense, obsessive child, dogged by feelings of inadequacy. You could say he was wired for the bitter schema of sin-and-salvation religion.

By the time he reached adolescence, Dallas's self-doubts were all-consuming. He "began to pray constantly for forgiveness," he later recalled, as many as "two to three hundred times each day." Seeking affirmation, he joined Young Life, the Christian youth-focused evangelism outfit. Christianity soon "became the heaviest burden I had yet encountered."

Despite this challenging start in life, Dallas had clear talents and attended Vanderbilt University, a private university in Nashville, Tennessee, known for its vast academic offerings, well-heeled student body, and vibrant Greek life. Dallas joined Sigma Nu and took business classes. But his heart was in the drama department, and he dreamed of making it big as an actor.

After graduating with honors, he moved to San Francisco. Blessed with photogenic looks, he modeled for "a major retail chain." "The money was good, but it was the clothing and attention that really appealed to me," he writes. "Hugo Boss and Armani were my favorites. Throw in some exquisite

Italian loafers and a brilliant designer tie, and with my hair gelled back, I was ready for action."

Soon Dallas was at the center of an energetic social whirl. "My party mates and I regularly rented stretch limos to weave through the streets in search of the hottest clubs," he says. People gave him the nickname "Mr. GQ." Men and women were drawn to him, and those connections started to yield fruit—and temptation.

He found his way into the real estate business, and then the money began to pour in. Dallas moved his mother and stepfather out west. In his early twenties, he and a woman named Toni had a child, a boy named Dallas. Toni "didn't put any pressure on me to support Dallas," he writes, though "she did give me the option of being part of his life." In those fast days and nights, however, he didn't make much of an effort. His life was focused on being "the bad-boy party animal of the Bay Area" with the "latest and greatest toys a man could buy."[2]

Even as he accumulated outward signs of success, Dallas couldn't shake the anxieties at his core. "I was completely empty, almost numb," he wrote. And then things really fell apart.

Dallas has publicly offered few details of the crimes he committed. What is known is that he was convicted of grand theft embezzlement and sentenced to prison. In addition, according to a 1995 article archived on SFGate.com, Dallas and his former company, Dallas Lucas, were fined a record $772,000 for having laundered campaign contributions to six Oakland City Council candidates.

As Dallas tells the story, he spent time in Susanville and then San Quentin, moving into a cell on the fourth tier of North Block, where his mother and stepfather were able to visit him weekly. It was there, he writes, that his life began to turn around. In his book, *Lessons from San Quentin: Everything I Needed to Know about Life I Learned in Prison*, Dallas describes the prison experiences that launched him on a trajectory that would land him at the center of a network of thousands of pastors, on the steering committee of Project Blitz, and in the cockpit of Christian nationalism's taxpayer-subsidized, data-driven voter turnout machine.

* * *

As Dallas became acclimated to life in prison, he says, he found that he preferred the "lifers" to the "short-timers." The latter tend to be younger, "self-absorbed," and focused on life after prison—less prone to surrender completely to their faith. The lifers, on the other hand, are much more likely to come to Jesus. With the assistance and mentorship of some of these lifers, Dallas deepened his connection to his faith and calmed his thought processes. He was able to gain mastery over compulsive behaviors, such as "washing my hands twenty to thirty times a day, hoarding books and magazines, obsessing over everything." After shifting his focus to God, "I quit the OCD behaviors cold turkey," he says. He also got a job at the prison's TV station, working his way up to producer and on-air host.

When he left prison, he was "mentally, physically, emotionally and spiritually fit—in the best shape of my life in each of those dimensions." In his book Dallas claims to visit San Quentin monthly to check in with his old buddies, who seem "peaceful and relaxed" and "always more than happy to provide me with a good life check."

Dallas had served his time, but he still hadn't paid his debts. He says that he owed "multiple fines, taxes, and other payments—one of the fines alone was $750,000."[3] He immediately looked for ways to make a living.

He worked for a time with Young Life, then for a Christian TV video company, Television Associates, utilizing skills he'd acquired at San Quentin. He also recommitted himself to his son. Then, on March 11, 1998, he had a holy visitation. "I believed God was telling me to start a satellite network that would deliver ministry training programs to churches around the country," he writes. In essence he conceived of the idea of building up a national network for communicating information and messaging to conservative evangelical pastors and through them to their congregations. As it turns out, this was exactly what the growing Christian nationalist movement needed.

With the help of Silicon Valley businessmen including Ken Eldred and Reid Rutherford and venture capitalist John Mumford, Dallas's Church Communication Network grew with exponential velocity. By the 2010s he was in regular contact with thousands of pastors, many leading movement figures, and "a variety of world-class business leaders."

But Dallas had a still bolder vision. Working with thousands of pastors allowed him to reach literally millions of congregants—which meant millions of potential voters. With the world of marketing and communications increasingly driven by data mining, he knew, there had to be a better way to mobilize the nation's Christian voters.

Dallas soon established a fruitful partnership with George Barna, the Ventura, California–based evangelical pollster and purveyor of nuanced analyses of Christian voter behavior in the aggregate. It was a match made in heaven. The two collaborated on a number of projects, including Dallas's autobiography and a collection of interviews with "master leaders" in ministry, business, and politics. But their ambitions were greater still. Dallas realized that his vast network might not only deliver information but collect data, and then turn around and use it to create more effective and impactful messaging. And now he had the resources to make it happen.

Bill Dallas and his team set up United in Purpose, or UiP, with the goal of creating a database to guide conservative Christian voter registration and voter turnout operations.[4] As Barna tells the story, UiP also played a vital role in fostering evangelical and conservative Christian unity. By November 2016, he writes, "there were roughly 75 faith-oriented non-profit organizations, along with a few thousand conservative churches in the nation, who strategically cultivated support for a variety of pro-life, pro-family, limited government candidates in swing states." UiP, Barna says, pulled them together. "The glue that bound together the entities in the United in Purpose partnership was their faith in Jesus Christ, their conservative Bible-based theology, and the shared notion that politics was one of the life spheres in which their faith should have influence."[5]

The initiative would prove so valuable to the movement that it catapulted Dallas into the upper echelons of power. His name appears on the Southern Poverty Law Center's leaked 2014 membership list for the Council for National Policy. When Donald Trump met privately with evangelical leaders in June of 2016, Bill Dallas organized the event, telling then *Time* magazine (now *New York Times*) reporter Elizabeth Dias, "We are trying to seek mutual understanding."[6] In advance of the meeting, billed as a "conversation," Fox News host Todd Starnes reported "rumblings" that "evangelical leaders are trying to turn Tuesday's meeting with Trump into a coronation."

In addition to Dallas, Barna, and Eldred, the organization's inner circle included some other familiar names. According to the 2016 and 2017 Form

990s for United in Purpose, which are publicly available through Candid, a collaboration between Guidestar and the Foundation Center Archive, David Barton acts as a "director," or consultant of some sort, contributing two hours per week to the cause but drawing no salary. Jim Garlow, the politically connected preacher with strong connections to the rising "global conservative movement," is another "director," according to the 2016 form 990 for United in Purpose Education, a division of UiP. According to the documents, Garlow volunteered a couple hours a week of his time to the cause. The UiP forms also show the seasoned Republican operative Robert D. McEwen—commonly known as "Bob"—contributing two hours a week in 2017 for a salary of $18,000, and eight hours per week in 2016 drawing a salary of $60,000.

It's not surprising to see David Barton's name pop up in this type of initiative: he's the Where's Waldo of the Christian nationalist movement. Garlow, too, is a recognizable figure in California's right-wing political scene; he was a key force behind the passage of the state's 2008 anti–marriage equality amendment, Proposition 8. Prior to the presidential election in 2016, Garlow warned his followers that Christians were close to the point when they would be compelled to "participate in very active civil disobedience" against an "anti-godly government." "Under no condition," he said, "do we have to follow laws that violate the word of God."[7]

Bob McEwen is a telling addition. After serving a dozen years as a member of Ohio's House of Representatives, McEwen, along with some associates, set up an investment bank and a lobbying and consulting firm in the D.C. area. His work as a lobbyist has put him on the payroll or in the company of a number of international political figures. McEwen also has longstanding ties to the Fellowship Foundation, also known as "the Family," whose fundamental mission is to create a ruling consortium of Christ-centered political and community leaders. The Fellowship Foundation is the organization behind the National Prayer Breakfast, an annual gathering of about 4,000 participants, hosted by members of Congress. The National Prayer Breakfast has long served as "a backdoor to American power," according to Jeff Sharlet, who has authored two books on The Family and executive produced a Netflix documentary on the topic. "Using the National Prayer Breakfast, they dispatch representatives to build relationships with foreign leaders," he explains, adding, "The more invisible you can make your organization, the more influence it will have."

McEwen also serves as executive director for the Council for National Policy.[8] This puts him in the driver's seat of the apparatus connecting "the doers and the donors," as Rich DeVos put it, of the Christian nationalist and conservative political machine.[9] Trump represents the change they have long been working toward. McEwen also has a decades-long history of experience in Russia and the former Soviet Union. In June 2019, just back from a visit to the Ukraine, McEwen joined the Conservative Book Club Podcast for an interview about his role at the CNP. "I have never been more optimistic about the future of my country than I am at this moment," he said.[10]

In 2015, Chris Vickery, an information technology specialist who at the time hunted for data breaches as a hobby, was sifting through the cyber universe when he came upon a massive file on 191 million U.S. citizens. The database, which Vickery downloaded and copied, contained data fragments offering bits of information belonging to registered voters, from cell phone numbers to evidence of gun ownership, all there for the taking. Pretty soon Vickery discovered a second breach involving 18 million Americans, this time with even more detailed information, including occupation and income levels, as well as lifestyle details such as religious views and affiliation, an interest in hunting or fishing, and whether the person was a fan of NASCAR or had a "Bible lifestyle."[11]

Vickery assumed that the second find either came out of or was in the process of enriching the 191 million file with additional data. "The table names were the same, and the usernames were the same for the database administrators," he told me.[12]

After some sleuthing, Vickery thought he had a clear idea of where it all came from. It linked, he said, to Pioneer Solutions Incorporated, which was run by Bill Dallas. Vickery pointed to other connections, too, including links between the data and a campaign titled "Champion the Vote," which, Vickery pointed out, was "run by United in Purpose."[13]

Presidential candidates and their supporters—on all sides of the political spectrum—were at the time investing massive amounts of money in data operations in order to target potential voters. For the 2016 election cycle, for instance, the Mercer family, which initially supported Ted Cruz before throwing their weight behind Donald Trump, were behind the now-shuttered political data firm Cambridge Analytica, which claimed to have developed "psychographic" profiles that could identify personality and political leanings, and which could be used to sway voting behavior. The billionaire brothers Charles and David Koch, mega-funders of the economic right, also invested big money in data operations and "persuasion models" to advance Republican candidates, in part through a data organization called i360.[14] And Democratic candidates were making use of their own data machines.

How, Vickery wondered, would a group such as United in Purpose have amassed files on virtually the entire voting population of the United States—and what exactly were they doing with the data? He searched for links between UiP and other large-scale data-mining operations such as Cambridge Analytica, which developed their voter databases by scraping data from Facebook and other means, and AggregateIQ, which has been embroiled in the Cambridge Analytica controversy over misuse of data in politics.

According to *Fast Company*, a smartphone app for the Ted Cruz campaign, Cruz Crew, was developed by AggregateIQ, the small Canadian data company that was the lead developer used by the data analytics consultancy Cambridge Analytica. Chris Wilson, founder and chief executive of the political marketing agency WPAi, which has been listed as the publisher of the Cruz Crew app, is a repeat guest on Tony Perkins's *Washington Watch* radio program; on June 20, 2016, Wilson and Dallas were featured in contiguous segments.

To be sure, the appearance of various data tools, methods, and individuals in close proximity in the hothouse world of political data operations does not mean that they are acting in coordination or violating the law. It could be that they are simply working independently toward a common goal. The real significance of Vickery's discovery was the number of voters about whom United in Purpose had collected information. UiP was in a position to select the targets for its messaging from almost the entire voting-age population of the United States.

Bill Dallas has not been shy in describing the massive reach of his data operation. "We have about 200 million files, so we have pretty much the whole voting population in our database," Dallas said in a September 5, 2016, interview with the Christian Broadcasting Network. "What we do is we track to see what's going to make somebody either vote one way, or not vote at all."[15] Other outlets, including *Forbes*, picked up on the stunning facts.[16]

So where did United in Purpose acquire information on pretty close to the entire voting age population? The answer is a bit of a mystery. UiP claims to buy lists and solicits Americans to fill in their own information through a variety of tools, including iVoterGuide. But one has to wonder what percentage of 180 million Americans would voluntarily sign over their data to a little-known company.

United in Purpose was just one of several entities on the right with access to comprehensive voter data. According to the Center for Media and Democracy, by November 2018 the Koch brothers–funded i360 had developed detailed "personality profiles" on 89 percent of the U.S. population and were microtargeting messages in ways that "revolutionized political communications."[17]

Data Trust, a private consultancy long used by the Republican National Committee, is another repository of voter data. According to UpGuard, the firm where Vickery presently serves as director of cyber risk research, a 2017 data breach, also discovered by Vickery, led to the personal information of "potentially near all of America's 200 million registered voters" and linked to "a publicly accessible cloud server owned by Republican data firm Deep Root Analytics."[18] Within the Deep Root Analytics database, according to UpGuard, "the folder 'data-trust' appears to contain nothing less than the full fruits of this RNC/Data Trust effort to house as comprehensive and detailed a repository of potential 2016 voter information." (As soon as Deep Root Analytics was made aware of the breach, they took action to secure the database.)

The utility of data, of course, consists in the ability to interact selectively and individually with voters. United in Purpose begins by assigning points to each individual in its database for characteristics that line up with conservative religious voting patterns. Individuals receive points if they are members of conservative churches or if they homeschool their children. They also get points if they appear to oppose marriage equality or abortion rights. They get additional points for certain interests or hobbies, such as hunting, fishing, or following NASCAR.

"If [your score] totaled over 600 points, then we realized you were very serious about your faith," Dallas explains.[19]

United in Purpose's first mission is to make sure that all 600-pointers are registered to vote. "We run that person against the voter registration database . . . If they were not registered, that became one of the key people we were going to target to go after," Dallas says.

For the 2012 election cycle, United in Purpose aimed to register 5 million conservative Christians—a number that Dallas believed could decide the presidency. In 2008, as he has pointed out, key states such as Florida, North Carolina, and Missouri were decided by slim margins. Registering conservative Christians could make a difference.

In order to persuade unregistered conservative Christians to register and vote, United in Purpose pursues various on- and off-line strategies. With a ready army of volunteers, many recruited from conservative churches by representatives of organizations such as the Family Research Council, UiP offers tools for making phone calls and knocking on doors.

According to a 2012 article in NPR, such volunteers were called "champions." Scott Spages, an evangelical activist from Davie, Florida, was recruited to the cause when a representative of the Family Research Council came to his church seeking volunteers.

"God says that when the righteous rule, the people rejoice, and when the wicked rule, the people groan," Spages said. "So as Christian[s], we are specifically called upon by the Bible and by God to raise up our leaders."[20]

The article follows Spages as he logs into a United in Purpose website allowing him access to information on unregistered conservative Christian voters in his area. The site offers Spages multiple ways to contact each voter, including phone numbers, email, and physical addresses, as well as a persuasive script so that he knows just what to say.

Another activist featured in the piece, Kay Clymer, an evangelical Tea Partier from Zanesville, Ohio, uses the data she gets from United in Purpose's Champion the Vote initiative to connect with like-minded believers. In addition to door-to-door canvassing, she spends several hours on the phone each day.

"I pray for a Red Sea experience like he did with the Egyptians—and then wash those people out that don't belong in office," she said. "And that's what keeps me going."

In advance of the 2016 election, Christian nationalist leaders stepped up their ground game. At his Road to Majority conference that year, Ralph Reed told the crowd about the force his group would bring to bear on the upcoming presidential race. "We will distribute 35 million nonpartisan voter guides to 117,000 thousand churches and houses of worship across this country," he vowed. "We will make 15 million phone calls from phone banks and volunteer centers. We will send out 20 million emails and texts to seven million voters of faith in battleground states . . . and, if they haven't turned in their vote by 4 P.M. that day . . . we're going to go to their house by car or van and knock on their doors." At the conference, Trump promised to uphold his part of the bargain, brandishing a list of potential Supreme Court appointees as though he were selling shiny new bonds for a casino development. "These judges are all pro-life!" he said.

All major political operations—of all parties—now rely on big data and activist networks to sharpen their effectiveness in election campaigns. Obama's successes in the 2008 and 2012 elections have been attributed in part to his superior data strategy. One key difference, however, is that United in Purpose's voter turnout machine is at the top of a long pyramid that largely operates in the religious sphere, almost all of which is exempt from taxes and shielded from public scrutiny.

Data gathering and operationalizing isn't cheap, of course. A 2011 article on United in Purpose published in the *Los Angeles Times* reported UiP's annual budget "in the millions of dollars."[21] Where does UiP get its money and other forms of support?

One source of support, no doubt, is United in Purpose chairman of the board Ken Eldred. Eldred was the cofounder and CEO of Inmac, the first company to sell computer-related products and accessories through direct-mail catalogs. The company expanded to multiple overseas markets, and by the time it was sold in 1996, it had an annual revenue of over $400 million. Eldred also founded several businesses, including the software company

Ariba Technologies, and "advises various Kingdom business ventures and ministries," according to his biography.[22] He is the author of several faith-based business titles, including *God Is at Work: Transforming People and Nations Through Business*. Eldred has donated generously to GOP campaigns, including those of Rick Perry and the disgraced former Alabama hopeful Roy Moore. At a breakfast hosted by UiP at the 2018 Values Voter Summit, Eldred said the upcoming midterm elections were about "judges, judges, judges" before leading the audience in prayer that "the Lord Jesus Christ would be the King of America once again."

According to United in Purpose's form 990s, their biggest funder by far is a single individual: Major General Vernon B. Lewis Jr., who lives in Marshall, Texas. Lewis led a distinguished military career in the Army and, when he retired in 1977, founded two businesses. The first was a military training and education company called Military Professional Resources Inc. (MPRI) that conducted military operations, intelligence analysis, and cyber operations; in 2014 the company agreed to pay a $3.2 million fine to resolve allegations of false labor charges on a contract to support the U.S. Army in Afghanistan.[23] Lewis's other company, Cypress International, describes itself as a consultancy specializing in support to the U.S. Department of Defense and other federal government agencies. The company claims to have "a deep understanding of business opportunities in the defense and homeland security sectors."[24]

Lewis also founded a conservative Texas online publication, the Lone Star Eagle, which offers syndicated content from Breitbart News Network and the Daily Caller. And his contributions in the political arena seem to extend beyond United in Purpose. His name appeared at the top of the sponsor's page for the Faith, Family, and Freedom Gala Dinner for the 2019 Values Voters Summit. At the dinner, Trump delivered a lengthy address with the customary mix of falsehoods, boasting, and invective, and he was received with multiple standing ovations.

In addition to attending several of Dallas's presentations at Values Voter summits and other events, I caught some of Dallas's appearances on a variety of Christian TV networks in the 2016 election cycle. In these interviews he revealed quite a bit about his role in the election.

On March 7, 2016, Dallas and Eldred appeared with Marcus and Joni Lamb on Daystar Television, a Christian broadcasting network, to deliver a clear message to viewers: Vote—the "right" way. As Eldred said, "It's not just voting. It's voting their principles. Their Christian principles."[25]

Lamb cut straight to those Christian principles. "Recently same-sex marriage became the law of the land," he said, knitting his fulsome eyebrows. "And principally it happened because Christians didn't vote in the presidential election, and Supreme Court justices who were very liberal were appointed to the bench. And they were the deciding votes and that becoming the law of the land, something that people thought would never ever happen. It's interesting that both Hillary Clinton and President Barack Obama, when they were running for president in 2008, both were against same-sex marriage but then they changed."

Turning to Dallas, Marcus repeated, "So, Bill, can it be reversed if we got the right kind of justices on [the Supreme Court]?"

Dallas was the practical one, the guy with the numbers and a plan. "Ninety million Christians, okay, and 39 million don't get involved," he said. "If they got involved, eventually the fragrance of this country would have a Christ-like fragrance. Which we all know we want; we just need to get involved. We're a sleeping giant. Christians are a sleeping giant. Let's get now involved in the process for cultural change!"

"What can churches do?" Marcus asked.

"They can go to championthevote.com," Dallas said. "We'll help the pastor determine who is registered or not registered in their congregation." Referring to United in Purpose's special toolkit for pastors, which he called "Pledge 75" tools, Dallas said, "We provide what we call 'turn-key'—or, like I make my brownies, 'just add water'—tools. Contact us! We have a ministry consultant who will work with each church to help them get their people out to vote on election day."

Smiling broadly, Marcus said, "This is something every church should be willing to get involved in. The way they do it is not partisan. They don't say, 'Vote Republican' or 'Vote Democrat,' or vote for this man or this woman; it's nothing like that at all. They're just saying, 'Christians, vote!' Then they trust the Lord and the Holy Spirit and their people that they'll then make the right choice."

"When we sit back and let the culture take over, it doesn't smell like us," Dallas said. "It doesn't smell with the biblical values."

By the half-hour mark, Lamb was in full persecution mode. "Let me say this, and this is going to be shocking for some of y'all . . . You know what's going to eventually happen in America if Christians don't vote and we don't get involved in the process? And the liberal groups see that they can just run roughshod over us? . . . There'll come a time when Christian television will be outlawed. There'll come a time that if a minister stands up and preaches the word of God against sin, it'll be considered hate crimes. And hate speech. And they will be arrested and thrown in prison just like in countries like Iran!"[26]

By now United in Purpose was embedded in the nexus of Christian nationalist power. The organization's voter registration and education initiative Champion the Vote was partnered with a number of other organizations, including the American Family Association, Concerned Women for America, Liberty Counsel, David Barton's Black Robe Regiment and WallBuilders, Students for Life, and more than a dozen others. Champion the Vote also linked online to Awake 88, the initiative described by Pastor J. C. Church in Unionville, North Carolina, and an initiative of Family Research Council.

United in Purpose's pastor-focused initiative, Project 75, aimed at "Mobilizing 75% of church members to VOTE." The program featured a Church Voter Lookup Tool, "the key to measuring your success in the Project 75 campaign."[27] Text on the Project 75 website advised that this tool "works exactly like the individual voter lookup below, but instead of looking up individuals one at a time, we run your church database all at once. You'll then receive a report that tells you what percentage of your congregation is registered to vote and what percentage actually voted in the last election! After each election, we provide you with a follow up report that shows the progress you're making." Other Project 75 offerings included an Individual Voter Lookup Tool, which might come in handy should a pastor care to see how a specific member of his congregation cast their vote. Project 75 also offered tools to facilitate voter registration drives at churches.

Project 75 was closely allied with another initiative called Let's Vote America. "Let's Vote America is a campaign of United in Purpose,"

according to archived website material, and "also works hand in hand with
Project 75." Prior to the 2016 election, UiP also hosted faith-focused "presi
dential forums" in battleground states such as Iowa, partnering with the
National Organization for Marriage, the Alliance Defending Freedom, and
the Christians United for Israel (CUFI) Action Fund, among others.

United in Purpose was now at the epicenter of a dense web of faith-
based initiatives aimed at turning out conservative Christians for Trump/
Pence. While each initiative had its own unique characteristics, they operated hand in glove as components of the sprawling Christian nationalist
machine. The religious right is not a single organization, and yet it is surprisingly well organized in a certain sense. It may be perceived as a grassroots
movement, not answering in a formal way to a command-and-control hierarchy. But it is the big-picture strategists who are, to a largely underappreci-
ated degree, acting as its architects and engineers.

In the run-up to the 2018 midterm elections, Dallas followed the rest of
the movement in doubling down on support for Trump, appearing on
Andrew Wommack's Truth & Liberty Coalition broadcast on August 27 to
discuss the Trump Russia scandal.

"Christians, we don't have the right to sit back and not engage. We have
a duty and a responsibility," said Dallas. "It is so important how we lay the
foundation of judges, both at the Supreme Court level and at the federal
levels, so that we get the right judges in place." Referring to a Christian
nationalist voter awareness event in the works for the following month,
which would be taking place at Wommack's Charis Bible College and
broadcast live all across the U.S., Dallas said, "This is the Super Bowl where
Christians are going to gather in our country."[28]

Wommack assured him that he was prepared to host the event. "I'm
going to be talking about Christians have a responsibility to get involved,"
Wommack said. Discussion immediately pivoted to the Founding Fathers
and how Christianity built America. "I've been doing a lot of research
lately," Wommack began to explain, "through David Barton . . ."

At some point in 2018 the website for United in Purpose was scrubbed.
Previously it had offered a window into the organization's three separate

components: the first, the American Culture and Faith Institute, focused on polling and research and headed by George Barna; a second focused around Dallas's Church Communication Network; and a third aimed at data. But much of the site was dismantled; all that remained was a splash page. Around this time United in Purpose filed a lawsuit against its data firm Trendmojo, Inc., in San Mateo County. The complaint asserted that the firm and its founder "are thieves" who have "embezzled and stolen millions of dollars from the Nonprofit Plaintiffs." But the lawsuit was dismissed after just sixteen days at the request of the plaintiffs.[29]

Nevertheless, the profile of the organization within the larger movement continued to climb. United in Purpose was a cosponsor of the 2018 Values Voter Summit in Washington, D.C, its logo repeating on publicity backdrops along with those of the Family Research Council and other top organizational players. In advance of the summit, United in Purpose held a ticketed breakfast event featuring Dallas, Eldred, and Faith & Freedom Coalition president Ralph Reed. "Remember how we were told we were going away? How we would recede as a political force?" Reed said to the crowd. "Not true, because the thing that matters is not your share of the population. That is declining. It's the share of the electorate." Reed nodded. "It only matters who actually turns out." As the crowd murmured its assent, he continued, "If you take evangelicals who are 27 percent of the electorate and you add to them 11 percent of the electorate that are frequent Mass-attending Catholics, folks, it's 38 percent of the electorate, and 56 percent of the entire Republican vote nationwide. If that vote goes away, the Republican party ceases to exist as a reliable political party."

United in Purpose also doles out awards to hard-right leaders. At the inaugural Impact Awards ceremony in 2017, which took place at the Trump International Hotel in Washington, D.C., awardees included the Federalist Society's Leonard Leo; Frank Gaffney, who has warned of a Muslim Brotherhood plot to infiltrate the conservative movement; and Hillsdale College president Larry Arnn—all of whom appear on the leaked membership list for the Council for National Policy.[30] An outstanding impact award went to Sean Hannity, and the organization gave its lifetime achievement award to Richard Viguerie. The awards were introduced by Virginia "Ginni" Thomas, president of Liberty Consulting and the wife of Supreme Court justice Clarence Thomas.[31] In 2018 it was Fox News host Mark Levin's turn to collect UiP's outstanding impact award. Ginni Thomas presided over that year's awards ceremony, too.[32] Meanwhile, 2018 tax filings for a new, Southland, Texas–based organization with a similar stated mission, USATrans-Form, appeared to have many of the same individuals at the helm, including Bill Dallas, Ken Eldred, Vernon Lewis, and Reid Rutherford.[33]

It remains to be seen whether United in Purpose's visibility outside of the Christian nationalist hothouse will increase as the 2020 presidential election approaches. In early 2018, before it was taken down, a question appeared on the UiP website: "Is it possible to transform American culture by bringing together conservative Christian organizations to act in unity to reach their shared goals?"[34] The answer, apparently, was "a resounding 'YES,' and we're just getting started. 'Transformation through Unity' is a reality that is building momentum as we look to 2018, 2020 and beyond."

CHAPTER 9

Proselytizers and Privatizers

A T THE HERITAGE Academy, a publicly funded charter school network in Arizona, according to a 2016 lawsuit, high school students are taught that "All things were created by God, therefore upon Him all mankind are equally dependent and to Him they are equally responsible." They are asked to memorize a list of "28 Principles" of "sound government," among which are that "to protect man's rights, God has revealed certain Principles of divine law" (the ninth Principle) and that "The highest level of prosperity occurs when there is a free-market economy and a minimum of government regulations" (the fifteenth Principle). To complete the course, students are told they are duty-bound to teach these principles to other individuals outside of school and family.[1]

The Texas-based Newman International Academy charter network, which presently operates seven schools, is named after Dr. Hepzibah Newman, CEO of an evangelistic organization, Brook of Life, which was established in February of 2011 "to preach the Gospel of the Lord Jesus Christ." Brook of Life runs before- and after-school programs that aim to lead elementary-age children to "worship" and prayer; the programs appear to be installed at every Newman International Academy charter school. Brook of Life's other founder is Dr. Lazarus K. George, whose wife, Dr. Sheba George, is the superintendent of Newman International Academies.

Also in Texas, Allen Beck, the founder of Advantage Academy, a four-campus charter school funded by taxpayers, has said he established the schools in order to bring "the Bible, prayer, and patriotism back into the public school system."[2] Students at Advantage Academy are also exposed to heavy doses of libertarian or free market economic ideology.[3]

The same pattern is evident at the American Heritage Academy (which is distinct from Heritage Academy), a two-campus charter school also located in Arizona. Describing itself as a "unique educational experience with old-fashioned principles that have worked for hundreds of years," the school celebrates a set of "Principles of Liberty" that include: "The role of religion is foundational"; "To protect rights God revealed certain divine laws"; and "Free market and minimal government best supports prosperity."[4]

These examples of church-school fusion are far from anomalous in the emerging charter school universe. Over the past four decades, Christian nationalists have achieved remarkable progress toward a longstanding goal: to convert America's public schools into conservative Christian academies, even as they weaken or even destroy public education altogether. And they have done so in large part by means of an alliance with education "reformers"—in particular, those reformers who are ideologically committed to the privatization of public education.

Hostility to public education among religious reactionaries has a long history. In 1979, Jerry Falwell made the agenda clear when he said he hoped to see the day when there wouldn't be "any public schools—the churches will have taken them over and Christians will be running them."[5] But the alliance between privatizers and proselytizers received a major boost in the 1990s in Michigan, the first state to feel the full combined force of economic and religious education reformers. The story really begins with the emergence of a particular kind of billionaire, and it reaches its apex when the daughter of one of those billionaires grew up and became the secretary of education for the United States.

A century and a half ago, members of the Christian Reformed Church, a small and unusually strict sect of Dutch Calvinists, settled the area around Holland, Michigan.[6] The group and region prospered. Yet the ultraconservative nature of their religion left a powerful imprint on the area. Until several years ago it was forbidden to serve alcohol at restaurants on Sundays.

The region is also known for the surprising number of billionaires it has produced, many of them ultraconservative in their politics. Chief among them were Richard DeVos Sr., the cofounder of Amway, a multilevel marketing business, and his business partner Jay Van Andel. Joining the ranks of the super-rich of Holland was Edgar Prince, an auto-parts magnate who shared with the DeVos family an affinity for conservative politics and antipathy toward organized labor.

The family summered at Castle Park, where the yacht club functioned as a lively social hub. In 1979, Prince's daughter Betsy married Richard DeVos Sr.'s son, Richard "Dick" Jr., making her Holland's version of a crown princess.

The Holland elite live large. Betsy DeVos's family owns or has owned a dozen-odd leisure boats, the flagship of which is a 163-foot, $40 million yacht called *Seaquest*, which boasts space for twelve guests and an equal number of crew.[7] They also reportedly own four airplanes and two helicopters.[8] One of their vacation homes, a sprawling 22,000-square-foot shingle-style summer mansion in Holland, Michigan, has a nautical design theme.[9] Like a well-run aristocratic family, the DeVoses know how to keep the locals happy. They invest in the community, paying for town restoration projects and other initiatives that make the clan popular here in a way that they are not in other parts of the country. It's what the clan does with its money beyond the flatlands of western Michigan that has had a profound impact on national politics.

In financial terms, in fact, the Christian right today is to a substantial extent the creation of the Michigan wing of the American plutocracy. Since the 1970s the late Richard DeVos Sr. and his wife and children, including Dick and Betsy, have been major funders of leading national groups on the religious right. The DeVos family donated millions of dollars to the militantly reactionary Coral Ridge Presbyterian Church, founded by the broadcaster D. James Kennedy, who instructed attendees at a 2005 conference organized by his ministry to "exercise godly dominion" over "every aspect and institution of human society."[10] Through their foundation, Betsy DeVos and her husband have donated to the Foundation for Traditional Values, a nonprofit with a mission "to restore and affirm the Judeo-Christian values upon which America was established."[11] DeVos money has flowed toward Steve Green's Museum of the Bible, where the donor wall acknowledges major gifts from multiple members of the extended clan.

Beginning in the 1970s, Richard DeVos and his wife and children have also worked systematically to build up some of the movement's leading free market policy groups, including the Acton Institute and the Mackinac Center for Public Policy.[12] Amway cofounder Van Andel, meanwhile, endowed and served as a trustee of Hillsdale College, which the religious right likes to cast as "the conservative Harvard"[13] and which counts Betsy DeVos's brother, Erik Prince, as an alum.

Edgar Prince and his wife, Elsa, were equally munificent with the seminal groups on the religious right. In 1983 they substantially contributed to the creation of the Family Research Council. The Edgar and Elsa Prince Foundation is a key backer of groups such as the Alliance Defending Freedom, the legal juggernaut of the religious right; Focus on the Family; and other like-minded organizations. Some of the leading figures of the movement, including Chuck Colson, James Dobson, and Gary Bauer, came to be family friends.

Betsy DeVos's brother, Erik Prince, founded the private contracting firm Blackwater and presently heads a private equity firm called Frontier Resource Group. He, too, has contributed to the Family Research Council and other advocates of "traditional family values" through the Edgar and Elsa Prince Foundation, where he served as vice president, as well as through a foundation he ran with his first wife, Joan.[14]

Erik, who was widowed after Joan lost her battle with cancer, is presently married to Stacy DeLuke. Possibly the two bonded over shared political passions; she reportedly posted pictures from inside the Trump campaign headquarters the night of the 2016 election.[15]

Prince has been uninhibited in his involvement in presidential and partisan politics. He donated $250,000 to support Trump's campaign effort. He has also acknowledged being present at a widely reported strategy meeting in August 2016 at Trump Tower. Other attendees reportedly included Donald Trump Jr., Joel Zamel, an Israeli expert in social media manipulation, and Lebanese American businessman George Nader, an advisor to the effective ruler of the United Arab Emirates. (In early 2019, Nader was placed in federal custody after FBI agents discovered sexually explicit videos of children in his possession and now faces additional charges of child sex trafficking.)

At the Trump Tower meeting, according to an article in the *New York Times*, Nader mentioned to Donald Trump Jr. that Saudi Arabia and the United Arab Emirates wished to help Trump win the election.[16] Prince has said the purpose of the meeting was "to discuss Iran policy."[17] Prince was also named in the investigation into Russian interference in the 2016 elections in connection with alleged meetings with foreign agents in the Seychelles.

The economic ideology that the Michigan billionaires have favored, not surprisingly, is of the kind that celebrates their own multilevel marketing fortunes as the mark of divine blessings. In this context, at least, Erik Prince's financial contributions to the Trump campaign were far from unusual. According to a 2014 article in *Mother Jones*, "Since 1970, DeVos family members have invested at least $200 million in a host of right-wing causes—think tanks, media outlets, political committees, evangelical outfits, and a string of advocacy groups."[18]

When it comes to efforts to eviscerate labor unions, the Holland elite can be counted upon to fund the necessary political campaigns with gusto. And when DeVos was heading into her Senate confirmation hearing for education secretary, twenty-two of the senators considering her nomination—including four of whom sat on the Senate education committee that oversees the process[19]—were recipients of the largesse of the DeVos family and their affiliated PACs, receiving in total nearly $900,000.[20] Commenting on her family's political giving, Betsy DeVos once wrote, "We expect a return on our investment."[21]

In the Devos-Prince universe, the economic activism and religious activism are often indistinguishable from one another. Shortly after its inception, the DeVos-funded Foundation for Traditional Values distributed a book, *America's Providential History*, which asserts that "a civil government built on Biblical principles provides the road on which the wheel of economic progress can turn with great efficiency."[22] According to a chapter titled "Principles of Christian Economics," "Secularists are cut off from the

Bible and the mind of Christ (the chief source of creativity), and so they get fewer ideas for inventing new and better tools."[23] Posing the question, "Why Are Some Nations in Poverty?" the book goes on to explain that "the primary reason that nations are in poverty is lack of spiritual growth ... Today, India has widespread problems, yet these are not due to a lack of food, but are a result of people's spiritual beliefs. The majority of Indians are Hindus."[24]

The book also offers a distinct perspective on education policy: "Privatizing education would be a great step forward in correcting the problems of modern day education."[25]

At some level, the world of the Holland plutocracy was always interested in the topic of education and fundamentally hostile to public education. In a 1986 sermon titled "A Godly Education," Pastor D. James Kennedy, whose ministry profited mightily from DeVos-Prince clan largesse, asserted that children in public schools were being "brainwashed in Godless secularism."[26] This harsh characterization no doubt met with approval by the family of the future education secretary. The foreword to a 2010 posthumously selected collection of Kennedy's work, *Well Done: A Christian Doctrine of Works*, was written by a Mr. Rich DeVos, who also used the occasion to praise Amway's expansion into Russia.[27]

The Devos/Prince-supported Family Research Council rather awkwardly advocated the abolition of the department that Betsy would one day come to lead. "The Department [of Education] is unconstitutional, ineffective, and wasteful. In short, it should be abolished ... Aim carefully and slay the dragon for once and for all," wrote Rob Schwarzwalder, then senior vice president of the Family Research Council, in 2010.[28] However, it was not until the late 1990s, when discussions about school vouchers and education reform began to gain traction across the country, that the heirs to the fortune—and in particular Betsy DeVos—likely realized the best way by far to advance their radical vision for America would be to mount a devastating assault on the nation's system of public schools.

Vouchers first came to prominence in the 1950s and '60s as a way to funnel state money to racially segregated religious academies.[29] In the aftermath of the *Brown v. Board of Education* decision of 1954, as we saw in chapter three, white Americans in the South organized massive resistance against federal orders to desegregate schools. While some districts shut down public schools altogether, others promoted "segregation academies" for white students, often with religious programming, to be subsidized with tuition grants and voucher schemes. Today vouchers remain popular with supporters of religious schools, many of whom see public education as inherently secular and corrupt.

Vouchers are also favored among disciples of the free market advocate Milton Friedman, who saw them as a step on the road to getting government out of the education business altogether. Speaking to an audience at a convention of the American Legislative Exchange Council in 2006, Friedman said, "The ideal would be to have parents control and pay for their school's education, just as they pay for their food, their clothing, and their housing." Acknowledging that indigent parents might be unable to afford their children's education in the same way that they might suffer food or housing insecurity, Friedman added, "Those should be handled as charity problems, not educational problems."[30]

Friedman was a free market fundamentalist, not a religious one. But his ideas were hailed by Christian conservatives, and the admiration was mutual. In 2004, when "school choice" pioneers Mae and Martin Duggan were honored at an event hosted by the Heritage Foundation for their work with Citizens for Educational Freedom, the pro-voucher group that Mae founded and that at one point represented three hundred voucher organizations, Friedman sent a letter praising the Duggans as "allies in a common cause."[31]

For many supporters, of course, the underlying motive for voucher programs is not to improve education but to eliminate nonsectarian education. As Mae Duggan once said, "We don't want people teaching humanism. Humanism is the basis of the public schools."[32] When Martin Duggan died in 2015, he and Mae were honored for their efforts by American Federation for Children—a charter lobbying and advocacy organization funded by the family of Betsy DeVos.

Up in western Michigan, the combination of religious conservatism and economic libertarianism in the voucher movement found a natural home.

In the mid-1990s the DeVos-backed Foundation for Traditional Values founded the Student Statesmanship Institute, which describes itself as "Michigan's premier Biblical Worldview & Leadership Training for High School Students." Betsy DeVos was listed on the SSI advisory board as recently as 2015 and has been featured as an active SSI participant nearly as far back as the program had a functional website. SSI, which presently holds summer camps in several states as well as yearlong programs and sundry workshops, functions as a pipeline for teens seeking to engage in right-wing political activism. Students participating in the SSI role-play as political leaders and participate in mock legislative hearings and committees. According to the SSI website, SSI "Legislative Experiences" have instructed students in topics such as "Laying a Biblical Foundation, Ambassadors for Christ, Christian Citizenship, Worldviews in Action," and "Science and the Bible."[33]

James Muffett, a "nationally recognized spokesperson for biblical values" who heads the Foundation for Traditional Values and is also the founder and head of the Student Statesmanship Institute, brings the program into Christian schools. "We just hope that God will give us the grace to see this program expand in the schools all throughout the state of Michigan and beyond," he says.[34] He also appears from time to time on the homeschooling conference circuit. At such events, public schools—or "government schools," as they are frequently referred to—are ritually maligned. Some of those conferences include screenings of the 2011 film *IndoctriNation*, which casts public schools as "a masterful design that sought to replace God's recipe for training up the next generation with a humanistic, man-centered program that fragmented the family and undermined the influence of the Church and its Great Commission."[35]

By the late 1990s, Betsy and Dick DeVos had thrown their weight behind the voucher movement. They helped build and lead national organizations that funded voucher interests in states across the country. These initiatives took the form of both nonprofit work and campaign finance work that helped elect pro-voucher politicians. As these efforts expanded, the DeVoses and their allies partnered with existing conservative and "free market" think tanks, including the Mackinac Center for Public Policy and the Acton Institute in Michigan, both DeVos-backed.

Soon those think tanks began to publish screeds denouncing the "command and control mentality" of the "government school," which "robs teachers and administrators of the joy and professionalism of their important work."[36] In an Acton Institute review of the book *Public Education: An Autopsy* by the libertarian author Myron Lieberman, William B. Allen praised the author's prescription for replacing public education with a for-profit model. "As public education fails and dies, it carries along the ghosts of natural abilities atrophied in young children who could not escape in time," Allen wrote. The solutions to America's educational challenges, he asserted, "must derive from the 'death of public education.'"[37]

At the heart of their voucher ambitions, the royals of Holland had a theocratic vision. In 2001, speaking at "The Gathering," an annual meeting of prosperous Christian philanthropists that has been associated with The Fellowship Foundation or "The Family," Betsy DeVos singled out education reform as a way to "advance God's Kingdom."[38] In an interview, she and her husband lamented that public schools had "displaced" churches as centers of the community, and said that school choice would lead to "greater Kingdom gain."

To put the DeVoses' contempt for public schools in a religious context, a helpful point of reference is the 2003 report from the synod, or general assembly, of the Christian Reformed Church in North America. At a five-day gathering, the Grand Rapids–based organization put out a report warning that "government schools" have "become aggressively and increasingly secular in the last forty years." Public schools, the report claims, are engaged in "a deliberate program of de-Christianization" that is at odds with Christian morality. "Not only does there exist a climate of hostility toward the Christian faith," the report continues, but "the legitimate and laudable educational goal of multi-culturalism is often used as a cover to introduce pagan and New Age spiritualities such as the deification of mother earth (Gaia) and to promote social causes such as environmentalism." The report goes on to champion "choice" and decry the efforts of "powerful lobbying groups" to resist "alternatives to public education such as charter schools and vouchers."[39]

In the 2000 election cycle, the DeVoses decided to place a huge bet on a Michigan ballot referendum in support of vouchers. The idea was to turn the state into an Ayn Randian paradise of privatized education in which public schools would wither as the field was turned over to entrepreneurs. The family and its allies poured millions of dollars into the campaign. Voters rejected the initiative by a two-to-one margin. But by then the DeVoses had begun to back charter organizations as part of their effort. Even after the ballot failure, the conflation of charters and vouchers would become a common feature of their tactics.

As the campaign-financing arm of the movement grew, so did the nonprofit arm. By 2009, Betsy DeVos had become chair of the major sister organizations of national pro-voucher nonprofits, Alliance for School Choice and Advocates for School Choice. As recently as July 2016, DeVos chaired the board of directors of the American Federation for Children, which works alongside the American Legislative Exchange Council to craft and support model "school choice" legislation.

One of the DeVoses' initiatives, a network of political action committees under the name All Children Matter, came under fire for violations of campaign finance rules, which included funneling $870,000 from its Virginia PAC to its affiliate in Ohio, skirting a $10,000 limit on contributions.[40] The group was issued a fine by the Ohio Elections Commission of over $5 million. In 2013 Ohio attorney general Mike DeWine obtained a court judgment to enforce the fine. But by that point, All Children Matter had closed down, and had no assets left to collect.[41]

By now the voucher movement had begun to shed its limited claims to respectability. The historian, education policy analyst, and former U.S. assistant secretary of education Diane Ravitch, an early proponent of vouchers, reversed her position, asserting that they were ineffective in dealing with persistent gaps in racial and economic equity.[42]

Numerous academic studies added to the doubts on vouchers' effectiveness. A 2007 study of Milwaukee schools by professors from three universities showed poor to mixed results for vouchers in that city. A study of Indiana's voucher program, substantially expanded by the state's then governor Mike Pence, found no change among student reading scores and achievement losses in mathematics. A 2016 study funded by the pro-voucher Walton Family Foundation and conducted by David Figlio and Krzysztof Karbownik for the Thomas B. Fordham Institute concluded that students who use vouchers tend to fare worse academically than closely matched peers who attend public schools. A 2017 Century Foundation report concluded that vouchers intensify racial and religious segregation. Another report, from the Economic Policy Institute, asserted that the loss of community-based schools makes it harder for poor families to access wrap-around services, such as job training, health care, and academic support, that can help lift them out of poverty. "All of these yield much higher returns than the minor, if any, gains that have been estimated for voucher students," wrote Martin Carnoy, a professor of education and economics at Stanford University, who authored the report.[43]

These setbacks did little to diminish the DeVos family's determination to take American education out of the dead hands of government. In a speech to the Heritage Foundation in 2002, Dick DeVos outlined new strategies for the movement, emphasizing the need to spend available funding on a system of "rewards and consequences" for state legislators.[44] He also drew attention to a critical insight that had emerged from the campaign: The idea of vouchers scared off many voters because it sounded like—indeed it was—a way of privatizing the school system. The DeVoses were slowly coming to the realization that charter schools might be the way to advance their aims.

In public confusion about the nature of charters, the DeVos family and their allies saw opportunity. A lightly regulated charter school industry, they realized, could achieve many of the same goals as voucher programs. They could drain funding from traditional public schools, deregulate the education sector, and promote ideological or even religious curricula—all without provoking the kind of resistance that vouchers received. Democrats, centrists, and secular education reformers who opposed voucher schemes were often favorably disposed to charters, which they saw as one of many tools available to public school systems.

In the aftermath of the 2000 voucher referendum failure, Betsy DeVos and her allies decided to shift their tactics and went all in on the charter movement. Many of the policy groups they funded followed suit. All became evangelists for "school choice," a label that conveniently blurs the distinction between charter schools and voucher programs—and between publicly accountable, well-regulated charters and those operating with minimal oversight. They also understood quite clearly that secrecy would be necessary. Dick DeVos advised a Heritage Foundation audience in 2002 that "we need to be cautious about talking too much about these activities."[45] The cause, he noted, "will go on quietly and it will go on in the form that often politics is done—one person at a time, speaking to another person in privacy."

A number of the most active boosters of DeVos's voucher movement rapidly joined the upper ranks of the new charter industry. J. C. Huizenga, a friend of the DeVos family from the yacht club scene at Castle Rock and a long-time voucher advocate whose name also appears in the leaked directory of the Council for National Policy, established National Heritage Academies, a Grand Rapids–based for-profit charter network that now has approximately ninety schools in nine states, making it the third-largest public charter operator in the country, according to the National Alliance for Public Charter Schools. Clark Durant, another voucher booster, opened his own chain of charters, the Cornerstone Education Group. Prince-backed Hillsdale College created a subsidiary, Barney Charter School Initiative, to move into the charter business. And longtime DeVos ally Foster Friess (a past president of the Council for National Policy, according to the Southern Poverty Law Center,[46] and the billionaire funder of other right-wing causes) joined the effort in promoting "charter schools, school choice, and innovative private sector solutions."

The DeVos vision for the charter industry, not surprisingly, had little room for government involvement. While many charter operators appreciate that sensible regulation and oversight are essential to a healthy charter sector, DeVos and her allies consistently undermined efforts to establish those safeguards. Through the Great Lakes Education Project, DeVos lobbied the Republicans in the Michigan legislature not just to expand charters but also to gut meaningful regulation.[47]

With DeVos money flooding the arteries of the state's political system, Michigan soon became a paradise for for-profit charter operators, most of them concentrated in urban areas. More than half of Detroit's children now attend charters—second in the nation only to New Orleans (and possibly Flint, Michigan)—and 80 percent of these are for-profit. The charter lobby not only secured the rights to massive expansion but also scored some lucra-tive tax breaks. Charter operators who own the property that they lease to their own schools demanded—and received—a tax exemption on that property, an arrangement that has become increasingly common around the country.[48]

The key to the charter boom was deregulation on a scale that would have made any devotee of Milton Friedman proud. "Michigan's laws are either nonexistent or so lenient that there are often no consequences for abuses or poor academics," concluded a 2014 article, the culmination of a yearlong investigation into Michigan charters, which was published in the *Detroit Free Press.* "Taxpayers and parents are left clueless about how charter schools spend the public's money, and lawmakers have resisted measures to close schools down for poor academic performance year after year."[49]

Meanwhile, in regions lacking in charter regulation and oversight, the sector has been a boon for profiteers. In Arizona, for example, with the approval of the Arizona State Board for Charter Schools, state representative Eddie Farnsworth reaped nearly $14 million in profit selling his four-school charter group to a nonprofit run by some of his pals. Glenn Way, founder of Arizona's American Leadership Academy, scored over $18 million in profit with no-bid contracts to build charters, paid for largely with public money. In Arizona, all of this is perfectly legal.[50]

The charter boom has also been, not coincidentally, a terrific develop-ment for theologically motivated charter operators. When Clark Durant founded Cornerstone in 1991, he intended to create private, religious schools with a clear dedicated mission of "lifting up a Christ-centered culture." As Allie Gross of Chalkbeat's Detroit office reported in 2017, principal Candace Brockman declared on the Cornerstone website that she "considers it a blessing to be able to educate children in a learning environment that places Jesus Christ first."[51] In a privately funded, faith-based educational setting, such goals would be appropriate. But four of Cornerstone's five schools are now publicly funded charters. When Gross toured one of the newly "de-converted" schools, she found religious posters on the wall and other markers of sectarianism.

"Pinpointing where the religious school ended and the charter school began was difficult," Gross wrote. "The school is also in the process of re-thinking how they can make sure influential texts, such as the Bible, are still, legally, underscoring lessons."[52]

Over at Hillsdale College's Barney Charter School Initiative, one doesn't have to peel back many layers to arrive at the ideological agenda. At the top of their web page is a link to *Imprimis*, a publication promoting a conservative political and religious agenda, with articles on "The Left's War on Free Speech" and "A More American Conservatism," and a piece titled "How to Think about Vladimir Putin." The latter defends the Russian dictator and assures readers that he is "not the president of a feminist NGO," "a transgender-rights activist," or "an ombudsman appointed by the United Nations to make and deliver slide shows about green energy."[53] The Barney Charter Initiative's former mission statement, which has since been taken down, declared that its goal was to "redeem" American public education and "recover our public schools from the tide of a hundred years of progressivism."[54]

Reporter Marianne Goodland of the *Colorado Independent* alleged that the Golden View Classical Academy, a charter school in Golden, Colorado, with "strong ties to billionaire industrialists David and Charles Koch's conservative political network" as well as links to the Barney Charter School Initiative, was offering students a religion-based curriculum. Such schools, she wrote, "have found a legal workaround, and many Democratic and Republican lawmakers are looking the other way."[55]

The bonanza for the charter operators proved to be a catastrophe for both the children of Michigan and the state's taxpayers. A 2017 NAACP task force report on the efficacy and impact of charters quoted a teacher in Detroit: "It's sad when you walk in a classroom here and you don't even know it's a biology classroom. We don't have the materials, we don't have the resources."[56] Speaking to the *New York Times*, Scott Romney, a board member of the civic and social justice organization New Detroit, said that the "point was to raise all schools" but instead "we've had a total and complete collapse of education in this city."[57] A yearlong investigation into two decades of Detroit charters by the *Detroit Free Press* uncovered grotesque levels of financial mismanagement. At some schools, operators were putting family and friends on the payrolls. A record number of for-profit charters refused to declare how they spend taxpayer money. School closures in Michigan have disrupted the education of nearly 25,000 students, 87 percent of whom are Black.[58]

For DeVos and her allies in the school choice movement, however, the disastrous consequences of deregulation of Michigan education were all the more reason to try harder next time. The plan now was to subject the rest of the nation to the same treatment.

As I traveled around the country in the course of my research, I began to notice a pattern. In the rural byways outside of Greenville, the strip malls of Phoenix, and the city blocks of Detroit, buildings that had once been solely intended for use as churches now housed charter schools, too. Some of the church-schools were led by pastors aiming to improve academic offerings for local youth. Others seemed to arise from a desire, on behalf of their leaders, for a fresh income stream. Still others seemed to be headed by religion-minded entrepreneurs from out of state. Several people told me the schools in their neighborhoods were utilizing academic workbooks from Abeka and other religious publishers, indoctrinating students in libertarian economics, or teaching Christian nationalist versions of American history. I went from supposing that these religion- and ideology-infused schools were quirky components of America's diverse education ecosystem to recognizing them as part of a larger trend.

I reached out to Vanessa Descalzi, a representative with the National Alliance for Public Charter Schools, which bills itself as "the leading national nonprofit organization committed to advancing the public charter school movement," for a list of the top twenty largest charter networks in the nation. I was curious to see if any of these networks were run by people with religious, partisan, or ideological agendas. The number that were surprised me.

Charter Schools USA, a Florida-based network of close to eighty charter schools operating in six states, is the fourth-largest charter operator in the country, right after DeVos buddy J. C. Huizenga's National Heritage Academies. Charter Schools USA founder Jonathan Hage, a former staffer at the Heritage Foundation, has a pattern of political giving to Republican politicians. He was rewarded by Florida governor Rick Scott with a seat on

Scott's education transition team; from his perch, Hage reportedly influenced changes to state law intended to make it easier for charter chains to open new schools. Charter Schools USA recently expanded into North Carolina, aided by such pro-charter politicians as the state's two Republican U.S. senators, Thom Tillis and Richard Burr, both of whom have been recipients of DeVos's political donations.

The sixth-largest network, Responsive Education Solutions, or ResponsiveEd, has collaborated with the Barney Charter School Initiative in the formation of the Founders Classical Academy, another charter network spinoff. According to the journalist Zack Kopplin, writing for *Slate* in 2014, biology workbooks used by Responsive Education Solutions "overtly and underhandedly discredit evidence-based science and allow creationism into public school classrooms." Other classroom materials seemed just as concerning. According to Kopplin, ResponsiveEd textbooks claimed that feminism "created an entirely new class of females who lacked male financial support and who had to turn to the state as a surrogate husband." In a section on the causes of World War I, Kopplin writes, "the study materials suggest that 'anti-Christian bias' coming out of the Enlightenment helped create the foundations for the war." Responding to the allegations, ResponsiveEd co-founder and CEO Chuck Cook issued a statement asserting, "There is much research to be done in this area of origins. Until more concrete answers are found, questions on how life originated will continue."

On October 16, 2017, a writer for the *HuffPost* who covered the controversy received a letter from ResponsiveEd pushing back on the charges. "While there were ambiguous references that did not violate state or federal law, ResponsiveEd nevertheless updated its curriculum to avoid any misinterpretation or confusion that ResponsiveEd was teaching creationism or otherwise endorsing or disapproving of religion," the notice read. "Creationism is simply not part of ResponsiveEd's science curriculum."[59]

ResponsiveEd grew out of a charter network, Eagle Educational Reform Systems, Inc. (initially called Eagle Project), founded by fundamentalist preacher Donald R. Howard in 1998. Howard, along with his wife Esther, also designed a "Biblically-based" Christian curriculum, Accelerated Christian Education, which has been used in religious schools around the world.

In 1979, Howard published a book, *Rebirth of Our Nation*, that bore a ringing endorsement from R. J. Rushdoony. "A war is on, and, if you are unaware of it, you will be on the casualty list of God and man," Rushdoony wrote. "The war is humanism's war on Christianity. In his book, *Rebirth of Our Nation*, Dr. Donald R. Howard gives us an account of that war, and some battle strategy. Read it, and join the battle."[60]

Of course, leaders of the new charter school offshoots of Howard's efforts likely understood that their ability to obtain taxpayer funding for their public charter schools rested on the appearance of respect for the separation of church and state. In 1998, Howard told the *Wall Street Journal*, "Take the Ten Commandments—you can work those as a success principle by rewording them. We will call it truth, we will call it principles, we will call it values. We will not call it religion."[61]

Imagine Schools, seventh on the list, was cofounded by Dennis and Eileen Bakke, who spend millions of dollars every year on a wide variety of domestic and international missionary projects through their faith-based nonprofit Mustard Seed Foundation. The Imagine Schools charter network has drawn scrutiny for lease arrangements that absorb large amounts of taxpayer funding. One Imagine Schools charter in Land O' Lakes, Florida, signed a lease from its landlord agreeing to a base rent of $757,989 per year; the landlord, Schoolhouse Finance, is a company that is also owned by Imagine Schools.[62]

The ninth-largest network in the country, Harmony Public Schools, is affiliated with the Turkish cleric Fethullah Gülen, leader of the transnational Islamic social and religious movement called the Gülen movement. Harmony schools have been accused of giving preference to Turkish teachers and vendors who are attached to the Gülen movement as well as abusing the visa program. The FBI has opened an investigation into whether Gülen followers are diverting money from their charters into the movement itself; several former teachers alleged they were forced to hand over part of their taxpayer-funded salaries for that purpose.[63]

According to the Center for Public Integrity, between 2006 and 2015 the Gülen religious movement funded more than one hundred and fifty international junkets for American lawmakers—some of whom later introduced resolutions supporting the nearly two hundred American charter schools linked to the movement. In addition to Harmony, Gülen-affiliated groups operate other charter networks in the United States, giving Gülen-affiliated schools robust representation within the charter sector.

Turkish president Recep Tayyip Erdoğan has accused Fethullah Gülen of leading a resistance front and has arrested and jailed tens of thousands of his alleged supporters. Setting aside the matter of Erdoğan's dictatorial leadership and other abuses of power, the question remains: Why is a somewhat secretive imam, the possible leader of a resistance campaign in his home country, running a sizable sector of the U.S. taxpayer-funded charter school movement within the U.S.?

In sum, about eight of the twenty largest charter operators in the country are under the control of individuals or groups of people for whom education "reform" is part of a clear partisan, religious, or ideological agenda.

Just as in Michigan, the waves of deregulation appear to have ushered in an epidemic of corruption in the charter sector. Every week, it seems, another item in what the *Washington Post* called the "charter scandal parade" makes the headlines. In its 2018 investigation into the Arizona charter sector, the *Arizona Republic*, part of the *USA Today* network, alleged that many charter schools in the state "have turned into cash cows through multi-billion-dollar business deals between charter schools and their founders."[64] A multipart investigation into Florida charter schools by the *South Florida Sun-Sentinel* reported that "unchecked charter-school operators are exploiting South Florida's public school system, collecting taxpayer dollars for schools that quickly shut down." Once schools close, "districts struggle to retrieve public money not spent on students."[65]

Nor have charter schools delivered on their boosters' oft-repeated promises of "racial equity." A 2017 investigation produced by the Hechinger Report, a nonprofit independent news agency focused on inequality and innovation in education, asserted that the charter school movement is prolonging racial segregation, citing an Associated Press analysis of nearly 7,000 charter schools. More than 1,000 of those schools, according to the report, had a minority enrollment of over 99 percent. Meanwhile a 2018 report coproduced by the Hechinger Report, NBC News, and the Investigative Fund concluded that loose laws allow elite charters to create policies that favor white students. A summary of the report cites the example of Lake

Oconee Academy in Greensboro, Georgia, which is largely white. Public schools in the surrounding area are 12 percent white and 68 percent Black.[66]

Still, the DeVos-supported apparatus continues to defend its record, massaging or cherry-picking evidence if need be. In 2018, *Michigan Capitol Confidential*, a nonprofit news service published by the Mackinac Center for Public Policy,[67] proclaimed, "The Numbers Are In: Detroit Charters Outperform Detroit District Schools." The article stated that some charter schools outperform some district schools in the English and math portions of Michigan's standardized test, the M-STEP. Buried in the piece is the fact that district schools are shown to outperform charters on important national measures, including SAT scores—even as they accept all students, including those with learning disabilities.

As in Michigan, charterization has produced a flurry of church-state mergers. Andrew Seidel, a constitutional attorney and the director of strategic response for the Freedom from Religion Foundation, says the organization has seen an uptick in complaints—about forty in the past five years—involving charter schools. They have included accounts of school officials leading students in prayer or forming unconstitutional partnerships with churches.

Frequently, cases stall because plaintiffs are afraid of being ostracized in their communities. Many parents are unwilling to expose their children to retaliation from teachers, administrators, and classmates. In the case of Heritage Academy in Arizona, a plaintiff accused the academy of teaching and endorsing religion in the classroom, violating the Constitution. But the federal judge barred him from proceeding as "John Doe" and required that he use his initials and those of his children, essentially killing the case; even their initials would have given away their identities.

"Most of the time, you don't know what goes on in the school unless you have kids there," says Richard Katskee, legal director for Americans United for Separation of Church and State, which represented the plaintiffs. "If you've chosen to send your kids there, you usually don't complain."

Americans United for Separation of Church and State also reports an uptick in cases brought to its doors. "Prior to 2007, we saw basically no complaints about charter schools," says Ian Smith, a staff attorney for Americans United. "After 2007, the number of complaints related to charter schools steadily increased to the point where we regularly review charter school–related submissions and write letters to charter schools about constitutional violations."

So far, just one complaint has led to the closure of a charter school on grounds of religion. Predictably, the religion in question was Islam. In 2009 the ACLU of Minnesota filed a federal lawsuit against the Tarek ibn Ziyad Academy (TiZA) alleging that TiZA, the Muslim American Society of Minnesota, and TiZA's landlords were linked by a complex set of overlapping relationships and that the school was endorsing Islam in connection with school activities. The school was shut down by the Minnesota Department of Education in 2011.[68]

Attempts to insert religion directly into the curriculum, in any case, are really only the most egregious examples of advancing the religious and ideological agendas of these charter operators. Other, subtler methods are often used to convey such messages. Some charter schools, often describing themselves as "classical academies," claim to teach "virtue," our "national heritage," and "the principles of the Founders." It requires further investigation to reveal that the heritage in question is a politicized and sectarian version, often one that springs directly from the talking points of David Barton.

Keith Becher, who was formerly employed by Pineapple Cove Academy, which is affiliated with the Pineapple Cove Classical Academy and a part of the Barney Charter School Initiative, describes what the soft establishment of religion in a charter school looks like on the ground. "They conduct orientations for parents, telling them how public education is ruining kids and we need to get back to how things used to be," he says. "A 'nondenominational' chaplain comes around and says stuff like 'America is a Judeo-Christian nation' founded on 'biblical principles.'" And, Becher adds, "everything is 'American exceptionalism,' Ayn Randian. If you're screwed, it's your fault."

Betsy DeVos came to the Department of Education with an abundance of contempt for the idea of public education and a near-total lack of experience in it, either as an educator or a parent. She soon lived down to expectations. In February 2017, at one of her first high-profile gatherings as education secretary, DeVos invited a number of participants to join her and

President Trump at the White House. "I'm really excited to be here today with parents and educators, representing traditional public schools, charter public schools, home schools, private schools—a range of choices," DeVos said. Of the nine invitees at the table, seven were homeschoolers, representatives from religious schools, and education reform advocates. Only two were representatives of traditional public schools, both working in special-needs education.

The pattern continued for the next two years. In August 2017, DeVos attended and led a roundtable of "education leaders" in Tallahassee, Florida. The leaders in question included six members of the Bethel Missionary Baptist Church, which convened the meeting, and several clergy from other Baptist and evangelical ministries. A dozen representatives of Florida universities, prominent school choice advocates, leaders of religious schools, five public school superintendents, elected Republican officials, and an office manager were also included. Not a single public school teacher or student was present.[69]

Afterward, Leon County superintendent Rocky Hanna, who attended the meeting, expressed his disappointment with DeVos. "It's obvious that the secretary and our federal government have very little respect for our traditional public school system," he said. "And it's insulting that she's going to visit the capital of the state of Florida to visit a charter school, a private school, and a voucher school"—but no traditional public schools.[70]

The Bethel Missionary Baptist Church, on the other hand, stands to benefit directly from the DeVos agenda. Their church-run school, the Bethel Christian Academy, is a voucher recipient. Approximately 73 percent of voucher schools across the country are Christian. Just 23 percent are nonreligious, with other religions accounting for an additional sliver of the pie. Like many other Christian schools receiving taxpayer subsidies, Bethel Christian Academy has utilized material from the Christian publisher Abeka, which is affiliated with Pensacola Christian College; its textbooks are also popular among Christian homeschooling families. The Abeka curriculum is rooted in themes that appear to fuse a biblical literalist understanding of Christian identity with right-wing economic ideology.

Abeka textbooks have come under fire for promoting creationism and denigrating non-Christian faiths. According to an Abeka textbook *World*

History and Cultures, Nelson Mandela, the South African leader who helped facilitate an end to apartheid, was a "Marxist agitator" who moved the country toward a system of "radical 'affirmative action.'" From an Abeka textbook titled *America: Land I Love*, kids might have read that "radical environmentalists" "worship" nature and "view mankind as the enemy of nature."[71] From that same textbook, children may have learned that it was Satan himself who "hatched the ideas of evolution, socialism, Marxist-socialism (Communism), progressive education, and modern psychology."[72]

The decentralized nature of the American school system begs the question as to how much of her "ed reform" agenda DeVos will be able to enact while serving as Trump's education secretary. Some of her critics take comfort in the thought that DeVos's programs are small drops in the education ocean or unlikely to survive passage through the political and bureaucratic channels of America's hyper-complex education system. But this would be to underestimate both the legitimizing effect of her ceremonial actions and the disruptive effect of the kinds of initiatives she is proposing.

As education secretary, DeVos presently controls various programs including the Expanding Opportunity Through Quality Charter Schools Program, or CSP. By September 2017 the program had awarded approximately $253 million in grants. The amounts of money don't seem that large in the context of America's education system. Furthermore, the program, which is in the new Every Student Succeeds Act, is highly competitive, requiring that grantees meet certain quality standards. But the Department of Education has the authority to add new priorities that applications have to address, giving DeVos the power to shape grant competition in specific ways.

Trump's first budget, released in early 2017, allocated $1.4 billion to bolster the school choice movement. A proposal released in February 2018 included $1.1 billion to be spent on private school vouchers and other school choice plans amid a 5 percent, or $3.6 billion, cut in the Education Department overall. DeVos's 2018 fiscal year budget called for an additional $1.4 billion for expanding "school choice," including a $250 million voucher increase and $160 million for a Charter Schools Program grant.[73] The amounts of money, to be sure, were part of a wish list and remained subject to congressional approval. But given DeVos's generous campaign contributions to the right-wing politicians who tend to advocate for "small government" in every other area, and lockstep endorsement of charters and "choice" by right-wing Republicans, it is not surprising that DeVos's education budgets and priorities have received favorable hearings. In September 2017, for instance, the state of Indiana was awarded a $59 million grant for charter schools' expansion, one of nine states to receive such awards, which totaled $253 million.[74]

Even if charter schools succeed in satisfying the criteria of church-state separation, including factually accurate lessons in history and science, a broader problem remains unaddressed: it isn't hard to imagine a future in which a small number of extremely wealthy individuals control large parts of America's system of public education. Is it wise for any society to entrust the education of its children to such an unrepresentative group with distinct interests and convictions?

To be sure, charter operators have a right to their religious beliefs and political views, and the presence of such viewpoints does not necessarily mean that their schools will be infused with them. There are many charter advocates who simply aim to deliver a quality education to America's children and who are dedicated to equity and transparency. Many argue passionately and persuasively about the importance of creating a diverse education ecosystem. It is also worth remembering that the charter movement in the United States is large, fragmented, and complex, and includes many individuals and groups that sincerely wish to promote and improve public education.

From the perspective of Christian nationalists and their allies, however, these earnest charter supporters must surely look like useful idiots. For DeVos and her army of think-tank warriors, "school choice" is part of an agenda of privatizing major public functions, including what is arguably one of the most important functions of government: education. This privatization, although it covers itself in libertarian rhetoric, is essential to the project of indoctrinating the next generation in the "right" ideology and the right religion—with the added benefit of funneling public dollars into the pockets of right-thinking businesspeople.

Which brings us to the deceptive nature of DeVos's doctrine of "choice." Public education came into existence to serve the common good. It is open to all and held to meaningful standards; that is why taxpayers support it. Choice can have a useful role to play. But reducing public education to a consumer experience for parents that allows them to "choose" to funnel taxpayer money into schools that discriminate, teach pseudoscience and fake history, and promote contempt for those who are different isn't a way to improve our system of education. It is really just a way to break our schools—and thus to fulfill D. James Kennedy's fervent wish that "children may be delivered from this godless brainwashing and receive a godly education as Thou hath commanded."[75]

CHAPTER 10

Theocracy from the Bench, or How to Establish Religion in the Name of "Religious Liberty"

WINTER GARDEN SEEMS a very unlikely place to have a religious war. A charming, family-friendly enclave just west of Orlando, the town has a population of 40,000 and is about 60 percent white, 25 percent of Latino origin and, as far as the eye can tell, moderately diverse in its religious and political perspectives. If you want to get certain things done through the city government, on the other hand, the peaceful appearance of religious pluralism dissipates quickly. Tim Grosshans and Joseph Richardson, two longtime residents with very different belief systems, know this aspect of life in Winter Garden very well.

Tim Grosshans, the senior pastor of First Baptist Church of Winter Garden, is a stout grandfather with a ready smile and a ruff of white hair encircling his bald pate. Notwithstanding his avuncular demeanor, Grosshans knows how to have a good time with the flashy and powerful. When Senator Marco Rubio, whose outreach director is a "personal friend," invited Grosshans to President Trump's State of the Union address, Grosshans apparently relished the opportunity to rub shoulders with local VIPs, including then reigning Miss America Cara Mund. "She was real chatty

[and] having the time of her life," Grosshans told a local newspaper. He also issued a favorable opinion on the physical attributes of the first lady: "She's as good looking in person as she is on television."[1]

Joseph Richardson belongs to that group of Winter Garden residents who are unlikely to be found in churches like that of Pastor Grosshans. A software engineer in his mid-fifties, he identifies himself as a "freethinker" and is an active member of the Central Florida Freethought Community. A slim, pensive man, he left behind a childhood in the Assemblies of God church, a deeply conservative Pentecostal denomination; became an Episcopalian in college; and eventually made his departure from Christianity at forty-nine. His journey was prompted by his concerns about, among other things, the treatment of LGBT Americans. "The 'love the sinner hate the sin' language in the church never translated into action that made sense to me," he says.

For several years Winter Garden has had a policy of opening certain official city meetings with an invocation or prayer. In the four years up through early 2019, the city opened eighty-four public meetings this way. One invocation came from a Jewish rabbi and one came from a Catholic priest. A third meeting commenced with a moment of silence, and in 2015, before the city adopted a restriction that invocators must represent a 501(c) (3) organization, a man who identifies as nonreligious was selected by the city commissioner to deliver an invocation that contained no reference to religion. The other eighty invocations were delivered by representatives of Protestant churches or religious groups, or by individuals or civic leaders delivering sectarian prayers.

Pastor Tim Grosshans alone accounted for three invocations, and other staff or members of his church contributed an additional five. Members of the First Baptist squad, like many of the other Protestant groups, seem proud of the explicitly sectarian character of their invocations. "It is in Jesus Christ's name that we pray for our leadership. Amen," said Jarian Felton, First Baptist Church's director of worship.[2]

Joseph Richardson first initiated a request for the opportunity to offer an invocation on May 9, 2014, four days after the Supreme Court issued its 5–4 decision in *Town of Greece v. Galloway*. The conservative majority in that case suggested that efforts to ban sectarian invocations at the start of official town meetings amounted to a violation of religious liberty, whereas such invocations posed no danger of establishing religion. Richardson's experience over the subsequent four years could make a mockery of the Court's reasoning. Indeed, it would be one of countless instances illustrating how Christian nationalists have gamed the American judicial system to advance an agenda of "religious liberty" that in reality serves to establish a very clear set of privileges for one variety of religion.

"I know they are sitting up there on that dais saying that what they've done is fair and equitable," says Richardson. "But it's obviously not. The spirit of the *Greece v. Galloway* decision was equal treatment. But the fact that the Supreme Court put their stamp of approval on sectarian invocation has made it so that legislators think they can insert their religious views into meetings and exclude the viewpoints of others who disagree with them."

Sectarian invocations before public meetings, like crosses placed on public lands, may appear to play a merely symbolic role in our governance and are therefore easily to dismiss. But they point to the broader privileging of conservative Christianity in America, including its superior access to sources of public money and the perversion of our most deeply held constitutional principles. They are part of the larger project to use the court system to "restore" a version of America that never was.

Not long after the election of Bill Clinton, Leonard Leo realized that the Christian right had little hope of winning the culture war at the ballot box. A Catholic ultraconservative, Leo was sure that the public, seduced by the shallow values of a liberalizing culture, would never voluntarily submit to the moral medicine needed to save the nation. The last best chance to rescue civilization, he concluded, was to take over the courts. If activists could funnel just enough true believers onto the bench, especially onto the Supreme Court, they just might be able to reverse the moral tide.[3]

"He figured out twenty years ago that conservatives had lost the culture war," said Leo's former media relations director, Tom Carter. "Abortion, gay rights, contraception—conservatives didn't have a chance if public opinion prevailed. So they needed to stack the courts."

Leo founded a student chapter of the Federalist Society while studying law at Cornell. In 1991 he went to work for the organization's national office in Washington, D.C. He set about building the conservative legal movement, forging alliances with prospective jurists and Republican leaders. The Federalist Society, which received some early funding from right-wing donors including the John M. Olin Foundation, the Scaife Foundation, and the free-market think tank Institute for Economic Affairs, became a kind of career center for the conservative young ideologues of the legal world. Undistinguished academic records might be forgiven provided an unwavering commitment to the cause could be verified. The best of the young talent was meticulously groomed through a program of rotating internships, clerkships, and interim appointments to the welcoming offices of plutocrat-funded think tanks and legal advocacy groups—"the carefully manicured terrarium of the conservative legal community," as the journalist Charles P. Pierce has described it. "Federalist Society member? Check. Clerkships for conservative Supreme Court Justices? Check . . . Wingnut culture-war bona fides? Check."[4]

When George W. Bush was elected president, Leo began working as an outside advisor. According to a 2003 email by a White House aide that was sent to, among others, Brett Kavanaugh, Leo was characterized as a point person for "all outside coalition activity regarding judicial nominations."[5] He became known as a moneyman who could be relied upon to drum up funding for promotional activities on behalf of judicial appointees, providing media training for key pundits or creating grassroots support through advertising campaigns and other means. He also joined the boards of various right-wing and conservative religious organizations, including the Catholic Association Foundation, which funded campaigns to oppose same-sex marriage, and Reclaim New York, whose directors included then Breitbart News chairman Steve Bannon and his billionaire backer Rebekah Mercer.

The Mercer family became major Federalist Society backers, too, donating nearly $6 million over a span of several years, according to the *Washington Post*. But even these munificent gifts were dwarfed by other contributions, often from unknown donors. Leo has advised or helped run over two dozen nonprofits, including the Freedom and Opportunity Fund, the BH Fund, and America Engaged. In 2016 and 2017 those three nonprofits, all of which named Leo as president in their tax filings, took in approximately $33 million. Some of the money was spent on the lobbying arm of the National Rifle Association and groups in the Koch orbit, including FreedomWorks and the Center for Individual Freedom.

One of Leo's guiding principles was a commitment to end abortion. The conservative legal activist Ed Whelan wrote, "No one has been more dedicated to the enterprise of building a Supreme Court that will overturn *Roe v. Wade* than the Federalist Society's Leonard Leo."[6] At a 2017 presentation at the Acton Institute outlining the Federalist Society's strategy to remake the federal judiciary, Leo said, "I would love to see the courts unrecognizable." Trump, he commented, is "the change we've been waiting for."[7]

In addition to advising Trump on his judicial picks, Leo and his allies have raised hundreds of millions of dollars—over $250 million between 2014 and 2017 alone, according to the *Washington Post*—in part to promote conservative policies, provide funding for right-wing TV pundits, and coordinate and finance campaigns for their judicial picks, including Brett Kavanaugh and Neil Gorsuch.

Leo's work builds on that of other great minds of the Christian right's legal juggernaut. In 1994, the Alliance Defense Fund (now Alliance Defending Freedom) was launched with the support of some of the heaviest hitters of the new Christian Right, including D. James Kennedy, founder of Coral Ridge Ministries; James Dobson, founder of Focus on the Family; Bill Bright, founder of Campus Crusade for Christ International (now Cru); Larry Burkett, president of Christian Financial Concepts; Donald Wildmon, president of the American Family Association; and radio host Marlin Maddoux.[8] The group secures its backing from financial heavyweights of the movement—among them the Edgar and Elsa Prince Foundation, the Bill and Berniece Grewcock Foundation, the Richard and Helen DeVos Foundation, and the Bolthouse Foundation. They also receive substantial funding from the National Christian Foundation, a "donor-advised fund" that reportedly raised over $1.5 billion in 2017.

Today, with an annual revenue of over $50 million, the Alliance Defending Freedom is a mainstay of the movement's plans for dismantling the wall of separation between church and state. The ADF is a key actor behind nearly every major case in the United States that is attempting to expand special privileges for conservative Christians. Its trophies include:

Masterpiece Cakeshop v. Colorado Civil Rights Commission; Burwell v. Hobby Lobby Stores, Inc.; Zubik v. Burwell; Citizens United v. Federal Election Commission; Trinity Lutheran Church of Columbia, Inc. v. Comer; and, of course, *Good News Club v. Milford Central School.*

Joining the ADF are a number of other legal advocacy groups with largely overlapping agendas. Jay Sekulow, who as of this writing serves as one of President Trump's counsels, helped Pat Robertson form the American Center for Law and Justice in 1990 with the idea of creating a right-wing alternative to the ACLU. In 1989, Mathew D. ("Mat") and Anita Staver established Liberty Counsel, which frequently shows up alongside the ADF and ACLJ in court. Becket, formerly known as the Becket Fund for Religious Liberty, whose founder, Kevin Hasson, said he created the organization in response to a "culture war" in the United States, also frequently joins the party. Together these right-wing legal advocacy groups have combined budgets of close to $100 million per year.

The ADF and its allies are as radical as they are rich. Alan Sears, who led the Alliance Defending Freedom for over two decades, announced his vision in the title of the 2003 book he cowrote with Craig Osten, *The Homosexual Agenda: Exposing the Principal Threat to Religious Freedom Today.* "The radical homosexual activist community has adopted many of the techniques used in Nazi Germany," he wrote.[9] Mat Staver of Liberty Counsel was just as quick to push the buttons of paranoia in his own 2004 book from the same publisher, *Same-Sex Marriage: Putting Every Household at Risk.* The Blackstone Institute, a learning center operated by the ADF to train up its army of lawyers, hopes to inspire a new generation of young attorneys. The organization seeks to "recover the robust Christendomic theology of the 3rd, 4th, and 5th centuries," according to text that appeared on the website of the Blackstone Legal Fellowship, an ADF fellowship program, in 2014.[10] The ADF has invoked key source texts of Christian Reconstructionism, and its faculty at one time included the omnipresent pseudo-historian David Barton, the R. J. Rushdoony–inspired Christian reconstructionist Gary DeMar, and the equally fanatical Andrew Sandlin, who served as executive vice-president of Chalcedon Foundation, coauthored a book with Rushdoony in 2000, and praised his mentor as a "champion of faith and liberty."[11]

In the public perception, the judiciary strategy of the Federalist Society, the ADF, and their allies appear to be centered on the issues of abortion, LGBT rights, and "religious freedom." In their own public relations messaging, the groups insist that their purpose is merely to defend "free speech" and the rights of persecuted Christians (along with the occasional token persecuted member of another faith). It would seem, however, the goal is to allow their version of Christianity, and their understanding of the Bible, to shape law and government. In recent years they have settled, paradoxically, on the rhetoric of "religious liberty" as the means to secure that goal.

The *Town of Greece v. Galloway* decision was just one in a string of victories, and far from the most important. It is, however, illustrative of the power of the Christian nationalist movement in the American judiciary today and the success of its Orwellian use of the term "religious liberty."

The case involved the town of Greece in upstate New York, which was in the habit of opening its municipal meetings with sectarian invocations—exclusively Protestant Christian in nature. Two townspeople of different faiths, Susan Galloway and Linda Stephens, complained that the process relegated them to second-class status and violated the First Amendment prohibition on the establishment of religion, and a number of lower courts agreed with them. But in May 2014 the Supreme Court gave the town its blessing and permitted the prayers to continue.

Christian nationalists were jubilant with the result. "It wasn't just an answer on prayer—it was an answer *to* prayer!" the Family Research Council exulted.[12] More important than the license to pray, the religious nationalists understood, was the legal reasoning encoded in the decision. The conservative majority in *Town of Greece* follows a logic that the ADF and its allies had been carefully constructing for years—one case at a time, one pliant Supreme Court justice at a time. That logic has implications that extend far beyond the matter of invocations at town meetings.

The first, crucial move in the logic of *Greece* is to reinterpret public acts that would appear to establish religion—such as officially sponsored invocations at the start of public meetings—as the personal speech of private individuals. Here the five conservatives then on the Supreme Court obediently followed the line of thought that the ADF and its allies provided in their briefs. If a clergyman appointed by the municipal government of Greece bids "All rise" before delivering a prayer, the majority decided, this is not an establishment of religion because the words do not come from the mouth of a public official. If town leaders respond with an "amen," that isn't establishment either because, just then, public officials are acting as private individuals, whose "religious liberty" is not to be denied.

The second, critical step in the logic embodied by the *Greece* decision is to deny that public perceptions of an establishment of religion have any meaningful legal weight. Thus, in response to the plaintiffs from Greece who (rather understandably) saw in the town's prayer practices an effort to favor one religion, Justice Anthony Kennedy sniped in his majority opinion, "Offense . . . does not equate to coercion." Justice Clarence Thomas, joined by Justice Antonin Scalia, drew out the critical implication: "To the extent coercion is relevant to the Establishment Clause analysis, it is actual legal coercion that counts—not the 'subtle coercive pressures' allegedly felt by respondents in this case." In other words, officially approved, relentlessly sectarian observance counts as establishment only if you are compelled to kneel by law.

The final, critical piece of the puzzle is to use the myth of neutrality as a justification for the establishment of the dominant religion. As long as we are looking at the letter of the law, towns like Greece are "neutral" with respect to religious viewpoint inasmuch as they purportedly allow citizens of all religious perspectives and sects to offer their own opening invocations. If conservative Christians happen to win the invocations sweepstakes, well then, that must be because they represent the majority of the town. Indeed, Justice Samuel Alito dismissed the blatantly sectarian history of the town of Greece's proceedings—Christian clergy had a lock on the slot for ten straight years—by pointing out that Jews represent a mere 3 percent of the local population and alleging that other groups are no larger.

Following the logic from beginning to end, it all amounts to saying that the "religious liberty" of the majority—or, at least, of the group that perceives itself to be in the majority, or maybe just a belligerent minority that happens to hold the reins of power—justifies the establishment of their religion. The only restriction—which turns out to be not much of a restriction at all—is that you can't force other people to kneel by law. You can just send them a very clear message that the people with power, and those who hope to remain in their favor, all happen to belong to the "correct" religion. Everyone else, apparently, will just have to suck it up. That, more or less, is what Joseph Richardson discovered in Winter Garden.

Richardson's initial offer, on May 9, 2014, to deliver the invocation at a city commission meeting was met with a polite response, but his request was deferred and subsequent efforts were rebuffed. "As a resident of Winter Garden, I would like our city to be known for its inclusiveness for all points of view and its respect for all individuals," Richardson wrote to the city clerk. "Opening up the commission meeting invocations to everyone would be a wonderful step in that direction." But openness was not forthcoming. After a period of reflection Richardson decided to make his case during the public comments period of city commission meetings. The commissioners were unmoved. Richardson returned again and again to politely request an opportunity to offer the invocation. All told, he appeared before thirty-five meetings.[13] At one meeting he was ejected for failing to stand for the Pledge of Allegiance.[14]

The city responded by instituting a rule that anyone wishing to perform an invocation must represent a 501(c)(3) organization.[15] The intent, Richardson believed, was to make it harder for nontheistic individuals like him to compete in the invocations contest. But Richardson, who happens to be a member of a 501(c)(3) called the Central Florida Freethought Community, was nonetheless able to supply the necessary documentation. Still no luck.

Richardson met with the city manager and multiple commissioners and followed up on those meetings with dozens of public records requests and emails. He circulated a nonbinding petition asking the city to either remove the discriminatory aspects of their invocation policy or to drop the invocations entirely. The city still rebuffed him. At a meeting on January 11, 2018, Richardson stated his case yet again during the public comments section.

"You have a policy that allows you to unfairly discriminate," Richardson stated, his voice firm but measured. "Meeting after meeting, month after month, your silence and inaction confers your consent for discrimination and exclusionary practices just as surely as if you crafted every word of this policy personally. I urge you to once again to reject discrimination, reject tribalism, reject exclusionary practices." In an audio recording of the event, after Richardson speaks, a member the audience can be heard loudly declaring, "Fake news!" Richardson claims that person was Linda Rees, the wife of the mayor.[16]

In May 2019, Richardson spoke at a final hearing as Winter Garden city commissioners debated whether to affirm their existing policy. After issuing yet another plea for inclusion, he was followed by Tim Grosshans, who stood up to air his views on the matter. "We heard clearly from the city manager that both the current and the proposed procedures are constitutional," Grosshans said. Adding, "I do think it needs to be inclusive for residents of Winter Garden," he said, "You have done well and I encourage you to continue to do so."[17] The commissioners voted to stay the course.

As of this writing, four years after making his initial request, Richardson has not been given the opportunity to deliver an invocation in Winter Garden. He has, however, been able to deliver invocations before public meetings at other Florida towns through the Central Florida Freethought Community. His speeches consist mainly of celebrations of Thomas Jefferson's Virginia Statute for Religious Freedom and appeals to the spirit of inclusion. Like other members of the CFFC, Richardson would prefer that cities and towns respect the diversity of their populations by skipping sectarian invocations altogether and focusing instead on rational deliberation over public policy matters that affect their residents. But as long as representatives of religious organizations insist on putting their stamp on proceedings, he feels his voice needs to be heard, too.

Meanwhile, on the other side of Winter Garden, even as Richardson continues his long slog for a symbolic recognition, Tim Grosshans has plenty of other fish to fry. He has no trouble securing invocation slots—he or his staff show up about every six months—so he invests his energy in other projects with more directly tangible benefits.

Grosshans sits on the board of Foundation Academy, a pre-K–12 school serving close to 1,000 students on two different campuses. His wife, Carol, serves as vice president of education. As of this writing, the school bills itself as "FBC [First Baptist Church] Winter Garden's largest ministry," and Grosshans delivered the 2019 commencement address.

Foundation Academy's 2016–17 student/parent handbook reflects the movement's normalization of gender hierarchy. It informs school families that the husband "has the God-given responsibility to provide for, to protect, and to lead his family," while "a wife is to submit herself graciously to the servant leadership of her husband, even as the church willingly submits to the headship of Christ."[18] The wife had indeed better be gracious, for she has the additional "God-given responsibility to respect her husband and to serve as his helper in managing the household and nurturing the next generation." In a section on "the Christian and the Social Order," the handbook identifies same-sex relationships as a form of "sexual immorality" and warns students and parents of the consequences: "We believe that any form (including practice, self-identifying statements, or public promotion) of homosexuality, lesbianism, bisexuality, bestiality, incest, fornication, adultery and pornography are sinful and may result in expulsion."[19] The handbook also makes clear that opposing abortion is part of being a good student: "We should speak on behalf of the unborn and contend for the sanctity of all human life from conception to natural death."[20]

None of which stands in the way of the Foundation Academy collecting public funds to carry out its mission. As a religious nonprofit, of course, the academy is exempt from some taxes and reporting requirements. More than that, it has a claim on direct subsidies from taxpayers through Florida's bountiful school voucher program. The school also accepts money from a state-funded school choice program called Step Up for Students, which grants the school up to $7,111 per qualifying child. Additional public funding is available through another state-funded program called the McKay Scholarship, which provides for students with learning and other disabilities.

Pastor Grosshans's friend Senator Marco Rubio is a big proponent of such "school choice" programs. In 2018, Rubio released a video celebrating "National School Choice Week," an initiative supported by voucher and charter lobbies and funded by the Gleason Family Foundation, which also funds the American Legislative Exchange Council (ALEC) and the libertarian Cato Institute.[21] Florida has one of the nation's largest private school voucher programs and in 2017 spent close to $1 billion on vouchers.[22] A reported 80 percent of the funds for such programs are funneled to religious schools throughout the state. Foundation Academy certainly appears to be thriving financially. It is presently embarking on a five-year expansion, which will include an athletic complex with a sophisticated, contemporary design, enlarged classroom capacity, and a fine arts building.

As a pastor, of course, Tim Grosshans is entitled to a minister's housing allowance—another unique subsidy to clergy and houses of worship that is not available to secular nonprofit groups and their leaders. According to IRS code, pastors are allowed to exclude the amount used to provide or rent a home or the fair market value of the home, including furnishings, property insurance, homeowners' association fees, utilities, even remodeling expenses from gross income. The Treasury Department rejected the ministerial housing exemption when it first came up in 1921, but Congress forced it through. With the overhaul of the tax code in 1954, housing or "parsonage" benefits were made more lenient, largely as part of Cold War efforts to promote religion.[23] Today, an estimated 80 to 90 percent of full-time clergy claim the housing allowance. In 2017, according to the Treasury Department, the exemption was predicted to cost approximately $9.3 billion in forgone taxes over the next decade.

The exemption is meant to apply only to a minister's primary residence, and is supposed to exclude commercial properties or vacation homes. While most pastors are moderately compensated, this rule has done little to slow the housing grift of mega-preachers, many within shouting distance of Winter Garden. Before her death in 2016, Jan Crouch, an Orlando televangelist known for her astonishingly buoyant hairstyles, cofounded with her husband, Paul, the Trinity Broadcasting Network, which was headquartered in Southern California and by 2010 was the third-largest over-the-air television station group in the country, that year receiving $93 million in tax-exempt donations.

The couple's vast portfolio grew to include more than thirty residences, many of them tax-free "parsonages," in Texas, Tennessee, Ohio, and Florida, paid for in cash. It also included a pair of planes valued at $8 million and $49 million. Trinity Broadcasting Network "ordained" employees as ministers, which allowed the Crouches and their network to escape paying social security tax. The Crouches enjoyed a lifestyle of thousand-dollar dinners, antiques paid for with TBN credit cards, and a $425,000 payoff, in 1998, to Enoch Lonnie Ford, a former employee of the network, on the condition that Ford keep quiet about what he claimed was a sexual encounter with Paul Crouch.[24]

In America today, there is nothing particularly remarkable about the financial pathways that lead from the public coffers to mega-preachers' lives of bounty. Trump adviser Paula White, former senior pastor of the Apopka, Florida–based New Destiny Christian Center and cofounder with her former husband of the Without Walls International Church, headed one of six ministries caught up in a lengthy investigation by the Senate Investigation Committee for alleged misuse of church funds and tax-exempt status.[25] The investigation also roped in the ministry of Georgia megapreacher Creflo Dollar, known for his collection of private jets and multimillion-dollar homes. Like White, Dollar resisted cooperating with an investigation into his various business entities, which included "private airports and aircraft leasing opportunities." The committee had questioned "the use of the church's tax-exempt status to avoid taxation" but eventually abandoned its efforts and called instead on pastors themselves to engage in "self-reform."[26] All around the country, the stories may vary in detail but they come down to the same bottom line. The ability to direct and protect the flow of public money toward religious groups, and above all religious groups with the correct creed, is an intended consequence of the "religious liberty" agenda.

In order to understand how the Alliance Defending Freedom and its political allies turned "religious liberty" into a gravy train of public money, it is important to take a closer look at some of the distortions in reasoning that they persuaded the Supreme Court to enshrine in law.

Starting in the 1980s, Jay Sekulow and others on the extreme wing of the religious right began to take a curious line of argument in Establishment Clause cases. In most such cases, there is a distinction between the First Amendment right to the free exercise of religion—such as a public school teacher's right to pray—and the First Amendment prohibition on the establishment of religion—such as an attempt by that public school teacher to lead students in prayer during class. Rather than invoke the Free Exercise Clause, however, Sekulow and his allies suddenly began to appeal to the Free

Speech Clause of the First Amendment. In an argument that formed the tip of the legal spear aiming at the Establishment Clause, they asserted that religion is just speech from a certain, religious point of view. And to prohibit speech of any type on the basis of viewpoint is, by definition, to violate the Free Speech Clause.

One could spill a lot of ink explaining why it is absurd to suppose that religion is not religion after all, but just speech from a religious point of view. But fine arguments are not necessary in this case because the Constitution itself supposes that religion is a category of activity distinct from speech. Why else would the First Amendment take the trouble to guarantee the freedom of religion and then turn around and add a separate and distinct guarantee of the freedom of speech? Indeed, the obvious fact that religion is a distinct activity is essential to make sense of the Establishment Clause, the very first clause of our First Amendment. Congress is proscribed from the "establishment of religion"—a concept easily grasped—but it isn't proscribed from the "establishment of speech," because the latter is nonsensical. What, after all, is the justification for religion's substantial and unique tax benefits if religion is nothing more than a form of speech like any other?

Supreme Court justice Byron White spotted the incoherent nature of this argument in a 1981 case *Widmar v. Vincent*, in which the Court decided that excluding a religious group from meeting on state university campus facilities amounted to a violation of its free speech rights. The opinion of the majority, White argued in his dissent, "is founded on the proposition that because religious worship uses speech, it is protected by the Free Speech Clause of the First Amendment." White concluded, "I believe this proposition is plainly wrong . . . Were it right, the Religion Clauses would be emptied of any independent meaning in circumstances in which religious practice took the form of speech."[27]

Yet subsequent legal advocates of the religious right seized on the opening created by the *Widmar* decision and generated other cases that followed a similar tack. "Our purpose must be to spread the gospel on the new mission field that the Lord has opened—public high schools," Sekulow told the supporters of the newly formed American Center for Law and Justice in 1990. "Yes, the so-called 'wall of separation' between church and state has begun to crumble."[28]

Rendering the Establishment Clause unintelligible, as far as the legal advocates for Christian nationalism were concerned, was a feature of the new line of argument, not a bug. Indeed, if they could recharacterize efforts to invest religion with the authority of government merely as the exercise of free speech rights, then the Establishment Clause would largely go away. Efforts to enshrine this novel line of constitutional misinterpretation achieved a critical victory in the 2001 case of *Good News Club v. Milford Central School*.

Good News Clubs, a widespread initiative sponsored by an organization called the Child Evangelism Fellowship, seek to convert children as young as four and five years old to a deeply reactionary form of evangelical Christianity. The organization installs the clubs as after-school programs in public elementary schools, both because that's where the youngest and most impressionable children are and, more importantly, because their presence in the schools often confuses small children into thinking that the public school endorses their particular religion. Public schools have a cloak of authority in the minds of small children. Most of them can't distinguish what is taught in school from what is endorsed by the school. They think that if something is being taught at their school, it must be what the school wants them to believe.

Prior to 2001, public schools across the United States generally excluded Good News Clubs out of Establishment Clause concerns (among other reasons). Indeed, for many years, public elementary schools routinely tended to exclude all religious groups from use of their facilities, just as they excluded, and continue to exclude, partisan political groups, for reasons that seemed obvious enough to all.

With *Good News Club v. Milford Central School*, Justice Clarence Thomas gave the Christian nationalists everything they asked for and more. Speaking for the conservative majority, Justice Thomas announced that in excluding the Good News Club because it was religious in nature, Milford Central School discriminated against its religious viewpoint, in violation of its right to free speech. There was no more reason to be concerned about the Establishment Clause, he further argued, than there would be if the school included a soccer club—which, he claimed, also involved speech from a certain point of view.

In his dissenting opinion, Justice John Paul Stevens easily spotted the absurdity. Schools in general still exclude partisan political groups from using their facilities—and yet no one supposes that in doing so they violate the free speech rights of those groups. Political groups are barred as a category on account of their nature, not their specific political views, and religious groups were barred in the same way—until Thomas, with guidance from the Alliance Defending Freedom, produced the palpable nonsense that excluding a group on the basis of its religious nature was to discriminate against its religious views. In reality, Thomas had simply obliterated religion as a meaningful category of activity, subject to constitutional constraints, such as the Establishment Clause.

Justice David Souter, in his dissent, saw even further into the potential consequences of such a breakdown in logic. If excluding a religious group on account of the fact that it is religious is a violation of its speech rights, then religious groups belong to a super-category of activity that can never be excluded from school (or other government functions). That is, while political groups, or sporting groups, or business groups, might be excluded on the basis of the nature of their activities without violating their speech rights, religion alone would have a trump card that guaranteed entry under all circumstances. Thus, Souter concluded, "this case would stand for the remarkable proposition that any public school opened for civic meetings must be opened for use as a church, synagogue, or mosque."[29]

The only part Souter got wrong was the bit about the synagogue and the mosque. Only conservative Christian churches stood a realistic chance of claiming the new bonanza. A religious group called The Satanic Temple proved the point. In the wake of the *Good News Club* decision, members of The Satanic Temple—a nontheistic religious order with chapters around the country and overseas—attempted to create after-school clubs of their own and install them in a handful of schools that had already accepted Good News Clubs.[30] A key difference was that, instead of teaching small children that without Jesus they would suffer eternal torment, as Good News Clubs do, The Satanic Temple clubs aimed to teach reason and empathy. They hired a curriculum specialist who produced detailed lesson plans focused on the principles of equality and kindness.

The schools could not slam their doors fast enough, throwing up a variety of procedural and legal hurdles. After news of their plan broke in the *Washington Post*, Satanic Temple leaders received multiple, often public, death threats. They weren't the only other group operating from a "religious viewpoint" effectively shut out from public schools: Wiccans, atheists, Muslims, and other minority religious groups have attempted similar gambits and been excluded from the schools through a variety of means. These episodes are a stark reminder of what I have amply documented in my last book: when members of minority or unpopular religions seek to exercise their "rights" in the same way conservative Christians do, they are frequently prevented from doing so. Public school buildings are not, as it turns out, a "viewpoint-neutral" forum, open in practice to all religions regardless of rank or social status, as the Alliance Defending Freedom argues. "Religious liberty" in America today is largely religious liberty for certain "approved" groups.

The legal powerhouses of the Christian right soon realized that their triumph in after-school programming had opened the door on yet other opportunities in church-state fusion. The same strategy for turning religious liberty into claims on public resources could be generalized to cover a variety of activities.

For example, around the time that Hurricane Sandy hit the eastern seaboard, it occurred to leaders of the legal movement that the new idea of religious liberty might unlock federal money for disaster relief. FEMA, after all, grants assistance to not-for-profit entities, such as shelters, disability and social service providers, child care centers, and others whose work is thought to be essential in the aftermath of disasters. So why shouldn't churches get in on the action?

Religious organizations have a tax exemption not because they provide essential services (some do and others don't), but because it has generally been felt that taxation would limit the freedom of exercise of religion that is guaranteed in the First Amendment. Precisely for that reason, religious organizations are exempt from reporting requirements imposed on those nonprofits that perform these essential services. They are also exempt from the nondiscrimination laws to which other nonprofit groups are compelled to comply.

But the more the legal powerhouses of the movement thought about it, the more denial of FEMA funds seemed like another case of religious discrimination. Keeping religious hands out of the public till was a violation of their religious freedom. By the time Hurricane Harvey hit Houston in late August 2017, the legal guns were armed and ready.

On September 4, 2017, even as the floodwaters from Harvey still swirled in the streets of Houston, three Texas churches filed suit alleging that FEMA's policy of excluding houses of worship from disaster relief funds was unconstitutional. The cause was taken up in a bill cosponsored by a number of right-wing politicians. The churches demanding federal money were free to buy insurance, just as businesses are. But they had not bothered to do so—it was too expensive, as one church representative claimed—so they were counting on the federal government to resolve their problems.

The demand for FEMA relief sounded innocuous at first. Who could object to helping out churches, especially those that offered aid to hurricane and flood victims in their hour of need? Some churches do provide essential services some of the time. And to the extent that they do, and if they should organize those activities with the kind of transparency, fairness, and accountability required of other nonprofits, few would argue with their claim to public money.

But two of the three churches in question did not lay claim to be providing essential services. And if they did, one wonders whether they would have provided those services with dignity to all members of the community, regardless of sexual orientation, ethnic background, or religious belief. Churches that filed the lawsuit belong to the Assemblies of God Pentecostal denomination, which issued in a statement of doctrine "that the growing cultural acceptance of homosexual identity and behavior (male and female), same-sex marriage, and efforts to change one's biological sexual identity are all symptomatic of a broader spiritual disorder that threatens the family, the government, and the church."[31] The Assemblies of God has also subscribed to the belief that "the spread of oriental [*sic*] religions and the occult in America has brought with it an increase in demon possession similar to that reported formerly by missionaries on foreign fields."[32]

Some churches in the area did, of course, open their doors to flood victims in order to provide shelter and other essential services. But many others did not, or at least not immediately—including the megachurch of "prosperity gospel" preacher Joel Osteen, who opened the doors to his 16,000-seat suburban facility only after he received a public drubbing.[33] Some private corporations, such as the Houston furniture showroom owned by Jim McIngvale, or "Mattress Mack," aided victims, too, offering food, shelter, and supplies in the immediate aftermath of the disaster—and yet none of those businesses laid claim to free insurance from the government. The argument for the FEMA money for church repair simply boils down to the complaint that the churches do not wish to purchase their own disaster insurance. "Wind storm insurance," explained a representative of one of the churches leading the lawsuit on a GoFundMe site, would cost "over $15,000 a year . . . that's simple [*sic*] not affordable." But why should taxpayers be on the hook for church facility insurance? Shouldn't "oriental" and "homosexual" taxpayers have a say?

As far as the Christian right was concerned, the answer was simple: religious liberty. "FEMA policy is patently unfair, unjustified and discriminatory," said New Jersey Republican Chris Smith in 2013 after he first introduced a bill in the House that would have compelled FEMA to underwrite church repairs.[34] At that time the Republican-controlled Senate balked, largely out of concern that such aid raised fiscal and constitutional issues. Just five years later, with Trump in office and the Republican Party controlled by the far right, the announcement by FEMA that houses of worship could now claim this special government benefit, too, was met with a collective shrug. The lines of separation between church and state were by now so blurred, the Establishment Clause so degraded, and the list of outrages over Trump-and-allies–related instances of graft and corruption so long and overwhelming that few people could muster the ability to notice or care.

The ultimate destination of the religious liberty gravy train is the school system. One way of securing government resources, Christian nationalists have realized, is to take a cheap ride on public school facilities. Today, thanks to national policy effectively legislated from the bench of the Supreme Court, churches can claim access to public facilities for their services, typically with below-market-rate facility use fees, on the grounds of "religious liberty." (Partisan political groups, on the other hand, have no such right.) A variety of religions and denominations have taken advantage of the opportunity, but the most aggressive by an overwhelming margin have been conservative evangelical churches that belong to national or international parachurch networks. For these groups, establishing churches in public schools has the added advantage of investing their activity with a high degree of public trust, especially among children and school families. Over the past two decades, vast networks of "church-planting" organizations have sprung up and rolled across the nation, effectively using taxpayer largesse to establish religion in the name of "religious liberty."

Church planting is now happening on an industrial scale, and it often takes place in neighborhoods that least expect it, with little or no input from the residents who are, in the end, subsidizing the process. Consider the town of Brookline, Massachusetts, which recently invested $120 million to make one of its elementary schools, known as the Coolidge Corner School, a top-drawer public school facility. Five days per week, the Coolidge Corner School's gleaming new complex houses a K–8 school for about eight hundred of the town's children. On the seventh day it turns into the City on a Hill Church, where hundreds of congregants fill the halls and multiple classrooms, gather for Bible study in the airy cafeteria, worship in the capacious auditorium, and make use of the school's sixty-three free underground parking spaces.

The town is presently poised to rename the Coolidge Corner School in honor of Florida Ruffin Ridley, a civil rights activist, educator, and suffragist who edited the country's first newspaper published for and by Black women. So it is perhaps interesting to note that the school that will likely soon bear Ruffin Ridley's name houses a church fighting the culture wars that drive support for a political party that has made voter suppression one of its principal and strategic imperatives.

The City on a Hill Church moved to the Coolidge Corner School after vacating another Brookline elementary school, the Driscoll School, which it had occupied for nearly eight years. In addition to weekly Sunday services, City on a Hill holds luncheons in the cafeteria on topics such as religiously righteous parenting and "exploring faith." The church even makes use of the expensive new school building on some weeknights. In this way City on a Hill is like other churches, except that many of its costs are borne by local taxpayers.

In lieu of rent, the church pays the town a "facility use fee," which is set at $100 per hour for a gym or auditorium and approximately $12.50 per classroom, according to the town's facility use forms—well below market rate for similarly sized facilities in the area. In many towns and cities, such fees are lower still, and sometimes the use of the facility is free. Naturally the town also charges for janitorial staff to clean the facility after it has been used. But paying people to clean up after you isn't "rent," as some public school church planters have characterized it. The real cost of occupying the space may be counted as a gift from the taxpayers.

The City on a Hill Church is a member of Acts 29, a parachurch network of approximately seven hundred churches worldwide. Each member church may have a distinct name, but all are united under the Acts 29 network umbrella, which has a codified structure of development and support for member pastors that ensures the doctrinal purity of every participating church.

The network was cofounded by Mark Driscoll, the controversial preacher who disparaged "sensitive emasculated men" and asserted, "We live in a pussified nation." He attracted further controversy after he blamed a celebrated pastor's affair with a male prostitute on the pastor's wife for "letting herself go." The late Christian author and columnist Rachel Held Evans castigated Driscoll for "degrading women, bullying men, and using hateful slurs to talk about LGBT people." In a widely circulated blog post she added, "Listen up, Church: Misogyny is real. Homophobia is real. And a man this notorious for both, a man this severely disturbed, should not be in a position of leadership in a church. He needs counseling, not a pulpit."[35]

Driscoll was eventually removed from his position following accusations of plagiarism, misuse of church funds, and abusive behavior—but not, apparently, for his views on gender order and contempt for gay people. On this count Acts 29 does not appear to deviate too far from its roots.

Women, according to an article in the Acts 29 online publication, are directed to "submit" to their husbands at home. According to an article on the Acts 29 website, "male headship and wifely submission" is something "God designed," and "we have no right to tamper with God's design."[36] It should come as no surprise, of course, that an Acts 29 doctrinal statement groups "homosexual behavior," together with "bestiality" and "incest" as worthy of condemnation.

Brookline's City on a Hill Church appears to be no less preoccupied with policing the line between pure and impure. In their written materials, which they hand out during their Membership Matters Course, a requirement for all new members, the church singles out other faith traditions to disparage, including Jehovah's Witnesses, Unitarians, "evangelical pragmatists," and "theological liberals who reject any notion of divine standards and judgment."[37] Like its parent network, Acts 29, the City on a Hill Church groups "homosexual behavior" together with "bestiality" and "incest" as worthy of condemnation.

City on a Hill insists on a "complementarian," "different-but-equal" theology that mandates the "Biblical role of pastor-teacher limited to males." The church's elders and deacons are uniformly male. Written materials for the church soften the imposition of gender hierarchies with some nice doublespeak about men's and women's "biblical equality." It's a way of assigning women and men distinctly unequal roles while assuring women they need not fret about their subordination because they are equal in the eyes of God. It sounds convoluted, but Robert Lewis Dabney would have gotten the point. "Higher and lower hold alike the same relation to the supreme ruler and ordainer of the commonwealth, God," he wrote, "yet they hold different relations to each other in society, corresponding to their differing capacities and fitnesses, which equity itself demands."[38] City on a Hill asserts that that "submission in roles is a reflection of the Trinity."[39] The organization regularly funnels a portion of the money it collects to a local antiabortion "crisis pregnancy center."

City on a Hill is able to thrive and grow precisely because so many of its essential expenses are covered by the taxpayer. After all, it did not pay to construct the Coolidge Corner School, nor did it cover any portion of the $120 million renovation. It does not have to purchase furniture, pay the heating bill, or contribute in any meaningful way to the building's ongoing operations and upkeep. It is perhaps for this reason that City on a Hill has become a "church-planting church," spawning new congregations in public schools in other parts of the city. It has also been able to acquire for its own use a three-story brownstone building with nine bedrooms and four bathrooms (according to the website RealtyTrac) in an area of Brookline where buildings of a similar size and location sell for over $1.5 million; City on a Hill appears to use the brownstone for housing, administration, and some smaller gatherings.[40]

The mingling of church and school comes at a time when many public school districts are under severe financial pressure. According to the Economic Policy Institute, underresourced schools have led to such dramatic declines in teacher pay that 59 percent of American public school teachers are supplementing their paychecks with additional paid work.

The state of Florida offers a clear example of the consequences of right-wing, "small government" policies. Between 2007 and 2015, public schools in Orange County, which includes the city of Orlando, suffered over $105 million in budget cuts—devastating losses that curtailed school administrators' ability to hire staff, maintain their facilities, and fund extracurricular activities.

In 2012, grappling with dwindling resources, overcrowded classrooms, and insufficient textbooks and supplies, Orange County Public Schools superintendent Barbara Jenkins announced an expanded outreach to faith organizations. "Our missions to better our community dovetail when churches, synagogues, and mosques and all faith-based organizations harness the power of volunteerism and servant leadership to benefit the region's youth," she said. Jenkins's plea was purposefully nonsectarian—and yet the "faith partners" for Orange County's schools were nearly all evangelical Christian.

Paradoxically, some of those groups did not appear to have faith in public education. The Venue Church in Apopka, Florida, which was planted inside a public school, used its website to "bemoan" the fact that "the school house has replaced the church house as the community building." Public schools, it added, are places where "morality is challenged and set." The church's purpose in becoming a "faith partner" with the school appeared to have little to do with education and everything to do with its own sectarian goals. "If you are looking to maximize missional money," the website continued, "the school campus is where you will yield the highest return on your investment." Indeed, as Georgia activist Terri Hoye, who champions church volunteers mentoring in public schools, said at a 2014 evangelical conference, "Once [the door to the public schools] is open, it is wide open."[41]

America's expanding network of quasi-state-funded churches have their eye on more than cheap or free facilities. Accessing taxpayer-funded school buildings to subsidize religion is a pauper's game compared to getting one's hands on the money that governments spend on the education that is supposed to go on inside those buildings. According to the National Center for Education Statistics, the United States spent $668 billion on public primary and secondary education for the 2014–15 fiscal school year. Christian nationalists understand that if they can capture a portion of that figure in the name of religious liberty, the money will flow without end.

It was on this account that Christian nationalists reacted ecstatically to the Supreme Court's June 2017 decision involving a church playground in Missouri. Hitherto, the state had declined to repair aging or lackluster church facilities, including playgrounds, out of Establishment Clause concerns. Now the Supreme Court ruled that churches may seek state money for new playground surfaces and other, ostensibly "nonreligious" needs. Of course, taking a few pennies from public money to pay for the resurfacing of a church playground is the kind of small potato that even the most resolute advocate of constitutional propriety might be willing to overlook. But the Christian nationalists behind the case understood very well what was at stake: where the case spoke of playgrounds and repair funds, the Alliance Defending Freedom and its allies saw the potential for schools and vouchers.

In *Trinity Lutheran Church of Columbia, Inc. v. Comer*, the Supreme Court majority, following the tortured legal theory enshrined in the *Good News Club* decision, agreed with plaintiffs that in excluding the church from public funding for its repairs, the state discriminated against its religious character. Under such a logic, of course, the Establishment Clause itself ceases to exist—or, rather, the government is effectively mandated to provide religious groups with public money, since failing to do so would amount to discrimination against their "religious viewpoint." In this case, the justices stopped short of saying whether the ruling applies to school voucher programs that might be used, in effect, to funnel money from the federal and state governments to churches. But the ADF and its allies are nothing if not patient.

Pastor Grosshans of Winter Garden, Florida, can count still more blessings from the powers that be. His son Joshua is a lawyer and he is married to a fellow lawyer, Jamie R. Grosshans. A graduate of Thomas Edison State College of New Jersey and the University of Mississippi School of Law, Mrs. Grosshans appears to have a thriving career. She clerked for the Civil Rights Division of the Department of Justice in Washington, D.C., and the United States Attorney's Office for the Northern District of Mississippi. She has served on the board of directors for the Central Florida Christian Legal Society and, according to a biography accompanying an article she wrote for a publication of the Christian Legal Society, "frequently provides pro bono representation for crisis pregnancy centers."[42]

Jamie Grosshans, not surprisingly, is an officer in the Central Florida Federalist Society. A look further back at her career shows that she was a Blackstone Fellow with the Alliance Defending Freedom. In short, she is a beneficiary of the vast support system for young conservative legal minds created and managed through the legal advocacy groups of the Christian right. In 2018 the grooming paid off when she was appointed by Governor Rick Scott as a judge with the Fifth District Court of Appeal.[43] According to the *Orlando Sentinel*, she is among eleven candidates for nomination to the Florida Supreme Court.[44]

Jamie Grosshans's climb up the right flank of the Florida judiciary mirrors the judicial takeover now occurring in the federal government, too. With Leonard Leo's assistance, by March 2019, eighty-six Trump nominees had been confirmed since Inauguration Day: two to the Supreme Court, thirty-one to courts of appeals, and fifty-three to district and specialty courts. Trump also nominated fifty-eight individuals to the federal courts. At that time there were 170 current and known future vacancies, giving Trump an opportunity to leave his mark on nearly 20 percent of the federal judiciary.

Among the many sordid legacies that the Trump/Pence administration will leave behind, perhaps the most damaging over the long term may well be the infiltration of America's judicial system with the progeny of the Federalist Society, the Alliance Defending Freedom, and their allies.

This is why Joseph Richardson keeps up his campaign, year after year, for what seems like symbolic representation in gatherings of local managers and lawmakers in Winter Garden, Florida. The symbol represents something far more profound, and more meaningful, than a twenty-second invocation. It is really about deciding what kind of nation the United States will become. Are we a nation in which one brand of religion enjoys a place of privilege? Are we a nation of laws—except in cases where the law offends the feelings of those who subscribe to our preferred religion? Will we recognize the equal dignity of all of our citizens? Or are we the kind of society that heaps contempt upon those groups that our national religion happens to despise?

CHAPTER II

Controlling Bodies: What "Religious Liberty" Looks Like from the Stretcher

O VER THE PAST decade, Christian nationalists have managed to convince many Americans that religious liberty is something that has to do with homophobic wedding cake bakers and florists. It's all about symbolic acts and offenses that cause harm only in the mind, or so many are led to conclude. We really don't get what the movement has in mind for us.

What today's Christian nationalists call "religious liberty" is in reality a form of religious privilege—for their kind of religion. But privilege is never free. It always comes at the expense of other people's rights. And the rights that are at stake here are not just about buying cakes and flowers.

The "religious liberty" of Christian nationalists can cost you your dignity, your health, your job, and even your life. I should know. I came close to paying for the "religious liberty" of others with my life. But before I share my experience, I want to tell the stories of those who have paid a much higher price.

Some years ago a medical doctor whom I'll call Dr. Reynolds worked at an HIV clinic at Yale New Haven Hospital, formerly the Hospital of Saint

Raphael, a Catholic entity. At present, an estimated one in six hospital beds in the United States is now in a Catholic-run medical facility. Like all Catholic health care facilities, including hospitals, clinics, and affiliated providers, Saint Raphael was governed by a set of Ethical and Religious Directives (ERDs), a numbered set of rules that reaffirm Catholic teachings as they relate to health care. The ERDs, which act as guidelines for all Catholic health care facilities and impose limitations on the types of services and procedures they are able to deliver, are laid down by the Vatican and codified by the United States Conference of Catholic Bishops.[1] They are the work of clergymen, not doctors. All employees of Catholic-affiliated hospitals and health care facilities must follow the directives as a condition of their employment. Many contractors and suppliers are also bound to the ERDs.

A condition of Yale New Haven Hospital's acquisition of Saint Raphael was that the ERDs must remain in place. So even though the HIV clinic at Yale New Haven Hospital was not a Catholic institution, it was compelled, as a term of the acquisition, to observe the ERDs. Such conditions are commonplace.

The ERDs are very clear on the subject of contraception. Directive 52 spells it out: "Catholic health institutions may not promote or condone contraceptive practices but should provide, for married couples and the medical staff who counsel them, instruction both about the Church's teachings on responsible parenthood and in methods of natural family planning."[2]

For Dr. Reynolds, Directive 52 presented a problem: some HIV medications, such as Efavirenz, which decreases the amount of HIV in the blood, are known to cause severe fetal malformities and other complications in pregnancy. Yet Dr. Reynolds was not allowed to prescribe medication for the explicit purpose of preventing pregnancy. "We still do not hand out condoms," she said. "We don't prescribe birth control."

Dr. Reynolds recalls an experience with one patient, a young woman with HIV, who she wished to put on Efavirenz. "It's a very potent antiviral medication, and has this very severe side effect of teratogenicity, which means it can cause severe harm to a developing fetus," Dr. Reynolds says. "She said she wasn't in a relationship and wasn't sexually active. I gave her the medication and told her, 'You shouldn't get pregnant if you're taking this.'" Because of the ERDs, Dr. Reynolds says, "I did not have the option of giving her birth control. I can do that by referring her out. But I could not prescribe birth control pills to prevent her from becoming pregnant on this med. She ended up getting pregnant and had a baby without a brain."

It is not terribly surprising, given Catholic doctrine on the topic, that the ERDs prohibit abortion. Directive 45 states, "Abortion (that is the directly intended termination of pregnancy before viability or the directly intended destruction of a viable fetus) is never permitted. Every procedure whose sole immediate effect is the termination of pregnancy before viability is an abortion, which, in its moral context, includes the interval between conception and implantation of the embryo." What many prospective patients don't know is that, as a consequence of this prohibition, many Catholic hospitals either ban outright or are reluctant to perform a number of miscarriage-related procedures that the Church chooses to characterize as abortion.

Mindy Swank of Illinois was one of those who found that out the hard way. Married and thrilled to be expecting her second child, she was at home one day when her water broke prematurely at twenty weeks. Through testing, she learned that the fetus had no chance of survival. But Swank was being treated at a Catholic hospital. The doctors at the hospital would not perform an abortion while there was still a fetal heartbeat—even though continuing the pregnancy put her health and life at risk. Mindy suffered through two weeks of emotional anguish as she waited for her body to complete the miscarriage on its own. Then one morning she woke up bleeding. She and her husband hurried to a different nearby hospital to ask them to treat her, but that hospital, too, adhered to Catholic "directives" and refused to induce labor. Over the next five weeks, desperate to obtain the medical care she needed, Mindy returned to that hospital multiple times and was consistently turned away. Nobody told her that she could get the abortion she needed at a non-Catholic hospital, and she continued to struggle with the emotional and physical strain. Then, at twenty-seven weeks, she began to hemorrhage. The hospital finally induced labor, and the baby died shortly after delivery.[3]

Tamesha Means, a Michigan mother of two, also found out the hard way. She was eighteen weeks pregnant when her water broke. With a rupture of membranes that early, the pregnancy was doomed. Means made her way to the nearest hospital, which happened to be a Catholic facility operated by Mercy Health Partners. An examination confirmed what she already suspected: the pregnancy was not viable. An "abortion," or termination, would have been the safest course of action, but instead, the hospital staff sent her home.

The next morning, bleeding and in pain, Means returned to the hospital. By now she was showing signs of infection, yet again she was turned away. As the pain intensified, she returned a third time. And yet again the hospital staff attempted to send her home. But as an administrator was filling out the discharge paperwork, Means began to deliver the products of the miscarriage, and only then did the hospital provide the medical care she needed.

The women who are harmed the most by these restrictions are often left incapable of telling their own stories. Dr. David Eisenberg, who was completing a residency at an Illinois hospital, recalls "the sickest patient I ever cared for during my residency." A young woman experiencing a miscarriage had sought care at a different hospital, which was a Catholic facility. Although her membranes had ruptured, the hospital denied steps to hasten the completion of the miscarriage. Ten days later the young woman transferred hospitals and fell under Dr. Eisenberg's care. By this point, Eisenberg recalls, she had a fever of 106 degrees and was "dying of sepsis." She survived, Eisenberg says, but suffered a cognitive injury as well as an acute kidney injury requiring dialysis. The woman spent nearly two weeks in the hospital, after which she was transferred to a long-term care facility.

"To this day I have never seen someone so sick—because we would never wait that long before evacuating the uterus" in a non-Catholic health care setting, says Eisenberg.

There is no official count of the number of pregnant women who have turned to Catholic hospitals and clinics when something goes wrong, only to be denied the medical care they need. And it is not easy to find women willing to publicize the most intimate details of traumatic experiences in order to "prove" to the world what should not have to be proven: that pregnancy carries significant risk of complications, and hospitals and medical professionals in a modern society ought to allow best practices, rather than religious dogma, to guide their protocols of care. It's also partly because patients do not necessarily know when they are being denied treatment on "ethical and religious" grounds. Hospitals are not required to explain why they are denying service or to inform their patients about other options for treatment. Evidently, the Ethical and Religious Directives do not prohibit the practice of deceiving patients.

Despite the challenges in collecting information, a 2016 report by the American Civil Liberties Union (for which I served as an investigator), titled "Health Care Denied: Patients and Physicians Speak Out About Catholic Hospitals and the Threat to Women's Health and Lives," detailed the ways in which women experiencing pregnancy complications, miscarriage included, frequently do not receive the kinds of medical care from Catholic facilities that other, non-Catholic hospitals routinely deliver.

A 2018 report by the Public Rights/Private Conscience Project, in conjunction with Public Health Solutions, explored the particular danger this arrangement poses to women of color.[4] "Pregnant women of color are more likely than their white counterparts to receive reproductive health care dictated by bishops rather than medical doctors," the authors wrote in the report, "Bearing Faith: The Limits of Catholic Health Care for Women of Color." Perhaps these facts go some way to explaining the alarming trends in maternal health, particularly among women of color. America's maternal mortality rate is the highest among nations in the developed world, and it is rising sharply, up over 26 percent between 2000 and 2014.[5] Black women are three to four times as likely as white women to die of pregnancy complications. This report finds that "in many states women of color disproportionately receive reproductive health care restricted by ERDs" and suggests that the consequent dangers "should be evaluated against the backdrop of vastly inferior health care delivered to women of color across the board."[6]

Many medical professionals privately express their frustration with the situation—but they, too, can be reluctant to go public with their stories. "Tricia," a thirty-one-year-old mother of three who works as an emergency medicine nurse at a Catholic hospital in northwest Indiana, also agreed to speak with me provided I use a pseudonym. ("All the medical facilities in this area are Catholic, so if I get fired, where am I going to work?" she says.)

According to Tricia, the emergency room at her hospital periodically turns away women experiencing miscarriages. "I only work one day a week there," she says, "but it happens a few times a year when I'm on duty, so I know it must happen more often than the times I've seen it."

Tricia recalls a nineteen-year-old woman who came to the emergency room seeking medical treatment for an ongoing miscarriage. Turned away twice, she developed complications. "She came in with a fever a few days later and they sent her home again. I don't think she was actively bleeding all that much, but the baby was already dead and she wasn't passing it on her own," says Tricia. "They said, 'It's just spotting and it will get worse, so let's just wait and see what happens.' They didn't even offer her methotrexate [a chemotherapy drug that will cause a woman to expel the products of a miscarriage]. They waited until her blood pressure was low and she was septic, and then they did the D&C.

"It was a lot to put her through," says Tricia. "She had to go through all that needless trauma—emotional, physical, and financial."

For Tricia, the denial of care at Catholic hospitals is also personal. Prior to the scheduled cesarean birth of her third child, Tricia decided, along with her husband, that their family was complete. The safest time for a woman to undergo a tubal ligation after childbirth is at the time of delivery. But the ERDs also prohibit "sterilization."

"So for me to get a tubal ligation," says Tricia, "I would have had to wait until after recovery from childbirth, then go out of network and find another doctor who doesn't know me or my medical history, travel to a non-Catholic hospital and have an unnecessary subsequent surgery, with all the expense, risk, and inconvenience.

"There is no other situation in which doctors and the hospital will decline to treat a patient who presents with a medical complication," she says, her voice rising in frustration. "Like if someone shows up with appendicitis, they won't decline to treat them and just say instead, 'Oh, you should go home; let's just wait and see what happens.'"

The power of imposing this kind of "religious liberty" on pregnant women isn't just for hospitals. Pharmacists, too, can now enjoy the privilege. Nicole

Arteaga, a first-grade teacher in Peoria, Arizona, found that out during an unexpectedly traumatic visit to her local Walgreens.

In June of 2018, Arteaga was pleased to discover that she was pregnant with her second child. But at the ten-week mark, her doctor delivered devastating news: The fetus had no heartbeat and the pregnancy was failing. At the doctor's suggestion, Arteaga decided to take misoprostol, a drug that antiabortion activists call an "abortifacient," rather than undergo a needless, invasive, and expensive surgery.

When she went to her local Walgreens to pick up the medication, however, the pharmacist refused to fill the prescription on the grounds of his own "ethical beliefs."

"I stood at the mercy of this pharmacist explaining my situation in front of my 7-year-old, and five customers standing behind only to be denied because of his ethical beliefs," she wrote on her Facebook page. "I left Walgreens in tears, ashamed and feeling humiliated by a man who knows nothing of my struggles but feels it is his right to deny medication prescribed to me by my doctor."[7]

According to today's Christian nationalists, this type of "religious refusal" is a shining example of "religious liberty" in action. It isn't.

Arteaga was eventually able to fill her prescription at another pharmacy. So the defenders of this form of privilege will say that no real damage was done. But this is quite false. The humiliation that Arteaga experienced was precisely the point of this bullying exercise in religious privilege. The pharmacist took advantage of an opportunity to announce, in public, that the United States government authorizes him to single out individuals who offend a certain narrowly defined set of religious beliefs, to discriminate against them, and to humiliate them.

The Ethical and Religious Directives of the Catholic Church aren't entirely focused on the reproductive lives of women. They also aim to control the ways that people spend their last days of life. John—the name has been changed—did not know this until it was too late.

In 2014, John was dying of brain cancer. He was residing in a hospice in Snohomish County, thirty-five minutes north of Seattle.[8] His condition was terminal, and he knew it. He likely faced complete incapacity and dementia. More than that, he knew that he almost certainly faced a painful end.

John asked his physician and the staff repeatedly for information on medically assisted death. In 2008, voters in the state of Washington had approved of a statewide "Death with Dignity" initiative that made it legal for physicians to provide aid in dying for people with terminal illnesses and fewer than six months to live. Exit polls showed that 49 percent of Protestants, 47 percent of Catholics, and 79 percent of those who claimed "no religion" voted in favor. John must have known something about the initiative, and now he wanted help.

But the hospice in which he was a patient was affiliated with Providence Health & Services, a large Catholic health care network, which necessarily adheres to the Ethical and Religious Directives. The ERDs prohibit not just aid in dying but certain palliative treatments. Directive 61 states: "Patients experiencing suffering that cannot be alleviated should be helped to appreciate the Christian understanding of redemptive suffering."[9]

Providence has a specific policy that prohibits referrals in connection with or even discussions with patients of the Death with Dignity Act. In keeping with company policy, John's physician and staff declined to answer his repeated pleas for information. The nurses who cared directly for John believed that they would be fired if they tried.

Somehow, John managed to get a gun into the hospice. On the last day of his life, he climbed into a bathtub, put the barrel in his mouth, and shot himself to death. We know of the story only because the nurses were so traumatized—and so angry at their employer for having compelled them to deny John the information that might have changed the outcome—that one filed a complaint with the state's department of health.

Mary Beth Walker, a spokesperson for Providence, called the death "tragic" but provided little information about the details of the event. She maintained that Providence "absolutely respects that patients have a right to ask" about the Death with Dignity Act. But she did not clarify whether the organization felt any obligation to answer their questions. The organization's policy statements, which the spokesperson forwarded to the press, stipulated that its staff and its contractors will not "participate in any way in assisted suicide." The department of health found no wrongdoing and concluded that facilities are not required to provide patients with information about the Death with Dignity Act.

The assertiveness of the Catholic hospital system in imposing its religious requirements on patients comes at a time of massive expansion.[10] Over the past decade the hospital system in the United States as a whole has been undergoing a process of consolidation and concentration, and Catholic hospitals are at the forefront of the charge. Behind the general trends are complex shifts in government policy. All hospitals are to some degree creatures of government, brought into being through regulatory systems and a huge flow of public money through entitlement programs such as Medicare and Medicaid as well as tax subsidies, land use agreements, and other governmental interventions.

As the consolidation of the industry advances, Catholic providers benefit from structural advantages that stem directly from their religious character. By virtue of their religious status, for instance, the Catholic operations have considerably more leeway to underfund pension plans.[11] Following the recent merger wave, over 16 percent of hospital beds in the United States are now in Catholic-run medical facilities. In some states the number exceeds 40 percent.[12]

The Catholic control over hospitals actually gives the Church an even wider reach over the rest of the medical system. Catholic hospitals seek to impose their ethical and religious directives on some of their business partners, too. According to Directive 72, "The Catholic party in a collaborative arrangement has the responsibility to assess periodically whether the binding agreement is being observed and implemented in a way that is consistent with the natural moral law, Catholic teaching, and canon law." In today's interconnected health market, this "ethical and religious" umbrella covers an expanding network of physicians, pharmacists, and specialist providers.

In Washington State, the consolidation of the industry has proceeded at a particularly vigorous pace. Three of the state's largest health care systems in the area—PeaceHealth, Providence Health & Services, and CHI

Franciscan Health—are Catholic entities, and they are expanding throughout the Northwest. Over 30 percent of all hospitals in the region now have a Catholic affiliation.

Because bishops and other religious authorities vary in their involvement with hospital protocol, some hospitals and clinics are more persnickety about adhering to the ERDs than others. At some facilities, administrators and doctors manage to create wiggle room that allows them to deliver some of the services that are technically prohibited. For instance, they may prescribe hormonal birth control if it is deemed a "medical necessity" unrelated to the prevention of pregnancy. Conversations between doctors and their patients are protected by confidentiality laws, and hospital administrators may not probe too deeply. At some Catholic facilities, medical professionals refer women in need of birth control or other forms of reproductive care to unaffiliated outside providers—such as a local Planned Parenthood.

But these concessions—or "workarounds," as they are sometimes referred to—sound more generous than they are. Forcing women to go through the side door to access essential forms of health care imposes logistical and financial burdens. It sends a clear message that they are unworthy of best-practices medical treatment and that female sexuality and reproductive health deserves to be shrouded in secrecy and shame.

In January 2018, the Trump administration established the Conscience and Religious Freedom Division in the Health and Human Services Office for Civil Rights. From the name of the new unit, an alien visitor might have supposed that the purpose of the office was to guarantee the rights of patients to receive equal care and respect, without regard to their religion or other matters of conscience. But the actual mission of the office is to make it easier for health care professionals to deprive patients of lawful, medically indicated services on the basis of their own religious beliefs.[13] Under the leadership of Roger Severino, a trial attorney with a history of right-wing legal activism and opposition to LGBT rights, the office was clearly intended to answer to the needs of avowedly religious people who do not wish to care for women in need of certain reproductive health services or LGBT Americans. Then on May 2, 2019, a "National Day of Prayer," President Trump proudly announced that the office had issued a rule on "Protecting Statutory Conscience Rights in Health Care," which allows health care providers, including physicians, nursing staff, participants in training programs—even X-ray technicians and schedulers—to refuse to serve or treat patients if it happens to offend their "religious beliefs or moral convictions."

It was just the latest example of the Trump administration privileging the "consciences" of certain groups at the expense of others. By now the Department of Labor had issued guidelines for federal contractors that said it's quite all right to violate antidiscrimination law against certain groups as long as they can claim they do so on account of their sincerely held religious beliefs.[14] In July 2018, then-Attorney General Jeff Sessions followed up with his own Religious Liberty Task Force, highlighting the Trump/Pence administration's true priorities.[15]

The biggest future gains for the Christian nationalist version of religious liberty, however, are likely to come from the Supreme Court. During the now-forgotten part of his Senate testimony, before questions about temperament and alleged past sexual aggressions consumed the proceedings, Judge Brett Kavanaugh signaled his concurrence with the theory of "religious liberty" animating the Trump administration. The two senators from Texas, Ted Cruz and John Cornyn, both praised Kavanaugh as a jurist who would uphold "religious liberty"—and all sides understood what this really meant: Kavanaugh's record confirms that he will uphold the religious privileges of conservative Christians at the expense of other people's rights.

In the case of the *Priests for Life v. United States Department of Health and Human Services*, Kavanaugh took the view that the requirement that nuns fill out a one-page form that would have exempted them from providing contraception coverage to their employees imposed a "substantial burden" on their organization's free exercise of religion. Clearly he keenly felt the nuns' anguish about sharing a government with women who can exercise control over their reproductive health.

But in *Garza v. Hargan*, he thought it was no real burden at all for a minor-aged girl, eighteen weeks pregnant and in federal custody, to be denied access to the abortion she desperately wanted. In that same decision—thankfully slapped down within days by the full bench of the court on which he sat—Kavanaugh characterized abortion as a "momentous life decision" and referred contemptuously to abortion rights—established in *Roe v. Wade* and other cases as constitutional in their foundation—as "abortion on demand." The very phrase, of course, was a dog whistle to the antiabortion movement.

Thus he offered a precise rendering of how "religious liberty" works in Christian nationalist circles today. You maximize the moral anguish of those whose "values" you share and protect their "rights" wherever possible. And you minimize the suffering of those who don't belong to the group and treat their rights as merely selfish demands.

Kavanaugh's record also showed that he would be happy to empower corporations to pursue the same vision of "religious liberty." He endorsed the *Hobby Lobby* decision, which allowed that corporation to use its religious beliefs to deny birth control coverage to its employees, regardless of their beliefs. In Kavanaugh's America, supported by the alliance of the Trump/Pence administration and the Christian nationalist movement, our schools, our corporations, and our government will work together to empower the partisans of one variety of religion and disempower the rest.

In the last days of December 2003, I was thirteen weeks pregnant and filled with joy at the prospect of having a second child. Then one afternoon I began to bleed heavily. After soaking a facecloth and then a hand towel in my own blood, I understood it was time to go to the emergency room. Leaving my toddler at home with my husband, I was loaded on to a stretcher and taken by ambulance to the nearest hospital. We were living in downtown Manhattan at the time, and so the ambulance took me to St. Vincent's Hospital, a Catholic facility in the West Village that has since been shuttered.

By the time I arrived, my blood pressure was running dangerously low and I felt that I was passing in and out of consciousness. I know now that what I needed then was a D&C, an abortion procedure to remove tissue from the uterus, and I needed it immediately to stanch the bleeding. But hours passed and I was left to hemorrhage alone. On several occasions hospital attendants came by to change my blood-soaked sheets, but no one would touch me. It didn't make any sense. When I pointed out to a passing ER doctor on duty what must have been obvious—that I was bleeding out—and begged her to conduct a basic examination, she balled up her fists, scrunched her face, and walked away. At some point I started shaking uncontrollably; I was going into shock. I later learned that I lost nearly 40 percent of my blood. Only then did the hospital provide me with the abortion that saved my life.

When I was transported home, via stretcher, my two-year-old didn't recognize me. "Who's that lady?" she asked my mother, who had flown in expecting the worst. It took weeks to recover from the loss of blood. It took much longer to stop reliving the experience in my head. I later inquired with the medical provider in order to review their records of the episode. I was able to confirm the amount of time that elapsed and the total loss of blood but found no explanation for the delay in treatment. In retrospect, given what I now know about the Ethical and Religious Directives, my best guess is that the hospital was willing to gamble with my life for the sake of preserving a child that was at that point nothing more than a fiction of their imagination.

CHAPTER 12

The Global Holy War
Comes of Age

A T A CROWDED outdoor café in Verona, Italy, on day two of the 2019 World Congress of Families, I find myself sitting one table away from Dominik Tarczyński, the far-right Polish politician. He is wearing a bright red MAGA hat and he is engaged in a lively conversation with Ed Martin, erstwhile CNN commentator and president of the Eagle Forum Education & Legal Defense Fund, a tax-exempt "pro-family" organization founded by Phyllis Schlafly.

The following day I catch Martin's talk at the conference, which brings together ultraconservative religious and political leaders from around the world. Resting beside him on the podium I see a red cap. This one reads "Make Europe Great Again."

Under President Trump, the United States has become a flashing red beacon of hope for a new, global, religious, right-wing populist movement. It calls itself a "global conservative movement" and claims that it seeks to "defend the natural family." But it's really about taking down modern democracy and replacing it with authoritarian, faith-based ethno-states. You could call it a kind of global holy war.

The Christian nationalist movement within the United States, which has been my subject in this book, is in reality just one piece of this increasingly interconnected, globe-spanning movement. This global holy war has nuances specific to different countries. But the striking thing about it is its consistency in tone and substance around the world.

The global holy war now defines itself against a single common, worldwide enemy: global liberalism. In one of the opening speeches at the World Congress of Families, I hear American radio host Steve Turley describe the common foe as "the anti-cultural processes of globalization and its secular aristocracy." The new movement, "this resistance, this religious renewal," Turley adds, "is as global as globalism itself."

Global liberalism, as the warriors see it, is a hydra. It has "multiple faces," says Ignacio Arsuaga, the founder and president of the ultraconservative Christian activist group CitizenGO, which is headquartered in Madrid and promotes culture war campaigns in dozens of countries. Taking his turn at the podium in Verona, Arsuaga goes on to name a hit list that will be familiar to anyone who has followed America's Christian nationalist movement: "radical feminists," "the abortion industry," and "the LGBT totalitarians."

In one of the breakout sessions at the congress, Alexey Komov, a Russian activist who has special interests in America's religious-right homeschooling movement[1] and Christian film industry,[2] adds biologists to the targets: "The scientific worldview, the Darwin theory, it's the same organizations, the same people who promote LGBT, gender rights . . . it goes in one package." He nods. "Gays and Darwin, somehow they are connected."

In Verona the new holy warriors reserve some of their greatest animus for migrants. Speakers at the congress warn repeatedly of a "demographic winter" and complain that "soon we will be extinct!" "What happens when our countries are overrun—it's happening in America—is that our families are destroyed," says Ed Martin. Perhaps the most celebrated speaker at the event is Deputy Prime Minister Matteo Salvini, a far-right politician who has made thinly veiled references to Italy's late fascist dictator Benito Mussolini, and who rose to power with rhetorical assaults on Italy's 5 million immigrants.

Like Christian nationalists in the U.S., the global holy warriors appear to enjoy nothing so much as tales of their own persecution. Here, of course, they are not speaking of the substantial, often violent persecution of Christians in countries in which they are actually targeted, such as Afghanistan, Somalia, Eritrea, and Sudan, but of an imagined martyrdom in Europe and the United States. Chairman of this year's World Congress of Families, Antonio Brandi, characterizes the struggle as nothing less than "a fight between good and evil."

Having long recognized the utility of an attack on truth itself, speaker after speaker pillories "fake news." "It doesn't matter if 10,000 articles tell lies about us, we walk in the footsteps of heroes," says Brian Brown, president of the International Organization for the Family, the sponsor of World Congress of Families.

The global holy war has an unmistakably theocratic vision for the future. "I think this collaboration, cooperation, this synergy between the church and the state in Russia, is the key to the defense of traditional family values," Komov says.

"Hungary has declared its commitment to the revitalization of Christian civilization," America's Steve Turley adds approvingly. "All the while Poland has formally declared Jesus Christ as Lord and King over their nation."

In his remarks, Ed Martin, who coauthored a book with the late Phyllis Schlafly and right-wing media personality Brett M. Decker titled *The Conservative Case for Trump*, offers "three key points" to summarize his vision: "Brexit, the borders, and the Bible." Martin adds, "The Donald Trump administration has been a blessing on America like we've never seen."

For a time traveler who may have missed out on the past two and half years, surely the most surprising feature of the new global holy war is the special status accorded to the United States under President Trump. "Donald Trump managed to score a historical victory against the entire U.S. mass media and mainstream political establishment, marking a turning point in the march against the global liberalism," says Levan Vasadze, a Georgian religious nationalist who doubles as a private equity investor with interests in Russia.

It would seem that President Trump supports Europe's new holy warriors unreservedly. In his talk in Verona, Martin quoted Trump's words on his visit to Warsaw in July 2016: "Just as Poland could not be broken, I declare today for the world to hear that the West will never, ever be broken.

Our values will prevail. Our people will thrive. And our civilization will triumph. So, together, let us all fight like the Poles—for family, for freedom, for country, and for God.'"

The bonds between the holy warriors and the Trump team are personal. At the Verona café outside the congress venue, I overhear Ed Martin urge his Polish fellow MAGA cap wearer Tarczyński to invite "Donald Jr." to an event. Then he coaches the Polish leader as he crafts a pair of tweets, instructing him to tag #realDonaldTrump. Martin also advises Tarczyński to tag Gateway Pundit, a conspiracy theory website that smeared survivors of the Marjory Stoneman Douglas High School shooting, alleging they were "heavily coached" crisis actors. He also recommends Jack Posobiec, famous for peddling the fraudulent Pizzagate myth. Tarczyński dutifully tags both.

"Jack's very savvy," said Martin. Glancing at his phone, Martin boasts that Steve Bannon has just texted him. Bannon is aiming to found an institute to support a global far-right Christian coalition, or what he calls "The Movement."

Ed Martin hails from the religious right, but Posobiec is more a figure of the alt-right. As the conversation in Verona attests, the two movements are increasingly finding common ground. Both fear and loathe the global liberal order; both are increasingly turning to a certain kind of national identity as the vector for solution. Increasingly, members of the two groups are making contact and working together. In the figure of Steve Bannon, who has called on "the Church militant" to "fight for our beliefs against this new barbarity," they may well have found a uniter.[3]

Sarah Posner, author of *Unholy: The Christian Right at the Altar of Donald Trump*, has documented these developments at length. "A turn against the liberal democratic values of the EU is exactly what many on the Christian Right are hoping for," she writes. "In an essay last year, [Allan] Carlson, the World Congress founder, scoffed at fears about Orban's autocratic rule and the eclipse of Enlightenment values. Instead, Carlson countered, 'May it be so!'"[4]

Back in the auditorium, I hear Jim Garlow, the politically connected preacher who has served as a director of a division of Bill Dallas's right-wing data-mining operation United in Purpose, speak proudly of his involvement in weekly Bible study classes in the U.S. Congress, the State Department, and the United Nations. "And so we find ourselves in the wonderful privilege of bringing specifically what does the word of God have to say about governmental issues," he says.

The bond between America's far-right and this global reactionary movement is also consecrated with money. The UK-based online political media platform openDemocracy, in partnership with the Independent Media Institute, published a report estimating U.S. Christian nationalist organizations have spent over $50 million in Europe over the past decade in an effort to influence the development of right-wing politicians and policies.[5]

The effects of their contributions are amplified by support from foreign allies. Princess Gloria von Thurn und Taxis, rumored to be a funder for Steve Bannon's planned "gladiator school for cultural warriors,"[6] has reportedly offered the use of her five-hundred-room palace in Regensburg, Germany, as a summer school.

With so much to celebrate and a world waiting to be conquered, the mood in Verona is both belligerent and triumphant. Warning the crowd of the urgent need to "break the ice cap of political correctness," Arsuaga said, "Please try to make liberal politicians and decision makers fear you."

"We are not medievalist throwbacks," Turley added. "We are the future. We are the prolife, pro-child, pro-family future, and there is nothing, absolutely nothing, the secular world can do about that."

As I listen in on the ebullient discussions in Verona, it strikes me that the imagined future of the global holy war looks a lot like the present in Russia. "In the Russian Federation the Orthodox Church has risen to a prominence not seen since the days of the czars," Steve Turley says in reverent tones. The enthusiasm of the crowd is palpable when Archbishop Antony of Vienna and Budapest, a young bearded man with a magisterial affect, rises to deliver a message from the Patriarch of Moscow, which he reads out in Russian.

Alexey Komov, a ubiquitous figure at the congress, seems determined to spread the Russian formula for church-state union around the world. He sits on the board of Arsuaga's CitizenGO and participates, along with two American activists, on a World Congress of Families panel on homeschooling. Komov, who litters his amiable presentations with casual references to "covfefe" and other terms of endearment for the American far-right, seems to have an intimate familiarity with the nuances of America's right-wing political scene. With his charming demeanor and youthful good looks, he reminds me of Maria Butina, the Russian student at American University who ingratiated herself to right-wing politicians through her embrace of America's pro-gun lobby and National Prayer Breakfast and has now been convicted for conspiring to act as an unregistered foreign agent. Komov assisted the Home School Legal Defense Association (HSLDA), along with the IOF and other organizations, in bringing a Global Home Education Conference to Russia in May 2018. The HSLDA's founder and former chairman, Michael Farris, currently serves at the CEO and General Counsel for the Alliance Defending Freedom. Like Brown, Farris too appears on the 2014 leaked membership list of the Council for National Policy.

"By networking with Russians, the HSLDA—now America's largest right-wing homeschooling association—has provided the Kremlin with a new avenue of influence over some of the most conservative organizations in the United States," writes the journalist Casey Michel, who has reported on the links between America's far right and Russia for ThinkProgress and other media outlets. "Russian ties to groups like the HSLDA demonstrate the Kremlin's broader attempts to hold sway over American policies."[7]

According to Michel, Komov has worked with Konstantin Malofeev, a Russian oligarch with links to pro-Russian military and political leaders in eastern Ukraine. Malofeev's television station, Tsargrad TV, which was launched with the help of former Fox News producer Jack Hanick, has provided a platform for the disgraced right-wing conspiracy theorist Alex Jones and the Russian philosopher Aleksandr Dugin. Dugin advocates for the establishment of a network of authoritarian, traditionalist ethno-states with Moscow at its center.[8]

The World Congress of Families got its start over twenty years ago when American and Russian activists and academics gathered in Russia to study issues of mutual interest. In 2018 the congress took place in the former Soviet republic of Moldova. In 2016 it was in the former Soviet republic of

Georgia, where members praised Putin's Russia and the Orthodox Church
as defenders of "Christian civilization" against a secular, decadent West.
Looking around at my fellow conference-goers, it occurs to me that if the
Russian government wanted to manipulate the politics of the West as effectively as it controls its own population, it could hardly have found a more
useful collection of people.

The World Congress of Families is for the generals of the global holy war.
The movement's strength in fact depends on its ground troops, operating
street by street and pew by pew. Or, in the case of the Child Evangelism
Fellowship, child by child. When I first reported in 2009 on the Good News
Club, the Child Evangelism Fellowship's flagship initiative for converting
very young children in public elementary schools, I focused on the American aspect of their work. But theirs is a global organization; at that time
their goal was to establish a presence in two hundred countries worldwide.
They have nearly reached that goal today.

In May 2017, more than 1,000 Child Evangelism Fellowship volunteers
and employees gathered at an evangelical conference center in Ridgecrest,
North Carolina, in honor of the ministry's eightieth anniversary. Ken Ham,
the notorious creationist, was featured as a keynote speaker. Ham has a
warm history with the CEF: two years previously the leaders of the organization "spent the entire day with us at the Creation Museum, plus took a
quick trip to the Ark Encounter construction site," he boasted on his blog.[9]

There was much to celebrate. The Child Evangelism Fellowship, which
targets children as young as four and five years old for conversion to a deeply
fundamentalist form of the evangelical Christian faith, grew at a slow and
steady pace for the first six decades after its founding in 1937. Then, in 2001,
the Supreme Court, dismissing concerns about the separation of church and
school, threw open the doors to America's public schools to the CEF. There
are now more than 4,000 CEF-sponsored Good News Clubs operating in
public elementary schools in the United States. Good News Clubs confuse
small children into believing that their school endorses the CEF's form of
Christianity, and they exploit that confusion to encourage children to
recruit their classmates to the clubs. As I have detailed in my book on the

topic, *The Good News Club: The Christian Right's Stealth Assault on America's Children*, Child Evangelism Fellowship representatives discovered long ago that the particular qualities that make children so vulnerable—their tenderness, their innocence, their eagerness to please and to trust—also make them a fruitful focus of missionary activity. In strategy meetings that I attended, public schools were referred to as "mission fields" and children as "the harvest."

In recent years the Child Evangelism Fellowship has lifted its sights from the children of America to the children of the world. In this respect the organization has tracked an important shift in the thinking of the leadership of the Christian nationalist movement. In 2009, the influential evangelical missions strategist Luis Bush announced a new, unifying vision for missionaries everywhere. He called it the "4/14 Window," and put his findings in a book titled *The 4/14 Window: Raising Up a New Generation to Transform the World*. The largest and most strategic group of people in the world, he observed, are children between the ages of four and fourteen, the stage of life at which most people form their religious identities. "Every major movement in history has grasped the need to target the next generation in order to advance its agenda and secure its legacy into the future," wrote Dr. Wess Stafford, president of the youth-focused ministry Compassion International, in the introduction to the book. "Political movements (like Nazism and Communism) trained legions of children with the goal of carrying their agenda beyond the lifetimes of their founders. World religions have done the same with the systematic indoctrination of their young—even the Taliban places great emphasis on recruiting children."[10]

The Child Evangelism Fellowship embraced this global vision unreservedly, and this is what made the 2017 conference in North Carolina remarkable. The international side of the organization was the star of the show. According to the CEF, there are presently over 75,000 Good News Clubs in about 180 countries around the world.

Today, Child Evangelism Fellowship's ministries contribute to budding theocracies in Latin America, the Caribbean, Africa, the Middle East, Europe, and—very soon, it hopes—North Korea. In a biography of the organization's founder, titled *The Indomitable Mr. O*, author Norman Rohrer boasts that "several countries of the world have adopted CEF materials taught by trained CEF workers as curriculum for mandatory religion classes in their schools." Reports from CEF workers around the world amplify the good news.[11] A CEF initiative in Brazil has embarked on a Tribal Children for Christ outreach, with a Leadership Training Institute session "only for the indigenous groups." A "program of CEF media ministry" in the Middle East region is broadcast "in many closed countries" through "social media and satellite," according to a CEF representative working in the area. In Zambia, as one worker exults, "Thank God the government has allowed us to minister freely in schools." A CEF regional director for the Bahamas reports that the organization "was invited to partner with the Royal Bahamas Police Force at its Annual Summer Camp 2018. Camps were held for six weeks at eight local schools in Nassau." Richard Acquaye, CEF director for Central and West Africa, succinctly articulated the underlying philosophy of the group to a Ghana newspaper reporter: "When the tree is tender you can easily mold it."[12]

North Korea appears to be a work in progress. The country is said to be one of the most hostile places in the world for freedom of religion, and citizens can be exiled to labor camps, tortured, and even murdered for possessing religious literature or materials. But that has only served to inspire Child Evangelism Fellowship president Reese Kauffman to announce as his first prayer goal for 2019 "that children in North Korea will have Good News Clubs." In a recent CEF document, members are exhorted to pray "that the Gospel Balloons will fly and reach every corner of North Korea, that these balloons will reach children and whoever reads the text printed on the balloons will be saved."[13]

In more accessible countries, the Child Evangelism Fellowship tends to partner with conservative local churches. A promotional video for CityKids, the CEF's latest ministry initiative focusing on European cities, shows a charming tot being greeted at the doors of a church by a friendly woman carrying a fistful of balloons.

The real backbone of this global movement is the growing and interconnected network of churches that emphasize strict interpretations of the faith. In many instances they are supplanting houses of worship that represent more traditional denominations. Sometimes these churches turn up where you would least expect, and they maintain ties with other, equally unexpected groups and institutions.

In England, for instance, where more than half the population say they have no religion and only 14 percent identified themselves as belonging to the Church of England, conservative church plants are making decisive inroads. While their edges tend to be softer, likely in response to cultural norms, the strictness at their core places them comfortably at the table of ultraconservative religious movements in America and beyond.

On a sunny Sunday in May 2018, I arrive in time for services at the Euston Church in central London. Housed in the rib-vaulted sanctuary of a neo-Gothic cathedral in Bloomsbury's Gordon Square, the church serves about 150 congregants. The vicar is Kev Murdoch, and I'm familiar with his theological views from his sermons, which are recorded and may be accessed online. "How Can a God of Love Send People to Hell?" is the title of one.[14] "It's not a nice subject for us to think about," he says in an apologetic tone. "Can it really be right that a God of love can put hell on decent people?" The answer is an unequivocal yes. "There will be no super-injunctions for anyone" who fails to accept a literalist interpretation of scripture, he argues. "Justice demands that there is a hell."

In front of every seat is a little square card, colored in red, with the words "Try Church" on one side. The other side asks the question, "IS GOD GOOD?" and reprints a quote from Richard Dawkins equating the notion of a vengeful deity with a "'capriciously malevolent bully.'" The card invites the public to "'Try Church' Sunday." I also learn that Dr. Andrew Sach, a pastor who obtained a doctorate in auditory neuroscience before shifting his career path to ministry, will deliver a talk, "Does Science Contradict Christianity?" "We dare you!" the card says.

The Euston Church presently rents space to hold its services at Church of Christ the King. The cathedral, which dates from the 1800s, is embellished with buttresses, turrets, and spires. It was originally built to accommodate the Catholic Apostolic Church, a Victorian-era sect also known as Irvingites, and for a time in the 1960s through the 1990s it served the Anglican chaplaincy to the nearby University of London. But student participation dwindled, and control of the facility was returned to Catholic

Apostolic trustees, who have leased the building since 2015 to Euston Church for a reasonable fee.

"We are part of the Church of England," a congregant explained to me when I attended services at Euston Church that Sunday morning in May 2018. "But like most Church of England churches, there are things that we think are really, really great, and there's parts that we don't agree with as much. So, for instance, we wouldn't do a gay wedding." In a February 27, 2017, sermon, Murdoch laid it out: "The battleground area, and I'm afraid it is a battleground, is sexuality." Pointing to certain passages in the Bible, he said, "All are unambiguously negative about gay sex."

Murdoch's comments clearly show where the Euston Church's sympathies lie in the schism that has threatened to tear apart the Church of England (part of the Anglican Communion) over the past decade. In 2008 an international faction of conservative Anglicans formed the Global Anglican Future Conference, or GAFCON. Although the Euston Church is not part of GAFCON, its leaders are in tune with sentiments of GAFCON's leader, Archbishop Nicholas Okoh of Nigeria, who declared in 2011 that "what is being known now as gay and homosexuality is contrary to God's plan for human sexuality and procreation. It is against the will of God, and nobody should encourage it, and those who do will earn for themselves the damnation of the Almighty."[15] GAFCON also opposes the ordination of women, which the Church of England has approved since 1992.[16] According to GAFCON representatives, the subordinate status of women in the church should mirror their natural submission at home. "God's good order does not envision nor permit women to exercise the ministry of headship in the family," wrote two church representatives who elaborated at length in a coauthored book.[17] Although GAFCON's base of support lies mostly outside the United Kingdom, with a large presence in Nigeria, Rwanda, Uganda, and other sub-Saharan African countries, as well as some number of churches in the Americas, its ambition is to retake the homeland. Okoh describes a plan "to help re-evangelize a nation that was once one of the greatest centers of Christian mission the world has ever seen but is now one of the most secular."[18]

The manpower driving the schism derives, in part, from the newly reactionary colleges and training institutes that feed into the Anglican hierarchy. According to Richard Howells, who was ordained in 1993 and presently serves as associate priest in the Nar Valley Group, Diocese of Norwich, the system has now passed a "tipping point."

"Moderate colleges are reduced in number, and therefore nowadays I would say three-quarters of the Church of England clergy are trained in an evangelical view of one kind or another," he tells me. Another factor driving the schism, he says, comes from conservative religious organizations such as Christian Concern, which promotes reactionary policy positions among the clergy through seminars, sponsored lectures, and other events.

Right-wing politicians and media personalities frequently mourn the emptying of England's historic churches, pointing out that more people go fishing on Sunday than attend church. Yet the conservative offshoots of Anglicanism are strengthening. In a survey of 185 English churches that opposed women bishops, two-thirds of those churches had grown in the past decade, with a third growing by over 33 percent every year, as reported in the UK weekly magazine the *Spectator*.[19] Approximately one in three congregants at those churches was younger than thirty. "For the rest of the church, the picture is miserable," according to the article. "The average age of a congregation is 62 and nearly half of English congregations have fewer than five members under 16." The situation bears similarity to that in the U.S., where mainline denominations are graying and thinning, while conservative evangelical plants thrive.

At Euston Church, the building may be historic but the service includes some distinctly American strands. The worship band mixes classic hymns, such as Charles Wesley's "And Can It Be," with American Christian music hits like "The Lion and the Lamb" by the Mobile, Alabama–based band Big Daddy Weave. The emphasis is on sin, salvation, and evangelism of the "unchurched." From the pulpit, Murdoch urged congregants to recruit other souls. "Wherever you go tomorrow, if you haven't yet told them that you are a Christian, tell them that you are a Christian," he said, his genial voice rising and falling. "Dare yourself to invite someone to church." Murdoch acknowledged that evangelism isn't always easy. "I feel very intimidated by secular London," he confessed, then reassured the group, "Take courage. The Lord stands beside you. He is totally *on it*."

Euston Church's Americanisms start to make sense when you learn that the church is a member of The Gospel Coalition. A powerful global alliance with nearly 8,000 affiliated churches in the U.S. alone, The Gospel Coalition was cofounded by the American pastors Don Carson and Tim Keller, the charismatic and influential guru of "church planting," the practice of sending out ministers to establish new congregations, often in rented or inexpensive facilities. Presently there are The Gospel Coalition–affiliated churches in 130 countries, and, like the Child Evangelism Fellowship, the organization recently launched a Europe- and urban-focused initiative called City to City Europe. "Cities are strategic places for gospel ministry and should receive missional priority at this point in history," Keller wrote.[20]

The Gospel Coalition has placed a new emphasis on planting churches in countries where liberalism flourishes, as well as in cities identified as "centers of influence." London checks both boxes.

While many of The Gospel Coalition's affiliated churches do a great job of emulating aspects of millennial culture, The Gospel Coalition teaches that same-sex relationships are sinful and insists on "male headship" at home and in church: "The man is the leader, and the wife is the follower," according to an article on the organization's online platform. In what reads like a form of Orwellian newspeak, the piece goes on to explain, "Her submissive role does absolutely nothing to diminish her equality with him as an image-bearer. In her humanity, she is his equal. In her role, she is submissive."[21]

The Gospel Coalition–affiliated churches are nevertheless often successful in university towns and areas where young professionals tend to congregate. The youth-focused culture of such church plants strikes some number of young people as fresh and authentic. In my experience chatting with younger congregants in the pews, I get a sense that some are there in search of an alternative to the present mating culture, with its consumerist orientation. Others are seeking refuge from the insecurities of the gig economy and even the existential dread of climate change, which offers them little vision or basis for creating a stable future. Smaller, midweek gatherings deliver instant fellowship. Such churches emphasize community and purvey doctrinal conformity in the language of personal growth. In an era of growing income inequality and diminishing expectations, they offer the hope of stability and purpose.

True to its ideological roots, the Euston Church believes it has enemies, and they aren't just "the homosexuals." The evildoers are above all the nonbelievers—as well as anyone who imagines that church and state should be kept apart. According to Murdoch, "secular thinking" is the way to spot the "enemies of the truth." In a sermon I attend, he advises, "Expect them to be divided among themselves, inconsistent in their arguments, expect them to overreach themselves . . . whether that's dictators promising to eradicate Christianity from their countries, or counselors trying to eradicate religion from the schools, as some want to in this borough."

After my visit to the Euston Church, I decide to check out their science-focused presentation by Dr. Andrew Sach, now available online. It turns out to be an extended tirade against atheism.[22] Sach, who represents himself as a reformed nonbeliever, alleges that questions about religion and science may be understood as a conflict "between two different philosophies. There's a conflict between the worldview of the Bible on the one hand, and the worldview of naturalism of atheism." Sach declines to clarify his own opinion of creationism, which is less acceptable in the UK than in the U.S. "I'm not going to tell you my view," he says, "because I don't want it to be the be-all and end-all today." But in the question-and-answer period, he makes clear his opinion that physical disabilities, disease, and earthquakes are all a consequence of the sin of disbelief.

"He made the world perfect," Sach said, "and we stuffed it up."

International church-planting networks and the organizations that support them increasingly cross borders in all directions. Another London church plant called Grace London is affiliated with a church-planting network, called the Advance movement, which got its start in Australia and has now reached into the United States. The Advance movement was founded and led by a man named P. J. Smyth for the "primary purpose of taking new ground for the Gospel in small towns, suburbs, cities, and nations." But, in an indication of the density of interconnections in the global network of new evangelists, Grace London periodically holds joint services, weekend retreats, and other activities with Reality Church London, a plant of the Carpinteria, California–based Reality Church, which also happens to be affiliated with The Gospel Coalition. Years ago, when I lived in Southern California, I periodically attended services at the Reality Church network's original founding church, so I am eager to visit its outpost here in London and learn more about its relationship with P. J. Smyth's Advance movement affiliate Grace London.

On a Sunday evening I enter a community center near Waterloo and find the Grace London/Reality Church London service in full swing. The congregation is young and multicultural; about a quarter are Asian or of Asian descent. "From life's first cry to final breath / Jesus commands my destiny," they sing the tuneful worship hit "In Christ Alone" with full-throated joy, raising their hands heavenward. At my seat I find a card telling me that Dr. Andrew Sach is scheduled to give a lecture here, too.

In front of me sits a woman with a flowing green top. A tall, androgynous friend is seated next to her. I strike up a conversation and ask the women their impressions of P. J. Smyth, the founder of the network to which Grace London belongs. They smile but indicate they don't know what I'm talking about. I find this troubling.

P. J. Smyth, now in his fifties, was raised in England, then moved with his parents to Zimbabwe and subsequently South Africa. P.J.'s father, John Smyth, an English lawyer who died in August 2018, once ran elite Christian summer camps for boys at Winchester College in Hampshire. But multiple allegations of physical and sexual abuse were lodged against him. Men who had attended the clubs as boys described how Smyth groomed them over time before compelling them to show him their genitals, then brutally beating them under the pretext that they were being punished for the "crime" of masturbation.

One victim who attended the camp and estimates he was one of twelve boys targeted by Smyth for beatings at that time described his experiences in an article for the *Telegraph*. Smyth was "particularly interested in the usual teenage stuff—masturbation, indecent thoughts, pornographic magazines," he wrote.[23]

When Smyth initiated the beatings, the victim says, they were cast as a necessary consequence of sin. "Quoting from the Bible—Hebrews in particular—he said it wasn't enough to repent for your sins; that they needed to be purged by beatings," the survivor writes. "I had to bleed for Jesus."[24]

"I was stunned by how hard he hit me that first time and gasped with what little breath I had left," the survivor wrote. "That was the first of the

8,000 or so strokes he would make on my bared bottom over the next four years; each and every stroke delivered with the same extraordinary ferocity."

Winchester College was made aware of the abuse but declined to report Smyth to the police. Instead he was "warned off" from the schools. Free to go elsewhere, he left the UK in the early 1980s and moved with his family to Zimbabwe, where he set up the Zambesi Ministries and ran a summer camps for boys from well-to-do families.[25]

At least five boys who had attended those Zimbabwe camps accused Smyth of abuse. Smyth was also formally charged with the killing of a Zimbabwe teen, Guide Nyachuru, whose body was found on the grounds of the school where the Zambesi holiday camps were held. In 2002, Smyth left Zimbabwe for South Africa, where he became an anti-LGBT activist.

Advance movement founder P. J. Smyth has claimed he was unaware of his father's behavior. "I never saw or heard anything that led me to suspect my father was engaged in the activities alleged," he wrote in February 2017. "I had a happy childhood at home, and my father disciplined me in a manner consistent with the laws and cultural trends of the UK at the time." He also said that "these are horrific allegations, and if proven true it is right that my father face justice."[26]

Some years previously, however, P. J. Smyth published a "Quick-Start Parenting" guide that was surely consistent with his father's approach to child-rearing.[27] In a section titled "Raising Obedient Children," he writes, "I really want to stress the importance of demanding immediate obedience." If a parent issues a request or order, and a child protests or even slightly delays in acquiescing, he continues, the father should hit the child.

"If there is so much as a squeak . . . ," he says, "then I pull the car over (even if we are later [sic] or on a highway) and smack the offending son."

Tender age is no excuse to abdicate from a father's apparent responsibility to beat his children. When his own children were still in high chairs, according to P. J. Smyth's guidebook, he trained them to obey by striking them whenever they reached for the salt. "I would smack their chubby little hand," he says, "just hard enough to sting them and shock them and provoke a few tears." Their next attempt to reach for the salt was met with "a slightly harder smack. And so it would go on. Guess who won? I did. Every time with every son. The issue was never the salt shaker. It was obedience."[28]

P. J. appears particularly proud of his nine-point plan of ritualistic corporal abuse.[29]

Tell them to "go to the bathroom," he instructs parents.

"Once the door is closed, I sit on the edge of the bath and they stand in front of me ..."

"Then say, 'turn around and hold the basin with both hands.'"

"Do not tolerate wriggling or trying to cover bottoms with hands."

"It should be hard enough to shock and provoke tears ..."

"Control the crying. No exaggerated or prolonged crying is allowed, and no sulking or bad attitude of any sort allowed."

If the process is not met with the expected response, according to the Advance movement founder, repeat beatings are necessary. "Go back to the bathroom and repeat the process until true repentance and submission is evident."

In what reads like a nod to his own father's strategy for realizing "the benefits of smacking," P. J. adds: "May I say at the outset that if the law of you [sic] country forbids this form of discipline, then I would recommend that you either fully obey the law, or move to another country where the government are not such a bunch of controlling sissies."[30]

What the pastor of Grace London leading today's services, Andrew Haslam, makes of P. J. Smyth and his father I cannot ascertain, although his contribution to the Advance movement website makes it clear that he is a proud and enthusiastic member of Smyth's organization. "I mentioned that we were looking at joining Advance," he writes on February 23, 2016. "This is now official, and it feels like a match arranged by God."[31]

It is clear that questions of gender order and masculine power preoccupy Haslam, too. He has also praised the controversial pastor Douglas Wilson, titling a February 15, 2014, blog post, "Profound, provocative, and prophetic—doug [sic] wilson on marriage," before it was taken down.[32] "This is the most provocative and helpful book on marriage that I have read," Haslam wrote, referring to a book authored by Wilson. "It is always a joy reading Doug Wilson ..." Wilson, the prolific theologian and pastor from Moscow, Idaho, with a somewhat agitated style, is infamous for his particularly perverse brand of antifeminism. "The sexual act cannot be made into an egalitarian pleasuring party," Wilson jabbers. "A man penetrates, conquers, colonizes, plants. A woman receives, surrenders, accepts." Wilson also writes that "women who genuinely insist on 'no masculine protection' . . . tacitly agree on the propriety of rape."[33]

Haslam, nevertheless, rewards Wilson with praise. "Men don't know how to lead, and they certainly don't know how to teach their family. It is on these themes that Wilson really hits hard, and hits below the belt," he wrote on his blog. "The tidal waves of cultural change have wreaked havoc with the family, and with godly masculinity, and it is now rare (in Britain at least) to find families that embody the scriptural values."[34] At the service I attend, he articulates his fervent wish to "see God revive family life along biblical lines."

Individuals with authoritarian dispositions tend to reinforce hierarchies in multiple spheres, and Haslam's erstwhile guru Doug Wilson was no different. An admirer of Rushdoony and other Reconstructionists, he hailed the "unexpected blessings of slavery" and has said that he believes LGBT people could be executed in certain circumstances. To be fair, he added that "killing homosexuals is pretty much a non-priority for me," since AIDS is claiming their lives already.[35]

No doubt this is a bridge too far for Haslam, who says gay people ought to simply forgo intimacy altogether. "For my friends who have grown up experiencing homosexual attraction but have also come to believe that Jesus is the Son of God, they have been willing to trade their sexual fulfilment [sic] in order to pursue a deeper satisfaction in following Christ," he says approvingly. "Literally every person who chooses to follow Jesus makes these painful and self-denying choices."[36]

I wave a friendly goodbye to the woman in the flowing green top and her androgynous friend on my way out the service. I wonder: Do they know about any of this?

As for P. J. Smyth, it now seems that he will be bringing his version of the gospel to America. According to their website, the Advance movement has planted or partnered with churches in Texas, Utah, California, Florida, and other states. Some Advance-affiliated churches hold Sunday services in taxpayer-funded buildings such as community centers and public elementary schools. In September 2016, the day after Donald Trump won the election, P. J. Smyth tweeted, "Political instability is a proven ally to gospel advance."

Then, in 2017, he accepted an invitation to head up the Covenant Life Church in Gaithersburg, Maryland.[37] Following a series of devastating child sexual abuse scandals, it seems Covenant Life was in the market for the kind of leadership that P. J. Smyth could offer. In 2012, the church had been hit with a class action lawsuit, and seven pastors were accused of engaging in a cover-up. A Montgomery County judge dismissed the suit citing various technicalities, "among them the state's restrictive civil statute of limitations for child-sex-abuse cases," according to a 2016 article in the *Washingtonian*. "The proceedings never delved into whether the allegations were true."[38]

The Child Evangelism Fellowship in its current, massive, global form is really a creation of the Alliance Defending Freedom, the legal advocacy nexus of Christian nationalism in the United States today. It was the ADF that guided the CEF through the American court system and toward the game-changing 2001 Supreme Court decision *Good News Club v. Milford Central School*, which effectively pried open the doors of every public elementary school in the nation to any Good News Club that wishes to be there. The Gospel Coalition, too, has drawn on the firepower of the ADF in building its network in the United States; the ADF has helped clear the way for the establishment of TGC-affiliated churches in taxpayer-funded spaces such as public schools and community centers. Not surprisingly, the international expansion of these groups also comes at a time of expansion for the ADF and its network.

Through offices in Mexico City, Vienna, Brussels, Strasbourg, London, New Delhi and other locations, the Alliance Defending Freedom exports the revolution, showing considerable skill in adapting to new cultural environments and political frameworks. Legal concepts that are workshopped in the U.S. are disseminated throughout the world. The goals of ADF International are consistent with those within the United States and rely on some of the same novel legal arguments and conceptions of "free speech" and "religious liberty."

ADF offices tend to be strategically located near centers of power. In Geneva, "we focus our legal advocacy efforts at the Human Rights Council, the Office of the High Commissioner on Human Rights, and the different bodies that monitor human rights treaties," according to the Alliance Defending Freedom International website.[39] In the U.S. the ADF's Washington, D.C., office is "strategically positioned to effectively engage with the OAS, which consists of Member States from Latin America, the Caribbean, the US, and Canada." New York offices, "just minutes away from UN headquarters," provide legal expertise "to Member States to ensure that the UN upholds the inherent dignity of every human person. Our specific areas of focus are the General Assembly, the Economic and Social Council (ECOSOC), and the functional commissions." The ADF also works "alongside a large network of allied lawyers throughout South Asia, Africa, and Oceana," and partners with other organizations that share their "vision for transforming the legal culture."[40]

ADF International has had some success in shaping public conversation on certain key issues. In 2017 a debate over end-of-life care for Charlie Gard, a child in a vegetative state, dominated the English media for several months. The framing of discussion, centered on the value of human life at its most vulnerable, was highly reminiscent of the debate that took hold around Terri Schiavo, which stormed through American politics in the early 2000s. Behind the scenes in both cases, the Alliance Defending Freedom was instrumental in launching and orchestrating the flurry of activity.

The Alliance Defending Freedom joins with other right-wing groups in weaponizing the idea of "free speech." In England, until quite recently, there was little public protest at women's reproductive health clinics. But as anti-abortion groups in the UK increase their visibility, protesters are becoming more aggressive and direct in their tactics. In 2018 a reproductive care clinic in Ealing, West London, was compelled to erect a "safe zone," also called an "exclusion zone," to protect clients from threats and intimidation. In England, that was a first. Opponents lost no time in casting the safety zone as discrimination against their right to free speech.[41]

Joining the Alliance Defending Freedom in the global expansion are a host of other right-wing, ultrareligious advocacy groups with a global reach. They include the National Organization for Marriage, the International Organization for the Family, and Family Watch International.

These U.S.-based groups are increasingly finding common cause with religious nationalist groups around the world, and they have begun to formalize their alliances through a variety of international organizations.

According to the Brussels-based policy and advocacy consultant Elena Zacharenko, there are hundreds of organizations pushing an ultraconservative agenda in courts and legislative tribunals across the European continent. Lobbying organizations include the European Center for Law and Justice (an international arm of the American Center for Law and Justice), which is active at the European Court of Human Rights in Strasbourg and at the European Parliament in Brussels. Other key organizations include European Dignity Watch, World Youth Alliance Europe, Fédération Pro Europa Christiana, and Dignitatis Humanae Institute, which is devoted to "pushing back the tide of radical secularism" and has been closely affiliated with Steve Bannon.[42] The organizations support and sustain political careers for those who share their goals. And, as in the U.S., their agenda is kept alive thanks to a flood of cash from conservative religious hierarchies and wealthy individuals.

"It is the same individuals involved in many of the (seemingly) different organizations, which creates an impression of many different movements supporting this agenda from the grassroots, while this is not necessarily the case," says Zacharenko. But over time, she points out, "the agenda has very much taken on a life of its own, and has unfortunately been adopted by some 'mainstream' politicians—in Poland, Hungary, Italy, Brazil, Croatia and elsewhere. It is therefore not something forcibly kept alive by a small number of radicals, but has entered and been embraced by some sections of the electorate."

Such groups have a solid toehold in eastern Europe, where persistent economic challenges, combined with falling birth rates, have contributed to existential questions about the very nature of nationhood. The most obvious signs of influence often appear on the familiar turf of the culture wars. In Poland the antiabortion cause was taken up by an organization of conservative lawyers, the Ordo Iuris Institute for Legal Culture, whose president is legal scholar Aleksander Stepkowski. Abortion is already prohibited in Poland in most instances, but exceptions are in place for rape and incest, for gross fetal abnormality, and to preserve the life of the mother. Ordo Iuris and its allies have tried to push through a new law that dispenses with some of those exceptions and would add sweeping and punitive language to the existing prohibitions.[43]

"Although a relative newcomer to the conservative Polish scene, Ordo Iuris has very quickly emerged as the leading organization advancing a drastically retrograde agenda ranging from a complete abortion ban to decriminalizing some forms of domestic abuse," says Neil Datta, executive director of the European Parliamentary Forum for Sexual & Reproductive Rights. "They are also very ambitious in reaching the highest levels of the Polish government and courts, and it would seem have plans to influence the EU and the UN."[44]

Efforts to impose further restrictions on abortion gave rise to massive protests. But the demonstrations, known as the "coat hanger rebellion,"[45] did little to derail the effort, which has the support of a small but vocal number of politicians as well as the backing of the Catholic hierarchies and appears to be part of a broader effort to change the culture. In 2018, new textbooks were introduced in Polish schools that present contraception as "dangerous" to women's health. And the proceedings only enhanced the stature of Stepkowski, the Polish legal scholar. On February 20, 2019, Poland's president appointed Stepkowski as a judge of the supreme court, which would make him the second Ordo Iuris activist already on the highest court of Poland. In 2019, CitizenGo launched a massive campaign in Poland to battle efforts to liberalize antiabortion law, spreading their message through billboards, mailings, and screenings of antiabortion films.

Europe's current spate of conservative activism and legislation, which appears to reverse the trend toward universal human rights, is not a result of spontaneous uprisings from ordinary citizens fed up with "the gays." In fact, this activism reflects an ongoing, well-funded, highly coordinated effort by multiple groups across states and even continents to roll back those rights in the EU and beyond.

American-origin groups like the Alliance Defending Freedom have been instrumental in shaping the emerging global movement toward reactionary religious nationalism. But there is another country that has played an exceptional role in the process, and that is Russia.

As on so many other fronts, Paul Weyrich got there first. Even before the collapse of the Soviet Union, Weyrich took a keen interest in Russian politics and religion.[46] He was among the first to grasp the potential for an alliance with religious conservatives in Russia and Eastern Europe. After the fall of the Soviet Union, Mr. Weyrich made multiple trips to Russia, eventually becoming a strong supporter of closer relations. As president of the Krieble Institute, a unit of another organization he cofounded called the Free Congress Foundation, Weyrich also supported democracy movements in eastern Europe, fostering political engagement and promoting the establishment of small businesses. In Hungary, he formed a partnership with Laszlo Pasztor. After serving a prison sentence for his activities with a pro-Nazi party, Pasztor made his way to the United States and took a key role in establishing the ethnic outreach arm of the Republican National Committee.[47] "The real enemy is the secular humanist mindset which seeks to destroy everything that is good in this society," Weyrich said.[48]

All told, Weyrich made more than a dozen trips to Russia and eastern Europe in the aftermath of the fall of communism. At the time of his death in 2008, even as he was riding high on a wave of plutocratic money in the United States, he was writing and speaking frequently in defense of Russia and facilitating visits between U.S. conservatives and Russian political leaders.[49]

Soon more Republicans began to experience a similar, extraordinary change of heart about their onetime enemy of all enemies. Around the time that Weyrich was first making contact with Russia, Brian Brown was growing up in the mainstream American world where the communist Soviet Union stood for the axis of all evil. But Brown's views on Russia changed as he rose the ranks of the religious right. A leading opponent of marriage equality, he began to meet Russians at international conferences on family issues. He found many kindred spirits. As cofounder and, later, president of the National Organization for Marriage, along with membership in the Council for National Policy and other right-wing interest groups, Brown visited Moscow four times in as many years. During one of his trips, in 2013, he testified before the Duma as Russia adopted a series of anti-LGBT laws.

"What I realized was that there was a great change happening in the former Soviet Union," Brown told the *Washington Post*. "There was a real push to re-instill Christian values in the public square."[50]

As the Republican nomination battle intensified, the burgeoning alliance between Russians and U.S. conservatives came into focus. The growing dialogue among international (often Russian or Russia-connected) political figures and members of the American right came at the same time that the Russian government stepped up efforts to cultivate and influence far-right groups in Europe. Russian oligarchs, having effectively deployed religious nationalism to gain control over their own population, readily grasped that it could be used to shape events in other countries, too. "Pro-family" politics, which purports to aid families but is in its largest part aimed at suppressing women's autonomy and LGBT rights, they understood, is an effective tool in uniting and mobilizing religious nationalists everywhere, which is in turn an excellent way to destabilize the Western alliance and advance Russia's geopolitical interests.

In short, Russian leaders see America's Christian right as a tremendously useful vehicle for influencing American politics and government in a manner favorable to Russian interests. Maria Butina, the Russian woman charged in 2018 with "acting as an agent of a foreign government," certainly understood the utility of the movement. When she set about "to establish a back channel of communication" with American politicians, it was not at all surprising that she would do so at the National Prayer Breakfast in Washington. Alexey Komov's dual interest in America's Christian home-schooling movement and faith-based film industry would appear to fit the pattern.

Russian leaders' evident interest in manipulating America's Christian nationalists for their own purposes did little to discourage those nationalists from clamoring for still more Russian involvement in American affairs. In the run-up to the 2016 election, the passion for Russian family values among America's religious extremists grew still more ardent. In 2013, Bryan Fischer, then a spokesman for the American Family Association, called Mr. Putin a "lion of Christianity." In 2014, Franklin Graham defended Mr. Putin for his efforts "to protect his nation's children from the damaging effects of any gay and lesbian agenda" even as he lamented that Americans have "abdicated our moral leadership." In December 2015, Mr. Graham met privately with Mr. Putin for forty-five minutes. And in March 2019, with the apparent blessing of Vice President Mike Pence—or so Graham says—Graham traveled to Russia to meet with a number of Russian religious and political leaders, such as Patriarch of the Russian Orthodox Church Kirill and Vyacheslav Volodin, a Kremlin official sanctioned by the U.S. government since 2014 for his role in Russia's invasion of the Ukraine. According to the social media account of one Russian official, the tête-à-tête was for the purpose of strengthening relationships between the U.S. Congress and the Duma.

On his own Facebook account on March 3, 2019, Graham obliquely dismissed to the Mueller investigation, writing, "#Collusion? I'm in Russia right now—Moscow to be exact—and I'm meeting with the Russian churches on how we can share with more young people about faith in Jesus Christ! That's not 'collusion' but it is collaboration for the sake of souls. #GoodNews."

The Christian nationalists' affection for Mr. Putin and all things Russian goes much deeper than a tactical alliance aimed at saving souls and defeating "homosexuals" and "gender ideology." At the core of the attraction lies a shared political vision. America's Christian nationalists have not overlooked Putin's authoritarian style of government; they have embraced it as an ideal. During the 2016 presidential campaign Mike Pence hailed Mr. Putin as "a stronger leader in his country than Barack Obama has been in this country."[51] The Christian nationalists haven't shied away from the fusion of church and state that characterizes Putin's regime. On the contrary, it appears they want to emulate it. They love Russia, it seems, because they hate America and its form of secular, constitutional democracy.

When Russians undertook a direct attack on American democracy in 2016 with the clear aims of electing Donald Trump as president and undermining Americans' trust in their system of government, Christian nationalist leaders did more than join Trump in the spurious cries of "No collusion." They joined him in denying that there ever was an attack. They cheered him on as he obstructed efforts to investigate the attack. And then they joined him in attacking Democrats, the FBI, the "fake media," the "deep state," and everyone else who suggested that investigating and countering an attack on America was a good idea.

It seems sadly fitting that so many of the self-anointed patriots of America's Christian nationalist movement should have found themselves working with foreign powers intent on undermining our national security, our social fabric, the integrity of our elections, and the future of American democracy. This is a movement that never accepted the promise of America. It never believed that a republic could be founded on a universal ideal of equality, not on a particular creed, or that it might seek out reasoned answers to humanity's challenges rather than enforce old dogmas. It never subscribed to the nation's original unofficial motto, *E Pluribus Unum*, that out of many, we could become one. From the beginning, its aim was to redeem the nation by crushing the pluralistic heart of our country. The day when it will have the power to do so is fast approaching.

EPILOGUE

THE RISE OF the religious right should be cause for alarm among all who care about the future of democracy in America. Yet it should not be the cause of despair. If Christian nationalism is a pathology rooted in America's past, as I have argued, so, too, may the cure draw in important ways from our history. Overcoming this kind of reactionary and authoritarian movement isn't just something Americans can do; it is what has made Americans what we are.

In this book I have focused on the organizations and the people behind the movement. What I have necessarily left out are the many Americans who are mobilizing to confront the threat. When right-wing ideologues have sought to disenfranchise voters, to pervert the meaning of freedom of conscience and freedom of speech, to target the rights of specific communities, and to defend criminal actions by their enablers, Americans have organized to meet the challenge.

While it is true that a sector of the media has essentially been enlisted in a propaganda campaign to stoke up nationalist impulses—working with far-right platforms as mouthpieces for disinformation and hate—there are many others that are working hard to bring the truth to light. The reason why Christian nationalist groups complain about government so loudly is that government often does intervene on the side of freedom; it was the government, after all, that went down to defend Black schoolchildren, the so-called Little Rock Nine, in Arkansas's infamous desegregation case. Similarly, when members of the movement attack those Christians who reject a theology of domination and inequality, it is because they know that a different embrace of Christianity undermines their empty claims of moral authority.

In addition, there are many legal advocacy groups committed to protecting individual rights, freedom of speech and conscience, and the separation of church and state, working in opposition to right-wing legal advocacy groups like the Alliance Defending Freedom. These organizations may not have as much money to devote to the cause, but their efforts are critical. Other organizations are devoted to promoting civic engagement, defending voting rights, and fostering access to comprehensive reproductive health care, scientific literacy and historical accuracy in schools, and the pursuit of justice in other arenas. Many faith groups are involved in seeking to restore the rights of the undefended and disenfranchised. All these groups and individuals working on different lines are advancing democracy against the claims of the radical right, and these are the Americans that inspire me. There are innumerable avenues of involvement, and they represent democracy in action. I believe they have the power to succeed, because they follow in the footsteps of those who have done so in the past.

The biggest fraud of Christian nationalism—that the United States was founded as a Christian nation—is also the movement's source of its greatest weakness. The mythologizers of Christian nationalism have hurled every distortion they can find at America's founders because they know that those same founders secured a truth that is fatal to their cause. The "wall of separation between Church & State" is not a latter-day fiction concocted by secular liberals, as Christian nationalists would have us believe. It is a phrase put to paper by Thomas Jefferson to describe a principle that was written into the Constitution and carved into history as a core achievement of the American Revolution. It is a principle understood by subsequent generations as essential to securing the lasting peace and prosperity of America's irreducibly pluralistic society. If we want to defend against Christian nationalists' distorted notion of "religious liberty," we don't need to find a new principle. We just need to reclaim the genuine religious freedom that our founders established and that most of our citizens cherish.

Today's movement leaders have declared a new holy war against America's ethnically and religiously diverse democracy. Yet the vision of a nation founded upon hierarchies enshrined in purportedly biblical law remains now, as it was with the Confederacy and Jim Crow, the foundation of a weak society, not a strong one. If we want to guard against demagogues and theocrats who wish to "redeem" America, we don't need a new theory of American democracy. We just need to recover and restore the vision of a nation dedicated to the proposition that all men and women are created equal.

Many leaders of the Christian right like to dress up in red, white, and blue and announce themselves as true patriots. But they are the same people who seek to pervert our institutions, betray our international alliances and make friends with despots, degrade the public discourse, treat the Constitution as a subcategory of their holy texts, demean whole segments of the population, foist their authoritarian creed upon other people's children, and celebrate the elevation of a "king" to the presidency who has made a sport out of violating democratic laws and norms. We don't need lessons on patriotism from Christian nationalists. We need to challenge them in the name of the nation we actually have—a pluralistic, democratic nation—where no one is above the law and the laws are meant to be made by the people and their representatives in accordance with the Constitution.

The version of the religious right that put Donald Trump in the White House is the one that stepped onto the national stage in 1980 with the election of Ronald Reagan. It gathered force with another iteration of its founding lie—that it represented the "moral majority" of the nation—and this lie is yet another source of its weakness. The movement does not speak for a majority. It is a militant minority. The 26 percent of the voting age population that voted for the movement's favored candidate in 2016 are far outnumbered by the slightly larger number of Americans who voted for a different candidate and over 40 percent of eligible voters that did not cast a ballot at all. We don't need to create a new majority; we just need to give our existing majority the power to which it is entitled.

Addressing gerrymandering, voter suppression, and other abuses of the electoral process that continue to hobble American democracy will be a central aspect of any effort to meet the challenge of Christian nationalism. Even more than the Republican Party itself, the movement's electoral power depends on its sway over primaries and general elections in states and districts that are disproportionately represented. A democratically elected government in America is much more likely to favor democracy over a theocratic order. Everything that restores the power of people to govern ourselves undermines the pretensions of those who would dominate us in the name of God.

There are of course many other threats facing our nation today. But the answers to those challenges are in some instances the same as the answers to religious nationalism. Reactionary authoritarianism doesn't come out of nowhere. It draws much of its destructive energy from social and economic injustices that leave a few with too much power and many others with too little hope. Rising economic inequality and insecurity has created a large mass of people, on all ends of the economic spectrum, who are anxious for their future and predisposed to favor calls for unity around an identity that targets others for vilification and degradation. And it has elevated the power of a small group of people with the means and desire to control the social order for their own benefit. Addressing inequality won't by itself resolve the challenges of the Christian nationalist movement, but it will take some air out of its bellows.

In some ways, Christian nationalism is the fruit of a society that has not yet lived up to the promise of the American idea. There is work to be done, but for now we are free to do it. We have met challenges in the past—well enough, at least, to make it to the present moment. Religious nationalists are using the tools of democratic political culture to end democracy. I continue to believe those same resources can be used to restore it.

ACKNOWLEDGMENTS

This work would not have been possible without the scholarship, assistance, and encouragement of so many others. Here I would like to acknowledge them, fully aware that I will not be able to name them all or thank them enough.

Many people invested their time and tested their patience relating their experiences to me, both on and off the record. I have acknowledged some directly in the text. Others, however, prefer to remain anonymous, and I thank them anonymously.

Some sections of the book draw on my journalism. Portions of this book appeared, in different form, in the *New York Times*, the *American Prospect*, the *Nation*, and the *Advocate*. It has been my very good fortune to work with some of the most talented editors in the field. They include Aaron Retica, Matt Seaton, Gabrielle Gurley, Kathryn Joyce, Amanda Teuscher, Harold Meyerson, Lizzy Ratner, Neal Broverman, Matthew Breen, and Marianne Partridge.

This book benefited from consultation with people with in-depth knowledge of the legal and policy landscape. Many of them are included in the following list, which is in no particular order and should not be taken to suggest that any of them endorse the views expressed in the book: Rob Boston, senior advisor for Americans United for Separation of Church and State; Jennifer E. Copeland, executive director of North Carolina Council of Churches; Rev. Jennifer Butler, founder and CEO of Faith in Public Life; Jennifer C. Pizer, law and policy director for Lambda Legal; Valerie Ploumpis, national policy director for Equality California; Katherine Franke, Kimberlé Crenshaw, Elizabeth Boylan, and Elizabeth Platt at the Law, Rights, and Religion Project at Columbia Law School; Miranda Blue, author at Right Wing Watch; Steve Martin, director of communications and development at the National Council of Churches; Caroline Fredrickson, president of the American Constitution Society; Will Harris, former global head of external communications at Marie Stopes; Samantha Sokol, legislative advocate at Americans United for Separation of Church and State; Maggie Garrett, vice president for public policy for Americans United for Separation of Church and State; Alison Gill, national legal and policy director at American Atheists; Téa Braun, director at Human Dignity Trust; Ira C. Lupu, professor of law at George Washington University; Mercedes K. Schneider, author at Teachers College Press; Andrew Seidel, director of strategic response at the Freedom from Religion Foundation; and Richard Katskee, legal director at Americans United for Separation of Church and State.

This project has also benefited from the direction of professional academic researchers and other experts. (I'd like to reiterate that the opinions expressed in this book should be blamed on me, not on those who have been generous enough to assist me.) Some of these experts are credited directly in the text. Others include Linda Woodhead, professor of politics, philosophy, and religion at Lancaster University; Randall Balmer, the John Phillips Professor in Religion at Dartmouth College; Warren Throckmorton, professor of psychology at Grove City College; Nancy MacLean, professor of history and public policy at Duke University; Angelia Wilson, Political Studies Association Chair at the University of Manchester; Julie Ingersoll, professor of philosophy and religious studies at University of North Florida; Richard Kahlenberg, Senior Fellow at The Century Foundation; Andreas Knab, former graduate student at Oxford University; Roberta Cook, cooperative and extension specialist and Lecturer Emerita in the Department of Agricultural and Resource Economics at the University of California Davis; Jill Hicks-Keeton, assistant professor of religious studies at the University of Oklahoma; Andrew Whitehead, associate professor of sociology at Clemson University; Hector Solon; Mark Chancey, associate professor in the Department of Religious Studies at Southern Methodist University; David Brockman, Nonresident Scholar at Rice University's Baker Institute for Public Policy; Eric C. Miller, assistant professor of education studies at Bloomsburg University of Pennsylvania; Mitchell Robinson, chair of music education at Michigan State University; Paul Weller, Emeritus Professor at the University of Derby; Bill Mefford, adjunct professor at Wesley Theological Seminary; and Professor Steven K. Green, the Fred H. Paulus Professor of Law and director of the Center for Religion, Law, & Democracy at Willamette University.

I owe so much to contemporary writers and researchers in this field, a large number of whom I quote directly, cite or otherwise acknowledge in the work. Other writers who have generously shared their ideas and offered their deep knowledge of America's religious landscape include Diana Butler Bass, Ann Neumann, Peter Montgomery, Bruce Wilson, Jonathan Larsen, Cole Parke, Pagan Kennedy, Doug Mesner, and Rachel Tabachnick.

A special thanks to Julie Silberger, Alissa Quart, Briallen Hopper, Maria Quintal Castillo, Frederick Clarkson, Maia Szalavitz, and Matthew Shakespeare for their generous assistance with various aspects of the work, including points of fact and language.

Then there are those who hosted me as I traveled for research on this book specifically, including Steve and Lorraine Saulovitch, Jill and Neil Levinson, David Lonsdale, Sara Lipton, Michelle Gittelman, Dana Lehmer, and David and Jocelyn Williamson.

I am especially grateful to all the staff at Bloomsbury for embracing and supporting the project. A special thanks to my brilliant editor, Anton Mueller, for his superlative guidance. Cheers to my agent, Andrew Stuart, for his literary acumen and friendship.

Above all I'd like to thank my husband, the writer Matthew Stewart.

NOTES

CHAPTER 1: CHURCH AND PARTY IN UNIONVILLE

1. Watchmen on the Wall, Testimonials, http://www.watchmenpastors.org /national-event-testimonials.

2. Dr. Kenyn Cureton, *Culture Impact Team Resource Manual: How to Establish a Ministry at Your Church* (Family Research Council, 2011).

3. Resisting the Green Dragon homepage, www.resistingthegreendragon.com. Archived March 15, 2016. Archived pdf on file at DeSmog blog.

4. "Cornwall Alliance for the Stewardship of Creation," DeSmog, www .desmogblog.com/cornwall-alliance-stewardship-creation.

5. John Bowden, "GOP Candidate Preaches That Wives Should 'Submit' to Husbands," *The Hill*, August 7, 2018.

6. Brian Tashman, "Charlotte Prayer Rally Repents for 'Homosexuality and Its Agenda That Is Attacking the Nation,'" Right Wing Watch, September 6, 2012, http://www.rightwingwatch.org/post/charlotte-prayer-rally-repents-for -homosexuality-and-its-agenda-that-is-attacking-the-nation.

7. Alexander Zaitchik and Daniel Adell, "Fringe Mormon Group Makes Myths with Glenn Beck's Help," *Intelligence Report*, February 23, 2011, https://www .splcenter.org/fighting-hate/intelligence-report/2011/fringe-mormon-group -makes-myths-glenn-beck%E2%80%99s-help.

8. Rob Boston, "Skouson's Scandalous Schools," Americans United for Separation of Church and State, October 2016, https://www.au.org/church-state /october-2016-church-state/featured/skousens-scandalous-schools; Carmen Green, "Students at an Ariz. Public Charter School Are Being Taught Religious Belief in Government Class, so Americans United Filed Suit," Wall of Separation Blog, September 07, 2016, https://www.au.org/blogs/wall-of -separation/students-at-an-ariz-public-charter-school-are-being-taught -religious-belief.

9. The suit was eventually dropped because the plaintiffs were unable to proceed anonymously. See Chapter 9, "Proselytizers and Privatizers."

10. Matthew Cole, "The Pentagon's Missionary Spies," *The Intercept*, October 26, 2015.

11. Sarah E. Jones, "Pentagon Problems: Family Research Council VP Once Paid Christian Missionaries to Spy for America," Americans United for Separation of Church and State, October 8, 2015, https://www.au.org/blogs/wall-of -separation/pentagon-problems-family-research-council-vp-once-paid -christian.

12. C. Peter Wagner, *Dominion! How Kingdom Action Can Change the World* (Chosen, 2008), 144, 148–49, 154–55.

13. Dan Wooding, "Never Surrender, Become 'Kingdom Warriors,'" https://www .identitynetwork.net/apps/articles/default.asp?blogid=0&view=post&articlei d=66032&fldKeywords=&fldAuthor=&fldTopic=0. Last accessed April 19, 2019.

14. www.potusshield.org. Last accessed February 17, 2019.

15. http://awake88.org/church-voter-analysis/. Last accessed July 15, 2019.

16. Rebecca Klar, "Christian Group Warns Against Rise of 'Christian Nation- alism,'" *The Hill*, July 29, 2019, https://thehill.com/homenews/news/455157 -interfaith-group-warns-against-creating-second-class-faiths-in-us.

17. Evangelical Environmental Network, "The Caring for Creation Pledge," www .creationcare.org, https://www.creationcare.org/the_caring_for_creation _pledge.

18. From FRC email dated October 25, 2018.

19. David Saperstein and Amanda Tyler, "Trump Has Vowed to Destroy the Johnson Amendment. Thankfully He Has Failed," *Washington Post*, February 7, 2018.

CHAPTER 2: MINISTERING TO POWER

1. "Capitol Ministries 20th Anniversary Report," https://www.e-digitaleditions .com/i/748914-20th-anniversary-report-capitol-ministries/5?m4=. Last accessed March 2019.

2. "Steve Taylor Working with Capitol Ministries to Make Disciples of Jesus Christ in the Political Arena," Capitol Ministries, https://capmin.org /resources/ministry-updates/steve-taylor-working-with-capitol-ministries -to-make-disciples-of-jesus-christ-in-the-political-arena. Last accessed March 1, 2019.

3. See warzone.cc, "Leadership" biographies, https://www.warzone.cc/leadership.

4. Von Lucas Wiegelmann, "Meet the Preacher Who Teaches the Bible to the U.S. Cabinet," *Welt am Sonntag*, October 29, 2017.

5. Ralph Drollinger, "The Profound Theological Importance of Husband-Wife Marriage," Capitol Ministries Members Bible Study, September 24, 2018, https://capmin.org/the-profound-theological-importance-of-husband-wife -marriage. Last accessed April 22, 2019.

6. "Protestant Pastors Name Graham Most Influential Living Preacher," LifeWay Research, February 2, 2010, https://lifewayresearch.com/2010/02/02/protestant -pastors-name-graham-most-influential-living-preacher.

7. John MacArthur, "The Willful Submission of a Christian Wife," Grace to You, February 19, 2012, https://www.gty.org/library/sermons-library/80-382/the -willful-submission-of-a-christian-wife.

8. Ibid.

9. Tom Krattenmaker, *Onward Christian Athletes: Turning Ballparks into Pulpits and Players into Preachers* (Rowman & Littlefield Publishers, 2009), 137.

10. Ralph Drollinger, *Rebulding America: The Biblical Blueprint*, 2nd ed. (Nordskog Publishing, 2016), 4–5.

11. Evan Halper and Jordan Rau, "Pastor's Remarks about Women Lawmakers with Young Children Spark Furor," *Los Angeles Times*, May 21, 2004; Evan Halper, "He Once Said Mothers Do not Belong in State Office. Now He Leads the Trump Cabinet in Bible Study," *San Diego Union-Tribune*, August 3, 2017.

12. Larry Mitchell, "Religious Right? Bible Teacher Hits Keene's Capitol Fellow-ship," *Chico Enterprise Record*, March 1, 2008.

13. Staff, "Capitol Ministries State Director Leaves, Joins New Christian Group," *Capitol Weekly*, November 12, 2009; "Religion-Politics Fight Flares over Bible Study Groups," *Capitol Weekly*, July 28, 2011.

14. Ralph Drollinger, "God's Word on Spanking," Capitol Ministries Members Bible Study, May 2, 2016, https://capmin.org/gods-word-spanking. Last accessed July 15, 2019.

15. Nina Burleigh, "Trump Cabinet Spiritual Advisor Shares His Views, and Some Find Them Spooky," *Newsweek*, October 31, 2017.

16. Ralph Drollinger, "Toward a Better Biblical Understanding of Lawmaking," Capitol Ministries Members Bible Study, February 17, 2014, https://capmin.org /toward-a-better-biblical-understanding-of-lawmaking. Last accessed July 15, 2019.

17. Ralph Drollinger, *Rebuilding America: The Biblical Blueprint*, 2nd ed. (Nordskog Publishing, 2016), 58.

18. Katherine Stewart, "The Museum of the Bible Is a Safe Space for Christian Nationalists," *New York Times*, January 6, 2018.

19. Ralph Drollinger, "Coming to Grips with the Religion of Environmentalism," Capitol Ministries Members Bible Study, April 2, 2018, https://capmin.org /coming-to-grips-with-the-religion-of-environmentalism.

20. Peter Montgomery, "EPA's Pruitt Hears from Bible Study Leader That 'Radical Environmentalism' Is a 'False Religion,'" Right Wing Watch, April 3, 2018, http://www.rightwingwatch.org/post/epas-pruitt-hears-from-bible-study -leader-that-radical-environmentalism-is-a-false-religion.

21. Robin Wright, "Pompeo and His Bible Define U.S. Policy in the Middle East," *New Yorker*, January 10, 2019.

22. https://www.wellversed.world

23. Ralph Drollinger, *Rebuilding America: The Biblical Blueprint*, 2nd ed. (Nordskog Publishing, 2016), 69.

24. "CM Ministry to Local Government Leaders Getting a Big Boost!" Capitol Ministries, undated, https://capmin.org/resources/ministry-updates/cm -ministries-to-local-government-leaders-getting-a-big-boost. Last accessed April 23, 2019.

25. "Please Pray for Plantings in Eastern European Nations," Capitol Ministries, undated, https://capmin.org/resources/ministry-updates/please-pray-ministry -plantings-eastern-european-nations. Last accessed April 23, 2019.

26. Ralph Drollinger, "Solomon's Advice on How to Eliminate a $20.5 Trillion National Debt," Capitol Ministries Members Bible Study, January 15, 2018, https://capmin.org/wp-content/uploads/2016/09/Solomons-Advice-on-How -to-Eliminate-a-20.5-trillion-Debt-by-Ralph-Drollinger-2018.pdf. Last accessed July 15, 2019.

27. Ralph Drollinger, "Toward A Better Biblical Understanding of Lawmaking," Capitol Ministries Members Bible Study, February 17, 2014, https://capmin.org /wp-content/uploads/2015/08/toward-a-better-biblical-understanding-of -lawmaking.pdf.

28. Ralph Drollinger, "Solomon's Advice on How to Eliminate a $20.5 Trillion National Debt."

29. Ralph Drollinger, "Government and Economics: Five Principles for Tax Policy," Capitol Ministries Members Bible Study, November 4, 2013, https:// capmin.org/government-and-economics-five-principles-for-tax-policy. Last accessed July 15, 2019.

30. Ibid.

31. Ralph Drollinger, "Toward A Better Biblical Understanding of Lawmaking."

32. Ralph Drollinger, "Theological Liberalism in America," Capitol Ministries Members Bible Study, April 1, 2019, https://capmin.org/theological-liberalism -in-america. Last accessed July 15, 2019.

33. Von Lucas Wiegelmann, "Meet the Preacher Who Teaches the Bible to the U.S. Cabinet," *Welt am Sonntag*, October 29, 2017.

34. Ralph Drollinger, "What the Bible Says About Our Illegal Immigration Problem," Capitol Ministries Members Bible Study, February 18, 2019, https://capmin.org /bible-says-illegal-immigration-problem-2. Last accessed July 15, 2019.

CHAPTER 3: INVENTING ABORTION

1. Hunter Schwarz, "Fox News Guest Says 'Frozen' Makes Men Look Like Villains and Fools. Welcome to the New Culture Wars," *Washington Post*, February 4, 2015.

2. "President of Concerned Women for America Penny Nance Talks About the #MeToo Movement," *Valley News Live*, October 18, 2018.

3. Michael Shear and Thomas Kaplan, "Political War over Replacing Kennedy on Supreme Court Is Underway," *New York Times*, June 28, 2018.

4. See Facebook video of March for Life speeches: https://www.facebook.com /ewtnonline/videos/live-march-for-life-ewtns-complete-coverage-part-2 /10155430019472582. Last accessed April 23, 2019.

5. Donald T. Critchlow, *The Conservative Ascendancy: How the GOP Right Made Political History* (Harvard University Press, 2007), 128; *Placerville Mountain Democrat*, March 29, 1985, https://mountaindemocrat.newspaperarchive.com /placerville-mountain-democrat/1985-03-29/page-6.

6. Richard Viguerie, *The New Right: We're Ready to Lead* (Viguerie Company, 1980), 55.

7. Randall Balmer, "The Real Origins of the Religious Right," *Politico*, May 27, 2014.

8. Viguerie, *The New Right*.

9. Randall Balmer, "By the Way: The Rove of the Religious Right, a Eulogy," *Religion Dispatches*, June 16, 2009, http://religiondispatches.org/iby-the-wayi -the-rove-of-the-religious-right-a-eulogy.

10. John Micklethwait and Adrian Woolridge, *The Right Nation: Conservative Power in America* (Penguin, 2004), 81.

11. "A Funding Father," *Washington Times*, September 19, 2003.

12. Viguerie, *The New Right*, 63.

13. Eric Heubeck, "The Integration of Theory and Practice," published on the Free Congress Foundation's website in 2001, archived at http://progressivevalues.org .s150046.gridserver.com/the-integration-of-theory-and-practice-a-program -for-the-new-traditionalist-movement.

14. See video: "Paul Weyrich—'I don't want everybody to vote' (Goo Goo)," uploaded by peoplefor, June 8, 2007, 40 sec, https://www.youtube.com/watch ?v=8GBAsFwPglw. Last accessed July 15, 2019.

15. Viguerie, *The New Right*, 79.

16. Ibid., 4.

17. Elizabeth Kolbert, "Firebrand: Phyllis Schlafly and the Conservative Revolution," *New Yorker*, October 30, 2005.

18. Interview with Sagar Jethani, "Conservative Icon Phyllis Schlafly: 'The Republican Party Is in the Hands of the Wrong People,'" Mic, May 24, 2013, https://www.mic.com/articles/43987/conservative-icon-phyllis-schlafly-the-republican-party-is-in-the-hands-of-the-wrong-people.

19. Viguerie, *The New Right*, 56.

20. Council for National Policy Membership Directory 2014, https://www.splcenter.org/sites/default/files/cnp_redacted_final.pdf.

21. Anne Nelson, *Shadow Network: Media, Money, and the Secret Hub of the Radical Right* (Bloomsbury, 2019).

22. Frances FitzGerald, "A Disciplined, Charging Army," *New Yorker*, May 18, 1981.

23. Blake Eskin interview with Frances FitzGerald, "Church and State," *New Yorker*, May 21, 2007.

24. Nancy D. Wadsworth, "The Racial Demons That Help Explain Evangelical Support for Trump," *Vox*, April 30, 2018.

25. FitzGerald, "A Disciplined, Charging Army."

26. Ibid.

27. Dr. Bob Jones Sr., "Is Segregation Scriptural?," address delivered over radio station WMUU, Bob Jones University, Greenville, S.C., April 17, 1960, https://docs.google.com/file/d/0B6A7PtfmRgT7QikzZEVXUThMLWc/edit.

28. Ibid.

29. Randall Balmer, "The Real Origins of the Religious Right," *Politico*, May 27, 2014.

30. Nancy MacLean, *Democracy in Chains: The Deep History of the Radical Right's Stealth Plan for America* (Viking, 2017), 68–69.

31. Glenda Elizabeth Gilmore and Thomas J. Sugrue, *These United States: A Nation in the Making 1890 to Present* (W. W. Norton, 2016), 550–51.

32. Harry R. Jackson Jr. and Tony Perkins, *Personal Faith Public Policy* (Frontline, 2008), 3.

33. Balmer, "The Real Origins of the Religious Right," *Politico*, May 27, 2014.

34. Linda Wertheimer, "Evangelical: Religious Right Has Distorted the Faith," NPR *Morning Edition*, June 23, 2006.

35. Ibid.

36. Balmer, "The Real Origins of the Religious Right," *Politico*, May 27, 2014.

37. Linda Greenhouse and Reva B. Siegel, "Before (and After) *Roe v. Wade*: Questions about Backlash," *Yale Law Journal*, 2011.

38. Daniel K. Williams, *Defenders of the Unborn: The Pro-Life Movement Before Roe v. Wade* (Oxford University Press, 2016), 237.

39. Jonathan Dudley, "When Evangelicals Were Pro-Choice," CNN Belief, October 30, 2012, http://religion.blogs.cnn.com/2012/10/30/my-take-when-evangelicals-were-pro-choice. Dudley is the author of *Broken Words: The Abuse of Science and Faith in American Politics* (Random House, 2011).

40. Johanna Schoen, *Abortion after Roe: Abortion after Legalization* (University of North Carolina Press, 2015), 151.

41. Patsy McGarry, "Catholic Church Teaching on Abortion Dates from 1869," *Irish Times*, July 1, 2013; Leslie Reagan, *When Abortion Was a Crime: Women, Medicine, and Law in the United States 1867–1973* (University of California Press, 1997), introduction.

42. Reagan, *When Abortion Was a Crime*, 11.

43. Horatio Robinson Storer, *Female Hygiene: A Lecture Delivered at Sacramento and San Francisco, by Request of the State Board of Health of California* (Campbell, 1872) 17–18.

44. Horatio Robinson Storer, *Why Not? A Book for Every Woman* (Boston: Lee and Shepard, 1866), 64, 85.

45. Reva Siegel, *Indiana Law Journal*, September 27, 2012, vol. 89:1365, 1366, http://ilj.law.indiana.edu/articles/7-Siegel11.pdf.

46. Daniel K. Williams, "The GOP's Abortion Strategy: Why Pro-Choice Republicans Became Pro-Life in the 1970s," *Journal of Policy History* 23, no. 4 (October 2011): 513–39.

47. Ibid.

48. Kevin Kruse, "Beyond the Southern Cross: The National Origins of the Religious Right," in *The Myth of Southern Exceptionalism*, Matthew D. Lassiter and Joseph Crespino, eds. (Oxford University Press, 2010), 299; Allan Carlson, *Godly Seed: American Evangelicals Confront Birth Control, 1873–1973* (Transaction, 2011).

49. Reagan, *When Abortion Was a Crime*, 7–8.

50. Joshua Holland, "When Southern Baptists Were Pro-Choice," *Bill Moyers*, July 17, 2014.

51. Lectures in American History, Modern Conservative Movement, https://www.c-span.org/video/?c3858491/phyllis-schlafly.

52. Phyllis Schlafly, "What's Wrong with 'Equal Rights' for Women?" from the Iowa State University Archives of Women's Political Communication, January 1, 1972.

53. "Betty Ford: A Gift to America," CBS News, July 10, 2011.

54. Barry M. Goldwater Jr. and John W. Dean, *Pure Goldwater* (Palgrave Macmillan, 2008), 347.

55. Box 27, folder "8/14-20/76 - Kansas City, Kansas-Republican National Convention (3)" of the Sheila Weidenfeld Files at the Gerald R. Ford Presidential Library, https://www.fordlibrarymuseum.gov/library/document/0126/46740330.pdf.

56. Daniel K. Williams, "The GOP's Abortion Strategy: Why Pro-Choice Republicans Became Pro-Life in the 1970s."

57. Phyllis Schlafly, *How the Republican Party Became Pro-Life* (Dunrobin, 2016).

58. John E. Yang, "Platform Dissenters Weld and Wilson Lose Convention Speaking Roles," *Washington Post*, August 11, 1996.

59. Neil J. Young, "Sermonizing in Pearls: Phyllis Schlafly and the Women's History of the Religious Right," *Los Angeles Review of Books*, September 7, 2016,

https://lareviewofbooks.org/article/sermonizing-pearls-phyllis-schlafly
-womens-history-religious-right/#!.

60. Damon Linker, *The Theocons: Secular America Under Siege* (Doubleday, 2006).

61. Sheldon Culver and John Dorhauer, *Steeplejacking: How the Christian Right Is Hijacking Mainstream Religion* (Ig, 2007), 22.

62. Ibid., 179.

63. Ibid., 10–12; Michelle Goldberg, *Kingdom Coming: The Rise of Christian Nationalism*, (W. W. Norton & Company, 2006).

64. Leon Howell, *United Methodism @ Risk: A Wake-Up Call* (Information Project for United Methodists 2003), 87.

65. Ibid., 94.

66. Michael Isikoff, "Christian Coalition Steps Boldly into Politics," *Washington Post*, September 10, 1992.

67. Jared Holt, "'Anointed' Trump Reaffirms His Promises to Religious Right Activists at 'Road to Majority,'" Right Wing Watch, June 26, 2019, http://www .rightwingwatch.org/post/anointed-trump-reaffirms-his-promises-to -religious-right-activists-at-road-to-majority.

68. Video interview with Buddy Pilgrim, at 30:27 mark: https://gcs-vimeo.akamai zed.net/exp=1552069292~acl=%2A%2F1138342612.mp4%2A~hmac=55dc8780cf 87a47503bd3d95abb98cd492206d2fcdf15c2540d7087d834bb245/vimeo-prod-sky fire-std-us/01/4694/11/298473481/1138342612.mp4. Last accessed March 1, 2019.

69. Camille Mijola, "I Went inside a Colombian 'Youth Camp' Run by Anti-Abortion Activists," openDemocracy, January 22, 2019, https://www .opendemocracy.net/en/5050/inside-colombian-youth-camp-anti-abortion -activists.

70. Elizabeth Dias, "After Viral Video, Families of Covington Are Swiftly Circling to Protect Their Boys," *New York Times*, January 21, 2019.

CHAPTER 4: THE MIND OF A WARRIOR

1. Loving v. Virginia, 388 U.S. 1 (1967), argued April 10, 1967, decided June 12, 1967.

2. Rebecca E. Klatch, *Women of the New Right* (Temple University Press, 1987), 47.

3. Kyle Mantyla, "Boykin: Jesus 'Was A Tough Guy, He Was A Man's Man,'" Right Wing Watch, November 18, 2013, http://www.rightwingwatch.org/post /boykin-jesus-was-a-tough-guy-he-was-a-mans-man.

4. Kyle Mantyla, "Boykin: When Jesus Comes Back, He'll Be Carrying an AR-15 Assault Rifle," Right Wing Watch, February 19, 2014.

5. Warren Throckmorton blog, "Mark Driscoll: 'We Live in a Pussified Nation,'" July 29, 2014, https://www.wthrockmorton.com/2014/07/29/mark-driscoll-year -2000-we-live-in-a-completely-pussified-nation.

6. Rachel Held Evans, "Inside Mark Driscoll's Disturbed Mind," July 29, 2014, https://rachelheldevans.com/blog/driscoll-troubled-mind-william -wallace.

7. Holly Pivec, "The Feminization of the Church: Why Its Music, Messages and Ministries Are Driving Men Away," *Biola* (Spring 2006).

8. Jim Domen, "Goliath MUST Fall," Church United blog, http://www .churchunited.com/goliath-must-fall. Last accessed July 15, 2019.

9. Jim Domen, "Church United Beginning," Church United blog, http://www .churchunited.com/church-united-beginning. Last accessed July 15, 2019.

10. Regional Briefings, http://www.churchunited.com/briefings. Last accessed July 15, 2019.

11. Erik Eckholm, "An Iowa Stop in a Broad Effort to Revitalize the Religious Right," *New York Times*, April 2, 2011.

12. Elizabeth Dias, "The Evangelical Fight to Win Back California," *New York Times*, May 27, 2018, https://www.nytimes.com/2018/05/27/us/politics/franklin -graham-evangelicals-california.html.

13. Josh Dulaney, "Preachers Under Fire: Politics from the Pulpit Breaks the Law, Some Say," *San Bernadino Sun*, December 23, 2012.

14. "Pastors Disrupt D.C.!" Advocates for Faith & Freedom blog, July 13, 2017, https://faith-freedom.com/blog/blog/pastors-disrupt-d-c.

15. Archived at prwatch.org, https://www.prwatch.org/files/52-1792772_990_2014 09.pdf, section 4c.

16. Jim Domen, "Goliath MUST Fall."

17. "Bishop Ed Smith Ministry Update," uploaded byZoe Christian Fellowship of Whittier, August 1, 2016, 10:21 min, https://www.youtube.com/watch?v =LZeusIR-R_M.

18. "Fresno Pastor Impacted by Washington, D.C. Tour," https://www.church united.com/impact.

19. "Temecula Pastor's Church Impacted,"https://www.churchunited.com/impact.

20. Bob Branch, "Finding Your Voice," sermon delivered at the Springs Commu-nity Church, July 16, 2017, https://www.thespringscc.org/sermons/finding-your -voice. Last accessed April 2019.

21. "120 California Pastors in California's Capitol Ready to Go Back to Their Church and Transform California for Christ Starting with Their Congrega-tions in Their City," Church United, posted May 17, 2018, https://www.facebook .com/1churchunited/videos/vb.1167182783344448/1748030321926355/?type=2 &theater. Last accessed April 1, 2019.

22. "Video: Awakening Tour Sacramento May 2018," https://www.churchunited .com/tours/sacramento. McCoy's quote is at the 12-second mark.

23. https://www.churchunited.com/tours/sacramento, at 15-second mark.

CHAPTER 5: UP FROM SLAVERY: THE IDEOLOGICAL ORIGINS OF CHRISTIAN NATIONALISM

1. W. Scott Lamb, "35th Anniversary of Ronald Reagan's 'I Know You Can't Endorse Me. But I Endorse You'—to Evangelicals," *Washington Times*, August 21, 2015.

2. Ibid.

3. Michael J. McVicar, "Reconstructing America: Religion, American Conserva-tism, and the Political Theology of Rousas John Rushdoony" (PhD diss., Ohio State University, 2010), 3.

4. Gary North, "R. J. Rushdoony, R.I.P.," LewRockwell.com, February 10, 2001

5. McVicar, "Reconstructing America," 5.

6. Julie J. Ingersoll, *Building God's Kingdom: Inside the World of Christian Recon-structionism* (Oxford University Press, 2015), 1.

7. Ibid., 2.

8. McVicar, "Reconstructing America," 9–10.

9. Walter Olson, "Reasonable Doubts: Invitation to a Stoning: Getting Cozy with Theocrats," *Reason*, November 1998.

10. Barbara Forrest and Paul R. Gross, *Creation's Trojan Horse: The Wedge of Intelligent Design* (Oxford University Press, 2004).

11. Frederick Clarkson, "Dominionism Rising: A Theocratic Movement Hiding in Plain Sight," Political Research Associates, August 18, 2016, https://www.politicalresearch.org/2016/08/18/dominionism-rising-a-theocratic-movement-hiding-in-plain-sight.

12. Ingersoll, *Building God's Kingdom*, 21.

13. Richard John Neuhaus, "Why Wait for the Kingdom? The Theonomist Temptation," *First Things*, May 1990, https://www.firstthings.com/article/1990/05/why-wait-for-the-kingdomthe-theonomist-temptation.

14. McVicar, "Reconstructing America," 5–9; Jeff Sharlet, *The Family: The Secret Fundamentalism at the Heart of American Power* (Harper Perennial, 2008), 44, 347.

15. Rousas John Rushdoony, *The Messianic Character of American Education* (Ross House Books, 1963), 337–339.

16. James D. Bratt, ed., *Abraham Kuyper: A Centennial Reader* (Erdmans, 1998), 461.

17. Michael J. McVicar, "The Libertarian Theocrats: The Long, Strange History of R. J. Rushdoony and Christian Reconstructionism," Political Research Associates, September 1, 2007, https://www.politicalresearch.org/2007/09/01/the-libertarian-theocrats-the-long-strange-history-of-r-j-rushdoony-and-christian-reconstructionism.

18. Larry B. Stammer, "The Rev. Rousas John Rushdoony; Advocated Rule by Biblical Law," *Los Angeles Times*, March 3, 2001.

19. Sean Michael Lucas, *Robert Lewis Dabney, A Southern Presbyterian Life* (P&R, 2005), 14.

20. Thomas C. Johnson, "Robert L. Dabney," *Kaleidoscope* (1899), 27, https://archive.org/details/kaleidoscope1899hamp/page/n8.

21. Robert L. Dabney, "The Negro and the Common School," *Discussions* 4 (Crescent Book House, 1897), 177.

22. Thomas Carey Johnson, "Summary View of the Man and His Service," *Life and Letters of Robert Lewis Dabney*, vol. 3 (Presbyterian Committee of Publication, 1903), 568.

23. Robert L. Dabney, "A Caution Against Anti-Christian Science," *Discussions*, vol. 3, "Anti-Biblical Theory of Rights," Presbyterian Committee of Publication, 1892; *Presbyterian Quarterly* (July 1888): 497.

24. Wallace Hettle, "The Minister, the Martyr, and the Maxim: Robert Lewis Dabney and Stonewall Jackson Biography," *Civil War History* 49, no. 4 (December 2003): 353–69.

25. Robert Lewis Dabney, "Christians Pray for Your Nation," editorial article in the *Central Presbyterian*, March 29, 1856.

26. Edward H. Sebesta and Euan Hague, "The US Civil War as a Theological War: Confederate Christian Nationalism and the League of the South," *Canadian Review of American Studies* 32, no. 3 (2002), http://www.theocracywatch.org /civil_war_canadian_review.htm.

27. Stephen R. Haynes, *Noah's Curse: The Biblical Justification of American Slavery* (Oxford University Press, 2002), 268, note 40; *The Southern Presbyterians* (Presbyterian Church in America Historical Center, 2003), 429, "Minutes of 1864," 293: http://www.pcahistory.org/ebooks/pcus/ch5.pdf.

28. *Macon Telegraph*, February 7, 1861.

29. Stephen S. Foster, *The Brotherhood of Thieves; or, a True Picture of the American Church and Clergy: A Letter to Nathaniel Barney, of Nantucket Concord, N.H.* (Parker Pillsbury, 1886, first published 1843), 36.

30. Cited in TPCW 6.135; *Christian Standard* (Charleston, S.C.), June 21, 1854.

31. See Stephen S. Foster, *Brotherhood of Thieves*, 38.

32. Ibid., 42.

33. Ibid., 37.

34. James G. Birney, *The American Churches: The Bulwarks of American Slavery* (Charles Whipple, 1842), 47; See also: Moses Stuart, *Conscience and the*

Constitution, with Remarks on the Recent Speech of the Honorable Daniel Webster (Forgotten Books, 2007), 1850.

35. John R. McKivigan, *The War Against Pro-Slavery Religion: Abolition and the Northern Churches, 1830–1865* (Cornell University Press, 1984), 30.

36. "The Bible View of American Slavery: A Letter from the Bishop of Vermont (New England) to the Bishop of Pennsylvania," reprinted from the *Philadelphia Mercury* October 11, 1863 (Saunders, Otley, 1863), 7; John Henry Hopkins, *A Scriptural, Ecclesiastical, and Historical View of Slavery* (W. I. Pooley, 1864), 5; and *The Bible View of Slavery* (Saunders, Otley, 1863), 6; see also reference to Hopkins in William Craft, *Running a Thousand Miles for Freedom; or, the Escape of William and Ellen Craft from Slavery* (William Tweedie, 1860), 96–97.

37. See Stephen S. Foster, *Brotherhood of Thieves*, 37; Nathaniel Taylor: http://www .yaleslavery.org/WhoYaleHonors/taylor.html.

38. "Rejoice that in this blessed country of free inquiry and belief, which has surrendered its creed and conscience to neither kings nor priests, the genuine doctrine of one only God is reviving, and I trust that there is not a *young man* now living in the United States who will not die an Unitarian.[i]," Thomas Jefferson to Dr. Benjamin Waterhouse, June 26, 1822; "Soon after I had published the pamphlet, Common Sense, in America, I saw the exceeding probability that a revolution in the system of government would be followed by a revolution in the system of religion. The adulterous connection of church and state, wherever it had taken place, whether Jewish, Christian, or Turkish, had so effectually prohibited, by pains and penalties, every discussion upon established creeds and upon first principles of religion, that until the system of government should be changed those subjects could not be brought fairly and openly before the world; but whenever this should be done, a revolution in the system of religion would follow. Human inventions and priestcraft would be detected, and man would return to the pure, unmixed, and unadulterated belief of one God, and no more. [i]," Thomas Paine, The Age of Reason, Foner (1995), 667.

39. *Collected Works*, a speech called "The Proclamation and the Negro Army," given during the Civil War, Frederick Douglass Papers, digital edition, 560.

40. PBS.org, American Colonization Society, 1816–65.

41. Mitchell Snay, *Gospel of Disunion: Religion and Separatism in the Antebellum South* (Cambridge University Press, 1993), 55.

42. The Rev. J. H. Thornwell, "Sermon Preached at the Dedication of a Church Erected in Charleston, S.C.: The Rights and Duties of Masters" (Steam-Power Press of Walker & James, May 26, 1850), 14.

43. Mitchell Snay, *Gospel of Disunion: Religion and Separatism in the Antebellum South* (Cambridge University Press, 1993), 186.

44. Robert Dabney, *Discussions by Robert L. Dabney, D.D., L.L.D.* vol. 4 (Mexico, Mo., 1897), 194, 205–08.

45. Robert Dabney, "Women's Rights Women," *Southern Magazine*, 1871 (Dabney Archive).

46. Robert Lewis Dabney, "Anti-Biblical Theories of Rights," *Presbyterian Quarterly*, July 1888 (Dabney Archive).

47. Ibid.

48. Ibid.

49. "Understanding R. J. Rushdoony," Mark Rushdoony, uploaded by Branch of Hope Church, January 19, 2016, 1:06:27, at 23:20 minute mark, text of a talk given September 16, 2005 at Chalcedon's 40th Anniversary Conference in Cummings, Georgia, https://www.youtube.com/watch?v=BQfK_5L82IQ.

50. Chris Smith, "Rousas John Rushdoony and the Rise of Christian conservatives," *California Magazine*, Cal Alumni Association, Fall 2012.

51. Mark R. Rushdoony, "Rousas John Rushdoony: A Brief History, Part II: 'You Are Going to Be a Writer," Chalcedon.edu, April 21, 2016, https://chalcedon .edu/magazine/rousas-john-rushdoony-a-brief-history-part-ii-you-are-going -to-be-a-writer.

52. Sebesta and Hague, "The US Civil War as a Theological War," 263.

53. Ingersoll, *Building God's Kingdom*, 16.

54. Sebesta and Hague, "The US Civil War as a Theological War."

55. Euan Hague, Heidi Beirich, and Edward H. Sebesta, eds., *Neo-Confederacy: A Critical Introduction* (University of Texas Press, 2008), 58.

56. Rousas John Rushdoony, *This Independent Republic* (Thoburn Press, 1978, 1964), 82.

57. Rousas John Rushdoony, *This Independent Republic* (Thoburn Press, 1954), 22.

58. Rousas John Rushdoony, *The Nature of the American System* (Ross House Books, 1965), 8.

59. Ibid., 7.

60. Rushdoony, *This Independent Republic* (Thoburn Press, 1954), 37.

61. Rousas John Rushdoony, *Politics of Guilt and Pity* (Craig Press, 1970), 19.

62. Rousas John Rushdoony, *Institutes of Biblical Law* (Presbyterian and Reformed Publishing Co., 1973), 251.

63. Rushdoony, *This Independent Republic* (Thoburn Press, 1964), 82–83.

64. Mark Potok, "Doug Wilson's Religious Empire Expanding in the Northwest," Southern Poverty Law Center, Intelligence Report (Spring 2004), https://www.splcenter.org/fighting-hate/intelligence-report/2004/doug-wilson%E2%80%99s-religious-empire-expanding-northwest.

65. Douglas W. Wilson: *Robert Lewis Dabney: The Prophet Speaks* (Vision Forum, 1999).

66. "The Bible, Slavery, and America's Founders," Wallbuilders.com, https://wallbuilders.com/bible-slavery-americas-founders. Last accessed July 15, 2019.

67. Sebesta and Hague, "The U.S. Civil War as a Theological War."

68. Billy Graham Center archives: "Papers of William Ashley 'Billy' Sunday and Helen Amelia (Thomson) Sunday, Collection 61," https://www2.wheaton.edu/bgc/archives/GUIDES/061.htm; http://are.as.wvu.edu/cbush.htm.

69. Robert Leeson, *Hayek: A Collaborative Biography, Part XI: Orwellian Rectifiers, Mises' "Evil Seed" of Christianity and the "Free" Market Welfare State* (Palgrave Macmillan, 2018), 361.

70. Rousas John Rushdoony, *Christianity and Capitalism* (Chalcedon Foundation, 2000; originally published by Coast Federal Savings Free Enterprise Department in the 1960s). Digital version pages 96, 119.

71. A. A. Hodge, *Popular Lectures on Theological Themes* (Presbyterian Board of Publications, 1887), 283–84.

72. Rushdoony, *Messianic Character of American Education*, 334–35.

73. Rousas John Rushdoony, "Intellectual Schizophrenia (Q & A)," tape code RR151B3, Chalcedon Archive.

74. Rushdoony, *Messianic Character of American Education*, 332, 108.

75. Anson Shupe, "Prophets of a Biblical America," *Wall Street Journal*, April 12, 1989.

76. D. James Kennedy, *A Godly Education*, sermon pamphlet (Coral Ridge Ministries, 1986), 20.

77. Ibid., 7.

78. Gary North "Announcing: The Ron Paul Curriculum Is Open for Business," April 06, 2013, https://www.garynorth.com/public/10862.cfm. See video at 25-second mark.

79. Gary North, "The Intellectual Schizophrenia of the New Christian Right," *The Failure of the American Baptist Culture*, vol. 1, *Christianity and Civilization* (Tyler, TX; Geneva Divinity School), 25

80. Milton Friedman, "The Role of Government in Education," *Economics and the Public Interest: Collected Works of Milton Friedman Project Records*, ed. Robert A. Solo (Rutgers University Press, 1955), 123–44.

81. Robert Dabney, "Secularized Education," *Discussions*, vol. 4 (Ross House Books and Sprinkle Publications 1979 [1897], 219, 8.

82. Mark R. Rushdoony, "Rousas John Rushdoony: A Brief History, Part VI: 'The Lord Will Perfect That Which Concerneth Me,'" Chalcedon.edu, December 17, 2016.

83. Frances FitzGerald, "A Disciplined, Charging Army," *New Yorker*, May 18, 1981.

84. "Prayer Targets: Biblical Basis for Testimony; Kavanaugh Confirmation; Pledge to Pray, Vote, and Stand," Watchmen on the Wall, October 03, 2018, https://www.frc.org/prayerteam/prayer-targets-biblical-basis-for-testimony-kavanaugh-confirmation-pledge-to-pray-vote-and-stand.

85. Ingersoll, *Building God's Kingdom*, 212.

86. Rev. David Woodfield, "The Eschatological Worldview of C. Peter Wagner and the New Apostolic Reformation," North-West University, in cooperation with Greenwich School of Theology, April 2017.

87. C. Peter Wagner, *Dominion! How Kingdom Action Can Change the World* (Chosen, 2008), 59.

88. Frederick Clarkson, "Christian Reconstructionism: 'Theocratic Dominionism Gains Influence Part 3,'" *Public Eye* (Political Research Associates), May 19, 1994.

89. Sarah Posner, "Amazing Disgrace: How Did Donald Trump—a Thrice-Married, Biblically Illiterate Sexual Predator—Hijack the Religious Right?" *New Republic*, March 20, 2017.

90. Press release from Christian Newswire, "Southern Baptist Pastor Submits Resolution Against Social Justice," May 14, 2018.

91. FitzGerald, "A Disciplined, Charging Army."

CHAPTER 6: THE USES AND ABUSES OF HISTORY

1. Steve Green, *Faith in America* (Looking Glass, 2011), 18.

2. Ibid., 18.

3. Ibid., 7.

4. Rob Boston, "Hobby Lobby Independence Day Ad Is a Real Mess," Americans United for Separation of Church and State, Wall of Separation Blog, July 6, 2017, https://www.au.org/blogs/wall-of-separation/hobby-lobby-s-independence-day-ad-is-a-real-mess.

5. Elizabeth Flock, "Hobby Lobby Thinks the Bible Can Save America. Now Its Museum Has to Convince Its Critics," PBS *News Hour*, July 18, 2017.

6. Steve Green, *Faith in America* (Looking Glass, 2011), 50.

7. Ibid., 77.

8. Nate Blakeslee, "King of the Christocrats," *Texas Monthly*, September 2006.

9. Jefferson's Letter to the Danbury Baptists, January 1, 1802, https://www.loc.gov/loc/lcib/9806/danpre.html.

10. Virginia Statute for Religious Freedom, Monticello.org.

11. Treaty of Peace and Friendship, signed at Tripoli, November 4, 1796.

12. Paul Blanshard, *Religion and the Schools: The Great Controversy* (Beacon, 1963).

13. Ulysses S. Grant speech before the Army of Tennessee, Des Moines, Iowa, 1875.

14. "Ten Steps to Change America," Wallbuilders.com, https://wallbuilders.com /ten-steps-change-america.

15. Dan Quinn, "David Barton, Jesus, and Taxes," Texas Freedom Network, tfnblog, March 26, 2011, https://tfn.org/david-barton-jesus-and-taxes.

16. Tanya Somanader, "Mike Huckabee Wants Every American to Be 'Forced at Gun Point' to Learn from Radical Historian," ThinkProgress, March 31, 2011, https://thinkprogress.org/mike-huckabee-wants-every-american-to-be -forced-at-gun-point-to-learn-from-radical-historian-5e33c5452b5a.

17. Will Bunch, "Glenn Beck's Plan to Save America . . . with Christian-Right Pseudohistory," *Philadelphia Enquirer*, February 9, 2010.

18. Jefferson's Letter to the Danbury Baptists, January 1, 1802.

19. "David Barton, America's Godly Heritage," uploaded by Sheldon Livesay, July 5, 2016, 50:56 min, https://www.youtube.com/watch?v=_2TOCXz X4NM.

20. David Barton, *The Myth of Separation* (WallBuilders Press, 1992), 42.

21. Rob Boston, "David Barton: Master of Myth and Misinformation," Institute for First Amendment Studies, June 1996, www.publiceye.org/ifas.

22. Barbara Bradley Hagerty, "The Most Influential Evangelist You've Never Heard Of," *All Things Considered*, NPR, August 8, 2012.

23. David Austin Walsh, "David Barton's *The Jefferson Lies* Voted the Least Credible History Book in Print," History News Network, July 16, 2012, https:// historynewsnetwork.org/article/147149#.

24. Hagerty, "The Most Influential Evangelist You've Never Heard Of."

25. Warren Throckmorton, "More of the Story Behind the Demise of David Barton's *The Jefferson Lies*," February 11, 2015, https://www.wthrockmorton.com /2015/02/11/more-of-the-story-behind-the-demise-of-david-bartons-the -jefferson-lies; Rob Boston, "The Barton Lies: Conservative Christian Scholars Debunk 'Christian Nation' Propagandist," Americans United for Separation of Church and State, Wall of Separation Blog, August 9, 2012, https://www.au .org/blogs/wall-of-separation/the-barton-lies-conservative-christian-scholars -debunk-christian-nation.

26. Elise Hu, "Publisher Pulls Controversial Jefferson Book, Citing Loss of Confidence," NPR, August 9, 2012.

27. https://www.drivethruhistory.com/series/american-history.

28. https://www.christianbook.com/drive-thru-history-america-foundations -character/9781414311838/pd/311834.

29. The Black Robe Regiment, Mission Statement, http://www.blackrobereg.org /mission.html. Accessed July 10, 2019.

30. Kyle Mantyla, "Jim Garlow to Head Gingrich's "Renewing American Leadership," Right Wing Watch, March 9, 2010, http://www.rightwingwatch.org /post/jim-garlow-to-head-gingrichs-renewing-american-leadership.

31. WallBuilders Profamily Legislative Network, "The ProFamily Legislators Conference," https://www.profamily.com.

32. "'Christian Nation' Guru Promoted Bush and GOP in 'Below the Radar' Scheme," Americans United for Separation of Church and State, a publication of, December 2004, https://www.au.org/church-state/december-2004 -church-state/people-events/christian-nation-guru-promoted-bush-and -gop-in.

33. Kyle Mantyla, "Brownback's Hero: Propagandist David Barton," Right Wing Watch, October 19, 2006, http://www.rightwingwatch.org/post/brownbacks -hero-propagandist-david-barton.

34. Patricia Murphy, "The Evangelical Power Broker behind Ted Cruz," *Daily Beast*, January 29, 2016.

35. David Barton, *Myth of Separation* (WallBuilders Press, 1992), 268.

36. "Johnson Amendment Is Limiting Our Free Speech and First Amendment Right," *WallBuilders Live!*, aired April 17, 2017.

37. David Brody, "David Barton Tells Brody File: Donald Trump's Using the CEO Model, Not Government Model," CBN News, September 9, 2016, https://www1.cbn.com/thebrodyfile/archive/2016/09/09/david-barton-tells -brody-file-donald-trumps-using-the-ceo-model-not-government-model.

38. "David Barton Talks on Brody File This Week," CBN News, September 15, 2016, https://www1.cbn.com/thebrodyfile/archive/2016/09/15/david-barton

-talks-trump-on-brody-file-this-week-says-he-doesnt-have-to-be-deep-on
-the-issues?amp.

39. Greg Price, "Donald Trump Opposition a Sign of End Times and 'Demonic' Right-Wing Pastor Claims," *Newsweek*, July 3, 2018.

40. Lance Wallnau, *God's Chaos Candidate: Donald J. Trump and the American Unraveling* (Killer Sheep Media, Inc., 2016), 30.

41. "Every Tribe Every Nation Making Bibles Accessible And Translating It Into All 6,000 Plus Languages," *WallBuilders Live!*, aired April 18, 2017, https://wallbuilderslive.com/every-tribe-every-nation.

42. "Hobby Lobby's Steve Green PART II—TheBlazeTV—The Glenn Beck Program - 2013.09.20," uploaded by Jared Law, September 20, 2013, 2:33 min, https://www.youtube.com/watch?v=Q7f_t6SihSU.

43. "Bible Museum Coming to D.C. This Fall with State of the Art Technology," *WallBuilders Live!*, May 1, 2017; "Part 1 - Behind the Scenes Setting Up the Museum—David Barton Talks About Some Items He's Brought," posted by Joel Helgeson, July 11, 2013, 2:50 min, https://www.youtube.com/watch?v=XWreybUjLrk.

44. Michelle Boorstein, "D.C.'s New Bible Museum Says It Wants to Avoid Politics. But Its Opening Gala Is at the Trump Hotel," *Washington Post*, November 15, 2017.

45. Candida Moss and Joel S. Baden, "Just What Is the Museum of the Bible Trying to Do?" *Politico*, October 15, 2017.

46. Michelle Boorstein, "Hobby Lobby's Steve Green Has Big Plans for His Bible Museum in Washington," *Washington Post*, September 12, 2014.

47. "Vice President Mike Pence Makes Surprise Appearance at FRC's Watchmen on the Wall Conference," May 31, 2018, http://nrb.org/news-room/articles/nrbt/vice-president-mike-pence-makes-surprise-appearance-frcs-watchmen-wall-conference.

48. See Generations website: https://www.generations.org/faqs/76.

49. See My Faith Votes website for October 24 event with Kirk Cameron: https://www.myfaithvotes.org/my-faith-votes-presents-kirk-camerons-revive-us-2-live-from-museum-of-the-bible-tuesday-oct-24.

50. "The Center for National Renewal," posted by Churches in Covenant, https:// vimeo.com/201143659.

51. "Capitol Ministries Leaders Come from Around the World for D.C. Fall Training Conference," Capitol Ministries, https://capmin.org/resources /ministry-updates/capitol-ministries-leaders-come-around-world-d-c-fall -training-conference.

52. John Hudson, "Ex-Palin Aide Lands Job at Trump's State Department," *Foreign Policy*, February 9, 2017.

53. Nicole Goodkind, "Here's What Ivanka Trump's Rabbi Thinks about Families Being Separated at the Border," *Newsweek*, June 20, 2018.

CHAPTER 7: THE BLITZ: TURNING THE STATES INTO LABORATORIES OF THEOCRACY

1. Frederick Clarkson, "'Project Blitz' Seeks to Do for Christian Nationalism What ALEC Does for Big Business," Religion Dispatches, April 27, 2018, http://religiondispatches.org/project-blitz-seeks-to-do-for-christian -nationalism-what-alec-does-for-big-business.

2. See Congressional Prayer Caucus Foundation, http://cpcfoundation.com/first -freedom-coalition-project-blitz. At that time, audio of two phone conferences was accessible on the website. Last accessed June 1, 2018; See Project Blitz Legislation Grid, "2018 Religious Freedom Measures," compiled by Congres- sional Prayer Caucus Foundation, https://drive.google.com/file/d/1aNCKlvh okEZZLLG5IhOskk1NjXw_7Y15/view.

3. "Lea Carawan—Cofounder and Executive Director, Congressional Prayer Caucus," *The Trey Blocker Show*, February 5, 2018, https://www.youtube.com /watch?v=AJHZ8OKPTEU.

4. See intregrityleadership.org: http://integrityleadership.org/about-us. Note point 2, "Integrity's Operating Strategy."

5. Buddy Pilgrim, "Freedom Is Under Attack," integrityleadership.org, June 4, 2017, http://integrityleadership.org/freedom-is-under-attack/; "Buddy Pilgrim—God and Money," *Life Today with James and Betty Robison*, light source.com, March 13, 2012, at 5:37 mark: https://www.lightsource.com/ministry /life-today/buddy-pilgrim-god-and-money-264143.html.

6. *Point of View* interview with Buddy Pilgrim, November 1, 2018, at 42–43:04 mark: https://pointofview.net/show/thursday-november-1-2018.

7. Project Blitz teleconference audio, February 13, at 22:55 mark; see Katherine Stewart, "A Christian Nationalist Blitz," *New York Times*, May 26, 2018.

8. "Encouraging Schools to Display Motto 'In God We Trust,'" Minnesota Senate Media Services, May 4, 2018, https://www.youtube.com/watch?v=SOS _Z5sW_QU.

9. "'In God We Trust' Motto Sparks Debate in Minnesota: 'How about Bringing Respect Back in Schools?'" Fox News Insider as seen on *Fox & Friends Weekend*, May 6, 2018.

10. At press time, Project Blitz organizers were discussing "strategic" rebranding and other organizational developments. Rob Boston, "Project Blitz Wants to Hide Its Christian Nationalist Agenda. It's Too Late for That," Americans United for Separation of Church and State, Wall of Separation Blog, November 08, 2019, https://www.au.org/blogs/project-blitz-exposed.

11. Moriah Balingit, "Does 'In God We Trust' Belong in Schools? More and More States Say Yes," *Washington Post*, December 1, 2018.

12. Congressional Prayer Caucus Foundation, "Report and Analysis on Religious Freedom Measures Impacting Prayer and Faith in America (2017 Version)," https://drive.google.com/file/d/0BwfCh32HsC3UYmVoNUp5cXZjT28/view. Last accessed July 15, 2019.

13. Teleconference audio, at 24:30 mark; also see Project Blitz download titled "Report and Analysis on Religious Freedom Measures Impacting Prayer and Faith in America" (2017 version), 23–34.

14. Teddy Wilson, "State-Level Republicans Pour Taxpayer Money into Fake Clinics at an Unprecedented Pace (Updated)," Rewire, February 16, 2018, https://rewire.news/article/2018/02/16/state-level-republicans-pour-taxpayer -money-fake-clinics-unprecedented-pace.

15. Olga Khazan, "Here's Why Hobby Lobby Thinks IUDs Are Like Abortions," *Atlantic*, March 12, 2014.

16. Esmé E. Deprez, "Abortion Clinics Are Closing at a Record Pace," *Bloomberg Businessweek*, February 24, 2016, https://www.bloomberg.com/news/articles /2016-02-24/abortion-clinics-are-closing-at-a-record-pace.

17. See Students for Life 2019 schedule: https://sflalive.org/schedule.

18. Sarah Kaplan, "Mississippi's Senate Just Approved a Sweeping 'Religious Liberty' Bill That Critics Say Is the Worst Yet for LGBT Rights," *Washington Post*, March 31, 2016.

19. James Dobson, *Parenting Isn't for Cowards: The You-Can-Do-It Guide for Hassled Parents* (Tyndale House, 2010).

20. James Dobson, *The Strong-Willed Child* (Tyndale House, 1978), 38.

21. Barbara Falconer Newhall, "James Dobson: Beat Your Dog, Spank Your Kid, Go to Heaven," Huffington Post, October 10, 2014, updated December 6, 2017.

22. Dr. James Dobson, "The Difference Between Childish Irresponsibility and Willful Defiance," Dobson Digital Library.

23. Ralph Drollinger, "God's Word on Spanking," Capmin.org, May 2, 2016, https://capmin.org/gods-word-spanking.

24. Katherine Stewart, "Why Mississippi's New Anti-LGBT Law Is the Most Dangerous One to Be Passed Yet," *The Nation*, April 8, 2016.

25. "Randy Forbes and Lea Carawan from CPCFoundation on Truth & Liberty Livecast," streamed live by Andrew Wommack, October 29, 2018, 59:01 min, at 14:40–15:00 mark, https://www.youtube.com/watch?v=Rpf3RplEMd4.

26. George Barna, *The Day Christians Changed America* (Metaformation, 2017), 55.

27. Brandon Showalter, "George Barna Explains How Christians Altered America's Future by Supporting Trump Last November," Christian Post, October 13, 2017, https://www.christianpost.com/news/george-barna-explains-how-christians-altered-americas-future-by-supporting-trump-last-november.html.

28. "Randy Forbes & Lea Carawan from CPCFoundation on Truth & Liberty Livecast," October 29, 2018, 11:55–13:15.

29. Ibid., 9:25–10:40.

CHAPTER 8: CONVERTING THE FLOCK TO DATA

1. Bill Dallas, *Lessons from San Quentin: Everything I Needed to Know about Life I Learned in Prison* (Tyndale House, 2009).

2. Ibid., 68–69.

3. Ibid., 11.

4. Matea Gold and Tom Hamburger, "Silicon Valley Gives Conservative Christians a Boost," *Los Angeles Times*, September 15, 2011.

5. George Barna, *The Day Christians Changed America* (Metaformation, 2017), 147–48.

6. Elizabeth Dias, "Inside Donald Trump's Private Meeting with Evangelicals," *Time*, June 21, 2016.

7. Kyle Mantyla, "Jim Garlow: 'Under No Condition Do We Have To Follow Laws That Violate The Word Of God,'" November 1, 2016, http://www.rightwingwatch.org/post/jim-garlow-under-no-condition-do-we-have-to-follow-laws-that-violate-the-word-of-god.

8. "The State of the Conservative Movement (Interview with Bob McEwen—Executive Director, Council for National Policy)," Conservative Book Club, podcast, episode 34, https://www.conservativebookclub.com/34261/podcasts/interview-bob-mcewen-cnp.

9. Jane Mayer, "Betsy DeVos, Trump's Big-Donor Education Secretary," *New Yorker*, November 23, 2016.

10. "The State of the Conservative Movement (Interview with Bob McEwen—Executive Director, Council for National Policy)," Conservative Book Club.

11. G. W. Schulz, "Are Christian Conservatives behind Breach of 18 Million Voter Records?" Reveal (Center for Investigative Reporting), March 2, 2016, https://www.revealnews.org/article/are-christian-conservatives-behind-breach-of-18-million-voter-records.

12. Author interview with Chris Vickery April 2019.

13. Author interview with Vickery; Thomas Brewster, "Right-Wing Company of Convicted Embezzler Turned Christian Linked to Huge Leak of Voter Records," *Forbes*, January 4, 2016.

14. U.S. Federal Election Commission, Disbursements, https://www.fec.gov/data/disbursements/?two_year_transaction_period=2018&data_type=processed&recipient_name=i360&min_date=01%2F01%2F2017&max_date=10%2F14%2F2018.

15. David Brody, "Brody File Exclusive: Evangelical Leader Says It's 'Still to Be Determined' Whether Evangelicals Will Show Up Strongly in November," CBN News, September 15, 2016, at 00:57 mark, https://www1.cbn.com/thebrody file/archive/2016/09/15/brody-file-exclusive-evangelical-leader-says-its-still-to -be-determined-whether-evangelicals-will-show-up-strongly-in-november.

16. Brewster, "Right-Wing Company of Convicted Embezzler Turned Christian Linked to Huge Leak of Voter Records."

17. Calvin Sloan, "Koch Brothers Are Watching You: And New Documents Reveal Just How Much They Know," Center for Media and Democracy's PRWatch, November 5, 2018, https://www.prwatch.org/news/2018/11/13413 /koch-brothers-are-watching-you-and-new-documents-reveal-just-how -much-they-know.

18. Dan O'Sullivan, "The RNC Files: Inside the Largest US Voter Data Leak," UpGuard, December 12, 2018, https://www.upguard.com/breaches/the-rnc -files.

19. Barbara Bradley Hagerty, "To Get Out the Vote, Evangelicals Try Data-Mining," *All Tech Considered*, NPR, February 27, 2012, https://www.npr.org /templates/transcript/transcript.php?storyId=147504999.

20. Ibid.

21. Matea Gold and Tom Hamburger, "Silicon Valley Gives Conservative Christians a Boost," *Los Angeles Times*, September 15, 2011, https://www.latimes.com /world/la-xpm-2011-sep-15-la-na-evangelical-outreach-20110916-story.html.

22. www.godisatwork.org/about.html

23. Department of Justice press release, "MPRI Inc. Agrees to Pay $3.2 Million for False Labor Charges on Contract to Support Army in Afghanistan," February 12, 2014, https://www.justice.gov/opa/pr/mpri-inc-agrees-pay-32 -million-false-labor-charges-contract-support-army-afghanistan.

24. See Cypressintl.com: https://www.cypressintl.com/who-we-are.

25. "Joseph Habedank, Bill Dallas, Dr. Ken Eldred, and David Hall," *Marcus & Joni Guests*, Daystar TV, March 7, 2016, http://www.daystar.com/guest-guide /marcus-joni-guests/dr-ken-elred.

26. Ibid.

27. See church voter lookup tools: http://churchesimpactingculture.com/voter
    -tools.

28. See video: "Bill Dallas on THE EVENT, Did Trump Break the Law?" *Truth
    & Liberty*, streamed live by Andrew Wommack, August 27, 2018, 1:01:04 hours,
    at 15:40 mark, https://www.youtube.com/watch?v=1SBksMK22Jo.

29. United in Purpose Education, a California Nonprofit Corporation; United in
    Purpose, a California Nonprofit Public Benefit Corporation v. Trendmojo, Inc,
    a California Corporation; Jay Bartels, an Individual; and Does 1 through
    100, case no. 18CIV02388, https://odyportal-ext.sanmateocourt.org/Portal
    -External/DocumentViewer/Embedded/784bsmjLEDcN414lnR4PIbS5som
    IrTbjSdkEEO5Wpqy_Zi-f3rzRfzqLWVLUAt7i_Mg102jVLdqoptOv5qI
    -JQn9mxiYe-NAr5vQvTToeHI1?p=0.

30. Council for National Policy Membership Directory 2014, https://www
    .splcenter.org/sites/default/files/cnp_redacted_final.pdf.

31. Peter Montgomery, "Ginni Thomas Gives Awards to James O'Keefe, Sean
    Hannity, Frank Gaffney & Other Right-Wing Activists," Right Wing Watch,
    December 7, 2017, http://www.rightwingwatch.org/post/ginni-thomas-gives
    -awards-to-james-okeefe-sean-hannity-frank-gaffney-other-right-wing
    -activists.

32. Video: "Mark Levin Receives United In Purpose's 'Outstanding Impact
    Award,'" CNSNews.com, December 5, 2018, https://www.cnsnews.com/video
    /mark-levin-receives-united-purposes-outstanding-impact-award.

32. USATransForm Form 990s: https://www.causeiq.com/organizations/view
    _990/824819179/3a1796585224e129a0d4f118c55f872b.

34. United in Purpose, https://www.contentofcharacterseries.com/united-in
    -purpose. Last accessed January 2018 on the United in Purpose website, unite
    dinpurpose.org.

CHAPTER 9: PROSELYTIZERS AND PRIVATIZERS

1. Billy Hallowell, "Charter School Gets Sued over History Course Some Say Is
   Too Religious," *Deseret News*, September 12, 2016.

2. Holly K. Hacker, "Reading, Writing, and Religion? Dallas-Area Charter
   Schools Come Under Fire (Again)," *Dallas News*, August 2016.

3. Christopher Line, "Getting God Out of Texas Charter Schools: Religious Exploitation Plagues Tax-Funded System," Patheos, August 9, 2016, https://www .patheos.com/blogs/freethoughtnow/getting-god-out-of-texas-charter-schools -religious-exploitation-continues-to-plague-the-charter-school-system.

4. See americanheritageacademy.org, "Principles of Liberty": http://www .americanheritageacademy.org/administration/principles_of_liberty.

5. Jerry Falwell, *America Can Be Saved!* (Sword of the Lord, 1979), 52.

6. Peter Daining, "West Michigan's 'Dutchness' Has Evolved to Be Quite Different from the Netherlands," *Holland Sentinel*, March 27, 2011.

7. "50-Metre $40-Million Superyacht *SeaQuest* Owned by Betsy DeVos Damaged," Yacht Harbour, July 26, 2018, https://yachtharbour.com/news/50 -metre-%2440-million-superyacht-seaquest-owned-by-betsy-devos-damaged -2627?src=_pos_1.

8. Beatrice Dupuy, "Very Rich Betsy DeVos Has 10 Boats, Two Helicopters, a Yacht Scheduler and a Lavish Lifestyle You Can't Afford," *Newsweek*, November 10, 2017.

9. Leanna Garfield, "Why Betsy DeVos's Summer Home Looks Like a 'Beached Whale,' According to an Architecture Critic," *Business Insider*, August 9, 2018.

10. Jane Lampman, "For Evangelicals, a Bid to 'Reclaim America," *Christian Science Monitor*, March 16, 2005, https://www.csmonitor.com/2005/0316/p16s01 -lire.html.

11. "Foundation for Traditional Values," Media Mouse, https://mediamousearchive .wordpress.com/resources/right/orgs/foundation-for-traditional-values.

12. Katherine Stewart, "Betsy DeVos and God's Plan for Schools." *New York Times*, December 13, 2016.

13. Jay Nordlinger, *National Review*, February 14, 2014.

14. Catherine Brown and Ulrich Boser, "The DeVos Dynasty: A Family of Extremists," Center for American Progress, January 23, 2017, https://www .americanprogress.org/issues/default/news/2017/01/23/296947/the-devos -dynasty-a-family-of-extremists; Anna Massoglia and Jack Noland, "Betsy DeVos and Her Big-Giving Relatives: Family Qualifies as GOP Royalty," OpenSecrets.org, December 1, 2016.

15. Jeremy Scahill, "Notorious Mercenary Erik Prince Advising Trump from the Shadows," *The Intercept*, January 17, 2017.

16. Mark Mazzetti, Ronen Bergman, and David D. Kirpatrick, "Trump Jr. and Other Aides Met with Gulf Emissary Offering Help to Win Elections," *New York Times*, May 19, 2018.

17. Brooke Seipel, "Erik Prince Acknowledges Attending 2016 Trump Tower Meeting 'to Talk about Iran Policy,'" *The Hill*, March 8, 2019.

18. Andy Kroll, "Meet the New Kochs: The DeVos Clan's Plan to Defund the Left," *Mother Jones*, January–February 2014.

19. Jack Smith IV, "This Is How Much It Cost Betsy DeVos to Become Education Secretary," Mic, February 8, 2017, https://www.mic.com/articles/167880/betsy-devos-total-campaign-donations-republicans-education-secretary-confirmation.

20. Michael Stratford, "Devos Heads into Confirmation with a Megadonor's Clear Advantage," *Politico*, December 20, 2016.

21. Jane Mayer, "Betsy DeVos, Trump's Big-Donor Education Secretary," *New Yorker*, November 23, 2016.

22. Mark A. Beliles and Stephen K. McDowell, *American Providential History* (Providence Foundation, 1989).

23. Ibid., 198.

24. Ibid., 200.

25. Ibid., 112.

26. D. James Kennedy, "A Godly Education" sermon pamphlet (Coral Ridge Ministries, 1986), 4.

27. Dr. D. James Kennedy and Dr. John B. Sorensen, *Well Done: A Christian Doctrine of Works* (Green Tree Press, 2010), xi–xiii.

28. Rob Schwarzwalder, "To Save Children, Cut Education," *Washington Times*, January 21, 2010.

29. Chris Ford, Stephenie Johnson, and Lisette Partelow, "The Racist Origins of Private School Vouchers," Center for American Progress, July 12, 2017, https://www.americanprogress.org/issues/education-k-12/reports/2017/07/12/435629/racist-origins-private-school-vouchers.

30. Milton Friedman at a speech delivered at a 2006 meeting of the American Legislative Exchange Council, http://library.fora.tv/2006/07/21/Milton _Friedman, last accessed September 12, 2017; Jonas Persson, "ALEC Admits School Vouchers Are for Kids in Suburbia," Center for Media and Democracy's PRWatch, July 22, 2015, https://www.prwatch.org/news/2015/07/12869 /alec-school-vouchers-are-kids-suburbia.

31. George A. Clowes, "'Never Give Up!'—An Exclusive Interview with Mae and Martin Duggan," Heartland Institute, December 1, 2004, https://www .heartland.org/news-opinion/news/never-give-up—an-exclusive-interview -with-mae-and-martin-duggan?source=policybot.

32. Rob Boston, "School Voucher Avalanche," Americans United for Separation of Church and State, February 2011, https://www.au.org/church-state/february -2011-church-state/featured/school-voucher-avalanche.

33. "LEAD Summer Camp," https://ssionline.org/lead/what-is-lead.

34. "The Onsite Program," https://ssionline.org/onsite, minute 3:05 of the video).

35. Adam Weinstein, "Who Paid for This Documentary Calling Public Schools Evil? (Video)," *Mother Jones*, March 30, 2011, https://www.motherjones.com/politics /2011/03/indoctrination-christian-anti-public-school-movie-home-school/.

36. Joseph P. Overton, "An Inside Look at the Government-School Mentality," Mackinac Center for Public Policy, September 23, 2002, https://www.mackinac .org/4674.

37. William B. Allen, "Public Education: An Autopsy," *Religion & Liberty* 4, no. 4 (July 20, 2010).

38. Benjamin Wermund, "Trump's Education Pick Says Reform Can 'Advance God's Kingdom,'" *Politico*, December 2, 2016.

39. Agenda for Synod 2003, Christian Reformed Church, June 14–21, 2003, https://www.crcna.org/sites/default/files/2003_agenda.pdf, 315–40.

40. Benjamin Wermund, "Trump's Education Secretary Pick Led Group That Owes Millions in Election Fines," *Politico*, November 29, 2016.

41. Ibid. According to an article in *Politico*, the state commission said the group "initially asked Ohio if this sort of spending was permissible. When the state said no, DeVos's group did it anyway." Tax filings from 2015 list DeVos as an

officer of All Children Matter. Donald Brey, the Ohio attorney representing the organization, asserted that DeVos was not directly involved in the case. "Her name never came up in any of the litigation," he said. "Nobody claimed she was responsible for anything All Children Matter did or didn't do."

42. Sam Dillon, "Scholar's School Reform U-Turn Shakes Up Debate," *New York Times*, March 2, 2010.

43. Martin Carnoy, "School Vouchers Are Not a Proven Strategy for Improving Sudent Achievement: Studies of U.S. and International Voucher Programs Show That the Risks to School Systems Outweigh Insignificant Gains in Test Scores and Limited Gains in Graduation Rates," Economic Policy Institute, February 28, 2017, https://www.epi.org/publication/school-vouchers-are-not-a -proven-strategy-for-improving-student-achievement.

44. "Heritage Foundation, December 3, 2002: DeVos Outlines Strategy in War on Public Education," uploaded by Bruce Wilson, May 1, 2011, 54:22 minutes, at 20:15 mark, https://www.youtube.com/watch?v=Xt9FmMrvJ3A&t=1874s. Last accessed May 14, 2019.

45. Ibid., 30:20 to 30:55 mark.

46. Heidi Beirich and Mark Potok, "The Council for National Policy: Behind the Curtain," Southern Poverty Law Center, Hatewatch, May 17, 2016, https://www .splcenter.org/hatewatch/2016/05/17/council-national-policy-behind-curtain.

47. Allie Gross, "Betsy DeVos's Accountability Problem," *Atlantic*, January 13, 2017.

48. Addison Wiggin, "Charter School Gravy Train Runs Express to Fat City," *Forbes*, September 10, 2013; Peter Greene, "How to Profit from Your Nonprofit Charter School," *Forbes*, August 13, 2018.

49. Jennifer Dixon, "Michigan Spends $1B on Charter Schools but Fails to Hold Them Accountable," *Detroit Free Press*, June 22, 2014.

50. Laurie Roberts, "Arizona Rep. Eddie Farnsworth Is a Charter School Million-aire—and You Helped Pay for It," *Arizona Republic*, September 11, 2018.

51. Allie Gross, "The Backdoor Voucher? How a Detroit School Created to Lift Up a 'Christ-Centered Culture' Found a Way to Get Public Dollars," Chalk-beat, May 18, 2017, https://www.chalkbeat.org/posts/detroit/2017/05/18/the -backdoor-voucher-how-a-detroit-school-created-to-lift-up-a-christ -centered-culture-found-a-way-to-get-public-dollars.

52. Ibid., published in the *Atlantic*, May 24, 2017.

53. Christopher Caldwell, "How to Think about Vladimir Putin," adapted from a speech delivered February 15, 2017 at a Hillsdale College National Leadership Seminar in Phoenix, Arizona, *Imprimis* 46, no. 3 (March 2017).

54. Marianne Goodland, "How Charter Schools Are Dodging Colorado Laws," *Colorado Independent*, May 1, 2016.

55. Ibid.

56. NAACP Task Force on Quality Education July 2017 Hearing Report, https://www.naacp.org/wp-content/uploads/2017/07/Task_ForceReport_final2.pdf.

57. Kate Zernike, "A Sea of Charter Schools in Detroit Leaves Students Adrift," *New York Times*, June 28, 2016.

58. Jennifer Chambers, "Michigan Charter School Closures Fire Up Education Debate," *Detroit News*, November 14, 2018.

59. Alan Singer, "Trump and the Religious Threat to Public Education," *HuffPost*, October 12, 2017, https://www.huffpost.com/entry/trump-and-the-religious -threat-to-public-education_b_59df46e4e4b075f45223a416.

60. Jonny Scaramanga, "Rebirth of Our Nation," Patheos, August 10, 2016, https://www.patheos.com/blogs/leavingfundamentalism/2016/08/10/rebirth -of-our-nation-review-introduction.

61. Zack Kopplin, "Texas Public Schools Are Teaching Creationism," *Slate*, January 16, 2014, https://slate.com/technology/2014/01/creationism-in-texas -public-schools-undermining-the-charter-movement.html; Max Brantley, "Charter School Leader Defends Creationism in Schools' Curriculum," *Arkansas Times*, January 19, 2014.

62. Jeffrey S. Solochek, "Imagine Charter Schools' Expensive Leases Draw Scrutiny," *Tampa Bay Times*, February 17, 2012.

63. Margaret Brennan and Jennifer Janisch, "Are Some U.S. Charter Schools Helping Fund Controversial Turkish Cleric's Movement?," *CBS This Morning*, CBS News, March 29, 2017, https://www.cbsnews.com/news/is-turkish-religious-scholar -fethullah-gulen-funding-movement-abroad-through-us-charter-schools.

64. "Charter Schools Are Big Business. Who's Making Money Off Public Education?" *Arizona Republic*, August 22, 2018.

65. Karen Yi and Amy Shipley, "Florida Charter Schools Unsupervised: Taxpayers, Students Lose When School Operators Exploit Weak Laws," *Sun Sentinel* (multipart investigation), http://interactive.sun-sentinel.com/charter-schools -unsupervised/investigation.html.

66. Emmanual Felton, "Nearly 750 Charter Schools Are Whiter Than the Nearby District Schools," Hechinger Report, June 17, 2018, https://hechinger report.org/nearly-750-charter-schools-are-whiter-than-the-nearby-district -schools.

67. https://www.mackinac.org/about.

68. Mike Mullen, "TiZA, Islamic-Themed Charter School, Closes for Good," Minneapolis City Pages, August 3, 2011, http://www.citypages.com/news/tiza -islamic-themed-charter-school-closes-for-good-6552473.

69. See White House press release: "Remarks by President Trump at Parent-Teacher Conference Listening Session," February 14, 2017, https://www .whitehouse.gov/the-press-office/2017/02/14/remarks-president-trump-parent -teacher-conference-listening-session; Valerie Strauss, "Who Was—and Wasn't—Invited to Betsy DeVos's Education Roundtable," *Washington Post*, August 30, 2017.

70. Ryan Dailey, "Superintendent Rocky Hanna Blasts Betsy DeVos Visit as 'Insulting,'" *Tallahassee Democrat*, August 29, 2017.

71. Deanna Pan, "14 Wacky 'Facts' Kids Will Learn in Louisiana's Voucher Schools," *Mother Jones*, August 7, 2012, https://www.motherjones.com/kevin-drum/2012 /08/photos-evangelical-curricula-louisiana-tax-dollars.

72. Rebecca Klein, "Voucher Schools Championed by Betsy DeVos Can Teach Whatever They Want. Turns Out They Teach Lies," *Huffington Post*, December 20, 2017.

73. White House "Fact Sheet": President Trump's FY 2018 Budget: https://www2 .ed.gov/about/overview/budget/budget18/budget-factsheet.pdf.

74. "Indiana Lands $59 Million for Charter School Expansion," *Indianapolis Business Journal* via Associated Press, September 28, 2017.

75. D. James Kennedy, "A Godly Education," 21.

CHAPTER 10: THEOCRACY FROM THE BENCH, OR HOW TO ESTABLISH
RELIGION IN THE NAME OF "RELIGIOUS LIBERTY"

1. Eric Gutierrez, "Winter Garden Pastor Attended Trump's SOTU," *West Orange Times & Observer*, February 15, 2018.

2. See video: https://drive.google.com/file/d/1_4b4Ad29PHBlufolD4SLiUTqX RXIxcPX/view.

3. Jeffrey Toobin, "The Conservative Pipeline to the Supreme Court," *New Yorker*, April 10, 2017.

4. Charles P. Pierce, "Alison Jones Rushing Is the Latest Conservative Wingnut to Join the Federal Court," *Esquire*, March 5, 2019.

5. Robert O'Harrow Jr. and Shawn Boburg, "A Conservative Activist's Behind-the-Scenes Campaign to Remake the Nation's Courts," *Washington Post*, May 21, 2019.

6. Ed Whelan, "Mistaken Attack by Andy Schlafly on Leonard Leo," National Review, December 9, 2016.

7. Ryan Lovelace, "Trump Advisor Leonard Leo Details Plan to Overhaul Judiciary," *Washington Examiner*, May 12, 2017.

8. Rob Boston, "The Alliance Defense Fund Agenda," Church & State, June 2004; Josh Israel, "The 800-Pound Gorilla of the Christian Right," ThinkProgress, May 1, 2014, https://thinkprogress.org/the-800-pound-gorilla-of-the-christian -right-89b8cfca7051.

9. Alan Sears and Craig Osten, *The Homosexual Agenda: Exposing the Principal Threat to Religious Freedom Today* (Broadman & Holman), 147.

10. Israel, "The 800-Pound Gorilla of the Christian Right."

11. P. Andrew Sandlin, "R. J. Rushdoony: Champion of Faith and Liberty," Chalcedon.edu, April 01, 2001, https://chalcedon.edu/magazine/r-j-rushdoony -champion-of-faith-and-liberty.

12. Katherine Stewart, "A Big Win for the Prayer Lobby," *New York Times*, May 8, 2014.

13. Playlist of public comments, uploaded by Central Florida Freethought Community: https://www.youtube.com/playlist?list=PL9ig3lMG3B8Fiwt8A Z2c4OnAKRWo1E9Ih.

14. "Joseph Richardson, Who Refused to Stand for the Pledge, Speaks to Media," *Orlando Sentinel*, undated, uncredited video, https://www.orlandosentinel.com /news/breaking-news/81282477-132.html.

15. See documentation, Resolution No. 16-02: http://cwgdn.com/DocumentCenter /View/390/Resolution-16-02-Amended-Invocation-Resolution-February-10 -2015-PDF.

16. Hemant Mehta, "An Atheist's Invocation Is Met with a Cry of 'Fake News' in LF," Friendly Atheist, January 13, 2018, https://friendlyatheist.patheos.com/2018 /01/13/an-atheists-invocation-request-is-met-with-cry-of-fake-news-in-fl.

17. May 9, 2019, 30:31–31:40 of the Facebook video at https://www.facebook.com /cflfreethought/videos/2054621198165207.

18. See Foundation Academy 2016–17 Student/Parent Handbook, Grades 7–12, page 8: https://fbcw.org/connect/foundation-academy, access date November 11, 2019.

19. Ibid., 36.

20. Ibid., 8.

21. Valerie Strauss, "It's National School Choice Week: What's That? (Possibly Not What You Think)," *Washington Post*, January 21, 2019.

22. Valerie Strauss, "Guess Which State Spends the Most Public Funds on Private and Religious School Education. Hint: Betsy Devos Has a House There," *Washington Post*, March 1, 2019.

23. Adam Chodorow, "The Parsonage Exemption," *UC Davis Law Review* 849, June 13, 2017, https://lawreview.law.ucdavis.edu/issues/51/3/Articles/51-3 _Chodorow.pdf.

24. Erik Eckholm, "Family Battle Offers Look Inside Lavish TV Ministry," *New York Times*, May 4, 2012.

25. Sarah Whitman, "Without Walls' Randy White Talks of Moving Forward," *Tampa Bay Times*, June 25, 2015.

26. Sarah Posner, "Creflo Dollar's Gulfstream for God?," CNN, March 19, 2015, https://www.cnn.com/2015/03/16/opinions/posner-creflo-dollar-gulfstream /index.html.

27. Supreme Court Justice Byron White dissent in Widmar v. Vincent 454 US 263 (1981).

28. CASEBulletin, July 1990, as cited in email to the author from Rob Boston, Americans United for Separation of Church and State, July 22, 2011.

29. See case details: Good News Club v. Milford Central School (99-2036) 533 U.S. 98 (2001), 202 F.3d 502, reversed and remanded, https://www.law.cornell .edu/supct/html/99-2036.ZD1.html.

30. Katherine Stewart, "An After-School Satan Club Could Be Coming to Your Kid's Elementary School," *Washington Post*, July 30, 2016.

31. See position paper "Homosexuality, Marriage, and Sexual Identity," General Presbytery of the Assemblies of God, session August 4–5, 2014: https://ag.org /Beliefs/Position-Papers/Homosexuality-Marriage-and-Sexual-Identity.

32. See position paper "Can Born-Again Believers Be Demon Possessed?" General Presbytery of the Assemblies of God, session May 1972, https://ag.org/Beliefs /Position-Papers/Demon-Possession.

33. Tom Porter, "Joel Osteen: Televangelist Whose Church Closed During Hurricane Harvey Tells Victims Not to Have 'Poor Me' Attitude," *Newsweek*, September 4, 2017.

34. "Bill to End Discrimination Against Houses of Worship Moves One Step Closer to House to Vote," U.S. Congressman Chris Smith Representing New Jersey's 4th District (U.S. House of Representatives website), December 1, 2017, https://chrissmith.house.gov/news/documentsingle.aspx?DocumentID =400790.

35. Rachel Held Evans, "Inside Mark Driscoll's Disturbed Mind," rachelheldevans .com, July 29, 2014, https://rachelheldevans.com/blog/driscoll-troubled-mind -william-wallace.

36. Bruce Ware, "Gender Moves?," Acts 29, June 4, 2015, https://www.acts29.com /gender-moves.

37. From "Membership Matters Course" pamphlet, City on a Hill Church, 8–9.

38. Robert Lewis Dabney, "Anti-Biblical Theories of Rights," *Presbyterian Quarterly* (1888), 23.

39. City on a Hill Church, "Membership Matters Course," 49.

40. See "Brookline Brownstone Walkthru #2" on Vimeo: https://vimeo.com /15743954.

41. Katherine Stewart, "The Movement to Put a Church in Every School Is Growing," *The Nation*, January 14, 2015, https://www.thenation.com/article /movement-put-church-every-school-growing.

42. Jamie Grosshans, "Missionary, Ambassador, Lawyer," *Christian Lawyer* (Fall 2016): 5.

43. See Florida Fifth District Court of Appeal: https://www.5dca.org/Judges /Judge-Jamie-R.-Grosshans.

44. Steven Lemongello, "Appeal Court Judge Jamie Grosshans Among 11 Nominees for Florida Supreme Court Seats," *Orlando Sentinel*, November 27, 2018.

CHAPTER 11: CONTROLLING BODIES: WHAT "RELIGIOUS LIBERTY" LOOKS LIKE FROM THE STRETCHER

1. *Ethical and Religious Directives for Catholic Health Care Services*, 6th ed. Copyright 2009, 2018, United States Conference of Catholic Bishops, http://www .usccb.org/about/doctrine/ethical-and-religious-directives/upload/ethical -religious-directives-catholic-health-service-sixth-edition-2016-06.pdf.

2. Ibid.

3. "Health Care Denied: Patients and Physicians Speak Out about Catholic Hospitals and the Threat to Women's Health and Lives," American Civil Liberties Union, May 2016, downloadable report at https://www.aclu.org /report/report-health-care-denied?redirect=report/health-care-denied.

4. Kira Shepherd, Elizabeth Reiner Platt, Katherine Franke, and Elizabeth Boylan, "Bearing Faith: The Limits of Catholic Health Care for Women of Color," Public Rights Private Conscience Project, Columbia Law School, https://www.law.columbia.edu/sites/default/files/microsites/gender-sexuality /PRPCP/bearingfaith.pdf.

5. Marian F. MacDorman, Eugene Declercq, Howard Cabral, and Christine Morton, "Is the United States Maternal Mortality Rate Increasing? Disentangling Trends from Measurement Issues," *Obstetrics & Gynecology* 128, no. 3 (2016): 447–55, https://www.ncbi.nlm.nih.gov/pmc/articles/PMC5001799/.

6. Shepherd, Reiner Platt, Franke, and Boylan, "Bearing Faith," 34.

7. Cydney Henderson and Bree Burkitt, "Arizona Walgreens Pharmacist Denies Mother Miscarriage Medicine Because of Moral Objection," *Arizona Republic*, June 24, 2018, story and video at https://www.wfaa.com/article/news /nation-now/arizona-walgreens-pharmacist-denies-mother-miscarriage -medicine-because-of-moral-objection/465-2c135b07-099f-419e-9ae7 -89fb44b4e806.

8. Nina Shapiro, "The Final Conversation: Are Patients Considering the 'Death with Dignity Act' Getting All the Information They Need?" *Seattle Weekly*, February 25, 2015: 6.

9. "Ethical and Religious Directives for Catholic Health Care Services."

10. "Rise in Catholic-Sponsored Hospitals Threatens Women's Health, New Report Finds," MergerWatch.org, December 18, 2013, http://www.mergerwatch .org/mergerwatch-news/2013/12/18/rise-in-catholic-sponsored-hospitals -threatens-womens-health.html; Katherine Stewart, "At Catholic Hospitals, a Right to Life but Not a Right to Death," *The Nation*, October 8, 2015.

11. Ronald Mann, "Opinion Analysis: Justices Unanimously Uphold ERISA Exemption for Church-Affiliated Pension Plans," SCOTUSblog, June 5, 2017, https://www.scotusblog.com/2017/06/opinion-analysis-justices-unanimously -uphold-erisa-exemption-church-affiliated-pension-plans.

12. "New Report Reveals 1 in 6 Hospital Beds Are in Catholic Facilities That Prohibit Essential Health Care for Women," American Civil Liberties Union, May 5, 2016, https://www.aclu.org/press-releases/new-report-reveals-1-6-us -hospital-beds-are-catholic-facilities-prohibit-essential.

13. Emmarie Huetteman, "At New Health Office, 'Civil Rights' Means Doctors' Right to Say No to Patients," KHN: Kaiser Health News, March 5, 2018, https://khn.org/news/at-new-health-office-civil-rights-means-doctors-right -to-say-no-to-patients.

14. Jacqueline Thomsen, "Trump Expands Federal Contractors' Ability to Cite Religious Freedom in Discrimination Cases," *The Hill*, August 17, 2018.

15. Tara Isabella Burton, "Jeff Sessions Announces a Religious Liberty Task Force to Combat 'Dangerous' Secularism," *Vox*, July 31, 2018.

CHAPTER 12: THE GLOBAL HOLY WAR COMES OF AGE

1. Casey Michel, "The Latest Front in Russian Infiltration: America's Right-Wing Homeschooling Movement," ThinkProgress, January 17, 2019, https://thinkprogress.org/americas-biggest-right-wing-homeschooling-group-has-been-networking-with-sanctioned-russians-1f2b5b5ad031.

2. Casey Michel, "How Russia Infiltrated the World of American Religious-Right Filmmaking," ThinkProgress, February 8, 2019, https://thinkprogress.org/how-russia-infiltrated-the-world-of-american-religious-right-film-making-movieguide-ted-baehr-alexey-komov.

3. Alexander Reid Ross, "Steve Bannon's Fascist Far Right Christian Army Is Marching on Liberal Europe—and on the Pope," Haaretz, April 22, 2019.

4. Sarah Posner, "The End of City on a Hill," Type Investigations, March 11, 2019, https://www.typeinvestigations.org/investigation/2019/03/11/european-american-christian-conservative-alliance.

5. Claire Provost and Adam Ramsay, "Revealed: Trump-Linked US Christian 'Fundamentalists' Pour Millions of 'Dark Money' into Europe, Boosting the Far Right," openDemocracy, March 27, 2019, https://www.opendemocracy.net/en/5050/revealed-trump-linked-us-christian-fundamentalists-pour-millions-of-dark-money-into-europe-boosting-the-far-right.

6. Jason Horowitz, "The 'It' '80s Party Girl Is Now a Defender of the Catholic Faith," New York Times, December 7, 2018.

7. Michel, "The Latest Front in Russian Infiltration: America's Right-Wing Homeschooling Movement."

8. Courtney Weaver, "God's TV, Russian Style," Financial Times, October 16, 2015.

9. Ken Ham, "Child Evangelism Fellowship Leaders at Museum," Answers in Genesis, Ken Ham Blog, December 21, 2015, https://answersingenesis.org/blogs/ken-ham/2015/12/21/child-evangelism-fellowship-leaders-museum.

10. Wess Stafford, introduction to Luis Bush, The 4/14 Window: Raising Up a New Generation to Transform the World (Compassion International, 2009).

11. See CEF World Day of Prayer 2018 booklet, https://static1.squarespace.com/static/5ae1da515ffd205aac4e25bc/t/5bbfce050852293cf2f967cc/1539296776297

/World+Day+of+Prayer+2018+booklet+%281%29.pdf. Last accessed July 15, 2019.

12. "Child Evangelism Conference Opens in Accra," GhanaWeb.com, July 8, 2004, https://www.ghanaweb.com/GhanaHomePage/NewsArchive/Child-evang elism-conference-opens-in-Accra-61246#.

13. See CEF World Day of Prayer 2018 booklet, p. 25. Last accessed July 15, 2019.

14. Kev Murdoch, "How Can a God of Love Send People to Hell?" http://www .eustonchurch.com/exploring.

15. "Nigeria: Anglican Primate Attacks Gay Marriage, Homosexuality," Virtue-online.org, September 20, 2011.

16. Although GAFCON has adopted a voluntary moratorium on the ordination of women, the issue remains a topic under dispute. See "Analysis: A Dilemma for GAFCON," Living Church, March 6, 2018, https://livingchurch.org/2018 /03/06/analysis-a-dilemma-for-gafcon. The Church of England has approved women's ordination since 1992: John Bingham, "Women in the Church of England: A Century of Waiting," *Telegraph*, January 26, 2015.

17. John W. Howe and Sam C. Pascoe, *Our Anglican Heritage: Can an Ancient Church Be a Church of the Future?* (Wipf and Stock, 2010), 194.

18. David W. Virtue, "GAFCON Chairman Hails First Ordination of Priests to the Anglican Mission in England," VirtueOnline, December 12, 2017, https:// virtueonline.org/gafcon-chairman-hails-first-ordination-priests-anglican -mission-england.

19. Isabel Hardman, "Conservative Anglicans' Emergency Plan to Escape Women Bishops," *Spectator* (UK), September 2014.

20. www.citytocityeurope.com/values.

21. Denny Burk, "5 Evidences of Complementarian Gender Roles in Genesis 1-2," March 14, 2014. https://www.thegospelcoalition.org/article/5-evidences-of -complementarian-gender-roles-in-genesis-1-2. Accessed July 15, 2019.

22. Dr. Andrew Sach, "Talk: Does Science Contradict Christianity?," Euston Church, March 16, 2016, http://www.eustonchurch.com/archive/2016/5/22 /does-science-contradict-christianity.

23. "John Smyth, the School Predator Who Beat Me for Five Years," *Telegraph*, February 5, 2017.

24. "Police Investigate Alleged 'Brutal Lashings' by Christian Leader," BBC Channel 4, February 2, 2017.

25. "Christian Lawyer Who 'Beat Boys' Was Charged over Zimbabwe Death," BBC Channel 4, February 3, 2017.

26. P. J. Smyth, "Open Letter from PJ Smyth," Covenant Life Church, February 4, 2017, https://www.covlife.org/blog/open-letter-from-pj-smyth. Last accessed April 24, 2019.

27. P. J. Smyth, *Quick-Start Parenting*, https://static1.squarespace.com/static /567931fc4bf118d6ee53d8cb/t/58ff0c045016e163f205e4e7/1493109769395/Quick+ Start+Parenting+-+PJ+Smyth.pdf. Last accessed April 24, 2019.

28. Ibid., 14.

29. Ibid., 16–17.

30. Ibid., 15.

31. Andrew Haslam, Grace London Newsletter #3, February 23, 2016.

32. Andrew Haslam, February 15, 2014, https://andrewhaslam.net/profound -provocative-prophetic. Last accessed April 1, 2018.

33. Libby Anne, "Doug Wilson: Women Who Reject Patriarchy Are Tacitly Accepting 'the Propriety of Rape,'" Patheos, March 14, 2016.

34. Andrew Haslam, February 15, 2014, https://andrewhaslam.net/profound -provocative-prophetic. Last accessed April 1, 2018.

35. Jonathan Merritt, "The Gospel Coalition and How (Not) to Engage Culture," *Religion News Service*, June 6, 2016; Douglas Wilson, "One of Those Circus Ponies," Blog and Mablog, June 23, 2013, https://dougwils.com/books/one-of -those-circus-ponies.html.

36. Andrew Haslam, "Are Christians Cherry-Picking Their Morals?" *Salt*, January 25, 2019.

37. Dave Chambers, "Son of Lawyer in 'Spanking' Documentary Heads US 'Megachurch' Embroiled in Sex Scandal," *Sunday Times* (South Africa), February 2, 2017.

38. Tiffany Stanley, "The Sex-Abuse Scandal That Devastated a Suburban Mega-church," *Washingtonian*, February 14, 2016, https://www.washingtonian.com/2016/02/14/the-sex-abuse-scandal-that-devastated-a-suburban-megachurch-sovereign-grace-ministries.

39. https://adfinternational.org/who-we-are/locations.

40. https://adfinternational.org/advocacy.

41. Dan Sabbagh, "Ban on Anti-Abortion Protests in London Clinic Dispropor-tionate, Court Hears," *Guardian*, June 7, 2018.

42. http://www.dignitatishumanae.com/index.php/about-us/about-the-institute.

43. Lidia Kurasinska, "This Ultra-Conservative Institute Has Infiltrated the Polish State, on a Relentless Quest to Ban Abortion," openDemocracy, July 30, 2018, https://www.opendemocracy.net/en/5050/ultra-conservative-institute-has-infiltrated-polish-state-to-ban-abortion.

44. Author interview with Neil Datta, February 27, 2019.

45. Cassandra Vinograd and Eva Gallica, "Abortion in Europe: 'Coat Hanger Rebellion' Grips Poland," NBC News, April 25, 2016, https://www.nbcnews.com/storyline/europes-abortion-fight/abortion-europe-coat-hanger-rebellion-grips-poland-n559621.

46. Paul Weyrich, "American Media and Reporting on Russia," Town Hall, May 22, 2007.

47. Martin A. Lee, *The Beast Reawakens* (Routledge, 1999), 303; Chip Berlet and Holly Sklar, "Republicans with a Fascist Heritage: Laszlo Pasztor," Research for Progress, February 20, 1990, https://www.researchforprogress.us/topic/34162/tracking-right-wing-power/republicans-with-a-fascist-heritage-laszlo-pasztor.

48. "Paul Weyrich Obituary," *Telegraph*, January 26, 2009, https://www.telegraph.co.uk/news/obituaries/4143579/Paul-Weyrich.html.

49. Dr. Dmitry Gorenburg, *Renewing the US-Russian Strategic Partnership: Confer-ence Report*, Center for Strategic Studies, November 2000, 12; Paul Weyrich, "Why Is Western Media Bashing the New Russia?" Taki's Magazine, May 27, 2007, https://www.takimag.com/article/why_is_western_media_bashing_the_new_russia.

50. Rosalind Helderman and Tom Hamburger, "Guns and Religion: How American Conservatives Grew Closer to Putin's Russia," *Washington Post*, April 30, 2017.

51. Jonathan Martin and Amy Chozik, "Donald Trump Campaign Stands by Embrace of Putin," *New York Times*, September 9, 2016.

INDEX

Abeka, 199, 205–6
abolitionism, 107, 109, 112, 114, 115
abortion. *See also Roe v. Wade* (1973)
    as a political issue, 3, 10, 54, 69, 75, 76, 115,
      162, 215
    and crisis pregnancy centers, 161, 231
    Ralph Drollinger on, 48
    and Ethical and Religious Directives
      (ERDs), 237–38
    and global conservative movement,
      268–69
    Mark Harris on, 18
    and Hyde Amendment, 161
    Brett Kavanaugh on, 246
    lack of common ground on, 53
    late-term abortions, 77
    Leonard Leo on, 213
    and martyrdom narrative, 92
    Tony Perkins on, 15
    prevalence of, 65–66
    as pro-life issue, 28, 55–57, 69, 74, 75–76,
      90, 92
    and religious right, 63–65
    and Republican Party, 54, 56–57, 66–69,
      74, 77, 161
    Phyllis Schlafly on, 67–68, 70
    and school vouchers, 219
    and state legislatures, 154, 160–62
    and TRAP laws, 161
    and U.S. Supreme Court, 54, 67
    and voter mobilization, 54, 176
Acton Institute, 188, 192–93, 213
Acts 29 parachurch network, 86, 229–30
Adams, John, 131
Advance movement, 261–66
Advantage Academy, 186

Affordable Care Act, 30, 92, 96, 144
AggregateIQ, 175
Ahmanson, Howard, Jr., 8, 103, 121
Alianza de Pastores Unidos de San Diego,
    79–81, 92
Alito, Samuel, 216
Alliance Defending Freedom
    and Andrew Brunson, 150
    and Child Evangelism Fellowship, 266
    and church-state separation, 213–16
    and Church United, 97
    and Michael Farris, 253
    funding of, 166, 188, 213, 214
    global expansion of, 266–67, 269–70
    and Green family, 139
    groups working in opposition to, 275
    judiciary strategy of, 214–16, 233–34
    and religious freedom, 215–16, 221, 224–25,
      266
    and United in Purpose, 182
Álvarez, Gloria, 94
American Center for Law and Justice, 150,
    214, 222
American Civil Liberties Union (ACLU),
    204, 214, 239
American Family Association, 74, 88, 140,
    157–58, 165–66, 181, 213, 271
American Federation for Children, 191, 194
American history
    and America's founding, 4, 122, 126–35,
      137–40, 144, 155, 182, 204, 275–76
    and Christian nation myths, 122, 127–28,
      275
    revisionist account of, 112, 137, 141, 199
American Legislative Exchange Council,
    60, 160, 191, 194, 219

A NOTE ON THE AUTHOR

KATHERINE STEWART is one of the leading authorities on the political aspects of the religious right. The author of *The Good News Club: The Religious Right's Stealth Attack on America's Children*, she contributes to the *New York Times*, *American Prospect*, the *Washington Post*, the *Nation*, the *Guardian*, the *Advocate*, and the *Atlantic*. In 2014 she was named Person of the Year by the national civil liberties group Americans United for Separation of Church and State.

www.katherinestewart.me